T0207408

Lecture Notes in Computer Science 14680

Founding Editors

Gerhard Goos
Juris Hartmanis

Editorial Board Members

The series Lecture Notes in Computer Science (LNCS), including its subseries Lecture Notes in Artificial Intelligence (LNAI) and Lecture Notes in Bioinformatics (LNBI), has established itself as a medium for the publication of new developments in computer science and information technology research, teaching, and education.

LNCS enjoys close cooperation with the computer science R & D community, the series counts many renowned academics among its volume editors and paper authors, and collaborates with prestigious societies. Its mission is to serve this international community by providing an invaluable service, mainly focused on the publication of conference and workshop proceedings and postproceedings. LNCS commenced publication in 1973.

Torben Ægidius Mogensen · Łukasz Mikulski
Editors

Reversible Computation

16th International Conference, RC 2024
Toruń, Poland, July 4–5, 2024
Proceedings

 Springer

Editors
Torben Ægidius Mogensen 🆔
Department of Computer Science
University of Copenhagen
Copenhagen Ø, Denmark

Łukasz Mikulski 🆔
Faculty of Mathematics and Computer
Science
Nicolaus Copernicus University
Toruń, Poland

ISSN 0302-9743   ISSN 1611-3349 (electronic)
Lecture Notes in Computer Science
ISBN 978-3-031-62075-1   ISBN 978-3-031-62076-8 (eBook)
https://doi.org/10.1007/978-3-031-62076-8

This Springer imprint is published by the registered company Springer Nature Switzerland AG
The registered company address is: Gewerbestrasse 11, 6330 Cham, Switzerland

If disposing of this product, please recycle the paper.

Preface

This volume contains the papers presented at the 16th International Conference on Reversible Computation (RC 2024) held on July 4–5, 2024 in Toruń, Poland.

There were 18 submissions, one of which was immediately rejected for being out of scope. Each remaining submission was reviewed by at least 3, and on average 3.2, program committee members. The committee decided to accept 13 papers for presentation at the conference and inclusion in the proceedings. This volume also includes 2 invited talks:

"Causal Debugging for Concurrent Systems (Tutorial)" by Ivan Lanese and Gregor Goessler

"Compositional Reversible Computation" by Jacques Carette, Chris Heunen, Robin Kaarsgaard, and Amr Sabry

The Reversible Computation conference series brings together researchers from computer science, mathematics, engineering, and physics to discuss new developments and directions for future research in the emerging area of Reversible Computation. This includes, for example, reversible formal models, reversible programming languages, reversible circuits, and quantum computing. The conference series is a major international venue for the dissemination of new results in reversible computations. The previous 15 conferences were held in the following locations: Giessen, Germany (2023), Urbino, Italy (2022), Nagoya, Japan (2021), Oslo, Norway (2020), Lausanne, Switzerland (2019), Leicester, UK (2018), Kolkata, India (2017), Bologna, Italy (2016), Grenoble, France (2015), Kyoto, Japan (2014), Victoria, Canada (2013), Copenhagen, Denmark (2012), Gent, Belgium (2011), Bremen, Germany (2010), York, UK (2009).

We are very grateful to the invited speakers and all authors of the submitted papers, as well as the members of the Program Committee for their excellent work in reviewing the papers and helping with the selection process. We also thank the additional external reviewers for their careful evaluation.

We thank the The Nicolaus Copernicus University in Toruń for hosting and supporting the conference and Springer for making these proceedings available. We also appreciate the EasyChair conference management system for making the reviewing process and proceedings production painless. Separate thanks are due to the Organizing Committee chaired by Kamila Barylska for the time and effort invested in the local organization of the event.

Lastly, we thank all the authors of papers and invited talks for their submissions and willingness to improve these as well as for interesting presentations at RC 2024 in Toruń.

April 2024

Torben Ægidius Mogensen
Łukasz Mikulski

Program Committee

Clément Aubert	Augusta University, USA
Kamalika Datta	University of Bremen/DFKI, Germany
Gerhard Dueck	University of New Brunswick, Canada
Robert Glück	University of Copenhagen, Denmark
James Hoey	University of Leicester, UK
Robin Kaarsgaard	University of Southern Denmark, Denmark
Ivan Lanese	University of Bologna, Italy
Andreas Malcher	University of Giessen, Germany
Uwe Meyer	Technische Hochschule Mittelhessen, Germany
Claudio Antares Mezzina	Università di Urbino, Italy
Łukasz Mikulski	Nicolaus Copernicus University, Poland
Torben Ægidius Mogensen	University of Copenhagen, Denmark
Iain Phillips	Imperial College London, UK
Krzysztof Podlaski	University of Lodz, Poland
Michael Kirkedal Thomsen	University of Oslo, Norway and University of Copenhagen, Denmark
Irek Ulidowski	University of Leicester, UK
Robert Wille	Technical University of Munich & SCCH GmbH, Germany
Shigeru Yamashita	Ritsumeikan University, Japan
Tetsuo Yokoyama	Nanzan University, Japan
Shoji Yuen	Nagoya University, Japan

Additional Reviewers

Choudhury, Vikraman
Deworetzki, Niklas
Hegerland Oldfield, Noah
Kole, Abhoy
Kristensen, Joachim
Kutrib, Martin
Medic, Doriana
Normann, Louis Marrott
Vadgaard, Lars-Bo Husted

Contents

Synthesis, Verification, and Analysis of Reversible and Quantum Systems

Invited Papers

Causal Debugging for Concurrent Systems

Ivan Lanese[1]([✉]) and Gregor Gössler[2]

[1] Olas Team, University of Bologna, INRIA, 40137 Bologna, Italy
`ivan.lanese@gmail.com`
[2] Univ. Grenoble Alpes, INRIA, CNRS, Grenoble INP, LIG, 38000 Grenoble, France

Abstract. Debugging concurrent systems is notoriously hard, since bugs may manifest only for some interleavings among the processes' execution, and since debugging them may involve analyzing multiple processes. We claim that two key ingredients for such an analysis are reversible execution, to explore a faulty computation back and forward, and causal analysis, to identify the causes of a visible misbehavior. In this talk we focus in particular on the use of reversible execution, as enabled by CauDEr, a reversible debugger for concurrent Erlang programs.

1 Introduction

As soon as one learns how to program, (s)he is faced with the challenges of debugging. Indeed, every programmer has experienced long and tedious debugging sessions, possibly ended with the discovery of very trivial bugs. While experience allows one to reduce the amount of trivial bugs, one is faced with programs which are more and more complex, and time spent in debugging remains consistent.

Concurrent programs may contain very hard to find bugs, the so called Heisenbugs, whose distinctive feature is that they manifest by producing some visible misbehavior only for some specific interleaving among the processes of a concurrent application. Interleavings are highly sensitive to factors beyond programmer's control, such as processor(s) speed, scheduling policy, interrupts, and others, what makes extremely hard to reproduce a desired scheduling. Folklore says that a concurrent program can run flawlessly for days in the programmer's premises, and fail as soon as started in front of the customer. Reality behind this folklore is that moving from programmer's to customer's machine may change some of the factors above, hence increasing the probability of failures, and of course, when such failures really occur, programmers experiencing them share the story, reinforcing the legend above.

In the present paper we do not discuss how to make such bugs manifest in the programmer's premises, but we tackle a related problem: how to catch those

---

The work has been partially supported by French ANR project DCore ANR-18-CE25-0007. The first author has also been partially supported by MSCA-PF project 101106046—ReGraDe-CS and by INdAM – GNCS 2023 project RISICO, code CUP_E53C22001930001.

T. Æ. Mogensen and L. Mikulski (Eds.): RC 2024, LNCS 14680, pp. 3–9, 2024.
https://doi.org/10.1007/978-3-031-62076-8_1

bugs, after they manifest at least once. Indeed, this includes two problems: how to reliably replay the corresponding misbehaviors after they manifest once, and how to find the bugs from their visible effect. We will show how to leverage the theory of causal-consistent reversibility [3] to this effect, and how this can be concretely done on Erlang programs using the reversible debugger CauDEr [1,10].

2   Rollback and Replay

As mentioned, we assume that we have been lucky enough to have seen a bug to manifest. Unfortunately, the bug may manifest only if a specific interleaving among actions occurs. If we keep no information on the execution, even if we provide the same input to the program, we have no guarantee that the bug occurs again. For instance, a process may expect 3 messages which can be either True or False, and the bug manifests, e.g., since the program prints True on the screen while the correct output would be False, only if the two first messages contain value True, and the last one value False. Note that here we have two sources of different behaviors: the values of the messages, and the order in which they are received. For simplicity assume that the input to the program determines the value of the messages, and that there is no synchronization so that the order in which they arrive only depends on the scheduling. Remembering the input allows us to replay an execution where two messages carry value True and one carries value False, but not to ensure the False message to be received last. A log of a computation allows us to keep track of all the events which may cause non-determinism, and executing a program (with the same inputs) by allowing actions only if they are compatible with the log allows us to reproduce the same behaviors. In order to identify messages, we assign them unique identifiers. In our example, assume the messages with True have identifiers 1 and 2, and the one with False has identifier 3. A log of the faulty computation states, e.g., that messages have been received in order 2, 1, 3. Any computation satisfying this condition will produce a wrong behavior, hence manifesting the bug.

We are now able to replay the computation and be sure to showcase the bug, causing a wrong output printed from the program. Clearly, chances are that the bug is not in the print instruction, but in some previous computation providing a wrong value to the print instruction. Since we are in a concurrent system, the computation may involve multiple processes, interacting with each other. Any such interaction creates a causal link between actions of (possibly different) processes, and actions of a single process are all linked by the program flow. Looking backwards, any action, specifically the print providing a wrong value, is determined by a tree of causes, spanning multiple processes. The bug is for sure one of these actions. Some actions, and even some processes, may not be involved in the tree, hence looking at them is not helpful to find the bug. Causal-consistent debugging [5] suggests the following algorithm to find a bug: explore the tree of causes backwards, starting from the visible misbehavior.

At every step, look at the involved data[1]: if all the data are correct, then try another branch, if the data are all wrong, go further backwards, if the data entering the action are correct, and the ones exiting from it are wrong, then the action is wrong and it is the bug looked for. In order to support such a debugging strategy, one should be able to go backwards to explore a past action in some branch of the tree of causes, go forward again if the selected branch does not contain the bug, while remaining in a computation showcasing the bug, and then go backwards again along another branch. Clearly reversible computation comes handy here. More precisely, we need to be able to find the direct cause of some wrong part of the state, such as the last assignment to a variable with a wrong value, or the send of a given wrong message, and to go back where such an action has been executed. Note that, in particular, the send of a given wrong message is in general not in the same process where the message is received, hence this requires to possibly explore multiple processes. In order to go back we will exploit *causal-consistent rollback* [9], which allows one to undo a given action, including all and only its consequences. Dually, we can go forward again using *causal-consistent replay* [11], which replays a given action (e.g., the print showcasing the bug), including all and only its causes, while respecting the log. These two primitives allows one to explore a computation backward and forward, remaining in a setting manifesting the bug, while undoing or redoing the minimal number of actions to reach a state where the target action has been undone or redone.

Causal Analysis. As a complementary technique to rollback and replay, we have been exploring the use of causal analysis to enable the debugger to automatically answer queries of the form "why is the output of my program True?". Indeed, the approach above does not distinguish among the causes of an action, requiring the programmer to explore all of them. Using causal analysis we can identify one or more events in the program execution that actually caused the wrong outcome [6]. The analysis is *counterfactual*, that is, based on the analysis of alternative executions, in order to determine whether the latter would have changed the outcome. As a particular case, the analysis is able to blame the outcome on non-deterministic choices in the program execution. Furthermore, it enjoys desirable properties such as stability of the analysis result under semantic equivalence of the program. The integration of causal analysis and rollback and replay is still future work.

The approach described above is general and can be ideally applied to any programming language. We will describe below how to apply rollback and replay in the concrete case of the Erlang programming language.

We are currently working on instantiating on Erlang the causal analysis as well, relying on a novel fine-grained semantics [2] which carefully describes the possible orders in which messages (and signals) are handled, which is the main source of non-determinism in Erlang.

---

[1] For simplicity, the description here focuses on wrong values, but a similar approach can be applied to control flow.

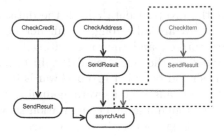

Fig. 1. The purchase workflow.

3   Causal-Consistent Debugging in CauDEr

The example above is not artificial, and it captures the essence of an actual case study, originally described in [12]. A simple Erlang implementation showcasing the misbehavior can be found in CauDEr [1] library of case studies. The case study implements a procedure for handling purchase orders, whose behavior is depicted in Fig. 1.

Before an order is placed, two conditions must be verified: the availability of the customer's credit, and the completeness of the address for delivery. The two independent checks CheckCredit and CheckAddress are performed concurrently. The results of the checks are sent to the asynchAnd procedure as soon as they are available. The asynchAnd procedure performs a short-circuit evaluation of n-ary AND: it waits for up to n values, but as soon as one is False, it immediately produces False as a result. If n True values are received, it sends the value True as a result.

Assume we perform perfective maintenance on this software: to avoid that clients wait for long periods of time, we make sure that the item is actually in stock before concluding the purchase. Thus, a new procedure checkItem implementing such a check is incorporated in the system (as shown in the dashed part of Fig. 1).

During testing, the program behaves as expected, however, when deployed on client's premises, it sometimes misbehaves. Indeed, it sometimes returns value True even if one of the conditions fails.

The bug is indeed dependent on the schedule, thus by running the program one most likely obtains the correct result, namely that the purchase is not authorized if at least one condition fails.

One can then run the program, instrumented by CauDEr tracer so to produce a log of the computation, and if (s)he is able to capture the misbehavior once, then (s)he can analyze it at will inside CauDEr, being sure that the misbehavior always manifests.

CauDEr interface can be seen in Fig. 2. We can see the code on the top-left, some useful commands on the top right, and information on the system and on the selected process (the one executing the asynchAnd) on the bottom.

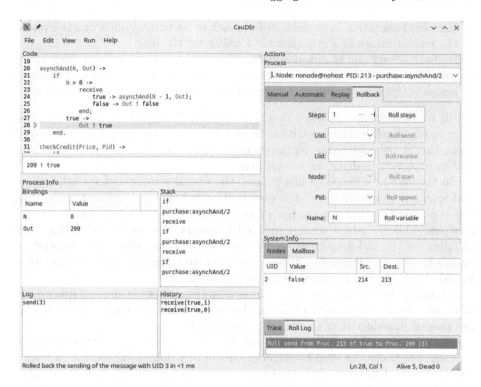

Fig. 2. CauDEr at work.

First one can select to replay the full log, so to execute the program till the end. Indeed the bug manifests: one check failed, yet the program reports that all the checks succeeded.

The result is taken from a receive, and it was inside message number 3. Then, we can use rollback to undo the send of message number 3. We reach exactly the state depicted in the figure. We can see, as expected, that the message comes from process asynchAnd. Looking at the history of the process (History frame in the center at the bottom) we see that the message has been sent after receiving only two values, what should be enough to understand which is the error. If we fail to notice this information in the history, we can execute backward step-by-step the code of the asynchAnd, and reasonably noticing the bug, when we reach the first invocation and look at the parameters.

4 Conclusion

We have shown, albeit in a minimal example, how to exploit causal-consistent debugging to find elusive bugs. We stress here a few aspects:

- a log provides a compact way to capture a family of computations which show some desired behavior, in particular the manifestation of a bug;

- backward execution in general, and rollback in particular, allow one to explore the tree of causes of a misbehavior, looking for the bug;
- rollback allows one to automatically navigate among processes, disregarding unrelated processes, hinting at the possibility that this debugging technique scales better than traditional approaches to programs with many processes.

While we believe this approach is very promising, being able to apply it to real large applications is far from trivial. Indeed, one needs to understand the causal semantics of the underlying language, to store history and causal information, and to exploit it to drive the computation.

In the case of a language like Erlang, the causal semantics for send, receive and spawn is relatively easy (it is essentially the happened-before relation [8]), but coping with other aspects has proved to require a detailed and non trivial analysis. This is indeed what happened to support primitives deadling with distribution [4], and primitives used to manage an imperative store associating names to process identifiers [7]. Notably, the latter highlighted challenges that would also emerge in languages with shared memory.

Managing history information requires a large amount of time and space overhead already in the sequential case, as shown by GDB, and smart optimizations are needed to reduce it as shown by UndoDB [13].

In order to use all this information to drive execution, CauDEr has been written essentially as a step-by-step interpreter of Erlang programs. As a result, constructs need to be implemented one by one, and one needs to follow Erlang evolution to avoid becoming outdated. This is a suitable strategy for a proof of concept, but an industrial implementation should be integrated with Erlang runtime support to avoid the above issues. However, this integration needs to be very deep, and it is not enough, e.g., to build on top of a classical debugger or a tracer.

References

1. CauDEr repository (2024). https://github.com/mistupv/cauder
2. Kong Win Chang, A., Feret, J., Gössler, G.: A semantics of core Erlang with handling of signals. In: Kulahcioglu Ozkan, B., Fernandez-Reyes, K. (eds.) Proceedings of the 22nd ACM SIGPLAN International Workshop on Erlang, Erlang 2023, Seattle, WA, USA, 4 September 2023, pp. 31–38. ACM (2023)
3. Danos, V., Krivine, J.: Reversible communicating systems. In: Gardner, P., Yoshida, N. (eds.) CONCUR 2004. LNCS, vol. 3170, pp. 292–307. Springer, Heidelberg (2004). https://doi.org/10.1007/978-3-540-28644-8_19
4. Fabbretti, G., Lanese, I., Stefani, J.-B.: Causal-consistent debugging of distributed Erlang programs. In: Yamashita, S., Yokoyama, T. (eds.) RC 2021. LNCS, vol. 12805, pp. 79–95. Springer, Cham (2021). https://doi.org/10.1007/978-3-030-79837-6_5
5. Giachino, E., Lanese, I., Mezzina, C.A.: Causal-consistent reversible debugging. In: Gnesi, S., Rensink, A. (eds.) FASE 2014. LNCS, vol. 8411, pp. 370–384. Springer, Heidelberg (2014). https://doi.org/10.1007/978-3-642-54804-8_26

6. Gössler, G., Stefani, J.-B.: Causality analysis and fault ascription in component-based systems. Theoret. Comput. Sci. **837**, 158–180 (2020)
7. Lami, P., Lanese, I., Stefani, J.-B., Sacerdoti Coen, C., Fabbretti, G.: Reversible debugging of concurrent Erlang programs: supporting imperative primitives. J. Log. Algebraic Methods Program. **138**, 100944 (2024)
8. Lamport, L.: Time, clocks, and the ordering of events in a distributed system. Commun. ACM **21**(7), 558–565 (1978)
9. Lanese, I., Mezzina, C.A., Schmitt, A., Stefani, J.-B.: Controlling reversibility in higher-order pi. In: Katoen, J.-P., König, B. (eds.) CONCUR 2011. LNCS, vol. 6901, pp. 297–311. Springer, Heidelberg (2011). https://doi.org/10.1007/978-3-642-23217-6_20
10. Lanese, I., Nishida, N., Palacios, A., Vidal, G.: CauDEr: a causal-consistent reversible debugger for Erlang. In: Gallagher, J.P., Sulzmann, M. (eds.) FLOPS 2018. LNCS, vol. 10818, pp. 247–263. Springer, Cham (2018). https://doi.org/10.1007/978-3-319-90686-7_16
11. Lanese, I., Palacios, A., Vidal, G.: Causal-consistent replay reversible semantics for message passing concurrent programs. Fundam. Inform. **178**(3), 229–266 (2021)
12. Stanley, T., Close, T., Miller, M.S.: Causeway: a message-oriented distributed debugger. Technical report, HP Labs (2009). HP Labs tech report HPL-2009-78
13. Undo Software. 6 things you need to know about time travel debugging. https://undo.io/resources/6-things-time-travel-debugging. Accessed April 2024

Compositional Reversible Computation

Jacques Carette[1][ID], Chris Heunen[2][ID], Robin Kaarsgaard[3][ID],
and Amr Sabry[4(✉)][ID]

[1] McMaster University, Hamilton, ON, Canada
[2] University of Edinburgh, Edinburgh, UK
[3] University of Southern Denmark, Odense, Denmark
[4] Indiana University, Bloomington, IN, USA
sabry@iu.edu

Abstract. Reversible computing is motivated by both pragmatic and foundational considerations arising from a variety of disciplines. We take a particular path through the development of reversible computation, emphasizing *compositional* reversible computation. We start from a historical perspective, by reviewing those approaches that developed reversible extensions of λ-calculi, Turing machines, and communicating process calculi. These approaches share a common challenge: computations made reversible in this way do not naturally compose locally.

We then turn our attention to computational models that eschew the detour via existing irreversible models. Building on an original analysis by Landauer, the insights of Bennett, Fredkin, and Toffoli introduced a fresh approach to reversible computing in which reversibility is elevated to the status of the main design principle. These initial models are expressed using low-level bit manipulations, however.

Abstracting from the low-level of the Bennett-Fredkin-Toffoli models and pursuing more intrinsic, typed, and algebraic models, naturally leads to rig categories as the canonical model for compositional reversible programming. The categorical model reveals connections to type isomorphisms, symmetries, permutations, groups, and univalent universes. This, in turn, paves the way for extensions to reversible programming based on monads and arrows. These extensions are shown to recover conventional irreversible programming, a variety of reversible computational effects, and more interestingly both pure (measurement-free) and measurement-based quantum programming.

Keywords: Rig Categories · Information Effects · Quantum Computing

1 Introduction

In 1992, Baker proposed "an abstract computer model and a programming language–Ψ-Lisp–whose primitive operations are injective and hence reversible" [7]. The proposal was motivated by both software engineering and physics.

The software engineering perspective, building on earlier insights by McCarthy [45] and Zelkowitz [59], recognizes that reversibility is a pervasive occurrence in a large number of programming activities:

The need to reverse a computation arises in many contexts–debugging, editor undoing, optimistic concurrency undoing, speculative computation undoing, trace scheduling, exception handling undoing, database recovery, optimistic discrete event simulations, subjunctive computing, etc. The need to analyze a reversed computation arises in the context of static analysis–liveness analysis, strictness analysis, type inference, etc. Traditional means for restoring a computation to a previous state involve checkpoints; checkpoints require time to copy, as well as space to store, the copied material. Traditional reverse abstract interpretation produces relatively poor information due to its inability to guess the previous values of assigned-to variables.

The more foundational physics perspective recognizes that a "physics revolution is brewing in computer science." This "physics revolution" traces to developments started 20 years earlier beginning with an analysis of logical (ir)reversibility and its connection to physical (ir)reversibility by Landauer [38]. This initial analysis demonstrated how an *isolated* irreversible computation can be embedded in a larger reversible one but failed to solve the problem of composing such embeddings. The solution to this puzzle was provided a decade later by Bennett [8]; it involved a general idiom compute-copy-uncompute that proved crucial for further developments. A few years later, Fredkin and Toffoli [19,55] finally designed a foundational model of composable reversible computations based purely on reversible primitives.

In our survey of part of the landscape of reversible computation, we start by reviewing the research initiatives whose goal is to develop a reversible programming language starting from existing (irreversible) languages. We will then consider the more foundational idea of taking reversibility as the main primitive notion, formalizing it, and extending it in principled ways to realize the full potential of the "physics revolution in computer science." In more detail, Sect. 2 reviews the early historical proposals for reversible computing characterized by using global history mechanisms. Section 3 discusses one of the crucial ideas necessary for compositional reversible computing: the compute-copy-uncompute paradigm. Sect. 4 exploits the power of categorical semantics to naturally express compositional reversible computing. Section 5 discusses general classes of reversible computational effects concluding with the "fundamental theorem of reversible computation." Section 6 shows that the categorical models for quantum computing are extensions of classical reversible models with computational effects. We conclude with an assessment of the broad impacts of "reversibility" on the discipline of computer science.

2   Reversibility from Global Histories

The most familiar sequential models of computation are the Turing machine and the λ-calculus. Both were proposed in the 1930s [16,57]. In the concurrent world, we have the influential models of *Communicating Sequential Processes* (CSP), the *Calculus of Communicating Systems* (CCS), and the π-calculus [28,46,47].

The methods used to derive a reversible variant of these models of computation are similar. In each case, additional constructs are added to record the information necessary for reversibility. In what follows, we discuss how to do this for the reversible extension of the λ-calculus [56] and the reversible extensions of CCS called *Reversible CCS* (RCCS) and *CCS with keys* (CCSK) [17,50].

The operational semantics of both sequential and concurrent programming languages is often specified using local reductions, e.g., $A \to B$. In a deterministic language A uniquely determines B but if the language is not reversible, the converse is not true. In other words, it is possible for have instances of reductions where both $A_1 \to B$ and $A_2 \to B$.

A straightforward way to ensure each reduction is reversible is to record additional information to disambiguate the lefthand sides. In the simplest case, we introduce a history mechanism H where we record the entire term on the lefthand side, i.e., the reductions above become:

$$\langle H \mid A_1 \rangle \to \langle H, A_1 \mid B \rangle$$
$$\langle H \mid A_2 \rangle \to \langle H, A_2 \mid B \rangle$$

An adequate history mechanism disambiguates which path the computation took to get to B, so that we now have enough information to reverse the reductions:

$$\langle H \mid A_1 \rangle \leftarrow_H \langle H, A_1 \mid B \rangle$$
$$\langle H \mid A_2 \rangle \leftarrow_H \langle H, A_2 \mid B \rangle$$

This simple scheme can be optimized in many ways to manage the history more efficiently. However, a fundamental limitation of this approach is that it fails to be *compositional*: Consider a term that includes both A_1 and A_2 as sub-terms and where A_1 should make a forward transition and A_2 make a backwards transition. Both sub-reductions require incompatible actions on the global history mechanism and direct composition is not possible. As the analysis of this problem in the context of CCSK shows [3], the best solution is to take reversibility as a basic building block, instead of a property to be achieved by extensions to an irreversible language.

3   Reversibility from Local Histories

In keeping with the approach above, Landauer observed that any Turing machine can be altered to operate reversibly by adding a dedicated *history tape* to it, recording each computational action on this tape as it occurs. However, Landauer also observed that, from a thermodynamic point of view, this approach

Stage	Tape 1	Tape 2	Tape 3
Initial configuration	Input	–	–
Compute	Output	History	–
Copy	Output	History	Output
Uncompute	Input	–	Output

Fig. 1. Bennett's construction of a standard reversible 3-tape Turing machine, starting from an arbitrary Turing machine instrumented to record its history on a dedicated tape.

Stage	Tape 1	Tape 2
Initial configuration	Input	–
Copy	Input	Input
Compute	Output	Input
Relabel	Input	Output

Fig. 2. An overly simple 2-tape Turing machine that "looks" like it operationally does the same as Bennett's construction.

is fundamentally unsatisfactory in that it merely *delays* rather than *avoids* the thermodynamic cost associated with the erasure of unwanted information [38]: to be able to reuse the tape, its contents must first be erased. To Bennett, this meant that the usefulness of a reversible computer hinged on the ability to avoid this problem, leaving behind "only the desired output and the originally furnished input" when it halts [8] (remarking that the preservation of the input is necessary to realize computable functions which happen to not be injective). This was likely the first instance of *reversibility as compositionality*, and has since been rediscovered numerous times in the context of circuits, programming languages, and categorical semantics.

It is amusing to note that "undo/redo" functionality in modern user-interfaces use either the *Command Pattern* or the *Memento Pattern*, which both amount to the non-composable Landauer encoding.

3.1 Bennett's Trick

The key insight behind Bennett's trick is that the use of *uncomputation* (i.e., inverse interpretation of a *reversible* Turing machine) can reduce the dependence on a computation history to the preservation of the input. This is done by proceeding in three stages (see Fig. 1): *compute* executes the Turing machine to obtain the output and its history, *copy* copies the output onto a dedicated output tape (assumed to be empty), and *uncompute* executes the Turing machine in reverse to reduce the output and history to the original input.

If we think of the computation history more generally as the garbage that is inevitably produced during computation (i.e., temporary storage needed during computation that can safely be discarded afterwards), Bennett's trick gives a reversible way of managing garbage without having to erase it outright. This allows procedures that use the same pool of temporary storage to be composed without incident, as they can all safely assume the store to be empty when needed. This technique is used to manage memory in, e.g., reversible programming languages [4] and reversible circuits [54].

Naïvely, one might suppose that a simpler approach (see Fig. 2) might work too. The problem is that this only works when the Turing machine is reversible to begin with! Furthermore, what is "Relabel"? Is that even an available operation on Turing machines? We could think of replacing Relabel with some kind of Swap operation, but since there is no guarantee that Input and Output are the same length, this operation is not reversible either without further assumptions. Another way to look at it: if one were working in a dependently typed language, Bennett's construction would require a proof that the history information is sufficient to actually drive the given Turing machine *deterministically* backwards.

3.2   Reversibility as a Local Phenomenon

While it seems clear that maintaining a history during computation is a general method for guaranteeing that the resulting Turing machine is reversible, it doesn't actually answer what it means for a Turing machine to be reversible in the first place.

Lecerf [40] answered this by defining a reversible Turing machine to be one where at each computational state, there is at most one *next* state and at most one *previous* state. We can express this more precisely using the judgement $\sigma \vdash c \downarrow \sigma'$, taken to mean that executing the command c while the machine is in state σ leads the machine to transition to the state σ'. The unicity of the next and previous states become the statements (see, e.g., [21]) that for all commands c and origin states σ, there is *at most* one next state σ' such that $\sigma \vdash c \downarrow \sigma'$ (forward determinism); and for all commands c and states σ', there is *at most* one origin state σ such that $\sigma \vdash c \downarrow \sigma'$ (backward determinism).

This establishes reversibility as a local phenomenon linked directly to compositionality: it is not enough to compute an injective function (a global property) to be reversible, it must also be done by taking only invertible steps along the way. Indeed, a defining consequence of this very strong conception of reversibility (amusingly dubbed the "Copenhagen interpretation" of reversible computation by Yokoyama [5,21]) is the property of *local invertibility*, allowing a reversible machine (or program) to be inverted by recursive descent over the syntax [20]. This idea was taken to its logical conclusion in the (explicitly compositional) denotational account of reversibility [35], where it was argued that a program should be considered to be reversible just in case it can be constructed by combining only invertible parts in ways that preserve invertibility. A reasonable place to take such denotational semantics is in categories of invertible maps, such as inverse categories [34,36] and groupoids [12,13].

4   Rig Groupoids

Category theory deals with abstractions in a uniform and systematic way, and is widely used to provide compositional programming semantics. We briefly discuss the types of categories that are useful in reversible programming: dagger categories and rig categories.

4.1 Dagger Categories and Groupoids

A morphism $f: A \to B$ is *invertible*, or an *isomorphism*, when there exists a morphism $f^{-1}: B \to A$ such that $f^{-1} \circ f = \mathrm{id}_A$ and $f \circ f^{-1} = \mathrm{id}_B$. This inverse f^{-1} is necessarily unique. A category where every morphism is invertible is called a *groupoid*. At first sight, groupoids form the perfect semantics for reversible computing. But every step in a computation being reversible is slightly less restrictive than it being invertible. For each step $f: A \to B$, there must still be a way to 'undo' it, given by $f^\dagger: B \to A$. This should also still respect composition, in that $(g \circ f)^\dagger = f^\dagger \circ g^\dagger$ and $\mathrm{id}_A^\dagger = \mathrm{id}_A$. Moreover, a 'cancelled undo' should not change anything: $f^{\dagger\dagger} = f$. Therefore every morphism f has a partner $f^\dagger$. A category equipped with such a choice of partners is called a *dagger category*.

A groupoid is an example of a dagger category, where every morphism is *unitary*, that is, $f^\dagger = f^{-1}$. Think, for example, of the category **FinBij** with finite sets for objects and bijections for morphisms. But not every dagger category is a groupoid. For example, the dagger category **PInj** has sets as objects, and partial injections as morphisms. Here, the dagger satisfies $f \circ f^\dagger \circ f = f$, but not necessarily $f^\dagger \circ f = \mathrm{id}$ because f may only be partially defined. In a sense, the dagger category **PInj** is the universal model for reversible partial computation [22, 36].

When a category has a dagger, it makes sense to demand that every other structure on the category respects the dagger, and we will do so. The theory of dagger categories is similar to the theory of categories in some ways, but very different in others [26].

4.2 Monoidal Categories and Rig Categories

Programming becomes easier when less encoding is necessary, i.e. when there are more first-class primitives. For example, it is handy to have type combinators like sums and products. Semantically, this is modeled by considering not mere categories, but monoidal ones. A *monoidal category* is a category equipped with a type combinator that turns two objects A and B into an object $A \otimes B$, and a term combinator that turns two morphisms $f: A \to B$ and $f': A' \to B'$ into a morphism $f \otimes f': A \otimes A' \to B \otimes B'$. This has to respect composition and identities. Moreover, there has to be an object I that acts as a unit for $\otimes$, and isomorphisms $\alpha: A \otimes (B \otimes C) \to (A \otimes B) \otimes C$ and $\lambda: I \otimes A \to A$ and $\rho: A \otimes I \to A$. In a *symmetric monoidal category*, there are additionally isomorphisms $\sigma: A \otimes B \to B \otimes A$. All these isomorphisms have to respect composition and satisfy certain coherence conditions, see [43] or [27, Chapter1]. We speak of a *(symmetric) monoidal dagger category* when the coherence isomorphisms are unitary. Intuitively, $g \circ f$ models sequential composition, and $f \otimes g$ models parallel composition. For example, **FinBij** and **PInj** are symmetric monoidal dagger categories under cartesian product.

$$b ::= 0 \mid 1 \mid b + b \mid b \times b \qquad \text{(value types)}$$
$$t ::= b \leftrightarrow b \qquad \text{(combinator types)}$$
$$i ::= id \mid swap^+ \mid assocr^+ \mid assocl^+ \mid unite^+l \mid uniti^+l \qquad \text{(isomorphisms)}$$
$$\mid swap^\times \mid assocr^\times \mid assocl^\times \mid unite^\times l \mid uniti^\times l$$
$$\mid dist \mid factor \mid absorbl \mid factorzr$$
$$c ::= i \mid c \, \mathring{\circ} \, c \mid c + c \mid c \times c \mid inv \; c \qquad \text{(combinators)}$$

Fig. 3. Π syntax

$$
\begin{array}{rcl}
id : & b \leftrightarrow b & : id \\
swap^+ : & b_1 + b_2 \leftrightarrow b_2 + b_1 & : swap^+ \\
assocr^+ : & (b_1 + b_2) + b_3 \leftrightarrow b_1 + (b_2 + b_3) & : assocl^+ \\
unite^+l : & 0 + b \leftrightarrow b & : uniti^+l \\
swap^\times : & b_1 \times b_2 \leftrightarrow b_2 \times b_1 & : swap^\times \\
assocr^\times : & (b_1 \times b_2) \times b_3 \leftrightarrow b_1 \times (b_2 \times b_3) & : assocl^\times \\
unite^\times l : & 1 \times b \leftrightarrow b & : uniti^\times l \\
dist : & (b_1 + b_2) \times b_3 \leftrightarrow (b_1 \times b_3) + (b_2 \times b_3) & : factor \\
absorbl : & b \times 0 \leftrightarrow 0 & : factorzr
\end{array}
$$

$$\frac{c_1 : b_1 \leftrightarrow b_2 \quad c_2 : b_2 \leftrightarrow b_3}{c_1 \, \mathring{\circ} \, c_2 : b_1 \leftrightarrow b_3} \qquad \frac{c : b_1 \leftrightarrow b_2}{inv \; c : b_2 \leftrightarrow b_1}$$

$$\frac{c_1 : b_1 \leftrightarrow b_3 \quad c_2 : b_2 \leftrightarrow b_4}{c_1 + c_2 : b_1 + b_2 \leftrightarrow b_3 + b_4} \qquad \frac{c_1 : b_1 \leftrightarrow b_3 \quad c_2 : b_2 \leftrightarrow b_4}{c_1 \times c_2 : b_1 \times b_2 \leftrightarrow b_3 \times b_4}$$

Fig. 4. Types for Π combinators

A *rig category* is monoidal in two ways in a distributive fashion. More precisely, it has two monoidal structures $\oplus$ and $\otimes$, such that $\oplus$ is symmetric monoidal but $\otimes$ not necessarily symmetric, and there are isomorphisms $\delta_L : A \otimes (B \oplus C) \rightarrow (A \otimes B) \oplus (A \otimes C)$ and $\delta_0 : A \otimes 0 \rightarrow 0$. These isomorphisms again have to respect composition and certain coherence conditions [39]. For example, **FinBij** and **PInj** are not only monoidal under cartesian product, but also under disjoint union, and the appropriate distributivity holds. Intuitively, given $f : A \rightarrow B$ and $g : C \rightarrow D$, $f \oplus g : A \oplus C \rightarrow B \oplus D$ models a choice between f and g, predicated on whether it gets an A or a B as choice of input.

4.3 The Canonical Term Model Π

Given a rig groupoid, we may think of the objects as types, and the morphisms as terms [41]. The syntax of the language Π in Fig. 3 captures this idea. Type expressions b are built from the empty type (0), the unit type (1), the sum type (+), and the product type ($\times$). A type isomorphism $c : b_1 \leftrightarrow b_2$ models a reversible function that permutes the values in b_1 and b_2. These type isomorphisms are built from the primitive identities i and their compositions. These isomorphisms correspond exactly to the laws of a *rig* operationalised into invertible transformations [12,13] which have the types in Fig. 4. Each line in the top part of the figure has the pattern $c_1 : b_1 \leftrightarrow b_2 : c_2$ where c_1 and c_2 are self-duals; c_1 has type $b_1 \leftrightarrow b_2$ and c_2 has type $b_2 \leftrightarrow b_1$.

To recap, the "groupoid" structure arises when we want all terms of our programming language to be typed, reversible and composable. The "rig" part, is a pun on "ring" where the removal of the "n" indicates that we do not have *negatives*. The multiplicative structure is used to model *parallel* composition, and the additive structure is a form of *branching* composition. All this structure is essentially forced on us once we assume that we want to work over the (weak) semiring of finite types with products and coproducts. We remark that in the categorical setting of Π, there are no issues in having terms like ($assocr^\times \times factor$) of the form ($c_1 \times c_2$) with c_1 is an isomorphism in the forward direction and c_2 is an isomorphism in the reverse direction. Composition is natural!

4.4   Finite Sets and Permutations

It is folklore that the groupoid of finite sets and permutations is the free symmetric rig groupoid on zero generators [6,37,39]. Given that the syntax of Π is presented by the free symmetric rig groupoid, given by finite sets and permutations, the folklore result can be formally established [15]. The formal connection provides an equational theory for Π that exactly includes all the necessary equations to decide equivalence of Π programs.

4.5   Curry-Howard

Reversible computation also brings new light to the Curry-Howard correspondance. The original correspondance, between type theory and logic, formally focuses on *equi-inhabitation*. This is because while logically A and $A \wedge A$ (as well as A and $A \vee A$) are logically equivalent, clearly, as types, A and $A \times A$ (similarly, A and $A + A$) are not equivalent. They are, however, equi-inhabited, i.e. we can show that $a : A$ if and only if $b : A \times A$, but the witnessing functions are not inverses. We can thus say that the Curry-Howard correspondance focuses on logically equivalent types (often denoted $A \Leftrightarrow B$).

In Π, we replace logical equivalence by equivalence $A \simeq B$. And what used to be a correspondance between classical type theory (involving types, functions and logical equivalence) and logic, transforms into a correspondance between reversible type theory (involving types, reversible functions and equivalences) and *algebra*, in this case rigs and their categorified cousins, rig categories. This picture emerged in the first looks at Π [12,13] and was shown to be *complete* more recently [15]. In other words, Π is the inevitable programming language that arises from universal reversible computing being semantically about **FinBij**.

5   Reversible and Irreversible Effects

Expressing reversibility in a categorical setting enables the integration of additional constructs using universal categorical constructions such as monads and arrows.

5.1   Frobenius Monads and Reversible Arrows

So far, we have modeled computations as morphisms in a category. But often it makes sense to separate out specific aspects of computation, distinguishing between *pure* computations, that only concern themselves with computing values, and *effectful* computations, that can additionally have side effects, such as interacting with their environment through measurement.

A *monad* T is a way to encapsulate computational side effects in a modular way. If A is an type, then $T(A)$ is the type of A with possible side effects. For example, for the *maybe* monad $T(A) = A + 1$, a term of type $T(A)$ is either a term of type A or the unique term of type 1, which may be thought of as an exception having occurred.

Regarding morphisms $A \to B$ as pure computations, computations that can have side effects governed by T are then morphisms $A \to T(B)$. For this to make sense, we need three ingredients, which are what makes T into a monad: first, a way to consider a pure morphism $A \to B$ as an effectful one $A \to T(B)$; second, to lift a pure morphism $A \to B$ to the effectful setting $T(A) \to T(B)$; and third, a way to sequence effectful computations $f \colon A \to T(B)$ and $g \colon B \to T(C)$ into $f \ggg g \colon A \to T(C)$. The resulting category of effectful computations is called the *Kleisli category* of the monad T [48].

What about the reversible setting? If the category of pure computations has a dagger, when does the category of effectful computations have a dagger that extends the reversal of pure computations? It turns out that this can be captured neatly in terms of the monad alone. The Kleisli category has a dagger if and only if the monad is a *dagger Frobenius monad* [26], meaning that

$$T(f)^\dagger = T(f^\dagger) \qquad \text{and} \qquad T(\mu_A) \circ \mu_{T(A)}^\dagger = \mu_{T(A)} \circ T(\mu_A^\dagger),$$

where $\mu_A \colon T(T(A)) \to T(A)$ is the sequencing of the identity $T(A) \to T(A)$, regarded as an effectful computation from $T(A)$ to A, with itself.

More generally, we can talk about *arrows* instead of monads. These still allow a sequential composition of effectful computations [29, 32], and still extend to the reversible setting [25].

5.2   The Fundamental Theorem of Reversible Computation

In this section, we define and further discuss the fundamental theorem of reversible computing in terms of *universal properties*. These are categorical properties that characterize the result of some construction in terms of its behavior only and not in terms of the particular construction itself. For example, singleton sets 1 are characterized by the fact that there is a unique function $A \to 1$ for any set A; notice that the property only speaks about morphisms into 1, and never about how 1 is built of a single element. We say that 1 is a *terminal object* in the category of sets and functions. In the opposite direction, the empty set is an *initial object*, meaning that there is a unique function $0 \to A$ for any set A. Similarly, the cartesian product $A \times B$ of sets can be characterized universally as a categorical *product* of A and B, and the disjoin union $A + B$ as a *coproduct*: these are the universal objects equipped with projections $A \leftarrow A \times B \rightarrow B$ respectively injections $A \rightarrow A + B \leftarrow B$ [41].

The fundamental theorem of reversible computing (originally proved by Toffoli for functions over finite collections of boolean variables [55]) can now be phrased categorically as follows [24].

We first recall the *LR-construction* [2] which turns a rig category into another category where I is terminal and 0 is initial. In more detail, morphisms $A \rightarrow B$ in the new category $\mathbf{LR}[\mathbf{C}]$ are morphisms $A \oplus H \rightarrow B \otimes G$ in the old category $\mathbf{C}$, which we identify if they behave similarly on the 'heap' H and 'garbage' G. The fundamental theorem of reversible computing follows by noting that there is an inclusion from the category $\mathbf{Bij}$ of sets and bijections to the category $\mathbf{Set}$ of sets and all functions. Then, by the universal property of the LR-construction, this inclusion factors through a functor $\mathbf{LR}[\mathbf{Bij}] \rightarrow \mathbf{Set}$. Any function in $\mathbf{Set}$ is in the image of this functor. In other words, any function $f : A \rightarrow B$ is of the form

$$A \xrightarrow{i} A + H \xrightarrow{\sim} B \times G \xrightarrow{\pi} B,$$

where I is a coproduct injection, π is a product projection, G is the garbage, and the function in the middle is a bijection.[1]

6 Quantum Effects

It turns out that the standard model of quantum computing is a dagger rig category. It is therefore natural to investigate the classical-quantum connection(s) by investigating the corresponding instances of rig categories.

6.1 The Hilbert Space Model

Quantum computing with pure states is a specific kind of reversible computing [49,58]. A quantum system is modeled by a finite-dimensional Hilbert space A. For example, *qubits* are modeled by $\mathbb{C}^2$. The category giving semantics to finite-dimensional pure state quantum theory is therefore $\mathbf{FHilb}$, whose objects are finite-dimensional Hilbert spaces, and whose morphisms are linear maps. Categorical semantics for pure state quantum computing is the groupoid $\mathbf{Unitary}$ of finite-dimensional Hilbert spaces as objects with unitaries as morphisms. Both are rig categories under direct sum $\oplus$ and tensor product $\otimes$.

The pure *states* of a quantum system modeled by a Hilbert space A are the vectors of unit norm, conventionally denoted by a *ket* $|y\rangle \in A$. These are equivalently given by morphisms $\mathbb{C} \rightarrow A$ in $\mathbf{FHilb}$ that map $z \in \mathbb{C}$ to $z|y\rangle \in A$.

---

[1] As noted earlier, Toffoli only proved this for finite sets. We thank Tom Leinster for the following neat proof for infinite sets. In a category with products, every morphism $f : A \rightarrow B$ factors as a split monic $(1, f) : A \rightarrow A \times B$ followed by a product projection $A \times B \rightarrow B$. But in $\mathbf{Set}$, split monics are exactly the same as injections, which are coproduct injections up to an isomorphism.

Dually, the functional $A \to \mathbb{C}$ which maps $y \in A$ to the inner product $\langle x|y \rangle$ is conventionally written as a *bra* $\langle x|$. Morphisms $A \to \mathbb{C}$ are also called *effects*.

In fact, **FHilb** is a dagger rig category. The *dagger* of linear map $f \colon A \to B$ is uniquely determined via the inner product by $\langle f(x)|y \rangle = \langle x|f^\dagger(y) \rangle$. The dagger of a state is an effect, and vice versa. In quantum computing, pure states evolve along unitary gates. These are exactly the morphisms that are unitary in the sense of dagger categories in that $f^\dagger \circ f = $ id and $f \circ f^\dagger = $ id, exhibiting the groupoid **Unitary** as a dagger subcategory of **FHilb**.

There is a way to translate the category **FPInj** of finite sets and partial injections to the category **FHilb**, that sends $\{0, \ldots, n-1\}$ to $\mathbb{C}^n$. This translation preserves composition, identities, tensor product, direct sum, and dagger: it is a dagger rig functor $\ell^2 \colon$ **FPInj** $\to$ **FHilb**, that restricts to a dagger rig functor **FinBij** $\to$ **Unitary**. Thus reversible computing (**FinBij**) is to classical reversible theory (**FPInj**) as quantum computing (**Unitary**) is to quantum theory (**FHilb**). In particular, in this way, the Boolean controlled-controlled-not function (known as the *Toffoli gate*), which is universal for reversible computing, transfers to a quantum gate with the same name that acts on vectors.

6.2   The Hadamard Mystery

Shi established that quantum computing can be characterized as a relatively small increment over classical computing [52]. The precise statement below is adapted from Aharonov's reformulation of Shi's result [1].

Theorem 1. *The set consisting of just the Toffoli and Hadamard gates is computationally universal for quantum computing. By computationally universal, we mean that the set can simulate, to within ϵ-error, an arbitrary quantum circuit of n qubits and t gates with only poly-logarithmic overhead in $(n, t, 1/\epsilon)$.*

The result may appear counter-intuitive since it omits any reference to complex numbers. The subtlety is that *computational universality* allows arbitrary—but efficient—encodings of complex vectors and matrices.

The significance of this result is the following. The Toffoli gate is known to be universal for classical computing over finite domains [55]. Thus, in one sense, a quantum computation is nothing but a classical computation that is given access to one extra primitive, the Hadamard transform.

Once expressed in rig categories, this result allows novel characterizations of quantum computing. The key to these characterizations is that quantum gates are *not* black boxes in rig categories: they are "white boxes" constructed from $\oplus$ and other primitives which means that can be decomposed and recomposed during rewriting using the coherence conditions of rig categories. For example, while a circuit theory will allow one to derive that $TT = S$, it is unable to provide justification for this in terms of the definitions of S and T. On the other hand, the rig model reduces this equation to the bifunctoriality of $\oplus$ and the definitions of S and T. This style of reasoning enabled two recent characterizations of quantum computing by (universal) categorical constructions. In the first paper [14], Hadamard is recovered by two copies of Π mediated by one equation for *complementarity*. In the second paper [11], Hadamard is recovered by postulating the existence of square roots for certain morphisms, i.e. the existence of morphisms $\sqrt{f}$ such that $\sqrt{f} \circ \sqrt{f} = f$.

6.3   Quantum Information Effects

Information effects [24,33] emulate the dynamics of open systems using the reversible dynamics of closed systems, by extending the latter with the ability to hide parts of the input and output spaces. This allows auxiliary states to be prepared and (parts of) the output to be discarded – as a consequence, measurement is recovered in the quantum case.

This idea comes from the theory of quantum computation, where *Stinespring's dilation theorem* [53] (see also [23,30,31]) provides a recipe for reconstructing the reversible dynamics of an irreversible quantum channel by outfitting it with an auxiliary system that can be used as a sink for the data that the process discards.

Concretely, given a quantum channel $\Lambda : H \to K$ (which can be thought of as a quantum circuit where measurements can occur), Stinespring's theorem argues that it is always possible to factor a quantum channel as an isometry (a kind of injective quantum map) $V : H \to H \otimes G$ followed by a projection $\pi_1 : H \otimes G \to H$. Note that projection is not as innocuous as it is in the classical case, since it may lead to the formation of probabilistic (mixed) states. In turn, it can be shown that every isometry can be realized by fixing a part of the input to a reversible (unitary) quantum map [30]: in other words, every isometry factors as an injection $\iota_1 : H \to H \oplus E$ (fixing a part of the inputs) followed by a reversible (unitary) quantum map $U : H \oplus E \to K$.

Putting these two factorizations together, we get that any quantum channel (i.e., irreversible quantum process) $\Lambda : H \to K$ factors (in an essentially unique way) into three stages:

$$H \xrightarrow{\text{prepare auxiliary state}} H \oplus G \xrightarrow{\text{reversible dynamics}} K \otimes E \xrightarrow{\text{discard environment}} K$$

Put another way, every quantum channel can be written as a unitary in which a part of the input (corresponding to the subsystem G above receiving a fixed state) and a part of the output (corresponding to the subsystem E above that is discarded after use) is hidden from view.

This factorization is clearly reminiscent of the fundamental theorem of reversible computing and the LR-construction of Sect. 5.2. More concretely, we define the hiding of the input and output through a stack of two separate effects, which turn out to correspond to *arrows*, and so give suitable notions of effectful programs with sequential and parallel composition. To that end, we define Π with allocation to have the same base types b as Π, and with the combinator type $b_1 \rightarrowtail b_2$. Terms in Π with allocation are given by the formation rule:

$$\frac{u : b_1 + b_3 \leftrightarrow b_2}{lift(u) : b_1 \rightarrowtail b_2}$$

That is, terms in Π with allocation are given by Π terms where part of their input is hidden. Additionally, we consider two terms in Π with allocation to be equal if they are equal up to an arbitrary term applied on the hidden part alone. These terms can be composed in sequence by:

$$lift(u) \ggg lift(v) = lift(assocl^+ \,\mathbin{\substack{\circ\\\circ}}\, (u \oplus id) \,\mathbin{\substack{\circ\\\circ}}\, v)$$

and it can be shown that this is associative, and that $lift(unite^+)$ acts as the identity with respect to composition. More generally, every Π term $u : b_1 \to b_2$ can be turned into one $arr(u) : b_1 \rightarrowtail b_2$ that acts as u does by letting it hide only the empty system, that is:

$$arr(u) = lift(unite^+ \,\mathbin{\substack{\circ\\\circ}}\, u)$$

Finally, it can be shown that this also allows a parallel composition $lift(u) \Whnew lift(v)$ to be defined, giving it all the structure of an arrow.

A consequence of these definitions is that can define a new term

$$alloc = lift(unite^+ l) : 0 \rightarrowtail b$$

which can be thought of as allocating a constant value from a hidden heap. It can be shown that this ability to allocate new constants is enough to extend Π with the ability to perform arbitrary injections $inl : b_1 \rightarrowtail b_1 + b_2$ and $inr : b_2 \rightarrowtail b_1 + b_2$, and to do classical cloning via a term $clone : b \rightarrowtail b \times b$. This is the first step of two in recovering open system dynamics from their reversible foundations.

The second step is a study in duality: to further extend Π with allocation and hiding, we introduce yet another arrow whose base types are the same as those of Π, and whose combinator types are given by a new type $b_1 \rightsquigarrow b_2$. Terms in this new layer are formed by the rule:

$$\frac{v : b_1 \rightarrowtail b_2 \times b_3}{lift(v) : b_1 \rightsquigarrow b_2}$$

and, by analogy to the previous definitions, one can define sequential and parallel composition, identities, and the lifting of arbitrary terms $v : b_1 \rightarrowtail b_2$ to $arr(v) : b_1 \rightsquigarrow b_2$ by adjoining the trivial system 1. This gives it the structure of an arrow. A consequence of this is that arbitrary data can now be discarded via a term $discard : b \rightsquigarrow 1$, and by combining this with parallel composition and the unitor $unite^\times : b \times 1 \rightarrowtail b$, we obtain projections $fst : b_1 \times b_2 \rightsquigarrow b_1$ and $snd : b_1 \times b_2 \rightsquigarrow b_2$, completing our journey from fully reversible to fully irreversible dynamics.

While it seems clear that we can recover irreversible classical computing from their reversible foundations by extending them with the ability to allocate constants and hide arbitrary data, it is less clear that one can also recover irreversible quantum computing this way. Surprisingly, this is so, with measurement (i.e., the map that sends a quantum state to its post measurement state after measurement in the computational basis) given the (classically nonsensical) term:

$$measure = clone \ggg fst : b \rightsquigarrow b.$$

and it can be verified that this recovers the usual Born rule assigning probabilities to classical measurement outcomes.

7   Conclusions and Future Research

Pragmatically, reversible computing, reversible programming languages, and bidirectional methods in computing have unified many of the original software engineering instances of reversibility which is clearly a positive contribution to the field of computer science.

But it has been 32 years since Baker stated that a "physics revolution is brewing in computer science" and it is fair to ask to what extent has this "revolution" been realized?

From the very beginning, one of the most common arguments for the physics revolution in computer science has been the potential to drastically reduce the energy needs of computation. The reasoning is that only irreversible operations need to dissipate heat and hence reversible computing can in principle operate near the thermodynamic limit. Despite its theoretical plausibility and its experimental validation [9,38], the promise of drastically more energy-efficient computers has not yet materialized.

We argue that the real revolution is more of a conceptual one, affecting what we mean by computation, logic, and information, and unifying them in ways that give new insights about the nature of logic and the fundamental limits of information processing by computers.

On the one hand, treating information as a first-class entity promotes several ad hoc techniques to the fold of well-established logical and semantic techniques. Examples includes the methods used in applications such as quantitative information-flow security [51], differential privacy [18], energy-aware computing [42,60], VLSI design [44], and biochemical models of computation [10].

On the other hand, reversible computing is the first key to understanding how Nature computes, how to integrate computational models with their physical environments, and to explore new modes of computation such as molecular computing, biologically-inspired computing, neuromorphic computing, emerging phenomena in complex systems, and of course quantum computing.

Acknowledgments. This material is based upon work supported by the National Science Foundation under Grant No. 1936353.

Disclosure of Interests. The authors have no competing interests to declare that are relevant to the content of this article.

References

1. Aharonov, D.: A simple proof that Toffoli and Hadamard are quantum universal (2003). arXiv:quant-ph/0301040
2. Andrés-Martínez, P., Heunen, C., Kaarsgaard, R.: Universal properties of partial quantum maps (2022). arXiv:2206.04814
3. Aubert, C.: The correctness of concurrencies in (reversible) concurrent calculi. J. Log. Algebraic Methods Program. 100924 (2023). https://doi.org/10.1016/j.jlamp.2023.100924
4. Axelsen, H.B.: Clean translation of an imperative reversible programming language. In: Knoop, J. (ed.) CC 2011. LNCS, vol. 6601, pp. 144–163. Springer, Heidelberg (2011). https://doi.org/10.1007/978-3-642-19861-8_9
5. Axelsen, H.B.: Private communication (2015)
6. Baez, J.C., Dolan, J.: From finite sets to Feynman diagrams (2000). arXiv:000413
7. Baker, H.G.: NREVERSAL of fortune—the thermodynamics of garbage collection. In: Bekkers, Y., Cohen, J. (eds.) IWMM 1992. LNCS, vol. 637, pp. 507–524. Springer, Heidelberg (1992). https://doi.org/10.1007/BFb0017210
8. Bennett, C.H.: Logical reversibility of computation. IBM J. Res. Dev. **17**(6), 525–532 (1973). https://doi.org/10.1147/rd.176.0525
9. Bérut, A., Arakelyan, A., Petrosyan, A., Ciliberto, S., Dillenschneider, R., Lutz, E.: Experimental verification of Landauer's principle linking information and thermodynamics. Nature **483**(7388), 187–189 (2012). https://doi.org/10.1038/nature10872
10. Cardelli, L., Zavattaro, G.: On the computational power of biochemistry. In: Horimoto, K., Regensburger, G., Rosenkranz, M., Yoshida, H. (eds.) AB 2008. LNCS, vol. 5147, pp. 65–80. Springer, Heidelberg (2008). https://doi.org/10.1007/978-3-540-85101-1_6
11. Carette, J., Heunen, C., Kaarsgaard, R., Sabry, A.: With a few square roots, quantum computing is as easy as Π. Proc. ACM Program. Lang. **8**(POPL), 546–574 (2024)
12. Carette, J., James, R.P., Sabry, A.: Embracing the laws of physics: three reversible models of computation. Adv. Comput. **126**, 15–63 (2022). https://doi.org/10.1016/bs.adcom.2021.11.009, https://www.sciencedirect.com/science/article/pii/S0065245821000838
13. Carette, J., Sabry, A.: Computing with semirings and weak rig groupoids. In: Thiemann, P. (ed.) ESOP 2016. LNCS, vol. 9632, pp. 123–148. Springer, Heidelberg (2016). https://doi.org/10.1007/978-3-662-49498-1_6
14. Carette, J., Heunen, C., Kaarsgaard, R., Sabry, A.: The quantum effect: a recipe for QuantumPi (2023). arXiv:2302.01885
15. Choudhury, V., Karwowski, J., Sabry, A.: Symmetries in reversible programming: from symmetric rig groupoids to reversible programming languages. Proc. ACM Program. Lang. **6**(POPL) (2022). https://doi.org/10.1145/3498667
16. Church, A.: A set of postulates for the foundation of logic. Ann. Math. **33**(2), 346–366 (1932). http://www.jstor.org/stable/1968337
17. Danos, V., Krivine, J.: Reversible communicating systems. In: Gardner, P., Yoshida, N. (eds.) CONCUR 2004. LNCS, vol. 3170, pp. 292–307. Springer, Heidelberg (2004). https://doi.org/10.1007/978-3-540-28644-8_19
18. Dwork, C.: Differential privacy. In: Bugliesi, M., Preneel, B., Sassone, V., Wegener, I. (eds.) ICALP 2006. LNCS, vol. 4052, pp. 1–12. Springer, Heidelberg (2006). https://doi.org/10.1007/11787006_1

19. Fredkin, E., Toffoli, T.: Conservative logic. Int. J. Theor. Phys. **21**(3), 219–253 (1982). https://doi.org/10.1007/BF01857727
20. Glück, R., Kawabe, M.: Derivation of deterministic inverse programs based on LR parsing. In: Kameyama, Y., Stuckey, P.J. (eds.) FLOPS 2004. LNCS, vol. 2998, pp. 291–306. Springer, Heidelberg (2004). https://doi.org/10.1007/978-3-540-24754-8_21
21. Glück, R., Yokoyama, T.: Reversible computing from a programming language perspective. Theoret. Comput. Sci. **953**, 113429 (2023). https://doi.org/10.1016/j.tcs.2022.06.010, https://www.sciencedirect.com/science/article/pii/S0304397522003619
22. Heunen, C.: On the functor ℓ^2. In: Coecke, B., Ong, L., Panangaden, P. (eds.) Computation, Logic, Games, and Quantum Foundations. The Many Facets of Samson Abramsky. LNCS, vol. 7860, pp. 107–121. Springer, Heidelberg (2013). https://doi.org/10.1007/978-3-642-38164-5_8
23. Heunen, C., Kaarsgaard, R.: Bennett and Stinespring, together at last. In: Proceedings 18th International Conference on Quantum Physics and Logic (QPL 2021). Electronic Proceedings in Theoretical Computer Science, vol. 343, pp. 102–118. OPA (2021). https://doi.org/10.4204/EPTCS.343.5
24. Heunen, C., Kaarsgaard, R.: Quantum information effects. Proc. ACM Program. Lang. **6**(POPL), 1–27 (2022)
25. Heunen, C., Kaarsgaard, R., Karvonen, M.: Reversible effects as inverse arrows. In: Proceedings of the Thirty-Fourth Conference on the Mathematical Foundations of Programming Semantics (MFPS XXXIV). Electronic Notes in Theoretical Computer Science, vol. 341, pp. 179–199. Elsevier (2018)
26. Heunen, C., Karvonen, M.: Monads on dagger categories. Theory Appl. Categories **31**, 1016–1043 (2016)
27. Heunen, C., Vicary, J.: Categories for Quantum Theory. Oxford University Press, Oxford (2019)
28. Hoare, C.A.R.: Communicating sequential processes. Commun. ACM **21**(8), 666–677 (1978). https://doi.org/10.1145/359576.359585
29. Hughes, J.: Programming with arrows. In: Vene, V., Uustalu, T. (eds.) AFP 2004. LNCS, vol. 3622, pp. 73–129. Springer, Heidelberg (2005). https://doi.org/10.1007/11546382_2
30. Huot, M., Staton, S.: Quantum channels as a categorical completion. In: Proceedings of the ACM/IEEE Symposium on Logic in Computer Science, vol. 35, pp. 1–13 (2019)
31. Huot, M., Staton, S.: Universal properties in quantum theory. In: Selinger, P., Chiribella, G. (eds.) Proceedings of the 15th International Conference on Quantum Physics and Logic (QPL 2018). Electronic Proceedings in Theoretical Computer Science, vol. 287, pp. 213–224. Open Publishing Association (2018).https://doi.org/10.4204/EPTCS.287.12
32. Jacobs, B., Heunen, C., Hasuo, I.: Categorical semantics for Arrows. J. Funct. Program. **19**(3–4), 403–438 (2009). https://doi.org/10.1017/S0956796809007308
33. James, R.P., Sabry, A.: Information effects. In: POPL 2012: Proceedings of the 39th Annual ACM SIGPLAN-SIGACT Symposium on Principles of programming languages, pp. 73–84. ACM (2012). https://doi.org/10.1145/2103656.2103667
34. Kaarsgaard, R., Glück, R.: A categorical foundation for structured reversible flowchart languages: soundness and adequacy. Log. Methods Comput. Sci. **14**(3) (2018)
35. Kaarsgaard, R.: The logic of reversible computing: theory and practice. Ph.D. thesis, Department of Computer Science, University of Copenhagen (2018)

36. Kastl, J.: Algebraische Modelle, Kategorien und Gruppoide, Studien zur Algebra und ihre Anwendungen, vol. 7, chap. Inverse categories, pp. 51–60. Akademie-Verlag, Berlin (1979)
37. Kelly, G.M.: Coherence theorems for lax algebras and for distributive laws. In: Kelly, G.M. (ed.) Category Seminar. LNM, vol. 420, pp. 281–375. Springer, Heidelberg (1974). https://doi.org/10.1007/BFb0063106
38. Landauer, R.: Irreversibility and heat generation in the computing process. IBM J. Res. Dev. **5**(3), 183–191 (1961). https://doi.org/10.1147/rd.53.0183
39. Laplaza, M.L.: Coherence for distributivity. In: Kelly, G.M., Laplaza, M., Lewis, G., Mac Lane, S. (eds.) Coherence in Categories. LNM, vol. 281, pp. 29–65. Springer, Heidelberg (1972). https://doi.org/10.1007/BFb0059555
40. Lecerf, Y.: Machines de Turing reversibles. Compt. Rendus hebdomadaires seances l'acad. sci. **257**, 2597–2600 (1963)
41. Leinster, T.: Basic Category Theory. Cambridge University Press, Cambridge (2014)
42. Ma, X., Huang, J., Lombardi, F.: A model for computing and energy dissipation of molecular QCA devices and circuits. J. Emerg. Technol. Comput. Syst. **3**(4) (2008). https://doi.org/10.1145/1324177.1324180
43. Mac Lane, S.: Natural associativity and commutativity. Rice Univ. Stud. **49**(4) (1963)
44. Macii, E., Poncino, M.: Exact computation of the entropy of a logic circuit. In: Proceedings of the Sixth Great Lakes Symposium on VLSI, pp. 162–167 (1996). https://doi.org/10.1109/GLSV.1996.497613
45. McCarthy, J.: The inversion of functions defined by Turing machines. In: C.E. Shannon, J.M. (ed.) Automata Studies, Annals of Mathematical Studies, pp. 177–181. No. 34. Princeton University Press (1956)
46. Milner, R.: A Calculus of Communicating Systems. Lecture Notes in Computer Science, vol. 92. Springer, Heidelberg (1980). https://doi.org/10.1007/3-540-10235-3
47. Milner, R.: Functions as processes. Math. Struct. Comput. Sci. **2**(2), 119–141 (1992). https://doi.org/10.1017/S0960129500001407
48. Moggi, E.: Notions of computations and monads. Inf. Comput. **93**, 55–92 (1991)
49. Nielsen, M.A., Chuang, I.: Quantum Computation and Quantum Information. Cambridge University Press, Cambridge (2002)
50. Phillips, I., Ulidowski, I.: Reversing algebraic process calculi. In: Aceto, L., Ingólfsdóttir, A. (eds.) FoSSaCS 2006. LNCS, vol. 3921, pp. 246–260. Springer, Heidelberg (2006). https://doi.org/10.1007/11690634_17
51. Sabelfeld, A., Myers, A.: Language-based information-flow security. IEEE J. Sel. Areas Commun. **21**(1), 5–19 (2003). https://doi.org/10.1109/JSAC.2002.806121
52. Shi, Y.: Both Toffoli and controlled-NOT need little help to do universal quantum computing. Quantum Info. Comput. **3**(1), 84–92 (2003)
53. Stinespring, W.F.: Positive functions on C*-algebras. Proc. Am. Math. Soc. **6**(2), 211–216 (1955). https://doi.org/10.2307/2032342
54. Thomsen, M.K., Kaarsgaard, R., Soeken, M.: Ricercar: a language for describing and rewriting reversible circuits with Ancillae and its permutation semantics. In: Krivine, J., Stefani, J.-B. (eds.) RC 2015. LNCS, vol. 9138, pp. 200–215. Springer, Cham (2015). https://doi.org/10.1007/978-3-319-20860-2_13
55. Toffoli, T.: Reversible computing. In: de Bakker, J., van Leeuwen, J. (eds.) ICALP 1980. LNCS, vol. 85, pp. 632–644. Springer, Heidelberg (1980). https://doi.org/10.1007/3-540-10003-2_104
56. van Tonder, A.: A lambda calculus for quantum computation. SIAM J. Comput. **33**(5), 1109–1135 (2004). https://doi.org/10.1137/S0097539703432165

57. Turing, A.M.: On computable numbers, with an application to the Entschei-dungsproblem. Proc. London Math. Soc. **s2-42**(1), 230–265 (1937). https://doi.org/10.1112/plms/s2-42.1.230, https://londmathsoc.onlinelibrary.wiley.com/doi/abs/10.1112/plms/s2-42.1.230
58. Yanofsky, N., Mannucci, M.A.: Quantum Computing for Computer Scientists. Cambridge University Press, Cambridge (2008)
59. Zelkowitz, M.V.: Reversible execution. Commun. ACM **16**(9), 566 (1973). https://doi.org/10.1145/362342.362360
60. Zeng, H., Ellis, C.S., Lebeck, A.R., Vahdat, A.: Ecosystem: managing energy as a first class operating system resource. In: Proceedings of the 10th International Conference on Architectural Support for Programming Languages and Operating Systems, ASPLOS X, pp. 123–132. Association for Computing Machinery, New York (2002). https://doi.org/10.1145/605397.605411

Models of Reversible Computation

Algorithmically Expressive, Always-Terminating Model for Reversible Computation

Matteo Palazzo[ID] and Luca Roversi[(✉)][ID]

Dipartimento di Informatica, Università degli Studi di Torino, Torino, Italy
{matteo.palazzo,luca.roversi}@unito.it

Abstract. Concerning classical computational models able to express all the Primitive Recursive Functions (PRF), there are interesting results regarding limits on their algorithmic expressiveness, meant as the possibility to naturally express algorithms with minimal computational cost. By introducing the reversible computational model $\mathsf{For_{est}}$, to our knowledge, we provide a first study of analogous properties, adapted to the context of reversible computational models that can represent all the functions in PRF. Firstly, we show that $\mathsf{For_{est}}$ extends Matos' linear reversible computational model M-SRL, the very extension being a guaranteed terminating iteration that can be halted by means of logical predicates. The consequence is that $\mathsf{For_{est}}$ is PRF-complete, because M-SRL is. Secondly, we show that $\mathsf{For_{est}}$ is strictly algorithmically more expressive than M-SRL: it can encode a reversible algorithm for the minimum between two integers in optimal time, while M-SRL cannot.

Keywords: Reversible computation · Loop-language · Primitive Recursive Functions · Algorithmic expressiveness

1 Introduction

In the context of classical computational models, there are established results concerning their algorithmic expressiveness. This term encompasses two aspects: efficiency, which is the ability to express algorithms with minimal computational cost, and flexibility, referring to the capacity to formalize algorithms in the most convenient and direct manner.

Colson and others [2,3] studied the efficiency of Primitive Recursive Functions (PRF), proving their *ultimate obstinacy property*. It means that many algorithms cannot be efficiently implemented by any term of PRF. Among them there are the algorithms to find the *minimum* between two values, which the literature see as a *least standard benchmark* to argue about the efficiency of a given computational model.

Matos [11] proves an analogous of *ultimate obstinacy property* for Meyer/Ritchie's LOOP [13], imperative computational model that characterizes PRF.

T. Æ. Mogensen and Ł. Mikulski (Eds.): RC 2024, LNCS 14680, pp. 31–49, 2024.
https://doi.org/10.1007/978-3-031-62076-8_3

```
0   // m,n ≥ 0, x=m, y=n, i=0, min=0, found=0
    min += x;
2   from ((i=0) or 0) to ((i=x) or (found=1)) {
        if (i=y) {
4           min -= x;
            min += y;
6           found += 1
        } else {skip}
8   }
    // min=min(m,n)
```

Listing 1.1. Term minPos in For$_{est}$ computing the function minimum in $\mathbb{N}$.

LOOP is PRF-correct and complete, representing all and only the elements in PRF. Roughly, LOOP is "obstinate" because its iterations cannot be interrupted as soon as necessary. They must unfold to their end even though the expected result is available before reaching the last iteration. Matos shows how to tame LOOP "obstinacy" by extending LOOP with conditional breaks and decrements, making the formalism non structured, however.

Motivations. If the algorithmic expressiveness of a computational model holds value in the classical setting, we posit that it assumes even greater significance in the context of reversible computation. This is due to the inherent challenge of formalizing algorithms that must be correct with respect to both forward and backward interpretation.

Contributions. Matos' *linear reversible* computational model M-SRL [10] is the natural counterpart of LOOP in a reversible setting. M-SRL is PRF-complete [12], and PRF-correct essentially because every instance of its iterative construct 'for r {P}' unfolds as many times as the initial value of r. A brief introduction of M-SRL is in Subsect. 4.1.

Inspiring to [11], we argue about why M-SRL cannot encode at least the algorithm for the minimum between two integer numbers with optimal cost.

To overcome M-SRL limitation, we introduce the computational model For$_{est}$, which we show it is: (i) always-terminating; (ii) reversible; (iii) able to simulate every M-SRL program, namely every PRF function; (iv) strictly more algorithmically expressive than M-SRL.

Point (iv) here above means that we can write *at least* Listing 1.1 in For$_{est}$. It is the *natural* implementation of the algorithm which *always computes* the *minimum* between two naturals m, n *efficiently*, namely in a number of steps of order equal to the least between m, and n.

In fact, we will see that For$_{est}$ can compute the minimum for *every pair of integers*, and this is possible because the iterative construct of For$_{est}$ is:

$$\textbf{from } (i=e_u \textbf{ or } e_{in}) \textbf{ to } (i=e_v \textbf{ or } e_{out})\{P\}, \tag{1}$$

where i is a variable and e_u, e_v are two expressions with values in $\mathbb{Z}$, while e_{in} and e_{out} are boolean expressions with values in $\{0, 1\}$. Construct (1) generalizes 'for r $\{P\}$' of M-SRL (Sect. 4 recalls it) by restricting Janus [7] iteration, Janus being (reversible) Turing-complete. In particular, (1) assures that $\mathsf{For_{est}}$ iterations simultaneously enjoy the two following features: (i) they can be halted by means of predicates, providing a more flexible control over the computation flow; (ii) $\mathsf{For_{est}}$ can be seen as a *paradigmatic structured programming*, possibly easing formal reasoning on it [4].

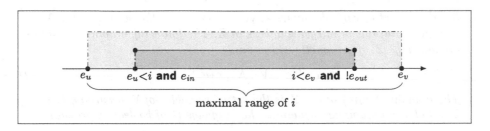

Fig. 1. The iteration of $\mathsf{For_{est}}$ starts/stops depending on e_u, e_v, e_{in}, and e_{out}.

Iteration in $\mathsf{For_{est}}$, *Intuitively.* We conclude this introduction by illustrating how (1) restricts the iteration in Janus. The body P of (1) cannot alter the variable i which drives the iteration. Entering the iteration is under the control of a logical disjunction with form $i=e_u$ **or** e_{in}. Analogously, exiting the iteration is under the control of a logical disjunction with form $i=e_v$ **or** e_{out}.

Assuming that e_u evaluates to u, and e_v to v such that $u \le v$, an iteration starts looping if i belongs to the interval $[u, v]$ and if $i=e_u$ **or** e_{in} holds. This means that if e_{in} holds, then the iteration can start with i assuming a value greater than u. Under the initial assumption, every iteration increments i by one unit. So, the iteration keeps going until $i=e_v$ **or** e_{out} holds true, namely until i reaches the upper bound v, or the exit condition e_{out} becomes true. Figure 1 visually summarizes how i moves inside the interval $[u, v]$, highlighting that the difference $v - u$ sets the maximum amount of iterations.

On the other side, if $u > v$ when the iteration starts, i must belong to the interval $[v, u]$, and the operational semantics of a loop develops a computation which is the inverse of the one just described. The flow-charts in Figs. 3 and 4, which we specialized from [17], will fully describe the computational flow of (1).

Structure of the Work. Section 2 introduces syntax and operational semantics of $\mathsf{For_{est}}$. Section 3 firstly shows that the operational semantics always terminates when interpreting a term P in $\mathsf{For_{est}}$, even though this does not mean that P always produces a meaningful state. Secondly, it shows that the function in Sect. 2, which defines P^- for any P in $\mathsf{For_{est}}$, actually yields the reverse of P. Section 4 translates M-SRL into $\mathsf{For_{est}}$, proving that the latter is complete with respect to the first one. Section 5 shows that $\mathsf{For_{est}}$ is algorithmically more expressive than M-SRL. Section 6 concludes, pointing to future and related work.

2   The Computational Model For$_{est}$

Concerning the algorithmic expressiveness, For$_{est}$ is defined by means of a syntax and of an operational semantics, designed to fall in between M-SRL and Janus.

Syntax. After some preliminaries (Definition 1) the structure of every term P is given together with its *domain* and *writable domain* to assure that For$_{est}$ contains the inverse of P itself (Definition 2).

Definition 1 (Arithmetic and boolean expressions).

1. *Let V be a set of variable names* x, y, ... *Let $\mathcal{N}$ be the set* $\{\ldots, \text{-}1, 0, 1, \ldots\}$ *of representations of integer numbers in $\mathbb{Z}$. The following grammar generates the language $\mathcal{Z}$ of arithmetic expressions:*

$$e, e' ::= V \mid \mathcal{N} \mid e\text{+}e' \mid e\text{-}e'. \tag{2}$$

   The domain $\text{Dom}(e)$ of $e \in \mathcal{Z}$ is the set of variables of V occurring in e.
2. *The following grammars generates the language $\mathcal{B}$ of boolean expressions.*

$$e, e' ::= 0 \mid 1 \mid !e \mid e \text{ or } e' \mid e \text{ and } e' \mid e_{\mathbb{Z}} = e'_{\mathbb{Z}} \tag{3}$$

   with $e_{\mathbb{Z}}, e'_{\mathbb{Z}} \in \mathcal{Z}$. The domain $\text{Dom}(e)$ of $e \in \mathcal{B}$ is the set of all the variables of V in e.

For example, (-1)+(x-3)-y $\in \mathcal{Z}$ and $\text{Dom}((\text{-}1)\text{+}(x\text{-}3)\text{-}y) = \{x, y\}$ while (3=y) or!(1=x+y) $\in \mathcal{B}$, and $\text{Dom}((3\text{=}y)\text{or!}(1\text{=}x\text{+}y)) = \{x, y\}$.

Definition 2 (Set $\mathcal{F}$ of well-formed terms). *The following grammar defines the language of raw terms:*

$$P, Q ::= \text{skip} \mid x\text{+=}e \mid x\text{-=}e \mid P;Q \mid$$
$$\text{if}(e)\{P\}\text{else}\{Q\} \mid \text{from}(i\text{=}e_u \text{ or } e_{in})\text{to}(i\text{=}e_v \text{ or } e_{out})\{P\}.$$

The second line contains the selection *with guard e and the* iteration *"$\text{from}(i\text{=}e_u$ or $e_{in})\text{to}(i\text{=}e_v$ or $e_{out})\{P\}$" that we call "from-to" with leading variable i.*

   For every raw term P, the domain $\text{Dom}(P) \subseteq V$ *and the* writable domain $\text{WDom}(P) \subseteq \text{Dom}(P)$ *are as follows:*

$$\text{Dom}(\text{skip}) = \emptyset$$
$$\text{Dom}(x\text{+=}e) = \text{Dom}(x\text{-=}e) = \text{Dom}(e) \cup \{x\}$$
$$\text{Dom}(P;Q) = \text{Dom}(P) \cup \text{Dom}(Q)$$
$$\text{Dom}(\text{if}(e)\{P\}\text{else}\{Q\}) = \text{Dom}(e) \cup \text{Dom}(P) \cup \text{Dom}(Q)$$
$$\text{Dom}\left(\begin{array}{l} \text{from}(i\text{=}e_u \text{ or } e_{in}) \\ \text{to}(i\text{=}e_v \text{ or } e_{out})\{P\} \end{array}\right) = \begin{array}{l} \{i\} \cup \text{Dom}(e_{in}) \cup \text{Dom}(e_{out}) \cup \\ \text{Dom}(e_u) \cup \text{Dom}(e_v) \cup \text{Dom}(P) \end{array}$$
$$\text{WDom}(\text{skip}) = \emptyset$$
$$\text{WDom}(x\text{+=}e) = \text{WDom}(x\text{-=}e) = \{x\}$$
$$\text{WDom}(P;Q) = \text{WDom}(P) \cup \text{WDom}(Q)$$
$$\text{WDom}(\text{if}(e)\{P\}\text{else}\{Q\}) = \text{WDom}(P) \cup \text{WDom}(Q)$$

$$\text{WDom}\left(\begin{array}{l}\texttt{from}(i=e_u \text{ or } e_{in})\\ \texttt{to}(i=e_v \text{ or } e_{out})\{P\}\end{array}\right) = \{i\} \cup \text{WDom}(P).$$

Finally, the set $\mathcal{F}$ *of* well-formed terms *exclusively contains* raw terms *in which:*

1. *every occurrence of* $\texttt{if}(e)\{P\}\texttt{else}\{Q\}$ *is such that* $\text{Dom}(e) \cap (\text{WDom}(P) \cup \text{WDom}(Q)) = \emptyset$;
2. *every occurrence of* $\texttt{from}\ (i=e_u \text{ or } e_{in})\ \texttt{to}\ (i=e_v \text{ or } e_{out})\{P\}$ *is such that* $(\{i\} \cup \text{Dom}(e_u) \cup \text{Dom}(e_v)) \cap \text{WDom}(P) = \emptyset$.

Listing 1.1 gives an example of a term in $\mathcal{F}$. Lines 4–7 have *domain* x, y, min, found and *writable domain* min, found. Neither min, nor found occurs in the domain of (i=y), (i=0), and (i=x) at lines 3 and 2, respectively. This is true in general. For any $P \in \mathcal{F}$, the notion *"writable domain"* implies that P cannot write into variables that belong to the domain of the guard of any selection, or into the leading variable or variables in domains of the bounds e_u, e_v of any iteration having P as a sub-term.

Definition 3 (Inverse of a term). *The inverse* P^- *of* $P \in \mathcal{F}$ *is as follows:*

$$(\texttt{skip})^- = \texttt{skip} \qquad\qquad (x\texttt{+=}e)^- = x\texttt{-=}e$$
$$(x\texttt{-=}e)^- = x\texttt{+=}e \qquad\qquad (P;Q)^- = Q^-;P^-$$
$$(\texttt{if}(e)\{P\}\texttt{then}\{Q\})^- = \texttt{if}(e)\{P^-\}\texttt{else}\{Q^-\}$$
$$\left(\begin{array}{l}\texttt{from}(i=e_u \text{ or } e_{in})\\ \texttt{to}(i=e_v \text{ or } e_{out})\{P\}\end{array}\right)^{-} = \begin{array}{l}\texttt{from}(i=e_v \text{ or } e_{out})\\ \texttt{to}(i=e_u \text{ or } e_{in})\{P\}.\end{array} \tag{4}$$

Clearly the image of $(\cdot)^-$ in Definition 3 is $\mathcal{F}$. Moreover, we underline that the function $(\cdot)^-$ is not applied to the rightmost P in (4) on purpose. The reason is that it is the operational semantics that let $\texttt{from}(i=e_v \text{ or } e_{out})\texttt{to}(i=e_u \text{ or } e_{in})\{P\}$ be the inverse of $\texttt{from}(i=e_u \text{ or } e_{in})\texttt{to}(i=e_v \text{ or } e_{out})\{P\}$. Let us see why, by assuming that e_u evaluates to u, and e_v to v in (4). The first case is with $u \leq v$. Then the operational semantics iterates P incrementing i *at the end* of each iteration. The second case is with $u > v$. Then the operational semantics iterates P^-, instead of P, decrementing i *at the start* of each iteration. The operational semantic of For_{est} in Definition 7 will formalize this behavior, Point 3. of Remark 2 will comment on it further, and Theorem 2 will finally prove the relation between every P and P^{-1}.

Operational Semantics. A state (Definition 4 below) sets the values of variables, allowing us to evaluate expressions (Definition 5 below). Figure 2 introduces the rules to interpret terms that belong to a syntax which extends $\mathcal{F}$ given in Definition 2. *This is necessary to formalize the behavior of a reversible computational model by means of a classical one.*

Definition 4 (States). *A state is a total map* $\sigma : V \to \mathbb{Z}$. *We write* $\sigma[x_1 \mapsto v_1 \ldots x_n \mapsto v_n]$ *to denote a state such that* $\sigma[x_1 \mapsto v_1 \ldots x_n \mapsto v_n](y) = v_i$, *if* $y = x_i$, *for any* $i \in \{1, \ldots, n\}$; *otherwise* $\sigma[x_1 \mapsto v_1 \ldots x_n \mapsto v_n](y) = \sigma(y)$. *The set* Σ, *ranged over by* $\sigma, \sigma' \ldots \tau, \tau' \ldots$, *contains all the possible states.*

Definition 5 (Evaluating arithmetic and boolean expressions). *Let $e \in$ $\mathcal{Z} \cup \mathcal{B}$. We write $\sigma, e \Downarrow n$ meaning that e evaluates to n in the state σ. If $e \in \mathcal{Z}$, the relation $\Downarrow$ can be defined obviously on the structure of e. Concerning boolean expressions, the meaning of $\sigma, e \Downarrow n$ is as follows:*

$$\sigma, 0 \Downarrow 0 \qquad\qquad\qquad \sigma, 1 \Downarrow 1$$

$$\sigma, (e{=}e') \Downarrow \begin{cases} 1 & \text{if } (\sigma, e \Downarrow n) \text{ and } (\sigma, e' \Downarrow n) \\ 0 & \text{otherwise} \end{cases}$$

$$\sigma, !e \Downarrow (1-m) \quad \text{if} \quad \sigma, e \Downarrow m \tag{5}$$

$$\sigma, (e \text{ and } e') \Downarrow (m \cdot n) \quad \text{if} \quad (\sigma, e \Downarrow m) \text{ and } (\sigma, e' \Downarrow n) \tag{6}$$

$$\sigma, (e \text{ or } e') \Downarrow (m + n - m \cdot n) \quad \text{if} \quad (\sigma, e \Downarrow m) \text{ and } (\sigma, e' \Downarrow n) \tag{7}$$

Remark 1. Clauses (5), (6), and (7) interpret boolean expressions by quadratic polynomials, yielding $\{0,1\}$ iff σ assigns values $\{0,1\}$ to every variable of $!e$, $(e \text{ and } e')$, $(e \text{ or } e')$. $\qquad\square$

$$\frac{\sigma, x \Downarrow n \qquad \sigma, e \Downarrow m}{\sigma \; x{+}{=}e \; \sigma[x \mapsto n+m]} \; \text{INC} \qquad \frac{\sigma, x \Downarrow n \qquad \sigma, e \Downarrow m}{\sigma \; x{-}{=}e \; \sigma[x \mapsto n-m]} \; \text{DEC}$$

$$\frac{\sigma, b \Downarrow 1 \qquad \sigma \; P \; \sigma'}{\sigma \; \text{if}(b)\{P\}\text{else}\{Q\} \; \sigma'} \; \text{IFTRUE} \qquad \frac{\sigma, b \Downarrow 0 \qquad \sigma \; Q \; \sigma'}{\sigma \; \text{if}(b)\{P\}\text{else}\{Q\} \; \sigma'} \; \text{IFFALSE}$$

$$\frac{}{\sigma \; \text{skip} \; \sigma} \; \text{SKIP} \qquad \frac{\sigma \; P \; \sigma' \qquad \sigma' \; Q \; \sigma''}{\sigma \; P;Q \; \sigma''} \; \text{SEQ}$$

$$\frac{\sigma \; \text{if}(e_u{<}{=}e_v)\{\text{assert}(e_u{<}{=}i \text{ and } i{<}{=}e_v);\text{assert}(i{=}e_u \text{ or } e_{in}); \atop \qquad \text{loop until}(i{=}e_v \text{ or } e_{out})\{P; i{+}{=}1; \text{assert}(!e_{in})\} \atop \}\text{else}\{\text{assert}(e_v{<}{=}i \text{ and } i{<}{=}e_u);\text{assert}(i{=}e_u \text{ or } e_{in}); \atop \qquad \text{loop until}(i{=}e_v \text{ or } e_{out})\{i{-}{=}1; P^-; \text{assert}(!e_{in})\}\} \; \tau}{\sigma \; \text{from}(i{=}e_u \text{ or } e_{in})\text{to}(i{=}e_v \text{ or } e_{out})\{P\} \; \tau} \; \text{FROMTO}$$

$$\frac{\sigma, e \Downarrow 1}{\sigma \; \text{assert}(e) \; \sigma} \; \text{ASSERT1} \qquad \frac{\sigma, e \Downarrow 0}{\sigma \; \text{assert}(e) \; \bot} \; \text{ASSERT0} \qquad \frac{}{\bot \; P \; \bot} \; \text{PROP}$$

$$\frac{\sigma, (i{=}e_v \text{ or } e_{out}) \Downarrow 1 \qquad \sigma \; \text{skip} \; \tau}{\sigma \; \text{loop until}(i{=}e_v \text{ or } e_{out})\{P\} \; \tau} \; \text{LOOPBASE}$$

$$\frac{\sigma, (i{=}e_v \text{ or } e_{out}) \Downarrow 0 \qquad \sigma \; P;\text{loop until}(i{=}e_v \text{ or } e_{out})\{P\} \; \tau}{\sigma \; \text{loop until}(i{=}e_u \text{ or } e_{out})\{P\} \; \tau} \; \text{LOOPREC}$$

Fig. 2. Operational Semantics on $\mathcal{F}_{ext}$.

Definition 6 (Extension $\mathcal{F}_{ext}$ of $\mathcal{F}$). *Let $\mathcal{F}_{ext}$ be $\mathcal{F}$ with boolean expressions $\mathcal{B}$ that also contain 'e_u<=e_v' and 'e_u>e_v', with $e_u, e_v \in \mathcal{B}$, and extended to contain:*

      assert(e)   **loop until**(e **or** e_{out}){P}

which are new terms. For example the following term is in $\mathcal{F}_{ext}$:

$$\textbf{if}(u\texttt{<=}v)\{\textbf{assert}(x\texttt{<}1);\textbf{skip}\}\textbf{else}\{\textbf{loop until}(z\texttt{>}2)\{\textbf{skip}\}\}. \qquad (8)$$

Definition 7 (Operational semantics of $\mathcal{F}_{ext}$). *Figure 2 introduces the rules to interpret terms of $\mathcal{F}_{ext}$. The rules derive three kinds of judgments: $\sigma\, P\, \tau$, $\sigma\, P \perp$, and $\perp P \perp$, for σ, τ in Σ, where $\perp$, which is not in Σ, denotes the result of a failing interpretation.*

    Interpreting P means to fix a state σ and to build a derivation tree with rules in Figure 2 whose conclusion can be either a successful $\sigma\, P\, \tau$, for some $\tau \in \Sigma$, or a failing $\sigma\, P \perp$, the latter generated if one judgment between μ **assert**(e) $\perp$ or $\perp Q \perp$ shows up while building the tree, for some μ, e, and Q.

Rules INC, DEC, IFFALSE, IFTRUE, and SKIP interpret terms in $\mathcal{F}_{ext}$ as expected. SEQ decomposes the evaluation of a sequence $P;Q$, to produce σ' required by Q the application of SEQ proceeds deterministically from left to right.

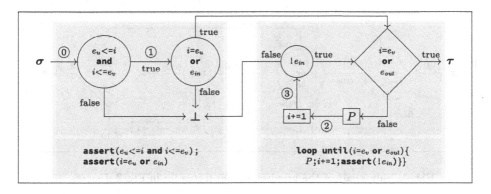

Fig. 3. Flow-chart of the premise of rule FROMTO in Fig. 2 if e_u<=e_v.

FROMTO interprets the eponymous term of $\mathcal{F}_{ext}$ in accordance to the flow-diagrams in Figs. 3, and 4 which, compared to the ones in [17], are *non standard*. We will comment on why in Remark 2, Point 6. Being σ an initial state, the premise of FROMTO triggers either IFTRUE or IFFALSE to interpret *exactly* one between the sequences:

$$\begin{aligned} &\textcircled{0}\textbf{assert}(e_u\texttt{<=}i \text{ and } i\texttt{<=}e_v);\textcircled{1}\textbf{assert}(i\texttt{=}e_u \text{ or } e_{in}); \\ &\textbf{loop until}(i\texttt{=}e_v \text{ or } e_{out})\{P;\textcircled{2}i\texttt{+=}1;\textcircled{3}\textbf{assert}(!e_{in})\} \end{aligned} \qquad (9)$$

$$\begin{aligned} &\textcircled{0}\textbf{assert}(e_v\texttt{<=}i \text{ and } i\texttt{<=}e_u);\textcircled{1}\textbf{assert}(i\texttt{=}e_u \text{ or } e_{in}); \\ &\textbf{loop until}(i\texttt{=}e_v \text{ or } e_{out})\{i\texttt{-=}1;\textcircled{2}P^-;\textcircled{3}\textbf{assert}(!e_{in})\} \end{aligned} \qquad (10)$$

by means of LOOPREC, LOOPBASE, ASSERT1, and ASSERT0. Numbers ⓪, ① ...
in (9) trace how (9) corresponds to the flow-chart in Fig. 3, which is interpreted if
$\sigma, (e_u \texttt{<=} e_v) \Downarrow 1$, i.e. if the argument of the selection in the premise of FROMTO,
holds true. Initially, the interpretation of (9) can yield $\bot$ in two cases because of
the first two **assert**. The first **assert** fails if $\sigma, (e_u \texttt{<=} i \text{ and } i \texttt{<=} e_v) \Downarrow 0$, i.e. the value
of i is not in $[u, v]$, assuming that e_u, e_v evaluate to u, v, respectively. Being the
first **assert** successful, the second one fails if $\sigma, (i \texttt{=} e_u \text{ or } e_{in}) \Downarrow 0$, i.e. the value
of i is greater than u but the value of e_{in} forbids to enter the loop, namely it
holds false. Otherwise, the construct **loop-until** starts and may keep unfolding
until neither i reaches v, nor e_{out} decrees to exit, namely it holds true. Rules
LOOPREC, and LOOPBASE govern the unfolding, generating:

$$P;②i\texttt{+=}1;③\texttt{assert}(!e_{in});P;②i\texttt{+=}1;③\texttt{assert}(!e_{in});\ldots \qquad (11)$$

which may be (abnormally) stopped, yielding $\bot$, as soon as P sets $!e_{in}$ to false.
If this happens, $\bot$ is propagated by means of PROP, leading to the failure of
the whole interpretation. If the argument $e_u \texttt{<=} e_v$ of the selection in the premise
of FROMTO holds false in the initial state σ, then (10) must be interpreted,
according the flow-chart in Fig. 4, whose behavior is analogous to the one in
Fig. 3.

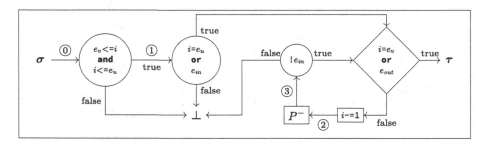

Fig. 4. Flow-chart of the premise of rule FROMTO in Fig. 2 if $e_u \texttt{>} e_v$.

Definition 8 (The computational model For$_{est}$). For$_{est}$ *has terms in* $\mathcal{F}$ *and*
operational semantics in Definition 7. *By* $P \in$ For$_{est}$ *we mean* $P \in \mathcal{F}$.

Remark 2. (For$_{est}$ **syntax and operational semantics**).

1. Definition 8 says that a term in For$_{est}$ cannot be written using the syntax in
   $\mathcal{F}_{ext}$: the terms of $\mathcal{F}_{ext}$ are *invisible* to a "programmer".
2. For$_{est}$ is designed to be *interpreted* deterministically. Given any $P \in \mathcal{F}$, two
   cases exist. On one side, P can be interpreted in state $\bot$ where only PROP
   applies, which keeps generating $\bot$. Otherwise, P is interpreted in $\sigma \in \Sigma$,
   where a single rule at a time applies, whose premises interpreted from left to
   right produce states in the expected order.

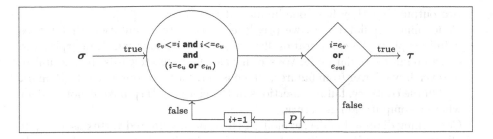

Fig. 5. The flow-chart of Fig. 3 in *standard* style [17].

3. Theorem 2 will formally show that the function in Definition 3 generates the inverse of any $P \in \mathcal{F}$, according to the operational semantics.

   A simple example should help to follow how the inversion of an iteration works. Let $P = $ **from**(i=-4 **or** 0)**to**(i=1 **or** 0){j+=1} and $\sigma \in \Sigma$ s.t. $\sigma(\text{i}) = -4$ and $\sigma(\text{j}) = 2$. Since -4<=1, the interpretation of P proceed forward, iterating j+=1 until i=1, making $|1 - (-4)| = 5$ iterations. The resulting state is therefore $\sigma' = \sigma[\text{i} \mapsto 1, \text{j} \mapsto 7]$. Now, let us interpret the inverse P^-, which is **from**(i=1 **or** 0)**to**(i=-4 **or** 0){j+=1}, starting from σ'. Since 1>-4 we proceed backward, iterating j-=1 until i=-4, making $|-4-1| = 5$ iterations yelding the starting state σ.

4. The rule FROMTO *explains the meaning* of **from-to** by means of the terms that already belong to $\mathcal{F}$. Up to **assert**, the unfolding of a loop relies on terms of M-SRL. A full internalization would require two further steps. In analogy to [12], the first one would be to express **if**(e){P}**else**{Q} through M-SRL. Secondly, it would be necessary to eliminate every **assert**, possibly by leveraging partial evaluation techniques [14] or tools for static analysis [9,16] developed for reversible computations. The consequence of such steps, would be to consider M-SRL as the core of $\mathcal{F}$, like R-CORE is for R-WHILE [5].

5. An alternative to invert **from-to** could be **morf**$(i=e_v$ **or** $e_{out})$**ot**$(i=e_u$ **or** $e_{in})$ {P} which would iterate P, decrementing i *at the start* of each iteration, and that we could use as follows:

$$\left(\begin{array}{l} \textbf{from}(i=e_u \textbf{ or } e_{in}) \\ \textbf{to}(i=e_v \textbf{ or } e_{out})\{P\} \end{array} \right)^- = \begin{array}{l} \textbf{morf}(i=e_u \textbf{ or } e_{out}) \\ \textbf{ot}(i=e_v \textbf{ or } e_{in})\{P^-\}. \end{array} \tag{12}$$

   That choice would be more coherent than (4) as compared to how Matos actually inverts LOOP s in M-SRL [11]. Our choice (4) is syntactically compact and would correspond to an iteration **for** r {Q} in M-SRL with **for** -r {Q} as its inverse such that, if $r < 0$, then Q^- is iterated $|r|$ times.

6. The syntax of the flow-charts in Figs. 3, and 4 does not conform to the one of established charts in [17], as pointed out by an anonymous reviewer. Indeed, *circular* nodes in Figs. 3, and 4, interpreted as **assert**, have one input and two output, while in [17] *assert nodes* have two input and one output. Moreover, the *diamond* nodes we introduce, interpreted as *selection*, have two input and

two output, but they have one input and two output in [17].

Concerning circular nodes, we privilege a visual representation that makes it fully explicit the computation flow of a failing **assert** which interpret the corresponding circular node. We see this as a first step towards the possibility to reversibly recover from failures, which is currently not possible (cfr. Remark 4.) On the contrary, failing assertions in the charts of [17] make it not evident where a computation get stuck.

Concerning diamond nodes, exploiting the typically unused vertex as an input allows us to avoid *join points* (cfr. [17]) which implies that we can adopt circle nodes as just described in the previous lines.

However, for completeness we add Fig. 5. Its flow-chart is both compliant with the established reversible flow-charts in [17] and is equivalent to the one in Fig. 3.   □

3   For$_{est}$ is Terminating and Reversible

The goal of this section is twofold. Firstly, it shows that, for every reasonable initial state, every $P \in$ For$_{est}$ terminates either by failing or by yielding a state (Theorem 1). Then, it establishes that P^- (Definition 3) truly represents the inverse of P, recovering the initial state from which P may have been interpreted.

The proofs of our goals will tacitly rely on the following fact, implied by the definition of the operational semantics:

Fact 1. Every non failing interpretation of $P \in$ For$_{est}$ from a state σ produces a final state τ, that preserves the read-only variables. Formally:

$$\forall P \in \mathsf{For}_{est}, \sigma, \tau \in \Sigma. \ \sigma \ P \ \tau \rightarrow (\forall x \notin (V \setminus \mathrm{WDom}(P)). \ \tau(x) = \sigma(x)). \quad \square$$

Theorem 1 (Termination). *Let* $P \in$ For$_{est}$*, and* $\sigma \in \Sigma$*. The interpretation of* P *starting from* σ*, either terminates in some* $\tau \in \Sigma$ *or fails. Formally:*

$$\forall P \in \mathsf{For}_{est}, \forall \sigma \in \Sigma. \ (\exists \tau \in \Sigma. \ \sigma \ P \ \tau) \vee (\sigma \ P \perp).$$

The proof is by induction on the structure of P. A case worth commenting is when P is **from**$(i{=}e_u$ **or** $e_{in})$**to**$(i{=}e_v$ **or** $e_{out})\{Q\}$. Let σ be an initial state. Let us assume that, initially, $\sigma, e_u{<}{=}e_v \Downarrow 1$. The assertions at ⓪, and ① in Fig. 3 must be checked. If $\sigma, e_u{<}{=}i$ **and** $i{<}{=}e_v \Downarrow 0$, namely i is not in the interval delimited by e_u, e_v, or $\sigma, e_{in} \Downarrow 0$ does not hold, then the iteration aborts, namely terminates, yielding $\perp$. Otherwise, the iteration starts, its termination depending on: (a) Q cannot write i and variables of e_u, e_v; (b) by induction Q terminates; (c) every iteration at ③ in Fig. 3 increments i. So, i will reach the upper bound e_v unless, meanwhile, e_{out} becomes true or $!e_{in}$ false, stopping the loop even earlier. Furthermore, the loop can also terminate earlier if Q aborts or the assertion at ③ fails.

Let us now assume $\sigma, e_v <= e_u \Downarrow 1$. Initially, i must be into the interval determined by e_v, e_u. Termination works as above, but in point (c). Every iteration at ② in Fig. 4 decrements i which will reach the lower bound e_v unless, meanwhile, e_{out} becomes true or $!e_{in}$ false. $\qquad\qquad\square$

Remark 3 (Failure and termination).

1. Theorem 1 just assures that the interpretation of $P \in \mathsf{For_{est}}$ terminates, saying nothing about *success* or *failure*. Assertions can stop the interpretation as soon as a state cannot assure that the interpreted term is reversible.
2. Let us recall [17, Proposition 1, pag 94]. It says that "*Well-formed reversible flow-charts, with finite atomic operations and finite configuration spaces always terminate*". We may ask, following an anonymous referee, if Theorem 1 can be an instance of [17, Proposition 1, pag 94]. Intuitively, Theorem 1 holds because the leading variable of every $\mathsf{For_{est}}$ iteration assumes at most all the values in a *finite* interval. Thus $\mathsf{For_{est}}$ **from-to** iterative constructive explores a finite configuration space and this suggests that Theorem 1 and [17, Proposition 1, pag 94] relate each other. Were we formalizing $\mathsf{For_{est}}$ operational semantics by using the same reversible flow-diagrams as [17], we believe Theorem 1 would become a direct corollary of [17, Proposition 1, page 94]. $\square$

Theorem 2 (Reversibility). *Let $P \in \mathsf{For_{est}}$, and $\sigma \in \Sigma$ an initial state. Then, P generates a state τ, namely $\sigma\,P\,\tau$ if and only if P^- generates σ, starting from τ. Formally: $\forall P \in \mathsf{For_{est}}, \forall \sigma, \tau \in \Sigma. \; \sigma\,P\,\tau \iff \tau\,P^-\,\sigma$.*

Remark 4. Theorem 2 says that P^- can recover the starting state σ exactly when the final state that P generates from σ is not $\bot$. $\qquad\qquad\square$

Clearly, one can simply say that $\mathsf{For_{est}}$ is reversible because it can be seen as a restriction of Janus. In any case, we briefly comment on how to prove Theorem 2. The proof splits into an 'only if' and an 'if' case, each proceeding by structural induction on the derivation with $\sigma\,P\,\tau$, or $\tau\,P^-\,\sigma$ as its conclusion, respectively.

The main intuition follows. Let $P \equiv \mathtt{from}(i=e_u \text{ or } e_{in})\mathtt{to}(i=e_v \text{ or } e_{out})\{Q\}$, and let $\sigma \in \Sigma$. Let us focus on the case $\sigma, e_u <= e_v \Downarrow 1$, the other $\sigma, e_u <= e_v \Downarrow$ 0 being analogous. Rules FORMAIN, IFTRUE and the repetition of LOOPREC and LOOPBASE unfold the **from-to** into a repetition of assertions, P and the increment of i. Since, if $\sigma\,P\,\tau$, we know how to prove:

$$\sigma \; \mathsf{assert}(u<=i \text{ and } i<=v); \mathsf{assert}(i=u \text{ or } e_{in});$$
$$[\mathsf{assert}(!(i=v \text{ or } e_{out})); P; i+=1; \mathsf{assert}(!(i=u \text{ or } e_{in}))]^m;$$
$$\mathsf{assert}(i=v \text{ or } e_{out}); \mathsf{assert}(u<=i \text{ and } i<=v) \; \tau,$$

for some $m \in \mathbb{N}$, the resulting code can be inverted. Once inverted, it can be wrapped into $\mathtt{from}(i=e_v \text{ or } e_{out})\mathtt{to}(i=e_u \text{ or } e_{in})\{Q\}$ which is the inverse of P.

Concerning the selection, reversibility follows from the fact that its branches cannot alter the value of the guard.

4   For_est is PRF-Complete Because M-SRL Is

Firstly, we briefly recall Matos' M-SRL from [10]. Secondly, we provide Definition 9, a function translating M-SRL to For_est. Theorem 3 relies on it to prove that For_est is complete w.r.t. M-SRL.

4.1   Recalling Matos' M-SRL

Standing for *Simple Reversible Language*, M-SRL is first introduced in [10] by Matos.

Syntax. M-SRL programs read from, and write into registers r, r1, ..., ranged over by r. Registers contain values in $\mathbb{Z}$. M-SRL has the following grammar:

$$P, Q ::= \textbf{INC } r \mid \textbf{DEC } r \mid P; Q \mid \textbf{for } r \; \{P\},$$

where r is any register. Concerning the iterative construct "**for** r $\{P\}$", r cannot occur in (the body) P.

Inversion. For each M-SRL program the *inverse* program is defined syntactically. Let P, Q two M-SRL programs. Then:

$$(\textbf{INC } r)^- = \textbf{DEC } r$$
$$(\textbf{DEC } r)^- = \textbf{INC } r$$
$$(P; Q)^- = Q^-; P^-$$
$$(\textbf{for } r \; \{P\})^- = \textbf{for } r \; \{P^-\}.$$

Semantics. The semantic of M-SRL is straightforward. **INC** r and **DEC** r respectively *increment* and *decrement* the value of a register r by one. The *series composition* of two programs is represented by $P; Q$. Finally, **for** r $\{P\}$ represents the *iteration*. If the value in r is positive, an iteration is equivalent to $P; \ldots; P$ with as many P as the value in r, register which cannot be written by P. If the value in r is negative, an iteration is equivalent to $P^-; \ldots; P^-$ with as many P^- as the *inverse* of the value in r.

By definition, M-SRL has no **if-then-else**. Using M-SRL terms, [12] encodes one in it.

Example 1. Addition in M-SRL can encoded as: **for** x $\{$**INC** y$\}$. After its execution y contains the value of the sum between x and y.

Remark 5. Notions like "domain/co-domain", "state", etc. defined for For_est obviously adapt to M-SRL. For example, $\sigma \, P \, \tau$ stands for "M-SRL program P with a domain compatible with state σ, produces a state τ". Moreover, variables in For_est are registers in M-SRL. $\square$

4.2   Translating M-SRL into For$_{est}$

The following notation eases the translation from M-SRL to For$_{est}$.

Notation 1 (Leading variables). If $P \in$ For$_{est}$, the set $l(P)$ of *leading* variables in P contains all the variables *leading* the unfolding of every **from-to** in P. Let $l(Q), l(Q')$ be given for any $Q, Q' \in$ For$_{est}$. Let $i \in V$, $e_u, e_v \in \mathcal{Z}$ and $e_{in}, e_{out} \in \mathcal{B}$. Then, $l(P)$ is empty for every $P \in$ For$_{est}$ but the two terms:

$$l(Q;Q') = l(Q) \cup l(Q')$$

$$l(\textbf{from}(i=e_u \ \textbf{or} \ e_{in})\textbf{to}(i=e_v \ \textbf{or} \ e_{out})\{Q\}) = \{i\} \cup l(Q).$$

Identifying the *leading* variables avoids name clashes when an iteration of M-SRL is mapped to a For$_{est}$ **from-to**.

Definition 9 (From M-SRL to For$_{est}$). *Let* $P, Q, Q' \in$ M-SRL *and* $r \in V$. *The map* $[\![\_]\!]$ *maps terms of* M-SRL *to terms in* For$_{est}$ *as follows:*

$$[\![\textbf{INC } r]\!] = r\texttt{+=1} \qquad [\![\textbf{DEC } r]\!] = r\texttt{-=1} \qquad [\![Q;Q']\!] = [\![Q]\!];[\![Q']\!]$$

$$[\![\textbf{for } r \ \{P\}]\!] = \textbf{from}(i\texttt{=0 or 0})\textbf{to}(i\texttt{=}r \ \textbf{or } \texttt{0})\{[\![P]\!]\};i\texttt{-=}r,$$

where $i \in V$ *is a* fresh *variable not in* $\{r\} \cup \mathrm{Dom}([\![P]\!]) \cup \mathrm{Dom}(P)$, *and* $\mathrm{Dom}(Q;Q')$ $\cap l([\![Q]\!]) = \mathrm{Dom}(Q;Q') \cap l([\![Q']\!]) = \mathrm{Dom}(\textbf{for } r \ \{P\}) \cap l([\![P]\!]) = \emptyset$.

An example: $[\![\textbf{for } r \ \{\textbf{INC } j\}]\!] = \textbf{from}(i\texttt{=0 or 0})\textbf{to}(i\texttt{=}r \ \textbf{or } \texttt{0})\{j\texttt{+=1}\};i\texttt{-=}r$.

Completeness. It is natural to require that $[\![P]\!] \in$ For$_{est}$ *simulates* any given $P \in$ M-SRL, which means that For$_{est}$ is complete w.r.t. M-SRL.

Notation 2. Let $\sigma, \hat{\sigma}$ be states in Σ, let P be a term in M-SRL or For$_{est}$.

1. We say "σ *and* $\hat{\sigma}$ *are equivalent w.r.t.* P", written $\sigma \simeq_P \hat{\sigma}$, when $\sigma(r) = \hat{\sigma}(r)$, for every $r \in \mathrm{Dom}(P)$, namely, if the two states have identical values on the variables of P.
2. We say "σ *is* P-*clean*", written $c(\sigma, P)$, when $\sigma(x) = 0$, for every $x \in l(P)$, namely when the state assigns 0 to every leading variable of P.
3. We say "$\hat{\sigma}$ *simulates* σ *w.r.t.* P", written $\sigma \sqsubset_P \hat{\sigma}$, if σ and $\hat{\sigma}$ are *equivalent w.r.t.* P and σ *is* $[\![P]\!]$-*clean*. $\qquad\square$

Theorem 3 (For$_{est}$ is complete w.r.t. M-SRL). *Let* $P \in$ M-SRL, *let* $\sigma, \tau \in \Sigma$ *s.t.* $\sigma \ P \ \tau$. *For any* $\hat{\sigma}$ *s.t.* $\sigma \sqsubset_P \hat{\sigma}$, *we can derive* $\hat{\sigma} \ [\![P]\!] \ \hat{\tau}$ *for some* $\hat{\tau}$ *s.t.* $\tau \sqsubset_P \hat{\tau}$.

As for the proof, it is by induction on the structure of P, remarking that Definition 9 assures $\mathrm{Dom}([\![P]\!]) = \mathrm{Dom}(P) \cup l([\![P]\!])$ with $\mathrm{Dom}(P) \cap l([\![P]\!]) = \emptyset$, for every M-SRL program P.

We intuitively illustrate the case when P is **for** r $\{Q\}$, for some r and Q. By definition, $[\![\textbf{for } r \ \{Q\}]\!]$ yields $\textbf{from}(i\texttt{=0 or 0})\textbf{to}(i\texttt{=}r \ \textbf{or } \texttt{0})\{[\![Q]\!]\};i\texttt{-=}r$, where $i \notin \{r\} \cup \mathrm{Dom}([\![Q]\!])$ and $l([\![Q]\!]) \cap \mathrm{Dom}(P) = \emptyset$. Let $\sigma, \tau \in \Sigma$ such that $\sigma(r) = v \geq 0$

and $\sigma \, P \, \tau$. The case with $v < 0$, is analogous. In order to return τ, P executes Q as many times as v, which we denote by $\sigma \, [Q]^v \, \tau$. Moreover, let $\hat{\sigma} \in \Sigma$ s.t. $\sigma \sqsubset_P \hat{\sigma}$, hence $\hat{\sigma}(i) = 0$, and let $\hat{\tau} \in \Sigma$ s.t. $\hat{\sigma} \, [\![P]\!] \, \hat{\tau}$. In order to produce $\hat{\tau}$, it can be shown that the rules in Fig. 2 imply "$[\![P]\!]$ executes '$[\![Q]\!]$;i+=1' v times, followed by i-=r", which we shorten as $\hat{\sigma} \, [[\![Q]\!] ; i\text{+=}1]^v ; i\text{-=}r \, \hat{\tau}$.

Now we are able to show that $\hat{\tau}$ *simulates* τ w.r.t. P, namely $\tau \sqsubset_P \hat{\tau}$.

1. To ease the proof of the main statement, we can show what follows.
   By induction on m, for every $\mu, \nu, \hat{\mu}$ s.t. $\mu \sqsubset_Q \hat{\mu}$, we can prove:

   $$\mu \, [Q]^m \, \nu \implies \hat{\mu} \, [[\![Q]\!] ; i\text{+=}1]^m \, \hat{\nu}$$

   where: (i) $\nu \sqsubset_Q \hat{\nu}$; (ii) $\hat{\nu}(i) = \hat{\mu}(i) + m$; and (iii) $\hat{\nu}(r) = \hat{\mu}(r)$, for some $\hat{\nu}$. Specifically, knowing that, by definition, $i \notin \mathrm{Dom}([\![Q]\!])$ we have that: (i) holds by applying the main statement, by induction, on Q; (ii) holds because i is incremented at every iteration; (iii) holds because, by definition of M-SRL and the translating function, $r \notin \mathrm{WDom}(Q) \cup \mathrm{WDom}([\![Q]\!])$.
2. Back to the main statement, we recall that, by assumption, $\sigma \, [Q]^v \, \tau$, and $\sigma \sqsubset_P \hat{\sigma}$ implies $\sigma \sqsubset_Q \hat{\sigma}$. So, the result in the previous point implies that:

   $$\hat{\sigma} \, [[\![Q]\!] ; i\text{+=}1]^v \, \hat{\tau}'$$

   where (i) $\tau \sqsubset_Q \hat{\tau}'$; (ii) $\hat{\tau}'(i) = \hat{\sigma}(i) + m = 0 + m = m$; and (iii) $\hat{\tau}'(r) = \hat{\sigma}(r) = m$, for some $\hat{\tau}'$.
3. The conclusion $\tau \sqsubset_P \hat{\tau}'$, follows by observing that it must be $\hat{\tau}(i) = 0$, because $\hat{\tau}$ results from executing i-=r starting from $\hat{\tau}'$.

Corollary 1 (For$_\mathrm{est}$ is PRF-complete). *Let $f \in \mathsf{PRF}$. There exists $P \in \mathsf{For}_\mathrm{est}$ that computes f.*

As for the proof, [12] implies that M-SRL is complete w.r.t. the class of *Reversible Primitive Permutations* which in turn is PRF-complete [8,9,15]. By transitivity, Theorem 3 implies that For$_\mathrm{est}$ is PRF-complete.

Remark 6. Since Corollary 1 shows that For$_\mathrm{est}$ is PRF-complete, and Theorem 1 implies that For$_\mathrm{est}$ is not Turing-complete, because it cannot develop infinite loops, we strongly believe that For$_\mathrm{est}$ is *weakly* PRF-*sound*, according to:

Definition 10 (For$_\mathrm{est}$is *weakly* PRF-sound). *For every $P \in \mathsf{For}_\mathrm{est}$, and $\sigma, \tau \in \Sigma$, if $\sigma \, P \, \tau$, namely P does not fail, then a primitive recursive $\hat{P} \in \mathsf{PRF}$ exists that computes the same function as P.*

We think that a proof of this would work in analogy to the one that LOOP is PRF-sound [13]. We leave it to future work. $\square$

5   For$_{est}$ is Algorithmically More Expressive Than M-SRL

So far we know that For$_{est}$ is M-SRL-complete. Here we show:

Theorem 4. For$_{est}$ *is strictly algorithmically more expressive than* M-SRL.

We can prove it in three steps: (i) we introduce a For$_{est}$ term determining the *sign* of an integer in time $O(1)$; (ii) we introduce another For$_{est}$ term computing the *minimum* between two integers m, n in $\min(|m|, |n|) + c$ steps, for some constant $c \in \mathbb{N}$; (iii) we argue about the non existence of a M-SRL program that can do same.

Computing the Sign in For$_{est}$. We determine the sign of $n \in \mathbb{Z}$ in $O(1)$ steps, which is optimal, as follows.

Definition 11 (Sign). *Let* sign *be the name for:*

$$\textsf{from } (i\texttt{=0 or 0) to } (i\texttt{=}x \textsf{ or } !(s\texttt{=0)}) \ \{s\texttt{+=1}\}$$

where x is the variable we want the sign of, and i, s the variables eventually containing the sign.

Starting from $\sigma \in \Sigma$ s.t. $\sigma(i) = 0$ and $\sigma(s) = 0$, we can see that σ sign $\sigma[i \mapsto v, s \mapsto v]$, where:

$$v = \begin{cases} 1 & \text{if } \sigma(x) > 0 \\ 0 & \text{if } \sigma(x) = 0 \ . \\ -1 & \text{if } \sigma(x) < 0 \end{cases}$$

The key point of sign is to fully exploit the interpretation given by the rule FROMTO which interprets {s+=1}, skip it, or interprets its inverse, according to the value in x, which can be greater, equal, or greater than 0, respectively.

Fact 2. Both time and space complexities of sign are in $O(1)$.   □

The behavior of sign can be traced back to how [12] encodes the sign function inside M-SRL. However, M-SRL iterations cannot be preemptively interrupted once the sign has been discovered, while For$_{est}$ ones can. Due to this, the sign algorithm in [12] has quadratic time and exponential space complexity. Thus, sign in Definition 11 is a first example of how "*escaping* from loops" extends For$_{est}$ algorithmic expressiveness as compared to M-SRL, possibly reducing drastically time complexity.

Computing the Minimum in For$_{est}$. We detail out the main ideas to write a For$_{est}$ term minGen, that computes the minimum between any $m, n \in \mathbb{Z}$ in time $O(\min(|m|, |n|))$. A possible implementation is in Listing 1.3.

Let x, y be two variables holding m and n, respectively. Let min, i, found be output and auxiliary variables, initially set to 0. The term minGen must start with two instances of sign to determine the sign of x, and y. Once the sign is known, minGen can distinguish among four scenarios:

```
0  // m,n ∈ ℤ⁻, x=m, y=n, i=0, min=0, found=0
   min += y;
2  from ((i=0) or 0) to ((i=-x) or (found=1)) {
     if (i=-y) { // |y| < |x| -> x < y
4      min -= y;
       min += x;
6      found += 1
     } else {skip}
8  }
```

Listing 1.2. Minimum in For_est between two negative values.

```
0  // m,n ∈ ℕ, x=m, y=n, i=0, sX = 0, sY = 0, min=0, found=0
   from ((i=0) or 0) to ((i=x) or !(sX=0)) {sX += 1};
2  i-=sX; // i = 0
   from ((i=0) or 0) to ((i=y) or !(sY=0)) {sY += 1};
4  i-=sY; // i = 0
   if(sX = 0 or sX = 1){ // x >= 0
6    if(sY = 0 or sY = 1){ // x >= 0 and y >= 0
       min += x;
8      from ((i=0) or 0) to ((i=x) or (found=1)) {
         if (i=y) {
10         min -= x;
           min += y;
12         found += 1
         } else{skip}
14     }
     } else{ // x >= 0 and y < 0
16     min += y
     }
18 } else{ // x < 0
     if (sY = -1){ // x < 0 and y < 0
20     min += y;
       from ((i=0) or 0) to ((i=-x) or (found=1)) {
22       if (i=-y) {
           min -= y;
24         min += x;
           found += 1
26       } else{skip}
       }
28   } else{ // x < 0 and y >= 0
       min += x
30   }
   }
```

Listing 1.3. Minimum in For_est between two numbers in ℤ.

1. Both x, and y are positive. In this case minGen must behave as minPos in Listing 1.1, which works as follows. It assumes that m in x is the minimum, setting min to it. Then, i counts from 0 to x. If i reaches y before getting to x, it means that y is the least value. So, minGen sets min to y, stopping the iteration by setting found to 1. Otherwise, min stays at x.
2. Only one between x, and y is positive. Then, minGen must set min to the variable containing the negative number, and this is trivial.
3. Both x, and y are negative. Then, minGen must behave as minNeg in Listing 1.2, analogous to minPos, but working on the absolute values of x, and y.

Since, by construction, sign costs $O(1)$, and every case is in $O(\min(|m|, |n|))$, the whole minGen costs $O(\min(|m|, |n|))$. Therefore, we can state:

Proposition 1. *There exists a term in* Forest *computing the minimum between* $m, n \in \mathbb{Z}$ *in time* $O(\min(|m|, |n|))$.

M-SRL *has no Optimal Minimum Algorithm.* We devise this proof following Matos. He proves an analogous of *ultimate obstinacy property* for LOOP languages [11]. Intuitively, we recall that for a computational model being *ultimately obstinate* means that some functions cannot be computed by its programs in optimal time because such functions are *non trivial*, namely they *cannot* have form $f(x_1, \ldots, x_n) = x_i + c$ [3].

Clearly, the *minimum* between m, n is non trivial, thus every program in M-SRL implementing it must be subject to two structural constraints. They must contain two registers, say rm, rn storing m, n respectively. Moreover, they must have form P_1 ; **for** r $\{P_2\}$; P_3 where r has to be one between rm and rn.

Let us assume that r is rm, the alternative choice being equivalent. For our purposes *the structure* of P_2 and P_3 is irrelevant, while the structure of P_1 is. P_1 can be empty, an explicit sequence of increments/decrements with fixed length, or even contain iterations, none of them led by rm or rn. Therefore, once we start interpreting **for** rm $\{P_2\}$, due to P_1 structure, rm contains $m + c$, for some constant $c \in \mathbb{Z}$, implying that the time complexity of **for** rm $\{P_2\}$ is at least $O(m)$. Clearly, if r were rn, the time complexity would be $O(n)$. This implies:

Proposition 2. *No* M-SRL *program exists that computes the minumum between* $m, n \in \mathbb{Z}$ *in time* $O(\min(|m|, |n|))$.

So, both Propositions 1, and 2 imply Theorem 4.

Remark 7. In Proposition 2 we use big-O notation in a very strict way. minGen computes the minimum between two numbers $m, n \in \mathbb{Z}$ in $\min(|m|, |n|) + c$ steps, with c a constant in $\mathbb{N}$.   □

6   Conclusions and Future Work

We addressed the problem of algorithmic expressiveness in a reversible setting. Our artifact is Forest, a reversible computational model where iterations always terminate, but can be interrupted preemptively. $\mathsf{For_{est}}$ is a meeting point between the two established and reversible computational models M-SRL and Janus. $\mathsf{For_{est}}$ is M-SRL and PRF-complete, but strictly more algorithmically expressive. It allows us to write an algorithm that computes the minimum between two integers m and n in $O(\min(m,n))$, which cannot be encoded in M-SRL with analogous optimal cost. The reason is that we can stop $\mathsf{For_{est}}$ iterations as soon as the expected result is available, while M-SRL iterations always unfold to the end.

Future Work. Even though $\mathsf{For_{est}}$ terms always terminate, this can be due to failing assertions. Clearly, assertions seems to be necessary for loops to have general exit condition. However, failing computations cannot be reversed. We aim to remove assertions to produce a computational model with same algorithmic expressiveness as $\mathsf{For_{est}}$, whose programs always terminate successfully. A possible strategy to follow is at least [16], where authors rely on SMT solvers to statically remove unnecessary assertions.

A further step we plan is to compare our work with the one of [1], which, in fact, inspired us. The authors of [1] introduce $\mathsf{Loop_{exit}}$. It is an *unstructured* conservative extension of LOOP models. The extension consists of introducing a statement exit which can break loops by jumping to end of a program. The main result in [1] is that $\mathsf{Loop_{exit}}$ is as algorithmically expressive as APRA, a PRF-sound and complete computational model obtained by restricting Gurevich *Abstract State Machines* [6]. In fact, in relation to the algorithmic expressiveness, we think that the most valuable goal would be to introduce a reversible version of APRA subsuming $\mathsf{For_{est}}$.

References

1. Andary, P., Patrou, B., Valarcher, P.: A representation theorem for primitive recursive algorithms. Fundam. Inform. **107**, 313–330 (2011)
2. Colson, L.: A unary representation result for system T. Ann. Math. Artif. Intell. **16**, 385–403 (1996)
3. Colson, L., Fredholm, D.: System T, call-by-value and the minimum problem. Theor. Comput. Sci. **206**, 301–315 (1998)
4. Dijkstra, E.W.: Go to statement considered harmful. In: Apt, K.R., Hoare, T. (eds.) Edsger Wybe Dijkstra: His Life, Work, and Legacy. ACM Books, vol. 45, pp. 315–318. ACM/Morgan & Claypool (2022)
5. Glück, R., Yokoyama, T.: A minimalist's reversible while language. IEICE Trans. Inf. Syst. **100**(5), 1026–1034 (2017)
6. Gurevich, Y.: Evolving algebras 1993: Lipari guide. In: Börger, E. (ed.) Specification and Validation Methods, pp. 9–36. Oxford University Press (1993)
7. Lutz, C.: Janus: a time-reversible language. Letter to R. Landauer (1986)
8. Maletto, G., Roversi, L.: Certifying algorithms and relevant properties of reversible primitive permutations with lean. In: Mezzina, C.A., Podlaski, K. (eds.) RC 2022. LNCS, vol. 13354, pp. 111–127. Springer, Cham (2022). https://doi.org/10.1007/978-3-031-09005-9_8
9. Maletto, G., Roversi, L.: Certifying expressive power and algorithms of reversible primitive permutations with lean. J. Log. Algebraic Methods Program. **136**, 100923 (2024)

10. Matos, A.B.: Linear programs in a simple reversible language. Theor. Comput. Sci. **290**(3), 2063–2074 (2003)
11. Matos, A.B.: The efficiency of primitive recursive functions: a programmer's view. Theoret. Comput. Sci. **594**, 65–81 (2015)
12. Matos, A.B., Paolini, L., Roversi, L.: On the expressivity of total reversible programming languages. In: Lanese, I., Rawski, M. (eds.) RC 2020. LNCS, vol. 12227, pp. 128–143. Springer, Cham (2020). https://doi.org/10.1007/978-3-030-52482-1_7
13. Meyer, A.R., Ritchie, D.M.: The complexity of loop programs. In: Proceedings of the 1967 22nd National Conference, ACM 1967, pp. 465–469. Association for Computing Machinery, New York (1967)
14. Normann, L., Glück, R.: Partial evaluation of reversible flowchart programs. In: PEPM, pp. 119–133. ACM (2024)
15. Paolini, L., Piccolo, M., Roversi, L.: A class of recursive permutations which is primitive recursive complete. Theor. Comput. Sci. **813**, 218–233 (2020)
16. Reholt, J.W., Glück, R., Kruse, M.: Towards a dereversibilizer: fewer asserts, statically. In: Kutrib, M., Meyer, U. (eds.) RC 2023. LNCS, vol. 13960, pp. 106–114. Springer, Cham (2023). https://doi.org/10.1007/978-3-031-38100-3_8
17. Yokoyama, T., Axelsen, H.B., Glück, R.: Fundamentals of reversible flowchart languages. Theor. Comput. Sci. **611**, 87–115 (2016)

A Toy Model Provably Featuring an Arrow of Time Without Past Hypothesis

Pablo Arrighi[1(✉)], Gilles Dowek[1], and Amélia Durbec[2]

[1] Université Paris-Saclay, Inria, CNRS, LMF, 91190 Gif-sur-Yvette, France
`pablo.arrighi@universite-paris-saclay.fr`
[2] CNRS, Centrale Lille, JUNIA, Univ. Lille, Univ. Valenciennes, UMR 8520 IEMN, 59046 Lille Cedex, France

Abstract. The laws of Physics are time-reversible, making no qualitative distinction between the past and the future—yet we can only go towards the future. This apparent contradiction is known as the 'arrow of time problem'. Its current resolution states that the future is the direction of increasing entropy. But entropy can only increase towards the future if it was low in the past, and past low entropy is a very strong assumption to make, because low entropy states are rather improbable, non-generic. Recent work from the Physics literature suggests, however, that we may do away with this so-called 'past hypothesis', in the presence of reversible dynamical laws featuring expansion. We prove that this is the case, for a reversible causal graph dynamics-based toy model. It consists in graphs upon which particles circulate and interact according to local reversible rules. Some rules locally shrink or expand the graph. Almost all states expand; entropy always increases as a consequence of expansion—thereby providing a local explanation for the arrow of time without the need for a past hypothesis. This discrete setting allows us to deploy the full rigour of theoretical Computer Science proof techniques. These objects are also interesting from a Dynamical Systems point of view, as a simple generalisations of cellular automatons exhibiting non-trivial behaviours.

Keywords: Models of computation · Cellular automata · Synchronous graph rewriting · Information theory · Invariants and termination

1 Introduction

In Short. The main contribution of this paper is a first rigorous proof that an arrow of time emerges from almost all configuration under some time-reversible dynamics, without the need for a past hypothesis. This problem pertains to a long 'foundations of Physics' tradition. But the novelty of our approach is precisely the deployment of theoretical Computer Science models and techniques, in order to formalise it and solve it. I.e. the problem is first transposed to the world of models of computation (cellular automata, graph dynamics, term algebras) and

© The Author(s), under exclusive license to Springer Nature Switzerland AG 2024
T. Æ. Mogensen and Ł. Mikulski (Eds.): RC 2024, LNCS 14680, pp. 50–68, 2024.
https://doi.org/10.1007/978-3-031-62076-8_4

information theory, and then addressed through the study of invariants and termination proofs. In the longer version of this paper [4], some natural variants of the model are also explored numerically.

The Problem. Physics laws are time-reversible, i.e. time evolution can be inverted, making no qualitative distinction between the past and the future. Yet, we clearly experience the fact that we cannot go back to the past. This discrepancy is referred to as the 'arrow of time problem'. It sets the requirement for an explanation of "how does the future versus past phenomenon that we witness in everyday life, arise from time-reversible dynamical laws alone". I.e. the aim of the game is to resolve this apparent paradox by pinpointing specific physical quantities that can be used as 'clocks', and then identifying the future direction to be the direction of increase of that quantity, thereby providing a time arrow.

Usually, these quantities are variants of the concept of entropy, and one shows that starting from a low entropy initial state, entropy typically increases even under a time-reversible law. Thus, in the conventional argument due to Boltzmann [14], "Time-reversible dynamical law + Past low entropy $\Rightarrow$ Arrow of time". This argument works even for systems of bounded size (e.g. a few of particles in a box). But it suffers three important criticisms: (i) By the Poincaré recurrence theorem, as we iterate the dynamics forward, the entropy typically increases... but then drops back, and increases, etc., as the dynamical system is necessarily (almost-)periodic. The criticism is usually dismissed by Physicists on the more practical ground that the recurrence period is beyond cosmological times, but in absolute terms this remains a valid criticism. (ii) Starting from an initial low entropy state and iterating the dynamics forward, entropy typically increases (the 'entropic clock's arrow' matches that of the external time-coordinate aka "dynamical clock"). However, had we applied the reversed dynamics instead, i.e. iterating the dynamics backward, entropy typically would have increased, too (the entropic clock's arrow does not match the dynamical clock's arrow) [19], as is quite often overlooked. (iii) The assumption that the initial state be of low entropy, also referred to as 'the past hypothesis' [1] is a very strong one. This is because generic states have maximal entropy. Hence, the presence of such an improbable state at dynamical clock time 0, remains a mystery, that again demands an explanation. We will review these points in Sect. 2.

Comparison with Related Models. In [15,16], Carroll and Chen try to fix the third criticism and provide the first plausible intuition why "Time-reversible dynamical law $\Rightarrow$ Arrow of time". Their key new ingredient is big bounce (big crunch then bang) then eternal expansion. Their discussion is left informal however, leaving plenty of room to discuss whether it really manages to do away with the past hypothesis [24–26]. In particular, they themselves raise the issue whether expansion mechanisms are actually compatible with reversibility.

Barbour et al. [10,11] use the $n-$body problem, with (non-local) Newtonian classical gravity turned on, as an enlightening analogy of big-bounce-then-eternal-expansion. The question whether their model really does away with the past hypothesis has been argued in [27]. Indeed as the considered bodies travel on a pre-existing infinite space, the analogy blurs out the requirement of finite but unbounded configurations, which is needed to make the argument rigorous. Moreover, the entropic clock (quantity measuring the microscopic disorder) is replaced by a non-standard "shape complexity clock" (quantity measuring the macroscopic clumping) in these works. The question whether expansion can be implemented as a local reversible mechanism also remains open in this strand of works [22].

The aim of this paper is to exhibit rigorously-defined local reversible dynamical laws (the local rule of reversible causal graph dynamics) for which we can prove that, for a rigorously-defined notion of entropy (alike that of perfect gas):

– Almost all states end up growing in size as we iterate the dynamics.
– Entropy always increases as size grows.

Thus we prove that an entropic clock direction emerges without the need to assume past low entropy. In other words the arrow of time is established from local reversible expansion mechanisms alone, doing away with the past hypothesis. This works because size as a function of dynamical clock time is almost always U-shaped. As almost all states are somewhere on this U-curve, their size will end up growing, and their entropy will end up increasing. They will do so forever, as configurations are of finite but unbounded size. Of course almost all states have, somewhere along the dynamical clock timeline to which they belong, some states of smallest size and lowest entropy, which may be dubbed as "initial". These particular states are non-generic, just like the minimum of any U-curve is non-generic. Because the U-curve is due to the dynamics alone, their existence is the result of dynamics alone.

Our toy model is set in $1 + 1$ spacetime. It consists in circular graphs upon which particles move and interact when they are closeby. Moreover, locally some patterns are interchanged, triggering shrinking or expansion of the circle. It is cast in the framework of reversible causal graph dynamics [6,8] and is inspired by the Hasslacher-Meyer model [21], for which there is numerical evidence of a U-shaped size curve, but no proof—this seems inherently hard to prove in fact [12]. There is no mention of the arrow of time nor entropy in their paper; moreover the sense in which it is reversible and causal is left informal and seems incompatible with quantum mechanics [3]. Instead, our toy model enjoys rigorous proofs of U-shaped size and entropy curves, as well as rigorous notions of reversibility [6] and causality (i.e. making sure that information propagates at a bounded speed with respect to graph distance), readily allowing for a quantum extension [5]. These results are provided in Sect. 3.

As far as we know, there are no other closely related models besides the above-mentioned ones. This may be because 1/ The fact that a time-reversible model always grows is somewhat counter-intuitive, 2/ Let alone proving it—as shown by the efforts of [12]. 3/ Interdisciplinary work is not so common on this topic. In particular, the theoretical Computer Science analysis that we deploy is a new player. We believe it brings simplicity, clarity and rigour to a long-standing issue.

2   The Conventional Argument

Entropy. Entropy was defined by Boltzmann in the 1870s:

Definition 1 [13]. *The entropy S of a macroscopic state is defined by :*

$$S = k.\ln \Omega \tag{1}$$

with k the Boltzmann constant and Ω is the number of microscopic configurations corresponding to the macroscopic state.

In this definition the word 'macroscopic state' refers to a set of values for the macroscopic properties of the system, such as its temperature, pressure, volume or density. Given a certain macroscopic state, a 'statistical ensemble' is a way to assign a probability distribution to the set of microscopic states that correspond to the macroscopic state. It is often reasonable to assume that the probability distribution be uniform (aka a 'microcanonical ensemble'). The probability p_i of a microscopic state x_i is then $p_i = \frac{1}{\Omega}$. The connection between the Shannon entropy [23] of this probability distribution, and the Boltzmann entropy of the macrostate, is then obvious:

$$S = -k \sum_{i=0}^{\Omega-1} p_i \ln (p_i) = -k \sum_{i=0}^{\Omega-1} \frac{1}{\Omega} \ln \left(\frac{1}{\Omega}\right) = k.\ln \Omega \tag{2}$$

For a dynamical system over the state space X, the microscopic states are simply the configurations $x_i \in X$ of the system. We formalize the macroscopic states as equivalence classes on X. The entropy function associates, to each microscopic state, the entropy of its macrostate.

Definition 2. *Consider X a set and $\equiv$ an equivalence relation on X. We define the entropy function $S : X \to \mathbb{R}$ associated with $\equiv$ as:*

$$S(x) = \ln \left(\|[x]\|\right) \tag{3}$$

with $[x]$ the $\equiv$-equivalence class of x and $\|[x]\|$ is its size.

The Case of Bounded Size Dynamical Systems. The second principle of thermodynamics states that "entropy increases in time". However, even for isolated, bounded size dynamical systems, the situation is not so obvious:

Remark 1. *Let X be a finite state space and $f : X \to X$ a bijection. For any entropy function S, and for any configuration $x \in X$, the sequence $(S(f^n(x)))_{n \in N}$ is periodic because the sequence $f^n(x)_{n \in N}$ is periodic. This implies that the sequence of entropy variations $(S(f^{n+1}(x)) - S(f^n(x)))_{n \in N}$ is itself periodic. If $(S(f^n(x)))_{n \in N}$ is not constant, then these entropy variations can be negative.*

How can we justify, then, that when we dilute a drop of dye in a sealed glass of water, entropy seems to just rise, unambiguously indicating an arrow of time? Besides the fact that in practice the glass is not quite a isolated system, and hence undergoes a not quite time-reversible dynamics, several other assumptions are implicit in this emblematic experiment.

First, the duration of such an experiment likely to be far too short to observe periodicity. Second, the drop of dye would likely have diluted just as well if it had undergone the time-symmetrized versions of Physics laws instead. In other words, entropy typically does increase when we start from a low entropy initial configuration... but it does so in both directions of the dynamical clock [19]. Third, we must realise that the experiment starts at a rather improbable time. Had current time been picked up at random within the period, there would be no reason to expect it to be a time of increase of entropy, rather than of decrease. Another way to say this is that the experiment starts from an improbable configuration. Indeed in any generic configuration the dye is diluted already; entropy is almost maximal already; and the entropy variation is zero on average, independently of t the number of steps between the two observations:

$$\sum_{x \in \Sigma} \left(S(f^t(x)) - S(x) \right) = \sum_{x \in \Sigma} S(x) - \sum_{x \in \Sigma} S(x) = 0. \tag{4}$$

In order to witness an arrow of time, we must start from a low entropy configuration, but in practice the equivalence relation and therefore the entropy function are chosen so that low-entropy configurations are non-generic.

Past Hypothesis. So, to this day, phenomena such as the dilution of the drop of dye in a glass of water, and the increasing entropy therein, are paradigmatic of current understanding of the arrow of time problem... and yet, a careful inspection of the assumptions underlying the conventional argument shows that it only displaces the problem. The question "Why do we observe an arrow of time" has become "Why was the Universe originally of low entropy?". This strong assumption of a low entropy initial configuration is referred to as the 'past hypothesis' [1], and was criticised right from its birth, on account of this unlikelihood [14]. Luckily, more recent accounts of the arrow of time suggest we could do without it [9,10,15,16]. The key ingredient is expansion.

3   Arrow of Time Without Past Hypothesis

In this section we prove via a toy model that an entropic arrow of time can originate from expansion, and that this expansion can be implemented locally and reversibly. In this model Remark 1 does not apply because, although each configuration is finite, the state space itself is infinite, as configurations can grow. That Remark 1 can be circumvented in an infinite state space is not surprising by itself: think of $\mathbb{N}$ the set of integers for instance. Each number can be written with a finite number of digits, but the set itself is of course infinite, and it is easy to define a non-periodic bijection on the set:

$$f(n) = \begin{cases} 0 \text{ if } n = 1 \\ n + 2 \text{ if } n \text{ is even} \\ n - 2 \text{ else} \end{cases} \tag{5}$$

What is much less obvious and harder to prove is the existence of a time-reversible, causal, homogeneous, ultimately expanding dynamics on generic configurations. We do not know of another such model.

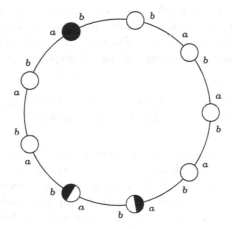

Fig. 1. *A configuration.* Each full half-disk represents the presence of an (undistinguishable) particle that is about to hop along the corresponding port.

3.1   State Space

The states of the model have one dimension, these are circular graphs. These circles are of unbounded but finite size, i.e. the infinite line is not allowed. The vertices are equipped with ports a and b, and edges go from port to port, each being used exactly once, as in Fig. 1.

Each vertex carries an internal state, amongst four possible states: 'containing no particle', 'containing a particle moving along port a', 'containing a particle moving along port b', 'containing two particles'. Notice that this set of internal states is the same as that used to model electrons in gas-on-grid methods [20], or in quantum walks to represent the spin of a fermionic particle such as the electron [2]. Later we will generalize this by associating, to each port of each node, not just one information bit, but two or three.

There is one subtlety: vertices are named, and these names form a little algebra. This is so that a vertex u may be able to split into $u.l$ and $u.r$, and later merge back into $u.l \vee u.r$, and that this be in fact the same as just u. There is no escaping this formalism in order to achieve both reversibility and local vertex creation/destruction [6], particularly if one wants to preserve causality in the quantum regime [3]. In order to remain self-contained, the full definition of these named graphs is provided in Appendix A.

We denote by C_n the set of circular graphs with $2n$ information bits per vertex (n per port). For any vertex x, we denote by $p_i(x)$ the value of the i-th bit of the port p of vertex x.

3.2   The Toy Model

Our main model ($\sqrt{\tau}I$) is inspired by the Hasslacher-Meyer dynamics [21]. It acts on the set C_1 and consists in composing two steps: I, then $\sqrt{\tau}$. Each of them is a reversible causal graph dynamics, thus so is their composition—the reader can refer to [6,8] for further theoretical aspects about reversible causal graph dynamics, including general definitions. Thus the whole dynamics is a time-reversible. It consists in a composition of steps which, taken individually, are time-symmetric [18]:

Definition 3. *A causal graph dynamics f is said to be* time-symmetric *if and only if there exists a causal graph dynamics T such that $T^2 = Id$ and $TfT = f^{-1}$.*

Step $\sqrt{\tau}$. Let τ be the operation that moves all particles along their corresponding port. The operation $\sqrt{\tau}$ is such $\sqrt{\tau} \circ \sqrt{\tau} = \tau$: it moves particles by half an edge instead, see Fig. 2a. One way of thinking about this operation is as inverting the roles of edges and nodes in the sense of taking the dual graph. Notice that alternatively, we could have used a (renaming-equivalent but less symmetrical) operation that moves only those particles associated to port b, but by a whole edge.

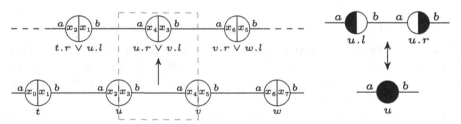

(a) *Step* $\sqrt{\tau}$. Each particle hops by half an edge. In other words, edges become vertices and vertices become edges. Particles keep their orientation.

(b) *Step* I. All occurrence of the two patterns are flipped for each other synchronously. This is unambiguous, as the patterns do not overlap.

Fig. 2. *Rules of the toy model.*

Definition 4 ($\sqrt{\tau}$). *Step $\sqrt{\tau}$ is defined for any graph $X \in \mathcal{C}_n$ as follows:*

- *$V(\sqrt{\tau}(X)) = \{u.r \vee v.l \mid \{u : b, v : a\} \in E(X)\}$*
- *$E(\sqrt{\tau}(X)) = \{\{x' : b, y' : a\} \mid u, x, y \in V(X) \text{ and } x' = u.r \vee x.l \text{ and } y' = y.r \vee u.l\}$*
- *$\forall x' \in V(\sqrt{\tau}(X))$, and for all $i \in [1, n], a_i(x) = a_i(u)$ and $b_i(x) = b_i(v)$, where u and v are the vertices of X such that $x'.l = u.r$ and $x'.r = v.l$ respectively.*

This step is both time-reversible and time-symmetrical, since

$$\sqrt{\tau}^{-1} = T\sqrt{\tau}T \tag{6}$$

with T the function exchanging the left and right information bits of each vertex.

Step I. Step I consists in splitting a vertex into two when it holds two particles, or conversely merging two vertices holding a pair of back-to-back particles, as in Fig. 2b. Thus, a vertex u such as $a_1(u) = b_1(u) = 1$ will produce two vertices $u.l$ and $u.r$ with $a_1(u.l) = b_1(u.r) = 1$ and $b_1(u.l) = a_1(u.r) = 0$. Conversely, two vertices u and v, with $a_1(u) = b_1(v) = 1$ and $b_1(u) = a_1(v) = 0$ will merge into a vertex $u \vee v$ such as $a_1(u \vee v) = b_1(u \vee v) = 1$.

This step is obviously time-reversible and time-symmetric, since it is involutive: $I^2 = Id$.

Spacetime Diagram. The evolution of a configuration under toy model $\sqrt{\tau}I$ can be represented in the form of a spacetime diagrams, e.g. Fig. 3 represents $\sqrt{\tau}I$. In these diagrams, the spatial dimension is represented horizontally, and dynamical clock time is represented vertically downwards. Each vertex is represented by a cell, separated from its neighbours with a vertical black line. Its internal state of a cell is captured by its colour. The cells are depicted in variable-sizes, allowing each split/merge to be done "on the spot".

3.3 Size Increases

The first observation that can be made from Fig. 3 is that the dynamics $\sqrt{\tau}I$, although time-reversible, grows the size of the graph. It does not grow from the borders, there are no borders, it just expands locally. The numerics in Fig. 4a suggest this is typical. We will now prove that this happens for almost all initial states. In fact, we will prove the stronger result that graphs always end up growing, and that the growth is strict as soon as they contain at least one particle of each type.

Intuitively this is due to the fact that vertex merger only occurs in the presence of a pattern which is unstable:

Lemma 1 (Merger Instability). *Let $X \in \mathcal{C}_1$ be a circular graph. Given a pair u and v of adjacent vertices of X, these are said to belong to a merger pattern if and only if $a_1(u) = b_1(v) = 1$ and $b_1(u) = a_1(v) = 0$. For any u, v forming a merger pattern in X, there are two vertices $u.r, v.l \in V((\sqrt{\tau}I)^{-1}(X))$ such that $u.r$ and $v.l$ form a merger pattern.*

Proof. By inspection of Fig. 5, which represents the pre-image of a merger pattern.

Let us fix notations before we state the expansion theorem. First, in what follows we will write (u_n) to designate the sequence $(u_n)_{n\in\mathbb{N}}$ in the absence of ambiguity. Second, we will use the following asymptotic notation:

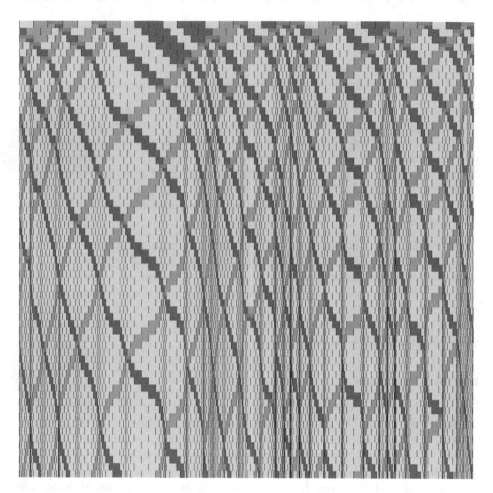

Fig. 3. *Spacetime diagram of dynamics* $\sqrt{\tau}I$. Dynamical clock time flows towards the bottom. Particles corresponding moving along port a (resp. b) are represented green (resp. blue). Observe how space keeps on expanding, making this spacetime diagram look like a curtain. (Color figure online)

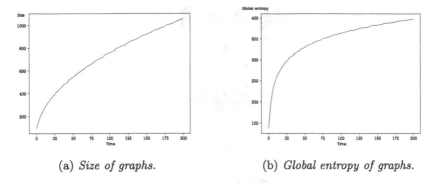

(a) *Size of graphs.*   (b) *Global entropy of graphs.*

Fig. 4. Typical size and entropy curves for dynamics $\sqrt{\tau}I$. The horizontal axis represents the number of steps of the dynamics, aka dynamical clock time. The initial configuration is drawn uniformly at random amongst all graphs of size 100.

Definition 5. *Let there be two sequences (u_n) and (v_n). We say that (u_n) is of the order of (v_n), and write $(u_n) = \Theta((v_n))$ if there exist positive numbers $a, b \in \mathbb{R}$ and $n_0 \in \mathbb{N}$ such that for all $n \geq n_0$, $a.v_n \leq u_n \leq b.v_n$.*

We have:

Theorem 1 (Expansion). *For any $X \in \mathcal{C}_1$ containing at least one particle of each type, let $u_n = |V\left(\left(\sqrt{\tau}I\right)^n(X)\right)|$. We have $(u_n) = \Theta((\sqrt{n}))$.*

Proof (Outline). As proved in Lemma 1 dynamics $\sqrt{\tau}I$ cannot create a merger pattern as they are stable by $(\sqrt{\tau}I)^{-1}$. This entails that any interference disrupting a merger pattern will permanently destroy it. We then prove, by means of a strictly decreasing measure, that such interference will occur if and only if the graph contains at least two particles going in opposite direction. Lastly we quantify the growth rate once all merger patterns have been removed from the graph, placing bounds corresponding to the best and worst case scenarios. The proof technique is thus akin to a program termination and complexity analysis proof. For readability, the technical details are given in Appendix B.

As can be seen in Fig. 4a, for a randomly chosen configuration, the asymptotic regime is reached quickly and is quite stable.

3.4   Entropy Increases with Size

It turns out that growth in the size of the graph implies growth of entropy, for a natural notion of entropy.

Indeed from this point on, we will focus on the entropy function associated with the following equivalence class: two configurations are considered equivalent if and only if they have the same size and the same number of particles. This entropy function can be seen as analogous to the one used in the study of perfect gases.

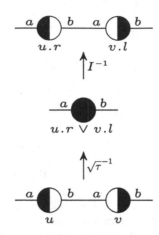

Fig. 5. *Instability of merger patterns under $\sqrt{\tau}I$.*

This is because the entropy of a perfect gas configuration is generally associated with the macroscopic properties of pressure, volume, temperature and number of particles. As these four variables are related by the perfect gas law, three are independent. Moreover, in our toy model the speed of the particles is constant, which makes it unnecessary to consider the temperature. We therefore have to consider just two variables amongst: the number of particles; the size of the graph (analogous to the volume); and the density of particles (analogous to the pressure).

We ignore the names of the vertices when counting the microstates corresponding to the macrostates, i.e. when counting the number of graphs of a given size and having a given number of particles. We denote $\binom{n}{p}$ the binomial coefficient p among n, i.e. $\binom{n}{p} = \frac{n!}{p!(n-p)!}$.

Definition 6. *The entropy function S' is defined by $S'(X) = \log(\binom{2|V(X)|}{p})$ where p is the number of particles in X.*

In the case of $\sqrt{\tau}I$ we have proven in Theorem 1 that $V(X)$ grows as a square root. Because this rule preserves the number of particles we automatically obtains the growth of entropy. But we can be more precise:

Corollary 1. *For any $X \in \mathcal{C}_1$ containing at least one particle of each type, let $e_n = S'(\sqrt{\tau}I)^n(X)$. We have $(e_n) = \Theta((\log(n)))$.*

Proof. Thanks to Theorem 1, we have that $(S'(\sqrt{\tau}I)^n(X))_{n\in\mathbb{N}} = \Theta(\log((\binom{\Theta(\sqrt{n})}{p})))$ Using the bounds $(\frac{a}{b})^b \leq \binom{a}{b} \leq e^b(\frac{a}{b})^b$ [17], and noting that p is constant, we obtain:

$$(S'(\sqrt{\tau}I)^n(X))_{n\in\mathbb{N}} = \Theta(p\log(\frac{\Theta(\sqrt{n})}{p})) = \Theta(\log(n^{1/2})) = \Theta(\log(n)) \quad (7)$$

Note that this corollary would apply equally well to any dynamics where the number of particles remains constant and the size of the graph grows polynomially (not necessarily as a square root).

The asymptotic regime of the size function was reached as soon as all the merger patterns were destroyed, cf. Fig. 4a. The same happens with global entropy, cf. Fig. 4b.

If we are only interested in whether entropy grows, without seeking to characterise its asymptotic behaviour, we can state a more general theorem, relating it to size growth. Indeed, under the assumption that the particles do not fill the whole space, nor disappear completely, then any dynamics that increase the size of the graph will also increase the entropy:

Theorem 2 (Entropy increases with size). *For all $X \in C_u$ and $f : C_u \to C_u$ such that :*

- $\lim\limits_{n \to +\infty} |V(f^n(X))| = +\infty$
- *$\exists m \in \mathbb{N}$ such that $\forall n \geq m, 1 \leq p_n \leq 2u \times |V(f^n(X))| - 1$ where p_n is the number of particles in the step in $f^n(X)$.*

We have that $\lim\limits_{n \to +\infty} S'(f^n(X)) = +\infty$.

Proof. Thanks to the second condition, we have for all $n \geq m$:

$$S'(f^n(X)) = \log(\binom{n}{p}_{2V(f^n(X))|}) \geq \log(\binom{2V(f^n(X))|}{1})) = \log(2V(f^n(X))|)$$

(8)

As $\log(2|V(f^n(X))|)$ tends to $+\infty$ when n tends to $+\infty$, this is also the case for $S'(f^n(X))$.

3.5   Recovering an Arrow of Time

With Theorem 1 and Corollary 1, we have proven that an entropic arrow of time emerges in some time-reversible, causal, homogeneous laws (namely the $\sqrt{\tau}I$ toy model), without relying on the past hypothesis. More precisely, we have proven that starting from almost all configurations, entropy ultimately grows as we iterate the dynamics. Intuitively, after a finite period of dynamical clock time, the entropic clock's arrow aligns with that of the dynamical clock. This solves criticism (*iii*) of the conventional argument. Notice how, ultimately, this resolution boils down to the fact that configurations are of finite but unbounded size. In this context, assuming that the universe "starts small" is reasonable, because for any configuration, there are many more larger configurations than smaller ones. The same happens with entropy: any starting value is small within the set of positive real numbers. In that sense past low entropy is no longer unreasonable, it is unavoidable.

An immediate consequence is that the toy model is not periodic, i.e. there is no recurrence time: this solves criticism (i) in a way more satisfactory manner than arguing that "there is a recurrence time but it is typically too big to be observed". Let us look at criticism (ii).

Since the system $\sqrt{\tau}I$ is time-reversible, one can naturally ask what happens if one tries to "go back in time", i.e. how a graph evolves when one applies the dynamics $(\sqrt{\tau}I)^{-1} = I^{-1}\sqrt{\tau}^{-1}$. Numerics suggest it also increases the size of the graph, but at a different rate, see Fig. 6a. We can prove it:

Theorem 3. *For any $X \in \mathcal{C}_1$ containing at least one particle of each type, the sequence $(|V((\sqrt{\tau}I)^{-n}(X))|)_{n\in\mathbb{N}} = \Theta(n)$.*

Proof. In the absence of patterns ⬤—⬤ , the size of the graph decreases strictly each time two particles meet. By conservation of momentum, the particles will continue to cross each other. Since the graph cannot decrease continuously a pattern ⬤—⬤ will inevitably form. As can be seen in the proof of Lemma 1, the pattern ⬤—⬤ is stable by $I^{-1}\sqrt{\tau}^{-1}$, and cannot be crossed by other particles. This implies that once such a pattern is present, any pair of particles not belonging to such a pattern can only collide once. When all these collisions have occurred, each application of $I^{-1}\sqrt{\tau}^{-1}$ increases the size of the graph by the number of patterns present. We can bound by $\min(n_a, n_b)$ the number of such patterns in X and its successors by $I^{-1}\sqrt{\tau}^{-1}$. Thus there exists $m \in \mathbb{N}$ such that for all $n \geq m$ we have:

$$|V((\sqrt{\tau}I)^{-m}(X))| + n \leq |V((\sqrt{\tau}I)^{-n}(X))| \leq |V((\sqrt{\tau}I)^{-m}(X))| + n\min(n_a, n_b) \quad (9)$$

By the same proof scheme as for Corollary 1, we obtain the entropy growth for $I^{-1}\sqrt{\tau}^{-1}$:

Corollary 2. *For any $X \in \mathcal{C}_1$ containing at least one particle of each type, let $e_n = S'(\sqrt{\tau}I)^{-n}(X)$. We have $(e_n) = \Theta(\log(n))$.*

Thus, a variation of criticism (ii) still holds, as entropy increases in both directions from a 'source'. But here, since the model is not periodic, there is a single such source: a possibility discussed under the name of 'Janus point' [9,10,15,16]. To move away from this region of minimal entropy, whether by iterating the forward dynamics or its reverse, means augmenting entropy and hence 'going towards the future'. The important point is the way in which this variation relates to the resolution of criticism (iii): it is no longer necessary to assume that the universe "started" in an improbable low-entropy state; as the existence of an arrow of time just follows from the existence of a minimal region, which itself is a direct consequence of the dynamical law.

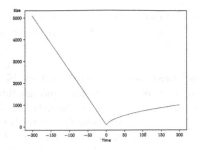

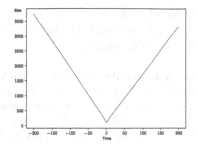

(a) *Typical curve of size of the graphs under $(\sqrt{\tau}I)^{-1}$ and $\sqrt{\tau}I$. The initial condition is drawn uniformly at random amongst graphs of size 100. We run the dynamics backwards and forward to explore negative and positive dynamical clock times.*

(b) *Typical curve of size of the graphs under $\sqrt{\tau}I_2$, a time-symmetrised version of $\sqrt{\tau}I$. The initial condition is drawn uniformly at random amongst graphs of size 100, thus particle density is high ~ 0.5.*

Fig. 6. Evolution of the size of a typical graph under $\sqrt{\tau}I)^{-1}$, $\sqrt{\tau}I$ and $\sqrt{\tau}I_2$.

4 Conclusion

This paper provides a first rigorous proof that an arrow of time emerges from almost all configuration under some time-reversible dynamics, without the need for a past hypothesis. The reversible dynamics in question is cast in the setting of reversible causal graph dynamics; the methods used pertain to the field of theoretical Computer Science. The proof works by showing that graph size increases, and that entropy increases with size, where entropy is defined as for perfect gases. It provides a local explanation for the origin of the arrow of time, by tracing it back to local, reversible expansion mechanisms acting over configurations of finite but unbounded size.

This explanation resolves two of the three main criticisms to the standard of the standard Boltzmann argument: there is no recurrence time, and no need to assume atypical initial conditions. One criticism still holds as there are successive configurations of minimal entropy from which two arrows of time flow in opposite directions. This idea is present in some cosmological models and popularized under the name or 'Janus point'.

We also show, numerically, in the longer version of this paper [4], that the explanation is compatible with fully time-symmetric dynamics, as well as periods of exponential growth.

In Thermodynamics, entropy increases globally, but locally it may well decrease and stabilize close to zero, reaching the so-called 'thermal death'. At which stage it becomes impossible to witness an arrow of time locally. The longer version of this paper also includes a theorem about the fatality of thermal death, and discusses delaying it.

We wonder whether the same argument can be made base on other notions of entropy, such as: metric entropy, topological entropy, or Von Neumann entropy (in the quantum regime).

Acknowledgements. We wish to thank Marios Christodoulou, Pierre Guillon, Benjamin Hellouin, Carlo Rovelli and Francesca Vidotto for many discussions and insights. This project/publication was made possible through the support of the ID# 62312 grant from the John Templeton Foundation, as part of the 'The Quantum Information Structure of Spacetime' Project (QISS). The opinions expressed in this project/publication are those of the author(s) and do not necessarily reflect the views of the John Templeton Foundation.

A   Named Graphs

Say as in Fig. 2b that some quantum evolution splits a vertex u into two. We need to name the two infants in a way that avoids name conflicts with the vertices of the rest of the graph. But if the evolution is locally-causal, we are unable to just 'pick a fresh name out of the blue', because we do not know which names are available. Thus, we have to construct new names locally. A natural choice is to use the names $u.l$ and $u.r$ (for left and right respectively). Similarly, say that some other evolution merges two vertices u, v into one. A natural choice is to call the resultant vertex $u \vee v$, where the symbol $\vee$ is intended to represent a merger of names.

This is, in fact, what the inverse evolution will do to vertices $u.l$ and $u.r$ that were just split: merge them back into a single vertex $u.l \vee u.r$. But, then, in order to get back where we came from, we need that the equality $u.l \vee u.r = u$ holds. Moreover, if the evolution is time-reversible, then this inverse evolution does exists, therefore we are compelled to accept that vertex names obey this algebraic rule.

Reciprocally, say that some evolution merges two vertices u, v into one and calls them $u \vee v$. Now say that some other evolution splits them back, calling them $(u \vee v).l$ and $(u \vee v).r$. This is, in fact, what the inverse evolution will do to the vertex $u \vee v$, split it back into $(u \vee v).l$ and $(u \vee v).r$. But then, in order to get back where we came from, we need the equalities $(u \vee v).l = u$ and $(u \vee v).r = v$.

Definition 7 (Names). *Let $\mathbb{K}$ be a countable set. The name algebra $\mathcal{N}[\mathbb{K}]$ has terms given by the grammar*

$$u, v ::= c \mid u.t \mid u \vee v \quad \text{with} \quad c \in \mathbb{K}, \ t \in \{l, r\}^*$$

and is endowed with the following equality theory over terms (with ε the empty word):

$$(u \vee v).l = u \qquad (u \vee v).r = v \qquad u.\varepsilon = u \qquad u.l \vee u.r = u$$

We define $\mathcal{V} := \mathcal{N}[\mathbb{K}]$.

The fact that this algebra is well-defined was proven in [6]. Now that we have a set of possible names for our vertices, we can readily define 'port graphs' (aka 'generalized Cayley graphs' [7]). Condition (10) will just ensure that names do not intersect, e.g. forbidding that there be a name $u \vee v$ and another $v \vee w$, so as to avoid name collisions should they split.

Definition 8 (Named graphs). *Let Σ be the set of internal states and π be the set of ports. A graph G is given by a finite set of vertices $V_G \subseteq \mathcal{V}$ such that for all $v, v' \in V_G$ and for all $t, t' \in \{l, r\}^*$,*

$$v.t = v'.t' \text{ implies } v = v' \text{ and } t = t' \tag{10}$$

together with

- *$\sigma_G : V_G \to \Sigma$ its internal states*
- *E_G a set of non-intersecting two element subsets of $V_G : \pi$, its edges.*

In other words an edge e is of the form $\{x : a, y : b\}$ and $\forall e, e' \in E_G., e \cap e' \neq \emptyset \Rightarrow e = e'$.

B   Proof of Theorem 1

Proof. First, it is argued that there is a time step m after which no more vertex mergers will occur. We denote $n_f(X)$ the number of merger patterns in X, and $d_f(X)$ the minimum distance between a merger pattern and a particle moving towards it (this includes a particle present in a merger pattern, and itself if there are no other particles). We will show that the pair $(n_f(\sqrt{\tau}I)^n(X), d_f(\sqrt{\tau}I)^n(X))$ decreases strictly in lexicographic order.

As we have seen in Lemma 1, a merger pattern cannot be created, and is destroyed on collision. We only need to prove that $d_{fu}((\sqrt{\tau}I)^n X)$ decreases strictly when $p(\sqrt{\tau}I)^n X)$ remains constant. Let u, v be two vertices of a merger pattern and p a particle such that u, v and p realise the distance $d_f(X)$. Two cases can occur, either p is itself part of a merger pattern, in which case there are no particles between the two merger patterns, or p is free moving, in which case there are only particles going in the opposite direction between p and u, v. In the first case, the two perform a fusion and there are no particles between the two merger patterns (so there is no division); the distance between the two patterns therefore decreases by 1. In the second case, the particle p will move towards the merger pattern, decreasing $d_{fu}((\sqrt{\tau}I)^n X)$.

In order to preserve the readability of the notations, we will denote (u_n) the sequence $(|V((\sqrt{\tau}I)^n(X))|)$. Thanks to the previous point, we know that there is a time step $m \in \mathbb{N}$ from which each collision of particles will cause the creation of an additional vertex, so the sequence u_n is necessarily increasing for all $n > m$. Since X contains at least one particle of each type, we have that for all $n \geq m$, the evolution of $(\sqrt{\tau}I)^n X$ during u_n time steps causes at least one collision. Similarly, we know that at most $c = 2n_a n_b$ collisions occur in the same time frame where n_a (resp. n_b) is the number of particles on the port a (resp. b). This allows us to obtain the following inequalities:

$$u_n + 1 \leq u_{n+u_n} \leq u_n + c \tag{11}$$

Let $(v_k)_{k \in \mathbb{N}}$ be the sub-sequence such that $v_0 = u_m$ and for all $k \in \mathbb{N}$, $v_{k+1} = u_{\text{ind}(k)+v_k}$, where $\text{ind}(k)$ is the function such that $\text{ind}(0) = m$ and for all $k \in \mathbb{N}, \text{ind}(k) = \sum_{i=0}^{k-1} v_i$. By induction, we prove that $u_{\text{ind}(k)} = v_k$:

$$u_{\text{ind}(k+1)} = u_{\sum_{i=0}^{k} v_i} = u_{v_k + \sum_{i=0}^{k-1} v_i} = u_{\text{ind}(k)+v_k} = v_{k+1} \tag{12}$$

This allows us to apply the inequality (11) on $v_{k+1} = u_{\text{ind}(k)+v_k}$. Combining (11) and (12), we obtain the linear growth of $(v_k)_{k \in \mathbb{N}}$:

$$v_k + 1 \leq v_{k+1} = u_{\text{ind}(k)+v_k} \leq v_k + c \tag{13}$$

Let us now focus on the growth of the index of $(v_k)_{k \in \mathbb{N}}$. By applying the inequalities of (13) to the definition of $\text{ind}(k)$ we obtain :

$$\sum_{i=0}^{k}(v_0 + i) \leq \sum_{i=0}^{k}(v_i) \leq \sum_{i=0}^{k}(v_0 + ci) \tag{14}$$

$$ku_m + \frac{k(k-1)}{2} = \sum_{i=0}^{k}(v_0 + i) \leq \text{ind}(k) \leq \sum_{i=0}^{k}(v_0 + ci) = ku_m + c\frac{k(k-1)}{2} \tag{15}$$

To conclude, let us return to the main sequence $(u_n)_{n \in \mathbb{N}}$. For a sufficiently large n, there exists $k \geq 4u_m + c$ such that:

$$\text{ind}(k) \leq n \leq \text{ind}(k+1) \tag{16}$$

This gives us, considering that $(u_n)_{n \in \mathbb{N}}$ is increasing, the previous Eq. (15) and that $k \geq 4u_m + c$ the following inequalities:

$$\text{ind}(k) \leq n \leq \text{ind}(k+1) \tag{17}$$

$$\implies ku_m + \frac{k(k-1)}{2} \leq n \leq (k+1)u_m + c\frac{k(k+1)}{2} \tag{18}$$

$$\implies k(2u_m + k - 1) \leq 2n \leq k(4u_m + c + ck) \tag{19}$$

$$\implies 2k^2 \leq 2n \leq (c+1)k^2 \tag{20}$$

$$\implies k \leq \sqrt{n} \leq \sqrt{\frac{(c+1)}{2}}k \tag{21}$$

$$\implies \sqrt{\frac{2}{c+1}}\sqrt{n} \leq k \leq \sqrt{n} \tag{22}$$

Since the sequence u_n is increasing, and using the inequalities (22) and (13), we can conclude with the following inequalities:

$$u_m + \sqrt{\frac{2}{c+1}}\sqrt{n} \le u_m + k \le v_k \le u_n \le v_{k+1} \le u_m + c(k+1) \le u_m + c + c\sqrt{n}$$

(23)

Thus, u_n is of the order of $(\sqrt{n})$.

References

1. Albert, D.Z.: Time and chance (2001)
2. Arrighi, P.: An overview of quantum cellular automata. Nat. Comput. **18**, 885 (2019). arXiv preprint arXiv:1904.12956
3. Arrighi, P., Christodoulou, D.Z., Durbec, A.: On quantum superpositions of graphs, no-signalling and covariance. CoRR, abs/2010.13579 (2020)
4. Arrighi, P., Dowek, G., Durbec, A.: A toy model provably featuring an arrow of time without past hypothesis. In: Proceedings of the 16th Conference on Reversible Computation (RC2024) (2024, to appear)
5. Arrighi, P., Durbec, A., Wilson, M.: Quantum networks theory. CoRR, abs/2110.10587 (2021)
6. Arrighi, P., Durbec, N., Emmanuel, A.: Reversibility *vs* local creation/destruction. In: Thomsen, M.K., Soeken, M. (eds.) RC 2019. LNCS, vol. 11497, pp. 51–66. Springer, Cham (2019). https://doi.org/10.1007/978-3-030-21500-2_4
7. Arrighi, P., Martiel, S., Nesme, V.: Cellular automata over generalized Cayley graphs. Math. Struct. Comput. Sci. **28**(3), 340–383 (2018)
8. Arrighi, P., Martiel, S., Perdrix, S.: Reversible causal graph dynamics: invertibility, block representation, vertex-preservation. Nat. Comput. **19**(1), 157–178 (2020). Pre-print arXiv:1502.04368
9. Barbour, J.: The Janus Point: A New Theory of Time. Random House (2020)
10. Barbour, J., Koslowski, T., Mercati, F.: Identification of a gravitational arrow of time. Phys. Rev. Lett. **113**, 181101 (2014)
11. Barbour, J., Koslowski, T., Mercati, F.: Janus points and arrows of time. arXiv preprint arXiv:1604.03956 (2016)
12. Baur, K., Rabin, J.M., Meyer, D.A.: Periodicity and growth in a lattice gas with dynamical geometry. Phys. Rev. E **73**(2), 026129 (2006)
13. Boltzmann, L.: Vorlesungen Über Gastheorie. Barth, Leipzig, 1. auflage edition (1896)
14. Boltzmann, L.: Lectures on Gas Theory. Courier Corporation (2012)
15. Carroll, S.M., Chen, J.: Spontaneous inflation and the origin of the arrow of time. arXiv preprint hep-th/0410270 (2004)
16. Carroll, S.M., Chen, J.: Does inflation provide natural initial conditions for the universe? Int. J. Mod. Phys. D **14**(12), 2335–2339 (2005)
17. Das, S.: A brief note on estimates of binomial coefficients (2015). https://www.semanticscholar.org/paper/A-brief-note-on-estimates-of-binomial-coefficients-Das/e0e703e1bbc914e563afb72480d7f915df79b834
18. Gajardo, A., Kari, J., Moreira, A.: On time-symmetry in cellular automata. J. Comput. Syst. Sci. **78**(4), 1115–1126 (2012)

19. Goldstein, S., Tumulka, R., Zanghì, N.: Is the hypothesis about a low entropy initial state of the universe necessary for explaining the arrow of time? Phys. Rev. D **94**, 023520 (2016)
20. Hardy, J., Pomeau, Y., de Pazzis, O.: Time evolution of a two-dimensional classical lattice system. Phys. Rev. Lett. **31**(5), 276–279 (1973)
21. Hasslacher, B., Meyer, D.A.: Modelling dynamical geometry with lattice gas automata. In: Expanded Version of a Talk Presented at the Seventh International Conference on the Discrete Simulation of Fluids held at the University of Oxford (1998)
22. Koslowski, T.A., Mercati, F., Sloan, D.: Through the big bang: continuing Einstein's equations beyond a cosmological singularity. Phys. Lett. B **778**, 339–343 (2018)
23. Shannon, C.E.: A mathematical theory of communication. Bell Syst. Tech. J. **27**(3), 379–423 (1948)
24. Vilenkin, A.: Arrows of time and the beginning of the universe. Phys. Rev. D **88**(4), 043516 (2013)
25. Wald, R.M.: The arrow of time and the initial conditions of the universe. Stud. Hist. Philos. Sci. Part B: Stud. Hist. Philos. Mod. Phys. **37**(3), 394–398 (2006). The arrows of time
26. Weaver, C.G.: On the Carroll-Chen model. J. Gen. Philos. Sci. **48**(1), 97–124 (2017)
27. Zeh, H.D.: Comment on the "Janus point" explanation of the arrow of time. arXiv preprint arXiv:1601.02790 (2016)

Reversibility with Holes
(Work in Progress)

Giovanni Fabbretti[1]([⊠]) [iD], Ivan Lanese[2] [iD], and Jean-Bernard Stefani[1] [iD]

[1] Univ. Grenoble Alpes, INRIA, CNRS, Grenoble INP, LIG, 38000 Grenoble, France
g.fabbretti8@gmail.com
[2] Olas Team, University of Bologna, INRIA, 40137 Bologna, Italy

Abstract. According to Landauer's principle, any non-reversible system can be made reversible -that is, capable of undoing its actions- by keeping information about the past of the computation. In the area of concurrent and distributed systems, this often takes the form of *memories*. Memories are special devices that keep track of past states of a system execution. Memories can be looked up to restore past states, upon necessity. This paper investigates and lays down ideas on how to achieve reversibility in systems that are subject to events that, as a side effect, erase some memories, creating then holes in the structure of memories. The chosen application area is concurrent and distributed systems, where the events erasing memories are the failure of nodes.

1 Introduction

A system is reversible if it is capable of executing not only in the standard, forward manner, but also backwards. Reversibility in computer science was first studied in the sixties in the seminal paper by Landauer [5] and then over the years flourished and appeared in many diverse application areas, from hardware [5] to formal languages such as CCS [1,9] and programming languages such as Erlang [8].

The vast majority of systems existing today have not been designed with reversibility in mind because they compute irreversible functions. However, one way to make them reversible is by employing *memories*. A memory is an artificial device that keeps track of the past state of a system execution that can be looked up to restore such past state later on, when needed.

In this paper we focus on concurrent and distributed reversible systems, relying on memories, for which *causal consistency*, proposed by Danos and Krivine in [1], is the most used notion of reversibility (alternative notions of reversibility are used, e.g., for biological systems [10]). Causal consistency states that an

The work has been partially supported by French ANR project DCore ANR-18-CE25-0007. The second author has also been partially supported by MSCA-PF project 101106046 - ReGraDe-CS and by INdAM – GNCS 2023 project RISICO, code CUP_E53C22001930001. The authors thank the anonymous reviewers for their useful comments and suggestions.

T. Æ. Mogensen and Ł. Mikulski (Eds.): RC 2024, LNCS 14680, pp. 69–74, 2024.
https://doi.org/10.1007/978-3-031-62076-8_5

action can be undone iff all of its consequences, if any, have been already undone. To check whether an action is a consequence of another one, memories need to keep trace of causal dependencies between past actions. Then, from memories it is possible to build the *causal graph* of the system execution - that is, an acyclic graph capturing causal relations between process states. Hence, before undoing an action, it suffices to check that it has no descendants in the causal graph.

To the best of our knowledge, a common assumption of the works on concurrent and distributed reversible systems relying on memories, such as [1,7,8], is that memories cannot be lost. However, in distributed systems this assumption is extremely challenging to fulfill at best. Indeed, distributed systems are notoriously subject to failures that affect the normal functioning of their nodes. Because of their structure, even relying on persistent storage may not easily solve the problem, because the failed node may not be readily accessible by, e.g., a human operator to retrieve memories.

In this paper, we study *causal-consistent rollback* [6], which allows one to undo an action in a causal consistent way, namely by undoing all and only its consequences. We propose two approaches for rollback in distributed systems subject to failures, which differ on the degree of cooperativeness that their nodes are willing to put in place.

We consider distributed systems where each node, locally, records, on volatile memory, all the actions, local or remote, performed by the processes it hosts. When a node fails all the processes and memories it was hosting are forever lost.

In the *non-cooperative* approach, the loss of memories creates *holes* in the system causal graph. We also assume that failures cannot be undone. Indeed, even if a node could be restarted the lack of information makes it impossible to restore its state prior to the failure. The resulting notion of reversibility, for the rollback algorithm to be causal consistent, requires to approximate causal dependencies.

In the *cooperative* approach, each node, besides locally recording the actions of the processes it hosts, when interacting with another node, copies on it the content of the memories related to the causes of the interaction. As a consequence of this copying mechanism, failures can be undone. When a failure is undone the rollback algorithm restores the last state known by the alive components of the system, available in the copied memories. This mechanism, inspired by the MANETHO rollback algorithm [3], makes so that when a locality fails, the only pieces of information lost are the ones which were only present on the failed node, either because they have never been copied elsewhere or because the nodes on which they were copied already failed. The resulting notion of reversibility never needs to over approximate causal dependencies between actions while undoing them.

Organization of the Paper. The paper is structured as follows. Section 2 describes the base framework common to non-cooperative and cooperative systems. Section 3 and Sect. 4 present non-cooperative systems and cooperative systems, respectively. Section 5 concludes the paper.

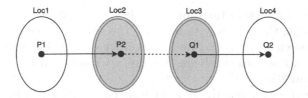

Fig. 1. Causal Graph: Dependencies

2 The Basic Framework

This section presents the basic reversible distributed systems on which we will discuss the two variants of rollback.

Processes are the smallest computational unit and are hosted inside nodes. The behavior of a node is defined by the behavior of the processes it hosts. Actions can either be local or remote. We assume that local actions can be either synchronous or asynchronous while remote actions are always asynchronous. Local actions do not interact with other nodes, like, e.g., a sys-call to open a local file, a local message exchange, etc. Remote actions interact with other nodes like, e.g., sending a message to another node, creating a new node, etc. Nodes are connected by links, which can fail and also be restored. We refer the reader to [4] for a thorough discussion of the calculus we intend to use.

When doing an action, a node also produces a memory to record the past state of the process doing the step. This memory is kept in the node's local volatile memory. If the action is remote, a memory is also produced in the target node and kept on its local volatile memory. We assume that memories, belonging to two different nodes, corresponding to a same interaction, can be matched. This could be achieved, e.g., by having the two memories sharing the same unique id.

Nodes can fail abruptly. Whenever a node fails, all the processes on it immediately stop working and all the memories on it are lost.

3 Non-cooperative Rollback

We now discuss how causal-consistent non-cooperative rollback ought to work in the context of the distributed systems described in Sect. 2.

In absence of failures, the rollback algorithm [6] works as follows. First, given a target action to undo, it identifies its consequences. Then, it undoes them following a reverse causal order.

In presence of a single failure, rollback works as follows. Given a target action, the rollback algorithm computes its consequences. If no consequence is an interaction with a failed node, then it proceeds as in absence of failures. If at least one of the consequences is a remote action, interacting with some action a on a failed node, say N_1, then ideally we should undo every remote interaction node N_1 had which is causally dependent on a, together with its consequences. However, N_1's causal graph, due to N_1 failure, is lost, hence it is impossible to know which of its interactions are causally dependent on a. Because of this lack of knowledge, the only way to undo all the consequences is to undo every interaction between N_1 and other nodes, together with their consequences. This may include many actions which are actually not consequences of a, hence it is an over approximation.

In presence of several failures, causal-consistent rollback gets even more intricate. Before discussing the general case, we first represent a concrete example of rollback in presence of two failed nodes in Fig. 1. A white, single-circled ellipse denotes a running node, while a red, double-circled ellipse denotes a failed node, dots inside ellipses denote processes and arcs (dashed or not) between dots denote interactions, causally linking states of two processes. Now, suppose we wish to undo the interaction between P1 and P2. Ideally, we should compute the set of consequences, which would be different if the dashed arc between P2 and Q1 existed or not. However, because of the failures of Loc2 and Loc3, it is impossible to determine if this dependency existed or not. Hence, again, the only way to be sure to undo all the consequences is to undo every interaction between the failed nodes, Loc2 and Loc3 here, and the other nodes. This includes in particular the interaction between Q1 and Q2 in Loc4.

In general, when several nodes fail, if at least a consequence of the target action interacts with a failed node, then, the only safe way to be causal consistent is to undo every interaction that every failed node had, together with its consequences. Whereas, if no consequence of the target action to undo is an interaction with a failed node, then rollback proceeds as in absence of failed nodes.

4   Cooperative Rollback

The distributed systems considered for cooperative rollback extend the base framework described in Sect. 2 as follows. Whenever there is a remote interaction between two nodes, besides recording locally the actions of the processes they host, the interacting process shares with the remote node its antecedent graph [3], i.e., the content of those memories recording the causes of the interaction. The redundancy of memories creates resilience to failures.

Indeed, when a node fails the only pieces of causal information that cannot be retrieved are those that either were never communicated to other nodes or that were communicated only to nodes that already failed.

As a consequence of redundancy the failure of a node can be undone, provided that there exists at least an alive node *remembering* an interaction with it. That is, we assume to have sufficient control over the system to be able to recreate nodes that failed. In undoing a failure, the rollback algorithm restores on the recovering node the processes it was hosting by retrieving their latest state from the corresponding memories on the other alive nodes. Conversely, if there is no alive node holding information about a failed node, then its failure cannot be undone.

We now discuss how causal-consistent rollback ought to work in this setting.

Given a target action, the rollback algorithm computes the set of consequences as usual. Then, it proceeds to undo them in a causal reverse order.

Here, we claim that the rollback algorithm can operate without requiring to approximate the set of consequences even in presence of failures. Indeed, in cooperative systems any alive process knows all the interactions, local or remote, that led to its current state. Hence, all the consequences of an action a can be retrieved by checking which processes descend from it. If a process does not have action a in its causes, then it is guaranteed to not be a consequence of a.

For example, let us see how the cooperative approach eliminates the need to approximate causal dependencies in the system of Fig. 1. Suppose, as before, that we wish to undo the interaction between processes P1 and P2. Here, since process Q2 on Loc4 is alive we can, by looking in Q2's memories, assert with certainty whether or not Q1 is a descendant of P2. In case Q1 descends from P2, and consequently from P1, then the actions to undo would be: i) interaction between Q1 and Q2; ii) failure of Loc3; iii) failure of Loc2; iv) interaction between P2 and Q1; v) interaction between P1 and P2. Whereas, in the case in which Q1 is not a descendant of P2, the actions to undo would be: i) failure of Loc2; ii) interaction between P1 and P2.

The mechanism proposed to propagate histories among localities in this section is similar to the one used in the MANETHO rollback algorithm [3]. Although at first the overhead imposed by duplicating memories may seem significant, this strategy has been already put in place successfully. Indeed, one can exploit various optimization techniques as, e.g., only copying the piece of past not already present in the remote locality, to reduce the overhead. We refer to [2] for further discussion on the topic.

5 Conclusion

In this paper we proposed ideas on how to achieve reversibility in systems that are subject to events that erase memories. The chosen application area is concurrent and distributed systems and the erasing events are failures. In Sects. 3 and 4 we identify two different approaches to causal-consistent rollback, which depend on the degree of cooperativeness of the underlying distributed system.

When localities are not cooperative, to ensure causal-consistency in the context of rollback, causal dependencies must be over approximated in case of failures. Without surprise, cooperation among localities enables strategies, like memory redundancy, to avoid the above mentioned over approximation. We remark that cooperation may not be possible since different nodes may obey to different authorities, or since the memory overhead required to replicate information may not be always desirable.

The cooperative and non-cooperative strategies described above are not the only possibilities. Indeed, by playing with the degree of cooperativeness, e.g., one could think to a system in which some nodes cooperate and some do not cooperate and by adding more hypothesis, as e.g., timestamps on interactions, many more interesting strategies, worth studying, emerge. The possible strategies can then be ordered on a spectrum according to their need of over approximation. As a first step, we chose the cooperative and non-cooperative strategies above as they well represent opposite extremes on the spectrum above.

References

1. Danos, V., Krivine, J.: Reversible communicating systems. In: Gardner, P., Yoshida, N. (eds.) CONCUR 2004. LNCS, vol. 3170, pp. 292–307. Springer, Heidelberg (2004). https://doi.org/10.1007/978-3-540-28644-8_19
2. Elnozahy, E.N.: Manetho: fault tolerance in distributed systems using rollback-recovery and process replication. Ph.D. thesis, Rice University (1993)
3. Elnozahy, E.N., Zwaenepoel, W.: Manetho: transparent roll back-recovery with low overhead, limited rollback, and fast output commit. IEEE Trans. Comput. **41**(5), 526–531 (1992)
4. Fabbretti, G., Lanese, I., Stefani, J.-B.: A behavioral theory for crash failures and Erlang-style recoveries in distributed systems. Technical report RR-9511, Inria (2023)
5. Landauer, R.: Irreversibility and heat generation in the computing process. IBM J. Res. Dev. **5**(3), 183–191 (1961)
6. Lanese, I., Mezzina, C.A., Schmitt, A., Stefani, J.-B.: Controlling reversibility in higher-order pi. In: Katoen, J.-P., König, B. (eds.) CONCUR 2011. LNCS, vol. 6901, pp. 297–311. Springer, Heidelberg (2011). https://doi.org/10.1007/978-3-642-23217-6_20
7. Lanese, I., Mezzina, C.A., Stefani, J.-B.: Reversibility in the higher-order π-calculus. Theor. Comput. Sci. **625**, 25–84 (2016)
8. Lanese, I., Nishida, N., Palacios, A., Vidal, G.: A theory of reversibility for Erlang. J. Log. Algebraic Methods Program. **100**, 71–97 (2018)
9. Phillips, I., Ulidowski, I.: Reversing algebraic process calculi. J. Log. Algebraic Methods Program. **73**(1–2), 70–96 (2007)
10. Phillips, I., Ulidowski, I., Yuen, S.: A Reversible process calculus and the modelling of the ERK signalling pathway. In: Glück, R., Yokoyama, T. (eds.) RC 2012. LNCS, vol. 7581, pp. 218–232. Springer, Heidelberg (2013). https://doi.org/10.1007/978-3-642-36315-3_18

Experiments in Reversible Programming

Exploring the Energy Overhead of Reversible Programs Executed on Irreversible Hardware

Lars-Bo Husted Vadgaard[1]([✉]) [iD], Maja Hanne Kirkeby[2] [iD], Ken Friis Larsen[3] [iD], and Michael Kirkedal Thomsen[1,3] [iD]

[1] Department of Informatics, University of Oslo, Oslo, Norway
{larsvad,michakt}@ifi.uio.no
[2] Roskilde University, Roskilde, Denmark
majaht@ruc.dk
[3] Department of Computer Science, University of Copenhagen,
Copenhagen, Denmark
kflarsen@di.ku.dk

Abstract. This paper investigates the energy efficiency of reversible programs executed on irreversible hardware. Motivated by Landauer's principle, which suggests that information loss during program execution increases energy consumption, we employ Intel's Running Average Power Limit (RAPL) technology to compare the energy consumption of "dereversibilised" reversible programs against that of straightforward irreversible implementations.

Preliminary results indicate that, while the memory handling of dereversibilised reversible programs does not necessarily improve overall energy efficiency, the energy overhead remains constant, ranging from 6% to around 240% over C depending on the abstraction level of the problem at hand. For dereversiblised Janus, one can expect an energy overhead of 100% or less when operating on data structures that are easily represented in the target language. One may expect an energy overhead of less than 30% for dereversibilised Hermes; however, its domain is more specific and thus resembles the target language more closely.

These findings indicate an interesting trade-off: dereversibilisation incurs a certain (constant) energy overhead, yet it uniquely produces two programs for the price of one. This will enable programmers to make informed decisions, balancing the energy overhead against the benefits of reversibility based on their specific needs. Future work will aim to further explore the impact of dereversibilisation on energy overhead and information security.

Keywords: Reversible programs · Energy efficiency · Dereversibilisation · Encryption

1 Introduction

The Information and Communications Technology (ICT) sector's energy consumption accounted for 7% of the global total in 2020, and data indicates that

T. Æ. Mogensen and L. Mikulski (Eds.): RC 2024, LNCS 14680, pp. 77–93, 2024.
https://doi.org/10.1007/978-3-031-62076-8_6

this number will increase in the coming years [1,2]. Though the world is moving towards green energy, the additional infrastructure needed to support a growing power demand will still result in an increased environmental cost in the form of mining, pollution, etc. With energy prices steadily increasing and environmental concerns becoming all the more prevalent, there is a strong incentive to study how and why different programs have different impacts on the energy consumption of computers.

It is known that the deletion of information (i.e. overwriting of bits) in a processor necessitates an amount of energy to be dissipated as heat. This principle is known as Landauer's principle [16], and it implies that the energy consumption of computations can be reduced in practice [7] (and, *in theory*, eliminated) by preventing the overwriting of bits.

The reversible computation model embraces Landauer's principle by making computations inherently non-destructive [6]. At a computational level, it is possible to design and implement programming languages that avoid the deletion of information [24,27] altogether and, thus, implement Turing completeness restricted to a reversible Turing machine model [4]. In fact, we can define reversible instruction set architectures and computing machines [25,26], to which we can make clean translations from high-level reversible programming languages [3,5].

However, current computing infrastructure predominantly relies on traditional, irreversible complementary metal-oxide semiconductor (CMOS) technology. This necessitates the *dereversibilisation* [10] of reversible programs for execution on these platforms, raising questions about the practical implications of Landauer's principle post-translation.

Beyond the theoretical appeal of reversible computing, one may postulate that practical aspects like linearity constraints and loss-less in-line data transformations present possible opportunities for energy optimisation. These features could aid optimising compilers and, thus, improve cache behaviour and memory allocation, suggesting an impact on energy efficiency beyond simply adhering to Landauer's principle.

As such, the goal of this work is to assess whether these characteristics translate into an energy efficiency advantage during dereversibilisation, or if they incur an quantifiable energy overhead; if a potential energy overhead is insignificant or insurmountable. By investigating this, we aim to identify the trade-offs between maintaining reversibility and the associated energy costs, thereby guiding programmers in making informed design decisions that balance these factors. Specifically, we dereversibilise some select reversible programs and compare the energy consumption of the resulting programs to that of straightforward irreversible implementations.

Structure: Section 2 discusses the methodology used for the experiment. In particular, it covers the set-up of the study and the steps taken to ensure consistent results. In Sect. 3, we describe the languages and specific programs used for the experiment. Section 4 gives a brief summary of the results, and Sect. 5 analyses the results with respect to the aforementioned energy overhead of dereversibilised reversible programs. Section 6 addresses an interesting aspect of dereversibilisation of Hermes programs in particular, and Sect. 7 concludes the study and suggests topics for further research. Finally, program artefacts and all measurements are available on GitHub.[1]

2 Methodology

We need to study how various effects of a reversible programming model impact the consumption of energy in a processor. To measure the energy consumption of the programs we use Intel's Running Average Power Limit (RAPL) [14]. This was chosen over other methods and tools such as external power meters, Turbostat [17] (which itself uses RAPL), and software profiling tools for how well it lends itself to a streamlined and reproducible experiment setup. Further, RAPL's measurements have been repeatedly shown to be highly correlated with the actual wall-plug power consumption [11,12,15], and RAPL has been used extensively to provide insights on energy efficiency of software [8,15,22].

RAPL utilises model-specific registers within the processor for estimating power consumption, differentiating it from external power measurement methods. Detailed in the Intel manual [14], RAPL provides an efficient mechanism for energy monitoring directly from the hardware, encompassing various processor domains such as DRAM, CPU cores (Power Plane 0 or PP0), the entire processor package, and uncore devices like GPUs (Power Plane 1 or PP1).

Despite its benefits, RAPL's use is subject to certain limitations. These include the potential for register overflow due to 32-bit energy counters, ± 0.02 ms variance in the timing of updates and with update delays with up to 0.14ms [12], dependency on specific driver support [14,15], and a focus on processor and memory that excludes other system components from its measurements [14,15]. As RAPL is dependent on processor architecture, its accuracy and set off vary across different processor models and manufacturers [11,12,15]; when performing measurements on a single machine, however, the demonstrated correlation between RAPL measurements the wall-plug power consumption will still yield statistically significant results. Further, specific features like Intel SGX or RAPL filtering can introduce data inaccuracies [13,18], but are turned off for this experiment.

The automated evaluation can be set up to mitigate the minor limitations of RAPL. In particular, we have taken the following steps to ensure a streamlined experiment.

- All C and C++ programs (both the dereversibilisations and the manual implementations) are compiled with the same compiler and optimisation flags. For this experiment it is version 11.4.0 of the GNU Compiler Collection using both the -O0 and the -O1 optimisation flags; see Sect. 3.3 for more details.
- All tests are executed on the same machine, ensuring comparability of the results due to the high correlation with the wall-plug power consumption.

---

[1] https://github.com/vadgaard/rc24-artefacts.

```
1   ...
2   for (i = 0 ; i < N ; i++){
3       // measure initial time
4       time_before = gettime(...);
5       // measure initial acc. energy consumption
6       rapl_before(...);
7
8       // execute the benchmark
9       system(command);
10
11      // computes the difference in acc. energy consumption
12      rapl_after(...);
13      // computes the difference in time
14      time_after = gettime(...);
15      time_spent = time_after - time_before;
16      ...
17  }
18  ...
19
```

Fig. 1. The structure of the measurements [21].

- There is minimal overhead when reading the energy registers before and after the execution of a program [15]. Our setup uses this approach. For each chosen program (see Sect. 3), we estimate the power consumption of running said program with varying input sizes. For each input size, we perform 40 measurements, and subsequently eliminate outliers using the Interquartile Range (IQR) method. In particular, negative accumulated energy values caused by 32-bit overflow are removed from the observations.
- All tests are designed to have wall times of more than 13ms to account for the variance in register updates. If necessary, the execution of a single compilation is repeated until a collective wall time of at least 13ms is achieved.
- RAPL filtering is turned off.
- When necessary, dereversibilisations are modified to accept data through standard input.
- Where convenient, some assertions produced during dereversibilisation are removed.

We measure both the execution time and the energy consumption of DRAM, CPU cores, and the entire process package. Figure 1 demonstrates the structure of these measurements with RAPL.

3   Evaluation

For this initial study we investigate two reversible programming languages, namely JANUS [27] and HERMES [20,23].

For each of these, we choose three programs to use in the study: run-length encoding, matrix multiplication, and binary tree creation and search for JANUS and the TEA, RC5, and Blowfish block ciphers for HERMES.

For this study, we will focus on the CPU power consumption; this is reasonably representative of all energy measurements. Still, all programs and measurements (including those of execution times and CPU, DRAM, and PKG energy consumptions) are available on the aforementioned GitHub repository.

3.1 JANUS Programs

JANUS has both a reversible interpreter and a compiler (or dereversibiliser) to C++ implemented in Haskell[2]. We use the compiler to produce a C++ program from each of the reversible JANUS programs; the energy consumption of running each of these dereversibilisations is then compared to that of running a simple hand-implemented C++ program with the same functionality. The JANUS programs work as follows.

Run-length encoding: This is implemented as a straightforward one-pass implementation and is intended to give a base-case for comparison. The array to be encoded is simply generated from random integers between 1 and 5, inclusive.

Matrix multiplication: The manual implementation will be the well-known, naïve $O(n^3)$ implementation. In contrast, the reversible implementation [19] first performs an inline LU-decomposition using Crout's method on the multiplicand. This provides two simple multiplications with the two triangular matrices after which the LU-decomposition is uncomputed.

In both versions, the matrices are filled with arbitrary values between 1 and 4, inclusive. Assertions have been removed in order to disregard the invertibility of the matrix; however, the overall work is the same and won't invalidate the generality of the program.

Binary tree creation and search: Because JANUS only supports integers and arrays, the reversible implementation [9] employs an abstraction where the binary search tree is represented using four integer arrays: one for node values, one for parents, one for left subtrees, and one for right subtrees. Each node in the tree is assigned an index within these arrays, and a heap pointer keeps track of available (i.e. unallocated) slots. The manual implementation, on the other hand, implements the search tree as a node structure containing the node value and one pointer for each of the subtrees.

In both the dereversibilisation and the manual implementation, the tree is generated such that roughly one half of all elements are put linearly in each subtree from the root, and a search for a bottom-most element is performed.

We argue that these programs are reasonably representative for JANUS: run-length encoding as a baseline program is simple and linear in both space and

---

[2] https://github.com/kirkedal/Jana-JanusInterp.

time; matrix multiplication has a larger time and space complexity with significantly more indexing in the data structures; and binary tree creation and search grows and operates on a more abstract data structure represented by index pointers.

All above-mentioned programs are only evaluated in the forward direction. Given that JANUS is locally invertible, they are expected to exhibit similar behaviour in both directions.

3.2   HERMES **Programs**

HERMES, similar to JANUS, has both a reversible interpreter and a compiler to C implemented in Moscow ML[3]. While JANUS is meant as a general-purpose reversible programming language, HERMES is focused towards symmetric encryption, and the choice of programs for HERMES reflects this more domain-specific nature of the language.

The methodology here is the same as for JANUS; that is, we compile the reversible programs to C and compare the energy consumption of running each of these to that of running a manual implementation with the same functionality. The HERMES programs work as follows.

TEA: Employs the TEA block cipher for encrypting and subsequently decrypting a specified number of 64-bit blocks. The key is 128 bits, and the algorithm iterates over 32 rounds for each block.

RC5: Uses the RC5 block cipher to encrypt and decrypt a given number of blocks. Each block is 64 bits, the key is 128 bits, and the algorithm iterates over 12 rounds for each block.

Blowfish: The Blowfish block cipher is here employed to encrypt and decrypt a specified number of 64-bit blocks. The algorithm iterates over 16 rounds for each block. While Blowfish in general supports variable-size keys, a 56-bit key was chosen for these measurements.

In each of the above-mentioned block ciphers, a fixed (arbitrary) key is used, and the 32-bit halves of each block are sequentially filled with increasing integers starting from 0. This approach ensures a consistent and straightforward data pattern for encryption and decryption processes across both versions of each evaluated block cipher. As each algorithm does the same operation on each 64-bit block, a linear increase in the energy consumption with increasing input sizes is to be expected.

3.3   Compilation of Programs

With this experiment we intend to investigate the potential benefit or overhead of the above reversible programs. The choice of compiler and optimisation flags does indeed have an influence on the measurements; however, this is not a study

---

[3] https://github.com/maltevelin/Hermes.

of the efficiency of compilers or the effects of compiler optimisations. We have therefore chosen the flags that provide little to no optimisation.

Specifically, we use version 11.4.0 of the GNU Compiler Collection[4]. This is the latest update (from May 2023) of GCC-11 that was first released (GCC version 11.1) in 2021. It is therefore considered stable and modern.

We have opted to compile the programs to be measured using the two optimisation flags `-O0` and `-O1`. To recap some of the most used optimisation flags[5]:

`-Og` behaves like `-O0`, but is better for debugging.
`-O0` disables most optimisations, which will optimise for compile time.
`-O1` performs simple optimisations to reduce code size and execution time, without impacting compilation time too much.
`-O2` adds all optimisations that do not involve a space-speed trade-off.
`-O3` performs more optimisations for especially loop and branching-flow.

As we want to investigate the effect of performing reversible computations, we do not want the compiler to optimise away *all* these effects. Further, the effect of compiler optimisations can be hard to predict; the choice and order of optimisations in (especially higher) optimisation flags are based on empirical studies of large benchmarks such as those defined by SPEC[6], which contain a large set of conventional irreversible programs. This can potentially give the irreversible programs a benefit over the reversible JANUS and HERMES programs, and to avoid this, we therefore only use `-O0` and `-O1`, effectively limiting the complexity of optimisations and better preserving the original program structure.

4   Results

The measurements with RAPL were performed on an Intel Core i5-6200U CPU with a base clock speed of 2.30 GHz, with all benchmark programs executed on a single core to ensure consistent performance analysis. The CPU features a dual-core architecture, where each core has access to its own dedicated L1 and L2 caches sized at 64 KiB and 512 KiB, respectively. Additionally, there is a shared L3 cache of 3 MiB available to both cores.

The JANUS measurements, along with those of their manual counterparts, are shown in Figs. 2, 3 and 4, and the Hermes measurements, along with those of their manual counterparts, are shown in Figs. 5, 6 and 7.

We can see from Fig. 2 that run-length encoding only incurs an overhead of around 28% over the manual implementation with optimisation turned off, while conservative optimisation reduces this overhead to around 17%. In Fig. 3, on the other hand, we see a clearer distinction between the reversible and conventional implementations of matrix multiplication. Both implementations run in $O(n^3)$ time with intuitive order of loop iterations that is not optimised for

---

[4] https://gcc.gnu.org/onlinedocs/gcc-11.4.0/gcc.pdf.
[5] https://gcc.gnu.org/onlinedocs/gcc/Optimize-Options.html.
[6] https://www.spec.org/benchmarks.html.

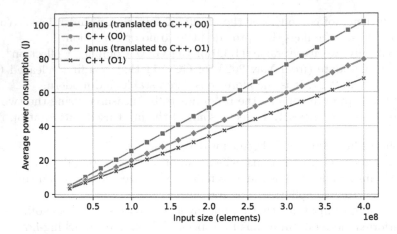

Fig. 2. Run-length encoding measured by average CPU power consumption for varying numbers of 32-bit integers encoded. Note that C++ (O1) and JANUS (O0) overlap.

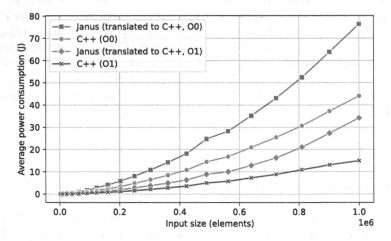

Fig. 3. Matrix multiplication measured by average CPU power consumption for varying numbers of 32-bit integers in each matrix.

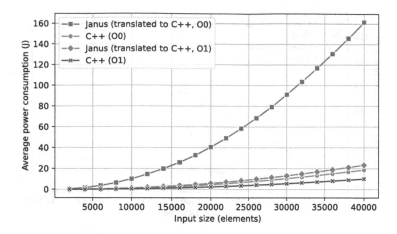

Fig. 4. Binary tree creation and search measured by average CPU power consumption for varying numbers of 32-bit integers inserted and subsequently searched through.

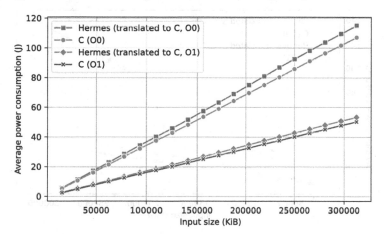

Fig. 5. TEA encryption and decryption measured by average CPU power consumption, with input data sizes expressed in kilobytes (KiB).

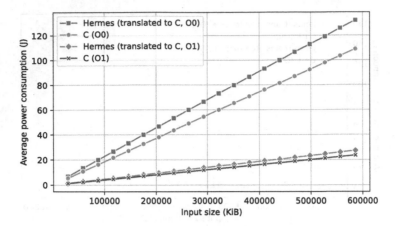

Fig. 6. RC5 encryption measured by average CPU power consumption, with input data sizes expressed in kilobytes (KiB).

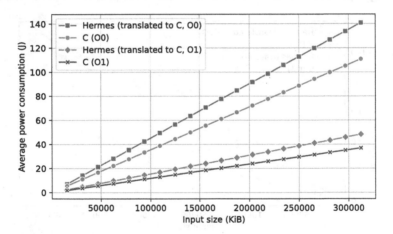

Fig. 7. Blowfish encryption and decryption measured by average CPU power consumption, with input data sizes expressed in kilobytes (KiB).

cache behaviour. However, the reversible version will actually make four $O(n^3)$ passes: LU-decomposition, multiplying the upper-triangular matrix, multiplying the lower-triangular matrix, and uncomputing the LU-decomposition. Comparing this to the single pass of the manual implementation, the results show an energy overhead of around 70% with no optimisation, though the overhead interestingly increases to around 80% with conservative optimisation at smaller input sizes, and even diverges with increasing sizes. The largest measurement multiplies two 1000×1000 (32-bit) `int` matrices and puts the result in a third matrix of the same size, which gives a total size of around 11.4 MiB. This will outsize all caches, and so we should see potential cache effects.

From Fig. 4, we see that the implementation of binary trees in JANUS demonstrates a significant overhead, peaking with no optimisation at around 800% compared to the manual implementation and at around 175% with conservative optimisation. The large overhead when using no optimisation is primarily due to the nature of how the binary search tree is represented in JANUS. In particular, any operation on the tree has to do up to k lookups in all four arrays that constitute the tree, where k is the height of the tree.

Figure 5 shows that the encryption and decryption of data using the TEA block cipher is closer to its manually implemented counterpart. Specifically, we see an overhead of only around 7% over the manual implementation regardless of the optimisation level. In contrast, Fig. 6 indicates that the reversible RC5 block cipher has a slightly greater overhead when utilising no optimisation at around 23% over the manual implementation, and at around 16% when utilising minimal optimisation. From Fig. 7, we see that the reversible Blowfish implementation comes close at around 28% over its manually implemented counterpart with no optimisation. Interestingly, like with matrix multiplication in Janus, the overhead increases once minimal compiler optimisations are applied.

The seemingly lower overhead of the dereversiblilised Hermes programs over their manual implementations is most likely due to the lower abstraction level of Hermes, along with the chosen algorithms being specific to its intended domain.

5   Reversible Programming and Energy Consumption

Following the approach of Pereira et al. [21], we can *normalise* the overhead of dereversibilised programs in an effort to put it into perspective. Here, a normalised overhead uses the energy consumption of C as a baseline, and the performance of any other language is expressed as a factor of this.

Conveniently, the HERMES overhead is trivially normalised; however, the JANUS overhead is not. For simplicity, we therefore multiply Pereira's inferred normalised C++ overhead of 1.34 with the overhead of the dereversibilised JANUS programs *over* C++, obtaining a conservative estimate of normalised overhead for JANUS.

Figures 8, 9 and 10 show the normalised energy overhead of the dereversiblilised JANUS programs. The linear, one-pass run-length encoding incurs an average energy overhead as low as approximately 57% when utilising compiler optimisations, giving a factor 1.57 that conservatively places it just below C++ itself in the previously mentioned study. Matrix multiplication, on the other hand, incurs a normalised overhead of around 130% when opting for no optimisation, indicating a rank between Lisp and OCaml in terms of energy efficiency. Finally, the overhead of binary tree creation and search averages at around 240% with conservative optimisation enabled, which would place it between Go and Dart. Taking the average of these, we get a factor of around 2.42, conservatively placing dereversibilised Janus between OCaml and Fortran

Given the limitations of the language, it is difficult to rank dereversibilised JANUS as a whole; in essence, the findings indicate that a ranking of dereversibilised JANUS should be based not on the language itself, but on a given JANUS program's *resemblance to the target language*, both with respect to the structure of the program, but also to the data that is operated upon.

Looking at run-length encoding, it is clear that the representation of the integer array—and the operations performed on it—in JANUS and C++ closely resemble each other. The operational cost of maintaining reversibility in JANUS is, in this case, not significant. In contrast, maintaining reversibility during matrix multiplication incurs a larger overhead, but *representing* the matrices does not. When representing and manipulating binary trees, both the cost of reversible operations and the higher level of abstraction contribute to the tenfold overhead that we see.

Thus, naïve dereversibilisation of JANUS programs can, depending on the situation, offer acceptable trade-offs in terms of energy consumption; it produces two programs for the price of one, and, if the abstraction level is reasonably low, the constant overhead should remain at 100% or less over the target language. Consequently, it is reasonable to expect some of the energy overhead incurred by the dereversibilisation of JANUS programs to be mitigated by appropriately extending JANUS with more control over the structure of data.

As one might expect, naïvely dereversiblised programs leave plenty of room for optimisation, so much so that we see a 4–5× improvement in the overhead of reversible binary tree creation and search. One interesting case, however, is reversible matrix multiplication when conservative optimisation is enabled; as we saw, the overhead diverges after passing an input size of 600.000; this indicates that are some significant optimisations that can't be performed, at least to the same degree, on the dereversibilised program. A similar phenomenon can be observed for reversible encryption and decryption with the BlowFish block cipher; though this does not diverge, the overhead increases when conservative compiler optimisations are applied. In the future, it would be interesting to look further into the nature of these optimisation, and why they do not apply as well to the dereversibilised program.

6 HERMES, RAPL, and Side-Channel Attacks

The HERMES program examples in this paper are all lightweight synchronous encryption algorithms. This is because HERMES was, in addition to being

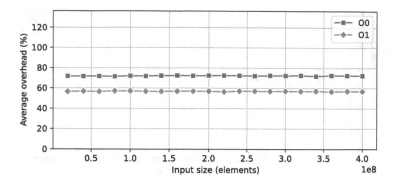

Fig. 8. Normalised energy overhead of run-length encoding.

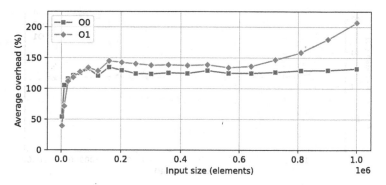

Fig. 9. Normalised energy overhead of matrix multiplication.

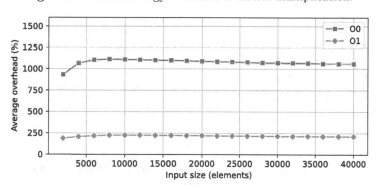

Fig. 10. Normalised energy overhead of binary tree creation and search.

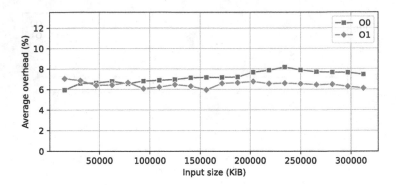

Fig. 11. Energy overhead of TEA encryption and decryption.

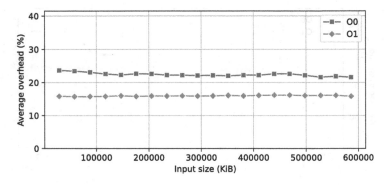

Fig. 12. Energy overhead of RC5 encryption and decryption.

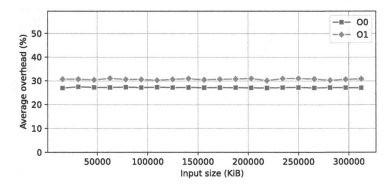

Fig. 13. Energy overhead of Blowfish encryption and decryption.

reversible, designed for implementing encryption algorithms while eliminating certain classes of side-channels [20,23]. The local reversibility of HERMES means that programs can run equally well forwards and backwards. This ensures that all variables are cleared after use, thus avoiding state information leakage. Furthermore, the language features a type system with secret and public types, which ensures that code written in HERMES is both information-flow secure and resistant to timing side-channel attacks.

The use of RAPL for HERMES programs is a confluence of ideas. It has been shown that RAPL can be used for software side-channel attacks [18]. By using RAPL to measure the energy usage of several OS security features it was possible to break synchronous AES encryption and address randomisation. Specifically, it is possible to make a statistical estimate of secret keys by measuring energy consumption of changes in multiplication and other timing-sensitive operations with different inputs. Though this is a known vulnerability, registered in several CVEs, and Intel have implemented a fix [13], the general problem is still relevant.

The goal of HERMES is to generate code for encryption algorithms that is resilient against exactly these kinds of side-channel attacks. The results in Figs. 11, 12 and 13 show an expected overhead of about 20–30%, with one algorithm, TEA, going as low as 10%. This would be a low price to pay for code that is more secure. However, more work is needed to investigate this in detail.

7 Conclusion

In this work, we assess the energy overhead of naïvely dereversibilised reversible programs. For this purpose, we have used RAPL along with the reversible programming languages JANUS and HERMES. Initial results show that a reasonable overhead can be achieved, but the viability ultimately depends on the goal of the programmer—and the nature of the program. Implementing an algorithm reversibly will yield two programs for the price of one, and a reasonably low abstraction level will incur a conservative overhead of around 100% or less over C. This has been indicated by the measurements of the dereversibilised JANUS programs, where a program more closely resembling the target language incurred a lower overhead, ranking JANUS just below Lisp from previous studies. This indication was further underscored by the low energy overhead of the dereversibilised HERMES programs, whose domain-specific nature makes them closely resemble the target language. This overhead was measured to be less than 40% over C, ranking HERMES just below C++ in terms of energy efficiency.

Further, the results also indicate that naïvely dereversibilised programs usually lend themselves well to compiler optimisations. Indeed, we saw a 4–5× improvement in one instance, binary tree creation and search. However, we also observed an instance, matrix multiplication, where the overhead no longer stays constant after applying these optimisation. It is left as possible future work, to investigate which compiler optimisation that gives the largest improvement for a larger benchmark of reversible programs.

Beyond its low energy overhead, HERMES' potential to mitigate side-channel attacks presents another factor to weigh in when considering the trade-offs of dereversiblisation. For future work, it would be interesting to study in depth the effect of HERMES dereversibilisation with respect to side-channel attacks and assess the viability of such a solution.

References

1. Andrae, A.S.G.: Hypotheses for primary energy use, electricity use and CO2 emissions of global computing and its shares of the total between 2020 and 2030. WSEAS Trans. Power Syst. **15**, 50–59 (2020). https://doi.org/10.37394/232016.2020.15.6
2. Andrae, A.S.G.: New perspectives on internet electricity use in 2030. Eng. Appl. Sci. Lett. **3**(2), 19–31 (2020). https://doi.org/10.30538/psrp-easl2020.0038
3. Axelsen, H.B.: Clean translation of an imperative reversible programming language. In: Knoop, J. (ed.) CC 2011. LNCS, vol. 6601, pp. 144–163. Springer, Heidelberg (2011). https://doi.org/10.1007/978-3-642-19861-8_9
4. Axelsen, H.B., Glück, R.: A simple and efficient universal reversible turing machine. In: Dediu, A.-H., Inenaga, S., Martín-Vide, C. (eds.) LATA 2011. LNCS, vol. 6638, pp. 117–128. Springer, Heidelberg (2011). https://doi.org/10.1007/978-3-642-21254-3_8
5. Axelsen, H.B., Glück, R.: Reversible representation and manipulation of constructor terms in the heap. In: Dueck, G.W., Miller, D.M. (eds.) RC 2013. LNCS, vol. 7948, pp. 96–109. Springer, Heidelberg (2013). https://doi.org/10.1007/978-3-642-38986-3_9
6. Bennett, C.H.: Logical reversibility of computation. IBM J. Res. Dev. **17**(6), 525–532 (1973)
7. Bérut, A., Arakelyan, A., Petrosyan, A., Ciliberto, S., Dillenschneider, R., Lutz, E.: Experimental verification of Landauer's principle linking information and thermodynamics. Nature **483**(7388), 187–189 (2012). https://doi.org/10.1038/nature10872
8. Eder, K., et al.: ENTRA: Whole-systems energy transparency. Microprocess. Microsyst. **47**, 278–286 (2016). https://doi.org/10.1016/j.micpro.2016.07.003
9. Glück, R., Yokoyama, T.: Constructing a binary tree from its traversals by reversible recursion and iteration. Inf. Process. Lett. **147**, 32–37 (2019). https://doi.org/10.1016/j.ipl.2019.03.002. https://www.sciencedirect.com/science/article/pii/S0020019019300523
10. Glück, R., Yokoyama, T.: Reversible computing from a programming language perspective. Theor. Comput. Sci. **953**, 113429 (2023). https://doi.org/10.1016/j.tcs.2022.06.010. https://www.sciencedirect.com/science/article/pii/S0304397522003619
11. Hackenberg, D., Schöne, R., Ilsche, T., Molka, D., Schuchart, J., Geyer, R.: An energy efficiency feature survey of the Intel Haswell processor. In: Proceedings of the 2015 IEEE 29th International Parallel and Distributed Processing Symposium Workshops, IPDPSW 2015, pp. 896–904 (2015). https://doi.org/10.1109/IPDPSW.2015.70
12. Hähnel, M., Döbel, B., Völp, M., Härtig, H.: Measuring energy consumption for short code paths using RAPL. Perform. Eval. Rev. **40**(3), 13–17 (2012). https://doi.org/10.1145/2425248.2425252
13. Intel Corporation: Running Average Power Limit Energy Reporting CVE-2020-8694, CVE-2020-8695 (2020). https://www.intel.com/content/www/us/en/developer/articles/technical/software-security-guidance/advisory-guidance/running-average-power-limit-energy-reporting.html. Accessed 29 Jan 2024
14. Intel Corporation: Intel 64 and IA-32 Architectures Software Developer's Manual (2023). https://www.intel.com/content/www/us/en/developer/articles/technical/intel-sdm.html. Accessed 29 Jan 2024

15. Khan, K.N., Hirki, M., Niemi, T., Nurminen, J.K., Ou, Z.: RAPL in action: experiences in using RAPL for power measurements. ACM Trans. Model. Perform. Eval. Comput. Syst. (TOMPECS) **3**(2), 1–26 (2018)

16. Landauer, R.: Irreversibility and heat generation in the computing process. IBM J. Res. Dev. **5**(3), 183–191 (1961)

17. linux.org: TURBOSTAT (2024). https://www.linux.org/docs/man8/turbostat. html. Accessed 08 Apr 2024

18. Lipp, M., et al.: Platypus: Software-based power side-channel attacks on x86. In: 2021 IEEE Symposium on Security and Privacy (SP), pp. 355–371 (2021). https:// doi.org/10.1109/SP40001.2021.00063

19. Madsen, F.M., Poulsen, D.R.: Reversible matrix multiplication in Janus (2011). Unpublished manuscript, DIKU, Department of Computer Science, University of Copenhagen, Presented at the DIKU workshop on Topics in Programming Languages, June 2011

20. Mogensen, T.Æ.: Hermes: A reversible language for lightweight encryption. Sci. Comput. Program. **215**, 102746 (2022)

21. Pereira, R., et al.: Ranking programming languages by energy efficiency. Sci. Comput. Program. **205**, 102609 (2021)

22. Rotem, E., Naveh, A., Ananthakrishnan, A., Weissmann, E., Rajwan, D.: Power-management architecture of the Intel microarchitecture code-named Sandy Bridge. IEEE Micro **32**(2), 20–27 (2012). https://doi.org/10.1109/MM.2012.12

23. Táborský, D., Larsen, K.F., Thomsen, M.K.: Encryption and reversible computations. In: Kari, J., Ulidowski, I. (eds.) RC 2018. LNCS, vol. 11106, pp. 331–338. Springer, Cham (2018). https://doi.org/10.1007/978-3-319-99498-7_23

24. Thomsen, M.K., Axelsen, H.B.: Interpretation and programming of the reversible functional language RFUN. In: Proceedings of the 27th Symposium on the Implementation and Application of Functional Programming Languages, IFL 2015, pp. 8:1–8:13. ACM (2016). https://doi.org/10.1145/2897336.2897345

25. Thomsen, M.K., Glück, R., Axelsen, H.B.: Towards designing a reversible processor architecture. In: Ulidowski, I. (ed.) Preliminary Proceedings of the Workshop on Reversible Computation, pp. 46–50 (2009)

26. Vieri, C.J.: Reversible computer engineering and architecture. Ph.D. thesis, MIT, EECS (1999)

27. Yokoyama, T., Glück, R.: A reversible programming language and its invertible self-interpreter. In: Partial Evaluation and Program Manipulation, PEPM 2007, pp. 144–153. ACM (2007). https://doi.org/10.1145/1244381.1244404

Towards Clean Reversible Lossless Compression
A Reversible Programming Experiment with Zip

Therese Lyngby[1](✉) , Rasmus Ross Nylandsted[1] , Robert Glück[1] ,
and Tetsuo Yokoyama[2]

[1] DIKU, Department of Computer Science, University of Copenhagen, Copenhagen,
Denmark
`therese.lyngby@di.ku.dk, kpn134@alumni.ku.dk, glueck@acm.org`
[2] Department of Electronics and Communication Technology, Nanzan University,
Nagoya, Japan
`tyokoyama@acm.org`

Abstract. Zip and unzip are everyday tools in today's digital world.
Since they are inherently inverse to each other, they are ideal for studying reversible computing methods on real-world problems.

In this work-in-progress study, we take steps to develop a reversible zip
tool. As a proof of concept, we designed clean (garbage-free) reversible
versions of two algorithms, which are officially recognized by the zip-
specification. Our design goal was not merely to achieve reversibility, but
rather to maintain the asymptotic complexity of the irreversible counterparts.

Because of their efficiency and different approaches to compression, we
chose the dictionary-based *Lempel–Ziv–Welch Compression* (LZW) and
the transformation-based *Burrows–Wheeler Transform* (BWT). As part
of the challenge, we found a way to zero-clear the LZW dictionary and
reversibly sort rotations for BWT. We have successfully created clean
reversible versions of both algorithms and fully implemented and tested
them in the reversible language Janus.

Our reversible LZW has a worst-case runtime of $\Theta(n)$, just like the
most efficient irreversible version. Our reversible BWT is, in the worst
case, a factor n^2 slower than the most efficient irreversible version.
There are currently no better trace-free reversible methods for lossless
compression.

Keywords: Clean reversible algorithms · Lossless compression
algorithms · Reversible software · Burrows–Wheeler transforms
(BWT) · Lempel–Ziv–Welch compression (LZW)

1 Introduction

Lossless compression algorithms have inverse counterparts in the form of
decompression algorithms. This makes them excellent candidates for studying
reversible computing methods, since reversible programming languages allow us

T. Æ. Mogensen and L. Mikulski (Eds.): RC 2024, LNCS 14680, pp. 94–102, 2024.
https://doi.org/10.1007/978-3-031-62076-8_7

to develop, verify, and maintain one algorithm rather than two mutually inverse compression/decompression algorithms. An important practical application for lossless data compression is the creation of zip-archives, where it is indispensable.

The zip-specification, created by PKWare in 1989 as a public domain alternative to proprietary formats, is now supported by many compliant programs. It lists the officially recognized compression methods, often combining multiple algorithms, like Deflate, which combines the LZ77 compression and Huffman coding [12].

This work-in-progress study addresses the challenge by creating reversible versions of two of these algorithms as a proof of concept to demonstrate that creating a clean (garbage-free) reversible zip-program with a constant space $O(1)$ overhead is possible. Our solutions outperform those generated by general methods, such as described in [2,8], by providing linear-time and linear-space reversible simulations that do not require the storage of global computation history.

The algorithms underlying the compression methods recognized by the zip-specification are classified into four categories: *1) dictionary-based algorithms* such as LZW; *2) statistical methods* such as Huffman coding, which use the frequency of characters; *3) transformation-based algorithms* like the Burrows–Wheeler transform, which aim at improving the compression ratio; and *4) special methods* like MP3 audio compression, which are lossy.

Based on our experience in developing reversible algorithms (e.g., [1,6]), we selected those algorithms that seemed most promising for efficient reversible implementation, while encompassing different categories. Therefore, we chose

- the dictionary-based *Lempel–Ziv–Welch compression* (LZW) and
- the transformation-based *Burrows–Wheeler Transform* (BWT).

The contributions of this study are as follows.

1. Development of two clean reversible algorithms for zip-compression.
2. Complete implementation of the algorithms in the reversible language Janus.[1]
3. Resolution of key programming challenges including zero-clearing of the LZW string-to-code dictionary and trace-free lexicographic rotation sorting.
4. Introduction of an asymptotically optimal linear time $\Theta(n)$ reversible LZW compression, requiring only constant extra space $O(1)$.

The results also highlight areas for improvement, particularly in the rotation sorting algorithm for the BWT and the constant factor of the LZW. However, to our knowledge, these are the first fully implemented reversible LZW and BWT algorithms for zip, which is the de facto standard of data compression. Previously, an irreversible inverse of the BWT was derived by equational reasoning [3].

Section 2 provides a brief review of the two algorithms along with the main challenges. The design of the clean reversible algorithms is described in Sect. 3, followed by an analysis of their asymptotic complexity in Sect. 4. Conclusions are drawn, and future work is discussed in Sect. 5.

We assume that readers are familiar with the basics of reversible programming and the reversible language Janus (e.g., [6,13]).

---

[1] https://tetsuo.jp/ref/RC2024/.

2 The Algorithms and Their Challenges

Reversible algorithms compute only injective functions, a necessity for any loss-less compression algorithm (otherwise data cannot be recovered by decompression). Because reversible algorithms are forward and backward deterministic, they cannot delete information in any computation step. Consequently, data structures cannot be overwritten. Instead, for reversible algorithms to be clean (garbage-free), methods for reversibly zero-clearing the input and all data structures after use are required, unlike irreversible (conventional) algorithms, which can delete them at any time. These characteristics pose challenges in designing the reversible zip-compression algorithms. We briefly summarize the two algorithms and point out the five main challenges. A programming perspective of reversible computing can be found elsewhere [7].

Challenges. In all clean reversible algorithms, we must 0) zero-clear the input.

LZW [11] improves on the original string-to-code dictionary-based LZ77 [15] by dynamically building the dictionary while compressing the input string.

Initially, the dictionary has one entry for each character in the fixed alphabet constituting the input string (e.g., the ASCII characters). LZW replaces each substring in the input that appears in the dictionary with the corresponding code. New dictionary entries are added when LZW encounters a substring not found in the dictionary. Thus, if the substring is repeated, it can be shortened to the code of the new entry. The dictionary has a fixed size of, e.g., 12-bit codes.

LZW returns *out*, the compressed *in*, as well as the new dictionary *dict*:

$$\text{LZW: } in \mapsto (out, dict) \tag{1}$$

Normally *dict* is then deleted. For an example of LZW see Fig. 1.

Challenges. To design a clean reversible LZW we need to 1) ensure that the updates and checks required to replace substrings are cleanly reversible, and 2) zero-clear the dictionary *dict* at the end.

BWT [4] transforms the input string by clustering identical characters, thereby improving the compression ratio of subsequent compression stages, such as run-length encoding. A reversible run-length encoder already exists [14]. Thus, we focus on the BWT.

Conceptually, BWT transforms the input string by creating a matrix containing all possible rotations of the string in its rows and sorting the rows lexico-graphically. The output of BWT is the last column of the matrix along with the index of the row containing the original input. In practice, the input is divided into blocks, each of which is transformed by BWT, and the matrix is represented efficiently by storing only the offset of each rotation in an array.

BWT returns *out*, the transformed *in*, as well as row index *idx* and *matrix*:

$$\text{BWT: } in \mapsto ((out, idx), matrix) \tag{2}$$

Normally the *matrix* is then deleted. Both *out*, i.e. the last column of the *matrix*, and *idx* are required for the inverse transform and cannot be deleted. For an example of BWT see Fig. 2.

Challenges. To design a clean reversible BWT we need to 3) ensure a clean reversible lexicographic sorting of the offset array and 4) zero-clear the offset array at the end.

3   Clean Reversible LZW and BWT

Given programs for computing an injective function and its inverse, a clean reversible program can be constructed using the Bennett method [2]. However, the resulting program requires several scans of the input and output, compromising the asymptotic complexity of either time or space, or both. The program also relies on a global computation history.

Our approach is to create two reversible procedures: Procedure p, which, given the input, computes the output and any auxiliary data, and procedure q, which, given the output, preserves it and computes the same auxiliary data as p. A clean implementation is achieved by *calling* p followed by *uncalling* q. In the case of LZW and BWT, this is accomplished by extending (1) and (2) as follows:

$$\text{Reversible LZW: } in \xmapsto{\text{lzw'}} (out, dict) \xmapsto{\text{build\_dict}^{-1}} out \tag{3}$$

$$\text{Reversible BWT: } in \xmapsto{\text{bwt'}} ((out, idx), matrix) \xmapsto{\text{build\_matrix}^{-1}} (out, idx) \tag{4}$$

Recall from Sect. 2 that idx in (4) is essential for the inverse transform of BWT.

Below, we use pseudo code similar to the extended version of Janus [13], further extended with a *dict* type for fixed-size dictionaries, and a zero-ended *string* type.

3.1   LZW

First, we develop the procedure lzw', which creates a compressed string out and a dictionary d from the string in (Listing 1.1). Figure 1 shows an example of lzw'.

```
1  procedure lzw'(string in, int i,
2                 string out, dict d)
3    call init_dict(d)
4    local int j = 0; curCode = 0
5    from i = 0 loop
6      call find_str(in, i, d, curCode)
7      out[j] <=> curCode
8      j += 1
9    until in[i] = 0
10   delocal int j = size(out); curCode = 0
```

Listing 1.1. Pseudo code for lzw'. Initially, in holds the input string, and i, out, d are zero-cleared. Afterwards, in is zero-cleared, i holds the input length, out the compressed string, and d the dictionary used for string compression.

In the from-until loop, the next substring to be replaced by its code and the next unseen substring added to the dictionary are found by the procedure find_str.

The inputs of find_str are the string in, an iterator i over in, the dictionary d, and the zero-cleared curCode. After a call, the replaced substring is zero-cleared in in, i points to the next non-zero character of in, d is extended with a non-matching substring, and curCode contains the code of the replaced substring.

```
1  procedure rev_lzw(string in, string out)
2    local dict d; int i = 0
3    call lzw'(in, i, out, d)
4    uncall build_dict(out, i, d)
5    delocal dict d; int i = 0
```

Listing 1.2. A reversible version of LZW

The procedure `find_str` assigns a unique code to every substring, creating a bijective mapping. This, along with other properties of the dictionary, enables the reversible construction of the procedure, which solves Challenge 1, making the replacement of strings cleanly reversible. Furthermore, after repeated calls to `find_str`, the entire input is zero-cleared, solving Challenge 0, zero-clearing the input. Due to space constraints `find_str` is not shown here.

For Challenge 2, zero-clearing the dictionary, we construct `build_dict` based on LZW decompression. This procedure takes the compressed string, rebuilds the dictionary, and computes the length of the original input.

By combining a call to `lzw'` with an uncall of `build_dict`, we achieve the clean reversible simulation of LZW, `rev_lzw` (Listing 1.2), as specified in (3).

3.2 BWT

The procedure `rev_bwt` in Listing 1.3 implements (4). See Fig. 2 for an example.

```
1  procedure rev_bwt(string in, string out, int idx)
2    local int[size(in)] offsets
3    call bwt'(in, out, idx, offsets)
4    uncall build_matrix(out, idx, offsets, in)
5    delocal int[size(in)] offsets
6
7  procedure build_matrix(string out, int idx,
8                         int offsets[], string in)
9    call gen_in(out, idx, in)
10   local int idx' = 0; n = size(in)
11   call bwt'(in, out, idx', offsets)
12   iterate int i = 0 to n - 1
13     out[i] -= in[(offsets[i] + n - 1) % n]
14   end
15   delocal int idx' = idx; n = size(in)
```

Listing 1.3. A reversible version of BWT

The matrix containing all rotations of the string `in` is represented by an array `offsets`.

To solve Challenge 3, making sorting the offset array injective, we exploit the fact that BWT only sorts string rotations given in a fixed order and that it stores the row index of the original string after sorting. These properties ensure that the sorting process is injective, enabling us to implement a trace-free sorting method that uses $O(n)$ space.

The uncall of `build_matrix` solves both Challenges 0, zero-clearing the input and Challenge 4, zero-clearing the offset array. Utilizing `out` and `idx`, `build_matrix` generates `offsets`. This is done by obtaining the original input from `gen_in` based on the original inverse transform [4, pp. 12–13]. Using `in` it is straightforward to rebuild the matrix by calling `bwt'`. Finally `out` is zero-cleared.

By combining a call to `bwt'` with an uncall of `build_matrix`, we obtain the clean reversible simulation of BWT, `rev_bwt` (Listing 1.3), specified in (4).

4 Time and Space Complexity

Given an injective program, we can always construct a clean reversible version. However, there is no guarantee that the time *and* space complexity of the original

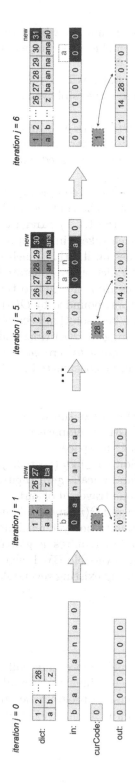

Fig. 1. An example of `lzw`' in Sect. 3.1 compressing the string "banana". Initially, the dictionary `dict` contains the English alphabet, in contains the input, and `curCode` and `out` are zero-cleared. After iteration 1, "b" is replaced by its code 2, which is moved from `curCode` to `out`, and `dict` is extended with the substring "ba". After 5 iterations, "an" is replaced by its code 28. After 7 iterations the string is fully compressed, `in` is zero-cleared, and `dict` is extended with several substrings of the input.

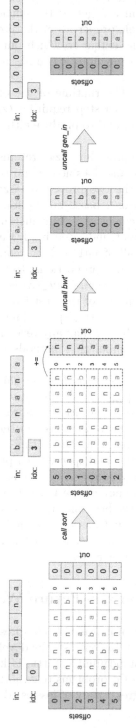

Fig. 2. An example of `rev_bwt` in Sect. 3.2 transforming the string "banana". The array `offsets` contains the offsets corresponding to the rotations of the original string. During the sorting phase, comparisons are made based on the characters at the positions indicated by `offsets`. After sorting the rotations, the index of `offsets` containing rotation 0 (the original string) is stored in the variable `idx` and the last character of each rotation is copied to `out`. `offsets` is zero-cleared by "unsorting", that is uncalling `sort`. `in` is zero-cleared by calling `gen_in`.

program can be preserved [2,8]. The challenge lies in determining how close the reversible program can get to the efficiency of the irreversible program while preserving desirable properties of the program.

We analyze the extent to which our reversible LZW and BWT algorithms have preserved the asymptotic complexity of their original, irreversible versions.

Reversible LZW. The runtime of the original LZW is $\Theta(n)$ [11]. It scans the input once, with each step requiring $O(1)$ time to check whether the current string exists in *dict* and to produce either no code or one. The generated output is not rescanned.

The reversible procedure `lzw'` retains the original algorithm's complexity. It runs in $\Theta(n)$ time and does not rescan the generated output. The runtime analysis is based on the two procedures `lzw'` and `find_str` (Sect. 3.1) `find_str` updates the iterator i based on the found substring, which takes time proportional to the increment of i. This incrementation continues until `in[i]` reaches the end of the input, indicated by 0. Finally, to clear the dictionary generated by `lzw'`, the uncall of `build_dict` scans the output once from the end to the beginning, taking time proportional to the size of the output, bounded by $O(n)$.

The reversible procedure `rev_lzw` is asymptotically the best solution because it matches the runtime of the best irreversible LZW running in $\Theta(n)$ time and requires only constant extra space. Thus, `rev_lzw` is *hygienic with zero-garbage bound* [1]. This is better than any reversible LZW that can be constructed using existing reversible simulation methods such as [2,8].

Reversible BWT. We consider the naïve BWT algorithm as outlined in the original paper [4, p. 2]. For simplicity, we assume an $O(n^2)$-time comparison sort for strings, hence the algorithm requires $O(n^3)$ time and $\Theta(n)$ space.

The complexities are preserved in the reversible version `rev_bwt` (Sect. 3.2), which calls `bwt'`, requiring $O(n^3)$ time and $\Theta(n)$ space, and uncalls `gen_input`, requiring linear time and space. Each procedure entails one traversal of `out`.

The reversible procedure `rev_bwt` requires $O(n^3)$ time and $\Theta(n)$ space, aligning with the efficiency of the naïve BWT algorithm. Despite not yet reaching the $\Theta(n)$ time of the best known irreversible version, `rev_bwt` requires no global computation history. Consequently, it is better than any reversible BWT algorithm that can be constructed from the naïve algorithm using existing reversible simulation methods such as [2,8].

5   Conclusion and Future Work

The development of irreversible compression algorithms spans more than half a century (e.g., [15]). In contrast, the development of such algorithms in reversible computing is just beginning. Little is known about reversible program design applied to real-world problems (e.g., [5,9,10]) and this is a main motivation for this work-in-progress study of lossless data compression.

This study presents steps towards reversible zip-compression. As a proof-of-concept, we illustrated that clean, trace-free reversible versions of LZW and BWT, both integral components of the zip-specification, can be designed and implemented. In particular, the reversible LZW is asymptotically optimal compared to the best irreversible counterpart, which runs in linear time and space. We conclude that techniques and tools developed in the field of reversible programming can be applied to the real-world challenges of lossless data compression and that key challenges can be solved efficiently, including the zero-clearing of the LZW dictionary, but also, that further improvements are possible and necessary.

Acknowledgement. The last author was supported by JSPS KAKENHI Grant No. 22K11983 and Nanzan University Pache Research Subsidy I-A-2 for 2023.

References

1. Axelsen, H.B., Yokoyama, T.: Programming techniques for reversible comparison sorts. In: Feng, X., Park, S. (eds.) APLAS 2015. LNCS, vol. 9458, pp. 407–426. Springer, Cham (2015). https://doi.org/10.1007/978-3-319-26529-2_22
2. Bennett, C.H.: Time/space trade-offs for reversible computation. SIAM J. Comput. **18**(4), 766–776 (1989). https://doi.org/10.1137/0218053
3. Bird, R.S., Mu, S.C.: Inverting the Burrows-Wheeler transform. J. Funct. Program. **14**(6), 603–612 (2004). https://doi.org/10.1017/S0956796804005118
4. Burrows, M., Wheeler, D.J.: A block-sorting lossless data compression algorithm. SRC Research Report 124, DEC Systems Research Center, Palo Alto, CA (1994)
5. De Vos, A., et al.: Designing garbage-free reversible implementations of the integer cosine transform. J. Emerg. Technol. Comput. Syst. **11**(2), 11:1–11:15 (2014). https://doi.org/10.1145/2629532
6. Glück, R., Yokoyama, T.: Reversible programming: a case study of two string-matching algorithms. In: Hamilton, G., et al. (eds.) Proceedings of the HCVS/VPT. EPTCS, vol. 373, pp. 1–13 (2022). https://doi.org/10.4204/EPTCS.373.1
7. Glück, R., Yokoyama, T.: Reversible computing from a programming language perspective. Theor. Comput. Sci. **953**, Article no. 113429 (2023). https://doi.org/10.1016/j.tcs.2022.06.010
8. Lange, K.J., McKenzie, P., Tapp, A.: Reversible space equals deterministic space. J. Comput. Syst. Sci. **60**(2), 354–367 (2000). https://doi.org/10.1006/jcss.1999.1672
9. Perumalla, K.S.: Introduction to Reversible Computing. CRC Press, Boca Raton (2013)
10. Schordan, M., et al.: Generation of reversible C++ code for optimistic parallel discrete event simulation. New Gener. Comput. **36**(3), 257–280 (2018). https://doi.org/10.1007/s00354-018-0038-2
11. Welch, T.A.: A technique for high-performance data compression. IEEE Comput. **17**(6), 8–19 (1984). https://doi.org/10.1109/MC.1984.1659158
12. Witten, I.H., Moffat, A., Bell, T.C.: Managing Gigabytes: Compressing and Indexing Documents and Images, 2nd edn. Morgan Kaufmann, Burlington (1999)

13. Yokoyama, T., Axelsen, H.B., Glück, R.: Principles of a reversible programming language. In: Proceedings of the Conference on Computing Frontiers, pp. 43–54. ACM (2008). https://doi.org/10.1145/1366230.1366239
14. Yokoyama, T., Axelsen, H.B., Glück, R.: Optimizing reversible simulation of injective functions. J. Mult.-Valued Logic Soft Comput. **18**(1), 5–24 (2012)
15. Ziv, J., Lempel, A.: A universal algorithm for sequential data compression. IEEE Trans. Inf. Theor. **23**(3), 337–343 (1977). https://doi.org/10.1109/TIT.1977.1055714

Reversible and Quantum Programming Languages

A Small-Step Semantics for Janus

Pietro Lami[1,2(✉)], Ivan Lanese[2], and Jean-Bernard Stefani[1]

[1] Univ. Grenoble Alpes, INRIA, CNRS, Grenoble INP, LIG, 38000 Grenoble, France
pietro.lami@inria.fr
[2] Olas Team, Univ. of Bologna, INRIA, 40126 Bologna, Italy

Abstract. Janus is an imperative, sequential language for reversibility. While heavily studied in the reversibility literature, to the best of our knowledge, no small-step semantics for it exists. Hence, we propose a small-step semantics for Janus and we prove it equivalent to a big-step semantics from the literature, for programs that have no runtime errors and no divergence. Our main motivation is to enable a future extension of Janus with concurrency primitives, which is more easily defined on top of a small-step semantics. As additional feature, a small-step semantics allows one to more easily distinguish between failing and non-terminating computations.

1 Introduction

Janus is the first structured reversible programming language, designed by Christopher Lutz and Howard Derby [8]. Janus is an imperative language, which supports deterministic forward and backward computation. This means that in Janus any forward computation can be undone by a finite sequence of backward steps.

The operational semantics of Janus was formally specified in [17,18,20]. The language and its semantics provide a solid foundation for further research and development in reversible computing. However, to the best of our knowledge, there are no small-step semantics of Janus in the literature. Indeed, the semantics mentioned above are all big-step.

Hence, the main contribution of this paper is to define a small-step semantics for Janus (using the syntax described in [20]), and proving it equivalent to the big-step semantics in the literature in absence of runtime errors and divergence (Theorem 1).

A main motivation for our work is that we are working towards an extension of Janus with concurrency primitives, namely we aim to add the possibility to create processes and to allow processes to communicate via message passing.

The work has been partially supported by French ANR project DCore ANR-18-CE25-0007. The second author has also been partially supported by MSCA-PF project 101106046—ReGraDe-CS and by INdAM – GNCS 2023 project RISICO, code CUP_E53C22001930001. The authors thank the anonymous reviewers for their useful comments and suggestions.

T. Æ. Mogensen and L. Mikulski (Eds.): RC 2024, LNCS 14680, pp. 105–123, 2024.
https://doi.org/10.1007/978-3-031-62076-8_8

$$\begin{aligned}
Programs \quad & p ::= s \ (\textsf{procedure } id \ s)^+ \\
Statements \quad & s ::= x \oplus = e \mid x[e] \oplus = e \mid \textsf{if } e \textsf{ then } s \textsf{ else } s \textsf{ fi } e \\
& \quad \mid \textsf{ from } e \textsf{ do } s \textsf{ loop } s \textsf{ until } e \mid \textsf{call } id \mid \textsf{uncall } id \mid \textsf{skip} \mid s \ s \\
Expressions \quad & e ::= c \mid x \mid x[e] \mid e \odot e \\
Constant \quad & c ::= -2147483648 \mid \cdots \mid 0 \mid \cdots \mid 2147483647 \\
& \oplus ::= + \mid - \mid \hat{\ } \\
& \odot ::= \oplus \mid * \mid / \mid \% \mid \& \mid \&\& \mid \parallel \mid \text{''}\mid\text{''} \mid < \mid > \mid = \mid ! = \mid <= \mid >=
\end{aligned}$$

with x variables and id identifiers

Fig. 1. Language syntax

This is a relevant aim since to the best of our knowledge, there are no pure concurrent reversible languages, namely concurrent languages which make no use of history information to enable reversibility. Indeed, all the concurrent reversible programming languages and calculi we are aware of use history information, as for instance in the cases of RCCS [3], CCSK [12], reversible π [1], reversible higher-order π [6] and reversible Erlang [7].

Notably, the semantics of the formalisms above are all small-step operational semantics, and this is the case also for the most well-known irreversible calculi for concurrency, such as CCS [9] and π-calculus [10]. Indeed, small-step semantics allows one to more easily describe the interleavings among the actions of different processes that take place in concurrent computations.

Summarizing, we believe that it makes sense to study extensions of Janus with concurrency primitives, and that defining a small-step semantics for Janus is a sensible first step in this direction.

Beyond this, small-step semantics and big-step semantics have their own strengths and weaknesses, as discussed, e.g., in [2,11], hence a small-step semantics adds a relevant tool for the study of Janus. We will show for instance that, as noted in [2], small-step semantics allows one to more easily distinguish between failing and non-terminating computations.

2   Background: Janus

Syntax. Janus [17,18,20] is a reversible imperative programming language designed to support both forward and backward computation. We show the syntax of Janus in Fig. 1 (w.r.t. [20] we drop variable declarations, since they are irrelevant for our discussion), where a program consists of a statement and a set of procedure declarations. A procedure declaration includes the keyword **procedure**, an identifier (the procedure name id), and a statement (the procedure body). A statement is a reversible assignment to a variable or an element of array, a reversible conditional, a reversible loop, a procedure call, a procedure uncall, a skip, or a statement sequence. A reversible conditional is formed by two predicates: the test that follows the keyword **if**, and the assertion that follows the keyword **fi**. If the test is true, the then-branch is executed, and afterwards the evaluation of the assertion must be true; if the assertion fails, the semantics

$$\text{CON} \ \frac{}{\sigma \vdash c \Downarrow \llbracket c \rrbracket} \qquad\qquad \text{VAR} \ \frac{}{\sigma \vdash x \Downarrow \sigma(x)} \qquad\qquad \text{ARR} \ \frac{\sigma \vdash e \Downarrow v}{\sigma \vdash x[e] \Downarrow \sigma(x[v])}$$

$$\text{BOP} \ \frac{\sigma \vdash e_1 \Downarrow v_1 \qquad \sigma \vdash e_2 \Downarrow v_2 \qquad \llbracket \odot \rrbracket(v_1, v_2) = v}{\sigma \vdash e_1 \odot e_2 \Downarrow v}$$

Fig. 2. Big-step semantics of expressions

of the conditional is undefined. Dually, if the test is false, the assertion must be false after execution of the else-branch. A reversible loop (from e_1 do s_1 loop s_2 until e_2) has two predicates, an assertion at the entry (e_1) and a test at the exit of the loop (e_2). Initially, assertion e_1 must be true and then s_1 is executed. The loop terminates if test e_2 is true; otherwise, s_2 is executed, after which e_1 must be false. Indeed, the assertion needs to be true at the first evaluation only. The loop is repeated as long as assertion and test are both false, and terminates when the test is true. A procedure call executes the procedure body in the global store. In this paper, we do not consider parameters or local variables. To pass values to and from a procedure, we use side effects on the global store. A procedure uncall computes the inverse function of the invoked procedure. An expression is a constant, a variable, an indexed variable, or a binary expression. A binary operator $\odot$ is an arithmetic $(+, -, *, /, \%)$, bitwise $(\&, |, \char`^)$, logical $(\&\&, ||)$, or relational operator $(<, >, =, ! =, <=, >=)$. For a deeper discussion we refer to [20].

Semantics. We describe only the semantics of statements, in a big-step style, and assume that procedure declarations are translated into a function Γ from procedure names to statements. We restrict the attention to programs where all the invoked functions have a definition. We consider the semantics in [20], but for loops we consider the equivalent but simpler semantics in [17,18]. Note that the definition of the semantics requires to extend the syntax of statements. Furthermore, the semantics for statements relies on an auxiliary semantics for expressions.

In Fig. 2 we show the rules for expressions. The rules have the form $\sigma \vdash e \Downarrow v$, where σ is a store, e is an expression and v is a value. A store σ is a function from variable names and indexed variable names to values. We denote with $\sigma[x \mapsto v]$ the update of σ which assigns value v to variable x. For simplicity we assume that σ is defined for all the variables used in the program, and we assume integer variables initialized with value 0.

In Fig. 3 we show the big-step semantics of statements. The rules have the form $\sigma \vdash s \Downarrow \sigma'$ where σ and σ' are stores, and s is a statement. The rules AssVAR and AssARR define the assignment. The assignment operator $(\oplus =)$ stands for $(+ =)$, $(- =)$, or $(\char`^ =)$.

A procedure call (defined by rule CALL) executes the procedure body $\Gamma(id)$ in the current store. A procedure uncall (defined by rule UNCALL) executes the inversion of the body of function $\Gamma(id)$. The inversion is computed thanks to the inverter function $\mathcal{I}$ (defined in Fig. 4), which given a statement computes

$$\text{AssVar} \frac{\sigma \vdash e \Downarrow v}{\sigma \vdash x \oplus = e \Downarrow \sigma[x \mapsto [\![\oplus]\!](\sigma(x), v)]}$$

$$\text{AssArr} \frac{\sigma \vdash e_l \Downarrow v_l \qquad \sigma \vdash e \Downarrow v}{\sigma \vdash x[e_l] \oplus = e \Downarrow \sigma[x[v_l] \mapsto [\![\oplus]\!](\sigma(x[v_l]), v)]} \qquad \text{Call} \frac{\sigma \vdash \Gamma(id) \Downarrow \sigma'}{\sigma \vdash \text{call } id \Downarrow \sigma'}$$

$$\text{UnCall} \frac{\sigma \vdash \mathcal{I}[\![\Gamma(id)]\!] \Downarrow \sigma'}{\sigma \vdash \text{uncall } id \Downarrow \sigma'} \qquad \text{Seq} \frac{\sigma \vdash s_1 \Downarrow \sigma' \qquad \sigma' \vdash s_2 \Downarrow \sigma''}{\sigma \vdash s_1 \, s_2 \Downarrow \sigma''}$$

$$\text{IfTrue} \frac{\sigma \vdash e_1 \Downarrow v_1 \quad \text{is\_true?}(v_1) \quad \sigma \vdash s_1 \Downarrow \sigma' \quad \sigma' \vdash e_2 \Downarrow v_2 \quad \text{is\_true?}(v_2)}{\sigma \vdash \text{if } e_1 \text{ then } s_1 \text{ else } s_2 \text{ fi } e_2 \Downarrow \sigma'}$$

$$\text{IfFalse} \frac{\sigma \vdash e_1 \Downarrow v_1 \quad \text{is\_false?}(v_1) \quad \sigma \vdash s_2 \Downarrow \sigma' \quad \sigma' \vdash e_2 \Downarrow v_2 \quad \text{is\_false?}(v_2)}{\sigma \vdash \text{if } e_1 \text{ then } s_1 \text{ else } s_2 \text{ fi } e_2 \Downarrow \sigma'}$$

$$\text{LoopMain} \frac{\sigma \vdash e_1 \Downarrow v_1 \quad \text{is\_true?}(v_1) \quad \sigma \vdash s_1 \Downarrow \sigma' \quad \sigma' \vdash (e_1, s_1, e_2, s_2) \Downarrow \sigma''}{\sigma \vdash \text{from } e_1 \text{ do } s_1 \text{ loop } s_2 \text{ until } e_2 \Downarrow \sigma''}$$

$$\text{LoopBase} \frac{\sigma \vdash e_2 \Downarrow v_2 \quad \text{is\_true?}(v_2)}{\sigma \vdash (e_1, s_1, e_2, s_2) \Downarrow \sigma}$$

$$\text{LoopRec} \frac{\sigma' \vdash e_1 \Downarrow v_1 \quad \begin{array}{c} \sigma \vdash e_2 \Downarrow v_2 \quad \text{is\_false?}(v_2) \quad \sigma \vdash s_2 \Downarrow \sigma' \\ \text{is\_false?}(v_1) \quad \sigma' \vdash s_1 \Downarrow \sigma'' \quad \sigma'' \vdash (e_1, s_1, e_2, s_2) \Downarrow \sigma''' \end{array}}{\sigma \vdash (e_1, s_1, e_2, s_2) \Downarrow \sigma'''}$$

$$\text{Skip} \frac{}{\sigma \vdash \text{skip} \Downarrow \sigma}$$

Fig. 3. Big-step semantics of Janus statements

another statement executing the inverse computation. Rule UNCALL is actually different from the one in [20], which is as follows:

$$\text{UnCall} \frac{\sigma' \vdash \Gamma(id) \Downarrow \sigma}{\sigma \vdash \text{uncall } id \Downarrow \sigma'}$$

However, [20, Theorem 4] states that $\sigma \vdash s \Downarrow \sigma'$ iff $\sigma' \vdash \mathcal{I}[\![s]\!] \Downarrow \sigma$ hence the two rules are equivalent. We prefer the one in Fig. 3, since it allows for a more direct correspondence with the small-step semantics. The execution of a statement sequence is defined by rule SEQ.

The conditional is defined by rules IFTRUE and IFFALSE, and which rule applies depends on the value of e_1 and e_2. Indeed, predicates is_true?(v) and is_false?(v) check the truth value of a value v. Notice that the semantics of conditional is defined only if the two expressions have the same truth value.

The loop is defined by three rules: a rule for entering the loop, LOOPMAIN, a rule for exiting, LOOPBASE, and a rule for iteration, LOOPREC. Rule LOOPMAIN requires the truth of assertion e_1 and then executes statement s_1. The execution of the loop terminates if test e_2 is true, with an application of rule LOOPBASE. Otherwise, the loop continues with rule LOOPREC, which executes s_2 and s_1, and which requires both test e_2 and assertion e_1 to be false. As for conditional,

$$\mathcal{I}_{op}[\![+]\!] ::= - \qquad \mathcal{I}_{op}[\![-]\!] ::= + \qquad \mathcal{I}_{op}[\![\char`^]\!] ::= \char`^$$
$$\mathcal{I}[\![x \oplus = e]\!] ::= x \; \mathcal{I}_{op}[\![\oplus]\!] = e$$
$$\mathcal{I}[\![x[e_1] \oplus = e_2]\!] ::= x[e_1] \; \mathcal{I}_{op}[\![\oplus]\!] = e_2$$
$$\mathcal{I}[\![\text{if } e_1 \text{ then } s_1 \text{ else } s_2 \text{ fi } e_2]\!] ::= \text{if } e_2 \text{ then } \mathcal{I}[\![s_1]\!] \text{ else } \mathcal{I}[\![s_2]\!] \text{ fi } e_1$$
$$\mathcal{I}[\![\text{from } e_1 \text{ do } s_1 \text{ loop } s_2 \text{ until } e_2]\!] ::= \text{from } e_2 \text{ do } \mathcal{I}[\![s_1]\!] \text{ loop } \mathcal{I}[\![s_2]\!] \text{ until } e_1$$
$$\mathcal{I}[\![\text{call } id]\!] ::= \text{uncall } id$$
$$\mathcal{I}[\![\text{uncall } id]\!] ::= \text{call } id$$
$$\mathcal{I}[\![\text{skip}]\!] ::= \text{skip}$$
$$\mathcal{I}[\![s_1 \; s_2]\!] ::= \mathcal{I}[\![s_1]\!] \; \mathcal{I}[\![s_2]\!]$$

Fig. 4. Inverter function for Janus statements

$$\text{CONS} \; \frac{}{\langle \sigma, c \rangle \to \langle \sigma, [\![c]\!] \rangle} \qquad \text{VARS} \; \frac{}{\langle \sigma, x \rangle \to \langle \sigma, \sigma(x) \rangle} \qquad \text{ARR1} \; \frac{\langle \sigma, e \rangle \to \langle \sigma, e' \rangle}{\langle \sigma, x[e] \rangle \to \langle \sigma, x[e'] \rangle}$$

$$\text{ARR2} \; \frac{}{\langle \sigma, x[v] \rangle \to \langle \sigma, \sigma(x[v]) \rangle} \qquad \text{BOP1} \; \frac{\langle \sigma, e_1 \rangle \to \langle \sigma, e_1' \rangle}{\langle \sigma, e_1 \odot e_2 \rangle \to \langle \sigma, e_1' \odot e_2 \rangle}$$

$$\text{BOP2} \; \frac{\langle \sigma, e_2 \rangle \to \langle \sigma, e_2' \rangle}{\langle \sigma, v_1 \odot e_2 \rangle \to \langle \sigma, v_1 \odot e_2' \rangle} \qquad \text{BOP3} \; \frac{[\![\odot]\!](v_1, v_2) = v}{\langle \sigma, v_1 \odot v_2 \rangle \to \langle \sigma, v \rangle}$$

Fig. 5. Small-step semantics of expressions

the semantics of loop is not defined if the value of assertions is not the required one. The SKIP rule does nothing. For a deeper discussion we refer to [17,18,20].

3   A Small-Step Semantics for Janus

In this section, we describe the small-step semantics for Janus that we propose, and prove it equivalent to the big-step semantics in the previous section. As for the big-step semantics, we need to extend the syntax of statements.

For the evaluation of expressions, we use the small-step semantics depicted in Fig. 5, where σ is a store and e and e' are expressions. Actually, we need to extend the syntax of expressions to also allow for values as leafs, to cope with partially evaluated expressions, such as $[\![3]\!] + 3$, where the first summand is the value 3 and the second one the corresponding constant. The evaluation stops when the expression reduces to a value v.

The rules for statements, depicted in Figs. 6, 7, 8 and 9, have either the form $\langle \sigma, s \rangle \to \langle \sigma', s' \rangle$, where σ and σ' are stores, and s, s' are statements, to denote a successful step, or the form $\langle \sigma, s \rangle \to \bot$ to denote a runtime error due to a failed assertion. In order to give a compact definition of the semantics, we use contextual rules to lift the evaluation of expressions and statements to larger contexts. To this end we need to define evaluation contexts.

Definition 1 (Evaluation contexts). *An* evaluation context *is a statement where a subterm is replaced by a* •*. We distinguish expression contexts* $C_e[•]$ *and statement contexts* $C_s[•]$*. We denote with* $C_e[e]$ *the statement obtained by*

$$\text{AssVarS} \quad \frac{}{\langle \sigma, x \oplus = v \rangle \rightarrow \langle \sigma[x \mapsto [\![\oplus]\!](\sigma(x), v)], \mathsf{skip} \rangle}$$

$$\text{AssArrS} \quad \frac{}{\langle \sigma, x[v_l] \oplus = v \rangle \rightarrow \langle \sigma[x[v_l] \mapsto [\![\oplus]\!](\sigma(x[v_l]), v)], \mathsf{skip} \rangle}$$

$$\text{CallS} \quad \frac{}{\langle \sigma, \mathsf{call}\ id \rangle \rightarrow \langle \sigma, \Gamma(id) \rangle} \qquad \text{UnCallS} \quad \frac{}{\langle \sigma, \mathsf{uncall}\ id \rangle \rightarrow \langle \sigma, \mathcal{I}[\![\Gamma(id)]\!] \rangle}$$

$$\text{SeqS} \quad \frac{}{\langle \sigma, \mathsf{skip}\ s_2 \rangle \rightarrow \langle \sigma, s_2 \rangle}$$

Fig. 6. Small-step semantics: rules for basic constructs

$$\text{CtxExp} \quad \frac{\langle \sigma, e \rangle \rightarrow \langle \sigma, e' \rangle}{\langle \sigma, C_e[e] \rangle \rightarrow \langle \sigma, C_e[e'] \rangle} \qquad \text{CtxStmt} \quad \frac{\langle \sigma, s \rangle \rightarrow \langle \sigma', s' \rangle}{\langle \sigma, C_s[s] \rangle \rightarrow \langle \sigma', C_s[s'] \rangle}$$

$$\text{CtxError} \quad \frac{\langle \sigma, s \rangle \rightarrow \bot}{\langle \sigma, C_s[s] \rangle \rightarrow \bot}$$

Fig. 7. Small-step semantics: contextual rules

replacing • *with expression* e *in expression context* $C_e[\bullet]$, *and* $C_s[s]$ *the one obtained by replacing* • *with statement* s *in statement context* $C_s[\bullet]$. *Contexts are defined as:*

$$C_e[\bullet] = x \oplus = \bullet \mid x[\bullet] \oplus = e \mid x[v] \oplus = \bullet \mid \mathsf{if}\ \bullet\ \mathsf{then}\ s_1\ \mathsf{else}\ s_2\ \mathsf{fi}\ e_2$$
$$\mid\ \mathsf{if}\ v_1\ \mathsf{then}\ \mathsf{skip}\ \mathsf{else}\ s_2\ \mathsf{fi}\ \bullet \qquad where\ \mathsf{is\_true?}(v_1)$$
$$\mid\ \mathsf{if}\ v_1\ \mathsf{then}\ s_1\ \mathsf{else}\ \mathsf{skip}\ \mathsf{fi}\ \bullet \qquad where\ \mathsf{is\_false?}(v_1)$$
$$\mid\ ((\bullet, e_1), s_1, e_2, s_2) \mid (e_1, (\mathsf{skip}, s_1), (\bullet, e_2), s_2)$$
$$\mid\ ((\bullet, e_1), (\mathsf{skip}, s_1), e_2, (\mathsf{skip}, s_2))$$
$$C_s[\bullet] = \bullet\ s$$
$$\mid\ \mathsf{if}\ v_1\ \mathsf{then}\ \bullet\ \mathsf{else}\ s_2\ \mathsf{fi}\ e_2 \qquad where\ \mathsf{is\_true?}(v_1)$$
$$\mid\ \mathsf{if}\ v_1\ \mathsf{then}\ s_1\ \mathsf{else}\ \bullet\ \mathsf{fi}\ e_2 \qquad where\ \mathsf{is\_false?}(v_1)$$
$$\mid\ (e_1, (\bullet, s_1), (e_2, e_2), s_2) \mid ((e_1, e_1), (\mathsf{skip}, s_1), e_2, (\bullet, s_2))$$

Rules AssVarS and AssArrS in Fig. 6 define the assignment. AssVarS evaluates the new value of a variable and updates the store, and AssArrS does the same with an element of an array.

A procedure call (defined by rule CallS) reduces to the procedure body $\Gamma(id)$, in the current store. A procedure uncall (defined by rule UnCallS) reduces to the inversion $\mathcal{I}[\![\Gamma(id)]\!]$ of the body of procedure id, retrieved using function Γ. Here $\mathcal{I}$ is the inverter function defined in Fig. 4.

$$\text{IFTRUEEND} \frac{\text{is\_true?}(v_1) \quad \text{is\_true?}(v_2)}{\langle \sigma, \text{if } v_1 \text{ then skip else } s_2 \text{ fi } v_2 \rangle \rightarrow \langle \sigma, \text{skip} \rangle}$$

$$\text{IFFALSEEND} \frac{\text{is\_false?}(v_1) \quad \text{is\_true?}(v_2)}{\langle \sigma, \text{if } v_1 \text{ then } s_1 \text{ else skip fi } v_2 \rangle \rightarrow \langle \sigma, \text{skip} \rangle}$$

$$\text{IFERROR1} \frac{\text{is\_true?}(v_1) \quad \text{is\_false?}(v_2)}{\langle \sigma, \text{if } v_1 \text{ then skip else } s_2 \text{ fi } v_2 \rangle \rightarrow \bot}$$

$$\text{IFERROR2} \frac{\text{is\_false?}(v_1) \quad \text{is\_true?}(v_2)}{\langle \sigma, \text{if } v_1 \text{ then } s_1 \text{ else skip fi } v_2 \rangle \rightarrow \bot}$$

Fig. 8. Small-step semantics: rules for if

The execution of a sequence is defined by rule SEQS, which removes the first statement if its evaluation is terminated. Notably, there is no rule for skip, since $\langle \sigma, \text{skip} \rangle$ denotes the end of the computation.

The rules in Fig. 7 describe how reductions of expressions (CTXEXP) and of statements (CTXSTMT) are lifted to larger contexts in successful steps. Similarly, rule CTXERROR lifts a runtime error.

The conditional (Fig. 8) is defined by four rules: IFTRUEEND, IFFALSEEND, IFERROR1 and IFERROR2. These rules are applied after having evaluated, using the CTXEXP and CTXSTMT rules, the test condition, the statement in the selected branch, and the assertion. The first two rules define a successful step when the test and the assertion are either both true (IFTRUEEND case) or both false (IFFALSEEND case). Rules IFERROR1 and IFERROR2 are used to signal a runtime error when the outcomes of the evaluation of the test and of the assertion differ. Notably, in such a case the big-step semantics is not defined.

The loop (Fig. 9) is defined by rules LOOPMAINS, LOOPEXP1T, LOOPENDS, LOOPEXP2F, and LOOPEXP1F. The interplay among these rules as well as the relations with the corresponding rules in the big-step semantics (cf. Fig. 3) is depicted in Fig. 10 to help the understanding. Rule LOOPMAINS enters the loop. Rule LOOPEXP1T is fired after the evaluation of the expression, performed thanks to rule CTXEXP. Rule LOOPEXP1T requires assertion e_1 to be true and it enables the execution of statement s_1, done using rule CTXSTMT. The execution terminates with rule LOOPENDS if test e_2 (evaluated via rule CTXEXP) is true. If the evaluation of test e_2 is false, instead, an iteration is needed, and rule LOOPEXP2F enables the execution of statement s_2 via rule CTXSTMT. Then, rule CTXEXP evaluates the assertion e_1, that must be false. This lead to another iteration using rule LOOPEXP1F. The assertion e_1 should be true at the first evaluation, and false in the others. When this is not the case rules LOOPERROR1 or LOOPERROR2 are fired, raising a runtime error. The big step semantics is undefined in these two last cases.

Before proving the equivalence between the big-step and the small-step semantics (when the execution terminates without runtime errors), we prove

$$\textsc{LoopMainS}\ \dfrac{}{\langle \sigma, \text{from } e_1 \text{ do } s_1 \text{ loop } s_2 \text{ until } e_2\rangle \rightarrow \langle \sigma, ((e_1, e_1), s_1, e_2, s_2)\rangle}$$

$$\textsc{LoopExp1T}\ \dfrac{\text{is\_true?}(v_1)}{\langle \sigma, ((v_1, e_1), s_1, e_2, s_2)\rangle \rightarrow \langle \sigma, (e_1, (s_1, s_1), (e_2, e_2), s_2)\rangle}$$

$$\textsc{LoopEndS}\ \dfrac{\text{is\_true?}(v_2)}{\langle \sigma, (e_1, (\text{skip}, s_1), (v_2, e_2), s_2)\rangle \rightarrow \langle \sigma, \text{skip}\rangle}$$

$$\textsc{LoopExp2F}\ \dfrac{\text{is\_false?}(v_2)}{\langle \sigma, (e_1, (\text{skip}, s_1), (v_2, e_2), s_2)\rangle \rightarrow \langle \sigma, ((e_1, e_1), (\text{skip}, s_1), e_2, (s_2, s_2))\rangle}$$

$$\textsc{LoopExp1F}\ \dfrac{\text{is\_false?}(v_1)}{\langle \sigma, ((v_1, e_1), (\text{skip}, s_1), e_2, (\text{skip}, s_2))\rangle \rightarrow \langle \sigma, (e_1, (s_1, s_1), (e_2, e_2), s_2)\rangle}$$

$$\textsc{LoopError1}\ \dfrac{\text{is\_false?}(v_1)}{\langle \sigma, ((v_1, e_1), s_1, e_2, s_2)\rangle \rightarrow \bot}$$

$$\textsc{LoopError2}\ \dfrac{\text{is\_true?}(v_1)}{\langle \sigma, ((v_1, e_1), (\text{skip}, s_1), e_2, (\text{skip}, s_2))\rangle \rightarrow \bot}$$

Fig. 9. Small-step semantics: rules for loop

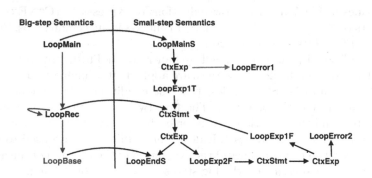

Fig. 10. Loop schema

an analgous result for the evaluation of expressions. We denote with $\rightarrow^*$ the reflexive and transitive closure of $\rightarrow$ and with $\rightarrow^+$ the transitive one.

Lemma 1.
$$\sigma \vdash e \Downarrow v \ iff \ \langle \sigma, e\rangle \rightarrow^+ \langle \sigma, v\rangle$$

where e does not contain values.

Proof. $\Rightarrow$: The proof is by induction on the derivation, with a case analysis on the last applied rule.

Con: we have that $\sigma \vdash c \Downarrow [\![c]\!]$. The thesis follows using rule CONS to derive $\langle \sigma, c\rangle \rightarrow \langle \sigma, [\![c]\!]\rangle$. The rules have no hypothesis.

Var: we have that $\sigma \vdash x \Downarrow \sigma(x)$. The thesis follows using rule VARS to derive $\langle \sigma, x\rangle \rightarrow \langle \sigma, \sigma(x)\rangle$. The rules have no hypothesis.

Arr: we have that $\sigma \vdash x[e] \Downarrow \sigma(x[v])$ with hypothesis $\sigma \vdash e \Downarrow v$. By inductive hypothesis we have $\langle \sigma, e \rangle \rightarrow^+ \langle \sigma, v \rangle$. Then we can apply rule ARR1 one or more times to derive $\langle \sigma, x[e] \rangle \rightarrow^+ \langle \sigma, x[v] \rangle$. The thesis follows using rule ARR2 to derive $\langle \sigma, x[v] \rangle \rightarrow \langle \sigma, \sigma(x[v]) \rangle$.

Bop: we have that $\sigma \vdash e_1 \odot e_2 \Downarrow v$ with hypothesis $\sigma \vdash e_1 \Downarrow v_1$, $\sigma \vdash e_2 \Downarrow v_2$, $[\![\odot]\!](v_1, v_2) = v$. By inductive hypothesis we have $\langle \sigma, e_1 \rangle \rightarrow^+ \langle \sigma, v_1 \rangle$, and $\langle \sigma, e_2 \rangle \rightarrow^+ \langle \sigma, v_2 \rangle$. Then we can apply rule BOP1 zero or more times to lift the first computation, and rule BOP2 zero or more times to lift the second one. The thesis follows using rule BOP3 with the last hypothesis.

$\Leftarrow$: The proof is by induction on the number of steps in the computation.

Base case: we have $\langle \sigma, e \rangle \rightarrow \langle \sigma, v \rangle$ in one step. We perform a sub-induction on the derivation of the step. We have a case for each rule.

    ConS: we have that $\langle \sigma, c \rangle \rightarrow \langle \sigma, [\![c]\!] \rangle$. The thesis follows using rule CON to derive $\sigma \vdash c \Downarrow [\![c]\!]$. The rules have no hypothesis.

    VarS: we have that $\langle \sigma, x \rangle \rightarrow \langle \sigma, \sigma(x) \rangle$. The thesis follows using rule VAR to derive $\sigma \vdash x \Downarrow \sigma(x)$. The rules have no hypothesis.

    Arr2: we have that $\langle \sigma, x[v] \rangle \rightarrow \langle \sigma, \sigma(x[v]) \rangle$. This case does not match the hypothesis, since $x[v]$ contains a value. Indeed, applications of ARR2 occur only as part of longer derivations which start with rule ARR1. We will prove below the case of ARR1 without relying on hypothesis on the case of ARR2.

    Bop3: we have that $\langle \sigma, v_1 \odot v_2 \rangle \rightarrow \langle \sigma, v \rangle$. As before, there is nothing to prove here since $v_1 \odot v_2$ contains values.

Inductive case: we have $\langle \sigma, e \rangle \rightarrow \langle \sigma, e' \rangle \rightarrow^+ \langle \sigma, v \rangle$. We perform a sub-induction on the derivation of the first step. We have a case for each rule.

    Arr1: we have $\langle \sigma, x[e] \rangle \rightarrow \langle \sigma, x[e'] \rangle \rightarrow^+ \langle \sigma, \sigma(x[v]) \rangle$. By rule inspection we know that first only rule ARR1 is applicable, followed by an application of rule ARR2. By considering the hypotheses of the applications of rule ARR1, we have that $\langle \sigma, e \rangle \rightarrow^+ \langle \sigma, v \rangle$. By inductive hypothesis we know that $\sigma \vdash e \Downarrow v$. We can derive the conclusion using rule ARR.

    Bop1: we have $\langle \sigma, e_1 \odot e_2 \rangle \rightarrow \langle \sigma, e_1' \odot e_2 \rangle \rightarrow^+ \langle \sigma, v \rangle$. By rule inspection we know that only rule BOP1 is applicable, and by considering the hypotheses of its applications, we have that $\langle \sigma, e_1 \rangle \rightarrow^+ \langle \sigma, v_1 \rangle$. Afterwards, the only applicable rule is BOP2, and from the hypotheses of the rule we have that $\langle \sigma, e_2 \rangle \rightarrow^+ \langle \sigma, v_2 \rangle$. In the end the only applicable rule is BOP3, and from the hypotheses of the rule we have that $[\![\odot]\!](v_1, v_2) = v$. By inductive hypothesis we know that $\sigma \vdash e_1 \Downarrow v_1$ and $\sigma \vdash e_2 \Downarrow v_2$. Thanks to this hypothesis of rule BOP3 we can derive the conclusion using rule BOP.

    Bop2: we have that $\langle \sigma, v_1 \odot e_2 \rangle \rightarrow \langle \sigma, e_2' \rangle$. There is nothing to prove here since $v_1 \odot e_2$ contains a value. $\qquad\square$

Now we prove the equivalence between the big-step and the small-step semantics of statements, when the execution terminates without runtime errors. The proof is not trivial, since not all the small-step rules have a direct correspondence in the big-step rules (see, e.g., Fig. 10 for the rules related to the loop), and since the loop relies on some runtime syntax for evaluation, differently from what happens for classical irreversible while loop semantics.

Theorem 1.
$$\sigma \vdash s \Downarrow \sigma' \ \text{iff} \ \langle \sigma, s \rangle \rightarrow^* \langle \sigma', \text{skip} \rangle$$

where expressions inside s do not contain values.

Proof. ⇒: The proof is by induction on the derivation, with a case analysis on the last applied rule.

We extend the inductive hypothesis to cover the additional case where s includes also the runtime syntax for big-step semantics (e_1, s_1, e_2, s_2), where we have:

$$\sigma \vdash (e_1, s_1, e_2, s_2) \Downarrow \sigma' \ \text{iff} \ \langle \sigma, (e_1, (\text{skip}, s_1), (e_2, e_2), s_2) \rangle \rightarrow^* \langle \sigma', \text{skip} \rangle$$

AssVar: we have $\sigma \vdash x \oplus = e \Downarrow \sigma[x \mapsto [\![\oplus]\!](\sigma(x), v)]$ with hypothesis $\sigma \vdash e \Downarrow v$. From Lemma 1 we deduce that $\langle \sigma, e \rangle \rightarrow^+ \langle \sigma, v \rangle$. The thesis follows using rule CTXEXP one or more times to lift the previous computation to $\langle \sigma, x \oplus = e \rangle \rightarrow^* \langle \sigma, x \oplus = v \rangle$. We conclude by applying rule ASSVARS to derive $\langle \sigma, x \oplus = v \rangle \rightarrow \langle \sigma[x \mapsto [\![\oplus]\!](\sigma(x), v)], \text{skip} \rangle$.

AssArr: we have $\sigma \vdash x[e_l] \oplus = e \Downarrow \sigma[x[v_l] \mapsto [\![\oplus]\!](\sigma(x[v_l]), v)]$ with hypothesis $\sigma \vdash e_l \Downarrow v_l$ and $\sigma \vdash e \Downarrow v$. From Lemma 1 we can derive $\langle \sigma, e_l \rangle \rightarrow^+ \langle \sigma, v_l \rangle$ and $\langle \sigma, e \rangle \rightarrow^+ \langle \sigma, v \rangle$. The thesis follows using one or more times rule CTXEXP and finally rule ASSARRS to derive $\langle \sigma, x[e_l] \oplus = e \rangle \rightarrow^* \langle \sigma, x[v_l] \oplus = e \rangle \rightarrow^* \langle \sigma, x[v_l] \oplus = v \rangle \rightarrow \langle \sigma[x[v_l] \mapsto [\![\oplus]\!](\sigma(x[v_l]), v)], \text{skip} \rangle$.

Call: we have $\sigma \vdash \text{call} \ id \Downarrow \sigma'$ with hypothesis $\sigma \vdash \Gamma(id) \Downarrow \sigma'$. By inductive hypothesis we have $\langle \sigma, \Gamma(id) \rangle \rightarrow^* \langle \sigma', \text{skip} \rangle$. Then the thesis follows using rule CALLS.

UnCall: we have $\sigma \vdash \text{uncall} \ id \Downarrow \sigma'$ with hypothesis $\sigma \vdash \mathcal{I}[\![\Gamma(id)]\!] \Downarrow \sigma'$. By inductive hypothesis we have $\langle \sigma, \mathcal{I}[\![\Gamma(id)]\!] \rangle \rightarrow^* \langle \sigma', \text{skip} \rangle$. Then the thesis follows using rule UNCALLS.

Skip: the thesis follows by executing a zero steps derivation.

IfTrue: by hypothesis we have that $\sigma \vdash e_1 \Downarrow v_1$, is_true?$(v_1)$, $\sigma \vdash s_1 \Downarrow \sigma'$, $\sigma' \vdash e_2 \Downarrow v_2$ and is_true?(v_2). From Lemma 1 we deduce that $\langle \sigma, e_1 \rangle \rightarrow^+ \langle \sigma, v_1 \rangle$ and $\langle \sigma', e_2 \rangle \rightarrow^+ \langle \sigma', v_2 \rangle$. By inductive hypothesis we have that $\langle \sigma, s_1 \rangle \rightarrow^* \langle \sigma', \text{skip} \rangle$. Then we can apply first one or more times rule CTXEXP to derive $\langle \sigma, \text{if} \ e_1 \ \text{then} \ s_1 \ \text{else} \ s_2 \ \text{fi} \ e_2 \rangle \rightarrow^+ \langle \sigma, \text{if} \ v_1 \ \text{then} \ s_1 \ \text{else} \ s_2 \ \text{fi} \ e_2 \rangle$, then zero or more times rule CTXSTMT to derive $\langle \sigma, \text{if} \ v_1 \ \text{then} \ s_1 \ \text{else} \ s_2 \ \text{fi} \ e_2 \rangle \rightarrow^* \langle \sigma', \text{if} \ v_1 \ \text{then} \ \text{skip} \ \text{else} \ s_2 \ \text{fi} \ e_2 \rangle$, then one or more times rule CTXEXP to derive $\langle \sigma', \text{if} \ v_1 \ \text{then} \ \text{skip} \ \text{else} \ s_2 \ \text{fi} \ e_2 \rangle \rightarrow^+ \langle \sigma', \text{if} \ v_1 \ \text{then} \ \text{skip} \ \text{else} \ s_2 \ \text{fi} \ v_2 \rangle$ and finally rule IFTRUEEND to obtain $\langle \sigma', \text{if} \ v_1 \ \text{then} \ \text{skip} \ \text{else} \ s_2 \ \text{fi} \ v_2 \rangle \rightarrow \langle \sigma', \text{skip} \rangle$. The thesis follows.

IfFalse: analogous to the one above.

LoopMain: we have $\sigma \vdash \text{from} \ e_1 \ \text{do} \ s_1 \ \text{loop} \ s_2 \ \text{until} \ e_2 \Downarrow \sigma''$ with hypotheses $\sigma \vdash e_1 \Downarrow v_1$, is_true?$(v_1)$, $\sigma \vdash s_1 \Downarrow \sigma'$, and $\sigma' \vdash (e_1, s_1, e_2, s_2) \Downarrow \sigma''$. From Lemma 1 we deduce $\langle \sigma, e_1 \rangle \rightarrow^+ \langle \sigma, v_1 \rangle$. Then, thanks to the two first hypotheses, we can apply rule LOOPMAINS, one or more times rule CTXEXP and finally rule LOOPEXP1T and obtain $\langle \sigma, \text{from } e_1 \text{ do } s_1 \text{ loop } s_2 \text{ until } e_2 \rangle \rightarrow \langle \sigma, ((e_1, e_1), s_1, e_2, s_2)) \rangle \rightarrow^+ \langle \sigma, ((v_1, e_1), s_1, e_2, s_2)) \rangle \rightarrow \langle \sigma, (e_1, (s_1, s_1), (e_2, e_2), s_2)) \rangle$. Thanks to the hypothesis $\sigma \vdash s_1 \Downarrow \sigma'$ we can apply the inductive hypothesis to obtain $\langle \sigma, s_1 \rangle \rightarrow^* \langle \sigma', \text{skip} \rangle$. Now, we can apply rule CTXSTMT zero or more times to lift the previous computation to $\langle \sigma, (e_1, (s_1, s_1), (e_2, e_2), s_2)) \rangle \rightarrow^* \langle \sigma', (e_1, (\text{skip}, s_1), (e_2, e_2), s_2)) \rangle$. We can finally apply the extended inductive hypothesis to derive $\langle \sigma', (e_1, (\text{skip}, s_1), (e_2, e_2), s_2)) \rangle \rightarrow^* \langle \sigma'', \text{skip} \rangle$.

LoopBase: we have $\sigma \vdash (e_1, s_1, e_2, s_2) \Downarrow \sigma$ with hypotheses $\sigma \vdash e_2 \Downarrow v_2$ and is_true?(v_2). From Lemma 1 we can deduce $\langle \sigma, e_2 \rangle \rightarrow^+ \langle \sigma, v_2 \rangle$. We can then use it to apply one or more times rule CTXEXP and then rule LOOPENDS to prove the thesis for the extended case of the inductive hypothesis.

LoopRec: we have $\sigma \vdash (c_1, s_1, e_2, s_2) \Downarrow \sigma'''$ with hypotheses $\sigma \vdash e_2 \Downarrow v_2$, is_false?$(v_2)$, $\sigma \vdash s_2 \Downarrow \sigma'$, $\sigma' \vdash e_1 \Downarrow v_1$, is_false?$(v_1)$, $\sigma' \vdash s_1 \Downarrow \sigma''$ and $\sigma'' \vdash (e_1, s_1, e_2, s_2) \Downarrow \sigma'''$. From Lemma 1 we deduce $\langle \sigma, e_2 \rangle \rightarrow^+ \langle \sigma, v_2 \rangle$ and $\langle \sigma', e_1 \rangle \rightarrow^+ \langle \sigma', v_1 \rangle$. By inductive hypothesis we know that $\langle \sigma, s_2 \rangle \rightarrow^* \langle \sigma', \text{skip} \rangle$ and that $\langle \sigma', s_1 \rangle \rightarrow^* \langle \sigma'', \text{skip} \rangle$.

We have to prove $\langle \sigma, (e_1, (\text{skip}, s_1), (e_2, e_2), s_2)) \rangle \rightarrow^* \langle \sigma''', \text{skip} \rangle$.

To do so, we can apply rule CTXEXP one or more times to obtain $\langle \sigma, (e_1, (\text{skip}, s_1), (e_2, e_2), s_2)) \rangle \rightarrow^+ \langle \sigma, (e_1, (\text{skip}, s_1), (v_2, e_2), s_2)) \rangle$. Then, we can apply rule LOOPEXP2F (since we know that the hypothesis holds) to obtain $\langle \sigma, (e_1, (\text{skip}, s_1), (v_2, e_2), s_2)) \rangle \rightarrow \langle \sigma, ((e_1, e_1), (\text{skip}, s_1), e_2, (s_2, s_2))) \rangle$, rule CTXSTMT zero or more times to derive $(\langle \sigma, ((e_1, e_1), (\text{skip}, s_1), e_2, (s_2, s_2))) \rangle \rightarrow^* \langle \sigma', ((e_1, e_1), (\text{skip}, s_1), c_2, (\text{skip}, s_2)))) \rangle$. Then we apply rule CTX-EXP one or more times to derive $\langle \sigma', ((e_1, e_1), (\text{skip}, s_1), e_2, (\text{skip}, s_2))) \rangle \rightarrow^+ \langle \sigma', ((v_1, e_1), (\text{skip}, s_1), e_2, (\text{skip}, s_2))) \rangle$, and finally rule LOOPEXP1F to get $(\langle \sigma', ((v_1, e_1), (\text{skip}, s_1), e_2, (\text{skip}, s_2))) \rangle \rightarrow \langle \sigma', (e_1, (s_1, s_1), (e_2, e_2), s_2))) \rangle$. We can now apply rule CTXSTMT zero or more times to lift $\langle \sigma', s_1 \rangle \rightarrow^* \langle \sigma'', \text{skip} \rangle$ to $\langle \sigma', (e_1, (s_1, s_1), (e_2, e_2), s_2)) \rangle \rightarrow^* \langle \sigma'', (e_1, (\text{skip}, s_1), (e_2, e_2), s_2)) \rangle$. We can finally apply the extended inductive hypothesis to obtain $\langle \sigma'', (e_1, (\text{skip}, s_1), (e_2, e_2), s_2)) \rangle \rightarrow^* \langle \sigma''', \text{skip} \rangle$. The thesis follows.

Seq: we have $\sigma \vdash s_1 \ s_2 \Downarrow \sigma'$ with hypothesis $\sigma \vdash s_1 \Downarrow \sigma''$ and $\sigma'' \vdash s_2 \Downarrow \sigma'$. By inductive hypothesis we have $\langle \sigma, s_1 \rangle \rightarrow^* \langle \sigma'', \text{skip} \rangle$ and $\langle \sigma'', s_2 \rangle \rightarrow^* \langle \sigma', \text{skip} \rangle$. The thesis follows by applying rule CTXSTMT zero or more times, then rule SEQS and finally using the inductive hypothesis.

$\Leftarrow$: The proof is by induction on the number of steps in the computation.

Base case: $\langle \sigma, \text{skip} \rangle \rightarrow^* \langle \sigma, \text{skip} \rangle$ in zero steps: then $\sigma \vdash \text{skip} \Downarrow \sigma$ using rule SKIP.

Inductive case: $\langle \sigma, s \rangle \rightarrow \langle \sigma', s' \rangle \rightarrow^* \langle \sigma'', \text{skip} \rangle$ and by inductive hypothesis we know that $\sigma' \vdash s' \Downarrow \sigma''$. We perform a sub-induction on the derivation of the first step. We have a case for each rule. Note that inductive hypothesis is only needed in some of the cases.

CtxExp: here we do a case analysis on the possible context:

$x \oplus = \bullet$: we have $\langle \sigma, x \oplus = e \rangle \to \langle \sigma, x \oplus = e' \rangle$. The only possibility for the subsequent steps is to apply zero or more times rule CTXEXP and then rule ASSVARS to obtain $\langle \sigma, x \oplus = e' \rangle \to^* \langle \sigma, x \oplus = v \rangle \to \langle \sigma[x \mapsto [\![\oplus]\!](\sigma(x), v)], \text{skip} \rangle$. Thanks to the hypotheses of the rules, we can deduce $\sigma \vdash e \Downarrow v$ from Lemma 1. We can derive the conclusion using ASSVAR.

$x[\bullet] \oplus = e$: we have $\langle \sigma, x[e_l] \oplus = e \rangle \to \langle \sigma, x[e'_l] \oplus = e \rangle$. The only possibility for the subsequent steps is to apply one or more times rule CTX-EXP to obtain $\langle \sigma, x[e'_l] \oplus = e \rangle \to^* \langle \sigma, x[v_l] \oplus = e \rangle \to^+ \langle \sigma, x[v_l] \oplus = v \rangle$. Then the only applicable rule for the next step is ASSARRS and the result is $\langle \sigma, x[v_l] \oplus = v \rangle \to \langle \sigma[x[v_l] \mapsto [\![\oplus]\!](\sigma(x[v_l]), v)], \text{skip} \rangle$. Thanks to the hypotheses of the rules, we can deduce $\sigma \vdash e \Downarrow v$ and $\sigma \vdash e_l \Downarrow v_l$ from Lemma 1. We can derive the conclusion using ASSARR.

$x[v] \oplus = \bullet$: as the second part of the previous case.

if $\bullet$ then s_1 else s_2 fi e_2: we have
$\langle \sigma, \text{if } e_1 \text{ then } s_1 \text{ else } s_2 \text{ fi } e_2 \rangle \to \langle \sigma, \text{if } e'_1 \text{ then } s_1 \text{ else } s_2 \text{ fi } e_2 \rangle$. For the subsequent steps we can only apply rule CTXEXP zero or more times, to derive $\langle \sigma, \text{if } e'_1 \text{ then } s_1 \text{ else } s_2 \text{ fi } e_2 \rangle \to^* \langle \sigma, \text{if } v_1 \text{ then } s_1 \text{ else } s_2 \text{ fi } e_2 \rangle$. The continuation of the computation depends on the truth value of v_1:

> **true:** by rule inspection we know that only rule CTXSTMT is applicable, and by considering the hypotheses of its applications, we have that $\langle \sigma, s_1 \rangle \to^* \langle \sigma', \text{skip} \rangle$. Afterwards, the only applicable rule is CTXEXP, and from the hypotheses of the rule we can derive $\sigma \vdash e_2 \Downarrow v_2$ from Lemma 1. Finally the only applicable rule is IFTRUEEND, and from the hypothesis of the rule we have that is_true?(v_2). By inductive hypothesis we know that $\sigma \vdash s_1 \Downarrow \sigma'$. We can derive the conclusion using rule IFTRUE.

> **false:** analogous to the true case.

if v_1 then skip else s_2 fi $\bullet$ where is_true?(v_1): we have
$\langle \sigma, \text{if } v_1 \text{ then skip else } s_2 \text{ fi } e_2 \rangle \to \langle \sigma, \text{if } v_1 \text{ then skip else } s_2 \text{ fi } e'_2 \rangle$. For the subsequent steps we can only apply zero or more times rule CTXEXP and then rule IFTRUEEND to obtain $\langle \sigma, \text{if } v_1 \text{ then skip else } s_2 \text{ fi } e'_2 \rangle \to^* \langle \sigma, \text{if } v_1 \text{ then skip else } s_2 \text{ fi } v_2 \rangle \to \langle \sigma, \text{skip} \rangle$. Then we know that $\sigma \vdash e_2 \Downarrow v_2$, $\sigma \vdash v_1 \Downarrow v_1$, is_true?$(v_1)$ and is_true?(v_2). Thanks to these hypotheses we can derive the conclusion using rule IFTRUE.

if v_1 then s_1 else skip fi $\bullet$ where is_false?(v_1): analogous to the previous case.

$((\bullet, e_1), s_1, e_2, s_2)$: the rule never matches our extended inductive hypothesis, hence there is nothing to prove.

$(e_1, (\text{skip}, s_1), (\bullet, e_2), s_2)$: the rule matches our extended inductive hypothesis only when $\bullet = e_2$. We have $\langle \sigma, (e_1, (\text{skip}, s_1), (e_2, e_2), s_2) \rangle \to \langle \sigma, (e_1, (\text{skip}, s_1), (e'_2, e_2), s_2) \rangle \to^* \langle \sigma', \text{skip} \rangle$. By rule inspection we know that the computation $\langle \sigma, (e_1, (\text{skip}, s_1), (e'_2, e_2), s_2) \rangle \to^*$

$\langle \sigma', \mathsf{skip} \rangle$ has a prefix, derived by applying at each step rule CTX-EXP, of the form $\langle \sigma, (e_1, (\mathsf{skip}, s_1), (e_2', e_2), s_2) \rangle \rightarrow^* \langle \sigma, (e_1, (\mathsf{skip}, s_1), (v_2, e_2), s_2) \rangle$.

By considering the hypothesis of the applications of rule CTXEXP we have that $\langle \sigma, e_2 \rangle \rightarrow^+ \langle \sigma, v_2 \rangle$. Now, we can have two possible continuations, depending on the truth value of v_2. If it is true, we can apply rule LOOPENDS, and the thesis follows applying rule LOOP-BASE. The second continuation is $\langle \sigma, (e_1, (\mathsf{skip}, s_1), (v_2, e_2), s_2) \rangle \rightarrow$
$\langle \sigma, ((e_1, e_1), (\mathsf{skip}, s_1), e_2, (s_2, s_2)) \rangle \rightarrow^+$
$\langle \sigma, ((v_1, e_1), (\mathsf{skip}, s_1), e_2, (s_2, s_2)) \rangle \rightarrow^*$
$\langle \sigma'', ((v_1, e_1), (\mathsf{skip}, s_1), e_2, (\mathsf{skip}, s_2)) \rangle \rightarrow \langle \sigma'', (e_1, (s_1, s_1), (e_2, e_2), s_2) \rangle$
$\rightarrow^* \langle \sigma''', (e_1, (\mathsf{skip}, s_1), (e_2, e_2), s_2) \rangle \rightarrow^* \langle \sigma', \mathsf{skip} \rangle$. The derivation is obtained by applying LOOPEXP2F, then one or more times CTX-EXP, zero or more times CTXSTMT, then rule LOOPEXP1F and zero or more times rule CTXSTMT. By considering the hypothesis of the applications of rule CTXEXP we have that $\langle \sigma, e_1 \rangle \rightarrow^+ \langle \sigma, v_1 \rangle$. By considering the hypothesis of the applications of rule CTXSTMT (the first time) we have that $\langle \sigma, s_2 \rangle \rightarrow^* \langle \sigma'', \mathsf{skip} \rangle$ and (the second time) $\langle \sigma'', s_1 \rangle \rightarrow^* \langle \sigma''', \mathsf{skip} \rangle$. Then by inductive hypothesis we have $\sigma \vdash s_2 \Downarrow \sigma''$ and $\sigma'' \vdash s_1 \Downarrow \sigma'''$. Then by applying the extended inductive hypothesis to the second part of the computation we know that $\sigma''' \vdash (e_1, s_1, e_2, s_2) \Downarrow \sigma'$. We can finally apply rule LOOPREC to derive $\sigma \vdash (e_1, s_1, e_2, s_2) \Downarrow \sigma'$, hence the thesis follows.

$((\bullet, e_1), (\mathsf{skip}, s_1), e_2, (\mathsf{skip}, s_2))$: the rule never matches our extended inductive hypothesis, hence there is nothing to prove.

CtxStmt here we do a case analysis on the context:

- s: we have that $\langle \sigma, s_1 \ s_2 \rangle \rightarrow \langle \sigma''', s_1' \ s_2 \rangle \rightarrow^* \langle \sigma'', s_2 \rangle \rightarrow^* \langle \sigma', \mathsf{skip} \rangle$. By inductive hypothesis we have $\sigma \vdash s_1 \Downarrow \sigma''$ and $\sigma'' \vdash s_2 \Downarrow \sigma'$. Then the thesis follows using rule SEQ.

  if v_1 then $\bullet$ else s_2 fi e_2 where is_true?(v_1): analogous to the second part of the case for rule CTXEXP with context equal to
  if $\bullet$ then s_1 else s_2 fi e_2 (the true subcase).

  if v_1 then s_1 else $\bullet$ fi e_2 where is_false?(v_1): analogous to the previous case.

  $(e_1, (\bullet, s_1), (e_2, e_2), s_2)$: the only possible match between the conclusion of the rule and the extended inductive hypothesis is when $s = \mathsf{skip}$, but in this case the premise of the rule is always false (skip cannot take any step), hence there is nothing to prove.

  $((e_1, e_1), (\mathsf{skip}, s_1), e_2, (\bullet, s_2))$: the rule never matches our extended inductive hypothesis, hence there is nothing to prove.

AssVarS: there is nothing to prove since the statement in the premise contains values.

AssArrS: as above, there is nothing to prove since the statement in the premise contains values.

CallS: we have $\langle \sigma, \mathsf{call} \ id \rangle \rightarrow \langle \sigma, \Gamma(id) \rangle$. By inductive hypothesis we have $\sigma \vdash \Gamma(id) \Downarrow \sigma'$. We can derive the conclusion using rule CALL.

UnCallS: we have $\langle \sigma, \text{uncall } id \rangle \rightarrow \langle \sigma, \mathcal{I}[\![\Gamma(id)]\!] \rangle$. By inductive hypothesis we have $\sigma \vdash \mathcal{I}[\![\Gamma(id)]\!] \Downarrow \sigma'$, hence we can derive the conclusion using rule UNCALL.

IfTrueEnd: there is nothing to prove since the statement in the premise contains values.

IfFalseEnd: analogous to IFTRUEEND.

LoopMainS: we have that
$\langle \sigma, \text{from } e_1 \text{ do } s_1 \text{ loop } s_2 \text{ until } e_2 \rangle \rightarrow \langle \sigma, ((e_1, e_1), s_1, e_2, s_2) \rangle \rightarrow^* \langle \sigma', \text{skip} \rangle$.
By rule inspection we know that the derivation of
$\langle \sigma, ((e_1, e_1), s_1, e_2, s_2) \rangle \rightarrow^* \langle \sigma', \text{skip} \rangle$ has the structure
$\langle \sigma, ((e_1, e_1), s_1, e_2, s_2) \rangle \rightarrow^+ \langle \sigma, ((v_1, e_1), s_1, e_2, s_2) \rangle \rightarrow$
$\langle \sigma, (e_1, (s_1, s_1), (e_2, e_2), s_2) \rangle \rightarrow^* \langle \sigma'', (e_1, (\text{skip}, s_1), (e_2, e_2), s_2) \rangle \rightarrow^*$
$\langle \sigma', \text{skip} \rangle$ where the steps in the first part are derived using rule CTX-EXP. Hence by taking the premises we know that there is a derivation $\langle \sigma, e_1 \rangle \rightarrow^+ \langle \sigma, v_1 \rangle$. Instead, the steps in the second part are derived using first rule LOOPEXP1T and then rule CTXSTMT zero or more times. Hence by taking the premises we know that there is a derivation $\langle \sigma, s_1 \rangle \rightarrow^* \langle \sigma'', \text{skip} \rangle$. By applying the inductive hypothesis we know that $\sigma \vdash s_1 \Downarrow \sigma''$. By applying the extended inductive hypothesis to the second part of the derivation we know that $\sigma'' \vdash (e_1, s_1, e_2, s_2) \Downarrow \sigma'$. Then we can apply rule LOOPMAIN and the thesis follows.

LoopEndS: the rule never matches our extended inductive hypothesis, hence there is nothing to prove.

SeqS: we have that $\langle \sigma, \text{skip } s_2 \rangle \rightarrow \langle \sigma, s_2 \rangle \rightarrow^* \langle \sigma', \text{skip} \rangle$, then using rule SKIP we have $\sigma \vdash \text{skip} \Downarrow \sigma$ and by inductive hypothesis we have $\sigma \vdash s_2 \Downarrow \sigma'$. Then the thesis follows using rule SEQ. □

4   Examples

We now present a few examples of use of our semantics, to clarify its use and features.

Example 1 (Iterative Fibonacci Computation). We show below the Janus code of the iterative computation of the Fibonacci function.

```
procedure main                procedure fib
    n+ = 4                        from x₁ = x₂ do
    x₁+ = 1                           x₁+ = x₂
    x₁+ = 1                           x₁ <=> x₂
    call fib                      loop
                                      n- = 1
                                  until n = 0
```

In the code, $x_1 <=> x_2$ denotes the swap of the values of variables x_1 and x_2. Extending our approach to cope with it is trivial, otherwise it can be translated as the sequence of assignments $x_1\hat{} = x_2 \quad x_2\hat{} = x_1 \quad x_1\hat{} = x_2$.

$$\ldots \rightarrow \qquad \langle \sigma, \mathsf{call}\ fib(x_1, x_2, n) \rangle$$

$$\textsc{Calls} \rightarrow \qquad \langle \sigma, \mathsf{from}\ x_1 = x_2\ \mathsf{do}\ x_1 + = x_2\ x_1 <\!=\!> x_2\ \mathsf{loop}\ n- = 1\ \mathsf{until}\ n = 0 \rangle$$

$$\textsc{LoopMainS} \rightarrow \qquad \langle \sigma, ((x_1 = x_2, x_1 = x_2), \begin{smallmatrix} x_1 + = x_2 \\ x_1 <\!=\!> x_2 \end{smallmatrix}, n = 0, n- = 1) \rangle$$

$$\textsc{CtxExp} \rightarrow^* \qquad \langle \sigma, ((\mathsf{true}, x_1 = x_2), \begin{smallmatrix} x_1 + = x_2 \\ x_1 <\!=\!> x_2 \end{smallmatrix}, n = 0, n- = 1) \rangle$$

$$\textsc{LoopExp1T} \rightarrow \qquad \langle \sigma, (x_1 = x_2, (\begin{smallmatrix} x_1 + = x_2 \\ x_1 <\!=\!> x_2 \end{smallmatrix}, \begin{smallmatrix} x_1 + = x_2 \\ x_1 <\!=\!> x_2 \end{smallmatrix}), (n = 0, n = 0), n- = 1) \rangle$$

$$\textsc{CtxStmt} \rightarrow^* \qquad \langle \sigma', (x_1 = x_2, (\mathsf{skip}, \begin{smallmatrix} x_1 + = x_2 \\ x_1 <\!=\!> x_2 \end{smallmatrix}), (n = 0, n = 0), n- = 1) \rangle$$

$$\textsc{CtxExp} \rightarrow^* \qquad \langle \sigma', (x_1 = x_2, (\mathsf{skip}, \begin{smallmatrix} x_1 + = x_2 \\ x_1 <\!=\!> x_2 \end{smallmatrix}), (\mathsf{false}, n = 0), n- = 1) \rangle$$

$$\textsc{LoopExp2F} \rightarrow \langle \sigma', ((x_1 = x_2, x_1 = x_2), (\mathsf{skip}, \begin{smallmatrix} x_1 + = x_2 \\ x_1 <\!=\!> x_2 \end{smallmatrix}), n = 0, (n- = 1, n- = 1)) \rangle$$

$$\textsc{CtxStmt} \rightarrow^* \quad \langle \sigma'', ((x_1 = x_2, x_1 = x_2), (\mathsf{skip}, \begin{smallmatrix} x_1 + = x_2 \\ x_1 <\!=\!> x_2 \end{smallmatrix}), n = 0, (\mathsf{skip}, n- = 1)) \rangle$$

$$\textsc{CtxExp} \rightarrow^* \quad \langle \sigma'', ((\mathsf{false}, x_1 = x_2), (\mathsf{skip}, \begin{smallmatrix} x_1 + = x_2 \\ x_1 <\!=\!> x_2 \end{smallmatrix}), n = 0, (\mathsf{skip}, n- = 1)) \rangle$$

$$\textsc{LoopExp1F} \rightarrow \quad \langle \sigma'', (x_1 = x_2, (\begin{smallmatrix} x_1 + = x_2 \\ x_1 <\!=\!> x_2 \end{smallmatrix}, \begin{smallmatrix} x_1 + = x_2 \\ x_1 <\!=\!> x_2 \end{smallmatrix}), (n = 0, n = 0), n- = 1) \rangle$$

$$\ldots \rightarrow^* \ldots \rightarrow^* \qquad \langle \sigma^m, (x_1 = x_2, (\mathsf{skip}, \begin{smallmatrix} x_1 + = x_2 \\ x_1 <\!=\!> x_2 \end{smallmatrix}), (\mathsf{true}, n = 0), n- = 1) \rangle$$

$$\textsc{LoopEndS} \rightarrow \qquad \langle \sigma^m, \mathsf{skip} \rangle$$

Fig. 11. Iterative Fibonacci with the small-step semantics (Color figure online)

We now show the evaluation of the code above, starting from the call statement, using both the small-step (Fig. 11) and the big-step (Fig. 13) semantics. Hence, both the evaluations start with the store $\sigma = \{n \mapsto 4; x_1 \mapsto 1; x_2 \mapsto 1\}$.

Clearly, the small-step semantics takes the form of a sequence of steps, while the big-step semantics gives rise to a single derivation. Notably, the intermediate stores are the same in both the cases. We report them here: $\sigma = \{n \mapsto 4; x_1 \mapsto 1; x_2 \mapsto 1\}$, $\sigma' = \{n \mapsto 4; x_1 \mapsto 2; x_2 \mapsto 1\}$, $\sigma'' = \{n \mapsto 4; x_1 \mapsto 1; x_2 \mapsto 2\}$, $\sigma^m = \{n \mapsto 0; x_1 \mapsto 8; x_2 \mapsto 13\}$.

We show in Fig. 12 as an example the derivation of the first step in the sequence denoted with a red $\rightarrow^*$ in Fig. 11 (small-step computation). $\Diamond$

Example 2 (Failing and non-terminating computations). As mentioned in the Introduction, the small-step semantics allows one to better distinguish between failing and non-terminating computations. We show this on the two sample programs below, that respectively exhibit a failing computation (on the left) and a non-terminating one (on the right).

```
procedure main                 procedure main
  from x₁ = 10 do                 from x₁ = 0 do
    x₂+ = x₁                        x₁+ = 1
  loop                           loop
    x₁- = 1                         x₂+ = x₁
  until x₁ = 0                    until x₁ = 0
```

$$\frac{\dfrac{\langle \sigma, x_2 \rangle \to \langle \sigma, 1 \rangle}{\langle \sigma, x_1+=x_2 \rangle \to \langle \sigma, x_1+=1 \rangle} \textsc{CtxExp}}{\langle \sigma, {}^{x_1+\ =\ x_2}_{x_1\ <=>\ x_2} \rangle \to \langle \sigma, {}^{x_1+\ =\ 1}_{x_1\ <=>\ x_2} \rangle} \textsc{CtxStmt}}{\langle \sigma, (x_1=x_2, ({}^{x_1+\ =\ x_2}_{x_1\ <=>\ x_2}\ ,\ {}^{x_1+\ =\ x_2}_{x_1\ <=>\ x_2}),n=0,n-=1)\rangle \to \langle \sigma, (x_1=x_2, ({}^{x_1+\ =\ 1}_{x_1\ <=>\ x_2}\ ,\ {}^{x_1+\ =\ x_2}_{x_1\ <=>\ x_2}),n=0,n-=1)\rangle} \textsc{CtxStmt}$$

Fig. 12. Derivation of the red step in Fig. 11

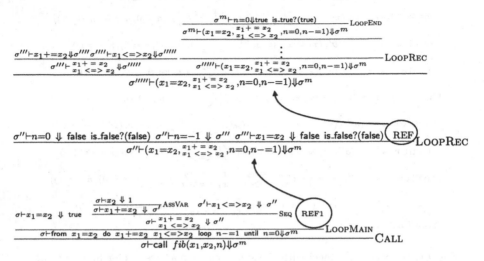

Fig. 13. Iterative Fibonacci with the big-step semantics

In both the cases, σ before the evaluation of the loop is $\sigma = \{x_1 \mapsto 0; x_2 \mapsto 0\}$. For the non-terminating computation, we assume (differently from [20]) that integer values are unbounded. The failing computation raises a runtime error due to the entry guard of the loop being false.

In both the cases, under the big-step semantics, no derivation exists. For the failing computation, we show below how such a derivation should terminate, but there is no applicable rule.

$$\frac{\sigma \vdash x_1 = 10 \ \Downarrow \ \text{false is\_false?(false)} \quad \dots}{\sigma \vdash \text{from } x_1 = 10 \text{ do } x_1+\ = 1 \text{ loop } x_2+\ = 1 \text{ until } x_1 = 0 \ \Downarrow \ ???} ???$$

For the non-terminating computation, the derivation is infinite hence one is not able to close it. A fragment of the infinite derivation is in Fig. 14. Using the small-step semantics, instead, on the failing computation we have a computation ending with the error state $\bot$:

$$\frac{\text{is\_false?(false)}}{\langle \sigma, ((\text{false}, x_1 = 10), x_1+\ = 1, x_1 = 0, x_2+\ = 1) \rangle \to \bot} \textsc{LoopError1}$$

In the non-terminating computation instead, we can derive an infinite amount of steps, that makes it visible how the computation evolves, as we can see in Fig. 15.

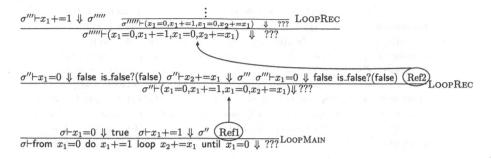

Fig. 14. Fragment of non-terminating derivation in big-step semantics

5 Related Work, Conclusion and Future Work

We proposed a small-step semantics for Janus, an imperative reversible programming language, and established its equivalence to existing big-step semantics. The Janus literature also covers extensions of Janus with other constructs, such as local variables [17,18] and stacks [17,18]. As immediate next step, we will extend our approach to cover such constructs as well. Beyond Janus, the literature on pure reversible programming languages includes also object-oriented languages such as ROOPL [4,15] and Joule [13], and functional languages such as RFun [19] and CoreFun [5]. They are all equipped with big-step semantics. Hence, as future work it makes sense to apply our approach to define small-step semantics for such languages as well.

The only small-step reversible semantics we are aware of are in the context of domain-specific languages for specifying assembly sequences in industrial robots [14,16]. However, the semantics of these languages is quite different from the one of Janus or functional or object-oriented reversible languages, since it involves the position and actions of the robot in the real world. Hence the relation with our work is quite limited. Also, they do not discuss big-step semantics, hence the issue of relating big-step and small-step semantics never emerges. As already mentioned in the Introduction, another promising area for future exploration is the integration of concurrency support into Janus. By enabling the creation of processes and enabling them to exchange messages, such an extension could allow one to write concurrent reversible programs. The definition of a small-step semantics provided in this paper is a relevant first step in this direction.

$$\cdots \rightarrow \qquad \langle \sigma, \text{from } x_1 = 0 \text{ do } x_1+\,= 1 \text{ loop } x_2+\,= x_1 \text{ until } x_1 = 0\rangle$$

$$\text{LoopMainS} \rightarrow \qquad \langle \sigma, ((x_1 = 0, x_1 = 0), x_1+\,= 1, x_1 = 0, x_2+\,= x_1))\rangle$$

$$\text{CtxExp} \rightarrow^* \qquad \langle \sigma, ((\text{true}, x_1 = 0), x_1+\,= 1, x_1 = 0, x_2+\,= x_1))\rangle$$

$$\text{LoopExp1T} \rightarrow \qquad \langle \sigma, (x_1 = 0, (x_1+\,= 1, x_1+\,= 1), (x_1 = 0, x_1 = 0), x_2+\,= x_1))\rangle$$

$$\text{CtxStmt} \rightarrow^* \qquad \langle \sigma', (x_1 = 0, (\text{skip}, x_1+\,= 1), (x_1 = 0, x_1 = 0), x_2+\,= x_1))\rangle$$

$$\text{CtxExp} \rightarrow^* \qquad \langle \sigma', (x_1 = 0, (\text{skip}, x_1+\,= 1), (\text{false}, x_1 = 0), x_2+\,= x_1))\rangle$$

$$\text{LoopExp2F} \rightarrow \langle \sigma', ((x_1 = 0, x_1 = 0), (\text{skip}, x_1+\,= 1), x_1 = 0, (x_2+\,= x_1, x_2+\,= x_1)))\rangle$$

$$\text{CtxStmt} \rightarrow^* \langle \sigma'', ((x_1 = 0, x_1 = 0), (\text{skip}, x_1+\,= 1), x_1 = 0, (\text{skip}, x_2+\,= x_1)))\rangle$$

$$\text{CtxExp} \rightarrow^* \langle \sigma'', ((\text{false}, x_1 = 0), (\text{skip}, x_1+\,= 1), x_1 = 0, (\text{skip}, x_2+\,= x_1)))\rangle$$

$$\text{LoopExp1F} \rightarrow \langle \sigma'', (x_1 = 0, (x_1+\,= 1, x_1+\,= 1), (x_1 = 0, x_1 = 0), x_2+\,= x_1))\rangle$$

$$\rightarrow \qquad \cdots$$

where: $\sigma = \{x_1 \mapsto 0; x_2 \mapsto 0\}$, $\sigma' = \{x_1 \mapsto 1; x_2 \mapsto 0\}$, $\sigma'' = \{x_1 \mapsto 1; x_2 \mapsto 1\}$

Fig. 15. Non-terminating computation in the small-step semantics

References

1. Cristescu, I., Krivine, J., Varacca, D.: A compositional semantics for the reversible pi-calculus. In: LICS, pp. 388–397. IEEE (2013)
2. Dagnino, F.: A meta-theory for big-step semantics. ACM Trans. Comput. Log. **23**(3), 20:1–20:50 (2022)
3. Danos, V., Krivine, J.: Reversible communicating systems. In: Gardner, P., Yoshida, N. (eds.) CONCUR 2004. LNCS, vol. 3170, pp. 292–307. Springer, Heidelberg (2004). https://doi.org/10.1007/978-3-540-28644-8_19
4. Haulund, T.: Design and implementation of a reversible object-oriented programming language (2017)
5. Jacobsen, P.A.H., Kaarsgaard, R., Thomsen, M.K.: CoreFun: a typed functional reversible core language. In: Kari, J., Ulidowski, I. (eds.) RC 2018. LNCS, vol. 11106, pp. 304–321. Springer, Cham (2018). https://doi.org/10.1007/978-3-319-99498-7_21
6. Lanese, I., Mezzina, C.A., Stefani, J.: Reversibility in the higher-order π-calculus. Theor. Comput. Sci. **625**, 25–84 (2016)
7. Lanese, I., Nishida, N., Palacios, A., Vidal, G.: A theory of reversibility for Erlang. J. Log. Algebraic Methods Program. **100**, 71–97 (2018)
8. Lutz, C., Derby, H.: Janus: a time-reversible language. Letter to R. Landauer **2** (1986)
9. Milner, R.: Communication and Concurrency, vol. 84. Prentice Hall Englewood Cliffs (1989)
10. Milner, R.: Communicating and Mobile Systems: The Pi Calculus. Cambridge University Press (1999)
11. Owens, S., Myreen, M.O., Kumar, R., Tan, Y.K.: Functional big-step semantics. In: Thiemann, P. (ed.) ESOP 2016. LNCS, vol. 9632, pp. 589–615. Springer, Heidelberg (2016). https://doi.org/10.1007/978-3-662-49498-1_23
12. Phillips, I., Ulidowski, I.: Reversing algebraic process calculi. J. Log. Algebr. Program. **73**(1–2), 70–96 (2007)
13. Schultz, U.P.: Reversible object-oriented programming with region-based memory management. In: Kari, J., Ulidowski, I. (eds.) RC 2018. LNCS, vol. 11106, pp. 322–328. Springer, Cham (2018). https://doi.org/10.1007/978-3-319-99498-7_22

14. Schultz, U.P.: Reversible control of robots. In: Ulidowski, I., Lanese, I., Schultz, U.P., Ferreira, C. (eds.) RC 2020. LNCS, vol. 12070, pp. 177–186. Springer, Cham (2020). https://doi.org/10.1007/978-3-030-47361-7_8

15. Schultz, U.P., Axelsen, H.B.: Elements of a reversible object-oriented language. In: Devitt, S., Lanese, I. (eds.) RC 2016. LNCS, vol. 9720, pp. 153–159. Springer, Cham (2016). https://doi.org/10.1007/978-3-319-40578-0_10

16. Schultz, U.P., Laursen, J.S., Ellekilde, L.-P., Axelsen, H.B.: Towards a domain-specific language for reversible assembly sequences. In: Krivine, J., Stefani, J.-B. (eds.) RC 2015. LNCS, vol. 9138, pp. 111–126. Springer, Cham (2015). https://doi.org/10.1007/978-3-319-20860-2_7

17. Yokoyama, T.: Reversible computation and reversible programming languages. Electron. Notes Theor. Comput. Sci. **253**(6), 71–81 (2010)

18. Yokoyama, T., Axelsen, H.B., Glück, R.: Principles of a reversible programming language. In: Proceedings of the 5th Conference on Computing Frontiers, CF 2008, pp. 43–54. ACM (2008)

19. Yokoyama, T., Axelsen, H.B., Glück, R.: Towards a reversible functional language. In: De Vos, A., Wille, R. (eds.) RC 2011. LNCS, vol. 7165, pp. 14–29. Springer, Heidelberg (2012). https://doi.org/10.1007/978-3-642-29517-1_2

20. Yokoyama, T., Glück, R.: A reversible programming language and its invertible self-interpreter. In: PEPM, pp. 144–153. ACM Press (2007)

Jeopardy: An Invertible Functional Programming Language

Joachim Tilsted Kristensen[1]([✉]) [ID], Robin Kaarsgaard[2] [ID],
and Michael Kirkedal Thomsen[1,3] [ID]

[1] Department of Informatics, University of Oslo, Oslo, Norway
{joachkr,michakt}@ifi.uio.no
[2] University of University of Southern Denmark, Odense, Denmark
kaarsgaard@imada.sdu.dk
[3] Department of Computer Science, University of Copenhagen, Copenhagen,
Denmark

Abstract. Reversible programming languages guarantee that their programs are invertible at the cost of restricting the permissible operations to those which are locally invertible. However, writing programs in a reversible style can be cumbersome, and may produce significantly different implementations than the conventional – even when the implemented algorithm is, in fact, invertible. We introduce Jeopardy, a functional programming language that guarantees global program invertibility without imposing local invertibility. In particular, Jeopardy allows the limited use of uninvertible – and even nondeterministic – operations, provided that they are used in a way that can be statically determined to be globally invertible. To this end, we outline an *implicitly available arguments analysis* and further approaches that can give a partial static guarantee to the (generally difficult) problem of guaranteeing invertibility.

Keywords: functional programming languages · program inversion · invertible computing · reversible computing

1 Introduction

Reversible programming languages guarantee program invertibility by enforcing a strict syntactic discipline: programs are comprised only of parts which are themselves immediately invertible (*locally invertible*), and these parts can only be combined in ways which preserve invertibility. In this way, the *global* problem of ensuring invertibility of an entire program is reduced to a *local* problem of ensuring invertibility of its parts. However, writing algorithms in the reversible style can be challenging: in a certain sense, it corresponds to requiring that programmers provide machine checkable proofs that their algorithms are invertible. As such, writing programs in these languages requires some experience, and can in some cases be notoriously hard. To mitigate the problem, this work investigates a more relaxed approach to reversible language design that enforces only (global) invertibility.

T. Æ. Mogensen and Ł. Mikulski (Eds.): RC 2024, LNCS 14680, pp. 124–141, 2024.
https://doi.org/10.1007/978-3-031-62076-8_9

We present the language Jeopardy: a functional language bearing syntactic resemblance to you garden variety functional programming language and, consequently, exhibits the expected semantics for programs running in the conventional direction. However, in order to support program inversion for a particular class of provably reversible programs that fail the syntactic condition of reversibility, we also seek to extend the semantics of Jeopardy to be *relational* in a conservative way. For example, consider the following program and its (manually implemented) inverse:

```
swap p =                          swap-inverse (b, a) =
  let a = first  p in              let p = second-inverse b in
  let b = second p in             let p = first-inverse  a in
  (b, a).                          p.
```

Not all parts of swap are invertible: for instance, first is not invertible at all. Nonetheless, swap clearly describes an invertible algorithm, as all of the information needed to reconstruct its input is contained in its output.

To strengthen our intuition about why swap is invertible, let us inspect the possible ways of implementing first or second. Both have to throw some information away, like so:

```
first  (a, _) = a.              first-inverse  a = (a, _).
second (_, b) = b.              second-inverse b = (_, b).
```

Because of this deletion of data, first and second are not information preserving transformations and it is this data loss that makes first and second non-invertible. However, when considered together as above, we see that the "*open*" part of their inverse function outputs (i.e., the underscore _, which can be thought of as a unification variable) can always be unified with a "*closed*" term (not containing such) from the other function.

Though there is a great deal of overlap between reversibility and invertibility, the notion of reversibility, as known from reversible computation, is philosophically distinct from the current work. In particular, we do not ask that programs are implemented only using small locally invertible parts, and cannot, as such, be cleanly mapped to a reversible low-level abstract machine or reversible hardware.

Related Work. Program inversion [4,23] concerns the automatic synthesis of the inverse to a given program (if such an inverse exists), while inverse execution seeks to interpret inverse programs from forward programs directly. Like compilation and interpretion, the two are connected by a *Futamura projection* [1,5]. Reversible programming [11,13,14,28,29,32,33], program inversion, and inverse execution have seen applications in areas as diverse as debugging [6, 18], high-performance simulation [25,26], quantum computing [3,9,10,30], and robotics [19,27], and is intimately connected with reversible models of computation [2,12,17]. The problem of deciding whether an algorithm is invertible is undecidable in general: for a language to guarantee that programs describe invertible algorithms, it must restrict *which* programs are allowed. For instance, a language may only permit locally invertible operations, such that their composition is invertible by construction: this is the case for Janus [21,33][1] and Theseus [14]. Languages which guarantee invertibility by allowing only such locally invertible operations are called *reversible*. Alternatively, a language may impose constraints that enforce function invertibility by global analyses, as has been done for RFun [28,32]. In this case, it turned out that enforcing a bidirectional first-match policy on choice points and requiring programs to be linear, was sufficient to guarantee invertibility without restricting computational power. Both the bidirectional branching and linear use of variables can be checked statically: the former by requiring syntactic orthogonality, and the latter through a linear typing discipline [7,31], as was also used in CoreFun [13]. Finally, a the class of *partially invertible functions*, meaning functions that become bijective when some inputs are fixed, can interact with reversible programs in a way that preserves invertibility by construction as has been done for the SPARCL programming language [22].

Structure. In the following section (Sect. 2) we introduce Jeopardy and its syntax. Section 3 will detail the reversible semantics, which includes rules for both forward and backward interpretation, while Sect. 4 suggests various strategies for conservatively relaxing the reversible semantics, and Sect. 5 discusses how one might implement such relaxations. Finally in Sect. 6 we conclude on what we have learned thus far. An implementation the reversible semantics of Jeopardy can be found at https://github.com/jtkristensen/Jeopardy, along with experimental implementations of the invertible semantics.

2   The Language

Jeopardy is a minimalistic first order functional language with user-definable algebraic data types and inverse function invocation. The latter is enabled by the special keyword **invert**. The syntax for algebraic datatype declaration differs slightly from the norm, in that a sum of products has to be declared using the keyword **data** rather than denoted directly in the program using the symbol $\cdot + \cdot$. This may seem odd to some theoretic computer scientists, but is common notation among programmers. The full grammar can be found in Fig. 1.

To clarify, a pattern p is either a variable or a constructor applied to (possibly zero) other patterns. A value v is a pattern that does not contain any variables. A program Δ is a list of mutually recursive function and datatype definitions, followed by a main function declaration. Functions are described by a name f, an input pattern, two type annotations (one for input and one for output), and a term t describing the functions body. A term is either a pattern, an application, or a case statement that branches execution. Application is special because the

---

[1] Often (as in Janus) local invertibility only guarantees invertibility of partial functions. This comes from the fact that control structures (like conditional and loops) require assertion of specific values.

$$x \in \textbf{Name} \qquad \text{(Well-formed variable names).}$$

$$c \in \textbf{Name} \qquad \text{(Well-formed constructor names).}$$

$$\tau \in \textbf{Name} \qquad \text{(Well-formed datatype names).}$$

$$f \in \textbf{Name} \qquad \text{(Well-formed function names).}$$

$$p ::= x \mid [c \; p_i] \qquad \text{(Patterns).}$$

$$v ::= [c \; v_i] \qquad \text{(Values).}$$

$$\Delta ::= f \; (p : \tau_p) : \tau_t \; = \; t \, . \, \Delta \qquad \text{(Function definition).}$$

$$\mid \textbf{data} \; \tau \; = \; [c \; \tau_i]_j \, . \, \Delta \qquad \text{(Data type definition).}$$

$$\mid \textbf{main} \; g \, . \qquad \text{(Main function declaration).}$$

$$g ::= f \mid (\textbf{invert} \; g) \qquad \text{(Function).}$$

$$t ::= p \qquad \text{(Patterns in terms).}$$

$$\mid g \; p \qquad \text{(Function application).}$$

$$\mid \textbf{case} \; t : \tau \; \textbf{of} \; p_i \to t_i \qquad \text{(Case statement).}$$

Fig. 1. The syntax of Jeopardy. The subscript notation denotes finite indexed sequences, ranging over the naturals, and starting from 0. For instance, a datatype declaration might look like `data natlist = [nil] [cons nat natlist]`.

$$[\![c \; t_i]\!]_{\Delta[\textbf{data} \; \tau=[c\tau_i]_j]} := \textbf{case} \; t_i : \tau_i \; \textbf{of} \; p_i \to [c \; p_i]$$

$$[\![(t_1, t_2)]\!]_\Delta := [\![\textbf{pair} \; t_1 \; t_2]\!]_\Delta$$

$$[\![t_1 : t_2]\!]_\Delta := [\![\textbf{cons} \; t_1 \; t_2]\!]_\Delta$$

$$[\![[]]\!]_\Delta := [\textbf{nil}]$$

$$[\![f \; t]\!]_{\Delta[f(\cdot:\tau):\cdot=\cdot]} := \textbf{case} \; t : \tau \; \textbf{of} \; p \to f \; p$$

$$[\![\textbf{let} \; p : \tau = t \; \textbf{in} \; t']\!]_\Delta := \textbf{case} \; t : \tau \; \textbf{of} \; p \to t'$$

$$[\![t']\!]_{\Delta[f(p_i:\tau_p):\tau_t=t_i.]} := [\![t']\!]_{\Delta[f(x:\tau_p):\tau_t=\textbf{case} \; x:\tau_p \; \textbf{of} \; p_i \to t_i]}$$

Fig. 2. Disambiguation of syntactic sugar.

operator may be a function symbol, denoting conventional application, or `invert` of a function symbol, applying the inverse of the corresponding function.

Running a program in the conventional direction corresponds to calling the declared main function on a value provided by the caller in an empty context. Similarly, running a program backwards corresponds to calling the main function's inverse on said value. Since function application is a term, reasoning about programs is reasoning about terms; as such, we will focus on terms from here on out. The syntax of terms has been designed to be small in order to make reasoning easier, at the cost of making programs harder to read and write. In the interest of writing intuitive program examples, we will use a couple of derived syntactic connectives that depend on the program Δ in which they are written, shown in Fig. 2.

2.1   Examples

In order to motivate the need for an invertible functional programming language, the following section compares programs written in the reversible style, to show that Jeopardy programs can get much closer to a conventional way of writing these programs. Suppose that we declared two datatypes **nat** and **pair** as follows:

```
data nat  = [zero] [suc nat].
data pair = [pair nat nat].
```

One may wish to add a pair of numbers, so we write an algorithm to do just that:

```
add ([zero ], n) = n
add ([suc k], n) = add (k, [suc n]).
```

Our algorithm **add** is not invertible because it is not injective since, e.g.

$$\text{add ([suc [zero]], [zero])} \equiv \text{add ([zero], [suc [zero]])}$$

even though

$$\text{([suc [zero]], [zero])} \not\equiv \text{([zero], [suc [zero]])}$$

However, since **add** *is* linearly typeable, the corresponding RFun and CoreFun programs will evaluate to a runtime error (as they should) upon calling **add** with an m that differs from [zero], as the result will not be syntactically orthogonal to the variable pattern n.

Now, suppose the caller of **add** happens to know the value of m in advance; meaning that m will be available in the future from the perspective of the inverse program. Then the case to use for inverse interpretation suddenly become unambiguous: either m is [zero] and we can unambiguously choose the first case, or m is [suc k], the caller now knows k, and can deterministically uncall **add** recursively in the second case. Therefore, the corresponding Jeopardy program will allow the programmer to call **add** in a context that knows about m as exemplified below:

```
fibber (m, n) = (add (m, n), m).

fib-pair [zero ] = ([suc [zero]], [suc [zero]]).
fib-pair [suc k] = fibber (fib-pair k).

fib n = (n, (first (fib-pair n))).

main fib.
```

Here, the function fib computes the pair containing n and the n'th Fibonacci number[2]. The helper function fib-pair becomes deterministic by the same trick as explained for add. Additionally, notice that even though the n is part of the output of fib, it is insufficient to uncompute fib by projecting out the input argument, since first is not invertible. As such, we either have to check that the second part of the output indeed does compute from n in the conventional direction, or we need to infer a unique environment in which the output was computed as we will discuss in Sect. 3.

Before moving on to doing so, we will further our intuition about what can be decided about invertible programs by considering the example of implementing map which has been specialised[3] to apply a specific function f:

```
data list = [nil] [cons nat list].
data pair = [pair list list].

reverse ([]      , ys) = ys.
reverse (y : xs, ys) = reverse (xs, y : ys).

f-iter ([]      , ys) = reverse (ys, []).
f-iter (x : xs, ys) = f-iter (xs, f x : ys).

map-f xs = f-iter (xs, []).

main map-f.
```

This definition of map-f is clearly invertible: As f-iter and reverse both move elements from the first to the second component a pair, and the first component of this pair always becomes smaller, so both algorithms terminate by size change termination [20]. Moreover the main function map-f always calls f-iter with an empty list as second argument, which in turn always call reverse with an empty list as second argument. We can make these cases explicit with a constructor like so

```
data argument-forms = [init list] [iter pair] [stop list]

f-iter [iter ([]      ,      ys)] =          [stop reverse (ys, [])  ].
f-iter [iter (x : xs, y : ys)] = f-iter [iter (xs, f x : y : ys)].
f-iter [init (x : xs,      [])] = f-iter [iter (xs, f x :      [])].

reverse [iter ([]      , ys)]     =          [stop ys            ].
reverse [iter (y : xs, ys)]    = reverse [iter (xs, y : ys)].
reverse [init (y : xs, [])]    = reverse [iter (xs, y : [])].
```

---

[2] It will never be possible to write an invertible implementation of the Fibonacci function that does not include something extra in its output, since the first couple of outputs has to be [suc [zero]] for two different inputs.

[3] The problem of extending an invertible (or even a reversible) programming language with (real) higher order functions will be worthy of its own paper.

which can be trivially and even tail-recursively inverted by just swapping inputs for outputs and putting recursive calls in front of the `iter` data structure as explained in [16], where we also show how such programs can be compiled into Janus-style loops.

However, for an interpreter to make this conclusion requires a non-trivial program analysis which cannot necessarily be performed inductively over the syntax of the program. In this particular case, the core difference between `fibber` and `map-f` is that the context in which `fibber` calls `add` provides information about the variable that `add` is branching on, making reverse pattern matching deterministic. In [15] we show how this relationship can be inferred in general.

3   Reversible Semantics

Aside from the special keyword `invert`, which invokes inverse interpretation of functions, Jeopardy is purposefully limited to garden variety syntactic constructs. It is desired that these constructs mean the conventional thing when interpreted in the conventional direction, and that more exotic constructions such as RFun's `rlet`-statement can be derived (in this case by combining `invert` with the case-statement and function application). It is likewise desired that such constructions mean the expected thing when inversely interpreted. In this section we present a *reversible* operational semantics for Jeopardy, in which all function definitions must be locally invertible.

The goal of this exercise is to ensure that invertible algorithms written in the reversible style are invertible in the same sense as that of corresponding programs written in languages that require programmers to formulate their algorithms in this way. In Sect. 4, we proceed to explaining how the reversible semantics can be relaxed to only require global invertibility. That is, to require a program's main function to be invertible, but not necessarily any other functions.

This reversible semantics is inspired by those of RFun and CoreFun, the main difference being a separation of concerns. For instance, the judgement rules of RFun can be read in two different ways. First, when read in the conventional direction, a term is evaluated to a value in an environment. Second, in the other direction, a resulting value is used to search a term for the unique environment in which that term would have yielded a particular result. In this regard, the semantics of Jeopardy programs are operationalised by four mutually recursive judgements; Figs. 3 and 4 show the judgements for interpretation, in the conventional and inverse direction, while Figs. 5 and 6 describe an algorithm for inferring unique environments under which terms (and inverted terms) evaluated to their canonical forms. We force this environment to be unique, by requiring that all terms are linearly typeable, meaning that any value of a given type must be used exactly once (and hence cannot be copied or deleted). Our type system ensures this by maintaining a set of explicitly disjoint typing environments Σ, following type system formalisation for CoreFun [13]. However, type checking has been factored out into four mutually recursive judgements: Figs. 7 and 8 about linear typing (and inverse linear typing), and Figs. 9 and 10 about environment uniqueness.

$$\boxed{\Delta\Gamma \vdash t \downarrow v} \text{ (for } t \text{ closed under } \Gamma)$$

$$\downarrow\text{Variable}: \frac{}{\Delta\Gamma \vdash x \downarrow v} \; (\Gamma(x) = v) \quad \downarrow\text{Constructor}: \frac{\Delta\Gamma \vdash p_i \downarrow v_i}{\Delta\Gamma \vdash [c\ p_i] \downarrow [c\ v_i]}$$

$$\downarrow\text{Cases}: \frac{\Delta\Gamma \vdash t \downarrow v \quad \Delta(\Gamma \circ \text{unify}(v, p_i)) \vdash t_i \downarrow v_i}{\Delta\Gamma \vdash \text{case } t : \tau \text{ of } p_i \rightarrow t_i \downarrow v_i} \; (\psi)$$

$$\downarrow\text{Application}: \frac{\Delta\Gamma \vdash p \downarrow v' \quad \Delta(\text{unify}(v', p')) \vdash t' \downarrow v}{\Delta[f\ (p' : \cdot) : \cdot = t']\Gamma \vdash f\ p \downarrow v}$$

$$\downarrow\text{Inversion}: \frac{\Delta\Gamma \vdash g\ p \uparrow v}{\Delta\Gamma \vdash (\text{invert } g)\ p \downarrow v}$$

Fig. 3. Interpretation in the conventional direction. The side condition (ψ) denotes the bidirectional first match policy as detailed in bullet point (2).

$$\boxed{\Delta\Gamma \vdash t \uparrow v} \text{ (for } t \text{ closed under } \Gamma)$$

$$\uparrow\text{Application}: \frac{\Delta\Gamma \vdash p \downarrow v' \quad \Delta[\![t' \downarrow v']\!] \rightsquigarrow \Gamma' \quad \Delta\Gamma' \vdash p' \downarrow v}{\Delta[f\ (p' : \cdot) : \cdot = t']\Gamma \vdash f\ p \uparrow v}$$

$$\uparrow\text{Inversion}: \frac{\Delta\Gamma \vdash g\ p \downarrow v}{\Delta\Gamma \vdash (\text{invert } g)\ p \uparrow v}$$

Fig. 4. Inverse interpretation for linear programs.

The motivation for producing explicit operational semantics for interpretation in both directions is to enable more fine grained program analysis, such as the ones outlined in Sect. 4. The remainder of this section will cover the meaning of each judgement of the reversible semantics along with its meta-theoretic properties, starting by programs that run in the conventional direction "from *top to bottom*". The corresponding judgement rules are therefore denoted by a downwards pointing arrow, and the form is $\Delta\Gamma \vdash t \downarrow v$, where Δ is a copy of the program text, Γ is a mapping between variable names and values, and the judgement reads "*in Δ, Γ stands witness that t evaluates to v in the conventional direction*".

1. The rules ↓Variable, ↓Constructor and ↓Application are the usual rules for looking up variables and applying first order functions. unify is the most general unifier as usual as well.
2. The ↓Cases rule says that when the selector term t evaluates to a value v, and v unifies with the ith pattern p_i, its corresponding term t_i evaluates to some value v_i under Γ and any bindings from unifying v and p_i, then the whole term evaluates to v_i. The side condition ψ is an abbreviation for the *symmetric first-match policy* [32], namely that we require p_j not to unify with v_i whenever $j < i$ holds, and that $\Delta[\![t_j \downarrow v_i]\!] \rightsquigarrow \Gamma$ should not hold for all such j either (this will be explained in greater detail later, as the rules are mutually recursive)x.
3. The ↓Inversion rule invokes inverse interpretation for function application, which can be seen in Fig. 4.
   Since the rules for inverse interpretation run in the opposite direction of the conventional one, their names have been annotated with an arrow pointing

$\boxed{\Delta[\![t \downarrow v]\!] \rightsquigarrow \Gamma}$ (for linear terms t)

$\rightarrow$Variable : $\dfrac{}{\Delta[\![x \downarrow v]\!] \rightsquigarrow \{x \mapsto v\}}$ $\rightarrow$Constructor : $\dfrac{\Delta[\![p_i \downarrow v_i]\!] \rightsquigarrow \Gamma_i}{\Delta[\![c\ p_i]\!] \downarrow [c\ v_i]\!] \rightsquigarrow \circ \Gamma_i}$

$\rightarrow$Cases : $\dfrac{\Delta[\![t_i \downarrow v_i]\!] \rightsquigarrow \Gamma_i \quad \Delta\Gamma_i \vdash p_i \downarrow v \quad \Delta[\![t \downarrow v]\!] \rightsquigarrow \Gamma}{\Delta[\![\mathbf{case}\ t : \tau\ \mathbf{of}\ p_i \rightarrow t_i \downarrow v_i]\!] \rightsquigarrow \Gamma_i \circ \Gamma}$ (ψ)

$\rightarrow$Application : $\dfrac{\Delta[\![t' \downarrow v]\!] \rightsquigarrow \Gamma' \quad \Delta\Gamma' \vdash p' \downarrow v' \quad \Delta[\![p \downarrow v']\!] \rightsquigarrow \Gamma}{\Delta[f\ (p' : \cdot) : \cdot = t'][\![f\ p \downarrow v]\!] \rightsquigarrow \Gamma}$

$\rightarrow$Inversion : $\dfrac{\Delta[\![g\ p \uparrow v]\!] \leftsquigarrow \Gamma}{\Delta[\![(\mathbf{invert}\ g)\ p \downarrow v]\!] \rightsquigarrow \Gamma}$

Fig. 5. Environment inference for linear programs. Again, the side condition (ψ) denotes the bidirectional first match policy as noted in bullet point (8).

$\boxed{\Delta[\![t \uparrow v]\!] \leftsquigarrow \Gamma}$ (for linear terms t)

$\leftarrow$Application : $\dfrac{\Delta[\![p' \downarrow v]\!] \rightsquigarrow \Gamma' \quad \Delta\Gamma' \vdash t' \downarrow v' \quad \Delta[\![p \downarrow v']\!] \rightsquigarrow \Gamma}{\Delta[f\ p' = t'][\![f\ p \uparrow v]\!] \leftsquigarrow \Gamma}$

$\leftarrow$Inversion : $\dfrac{\Delta[\![g\ p \downarrow v]\!] \rightsquigarrow \Gamma}{\Delta[\![(\mathbf{invert}\ g)\ p \uparrow v]\!] \leftsquigarrow \Gamma}$

Fig. 6. Inverse environment inference.

upwards. Furthermore, since the keyword `invert` can only appear in an application, there are only two rules.

4. Finally, in the $\uparrow$Application rule, the looming problem of inverse interpretation of functional programs emerges from hiding. The rule says that if the argument to an inverse function evaluated to some value v', and the body of the corresponding function in the source program evaluated to v' in the conventional direction because of a unique environment Γ', then the result of the inverse function is the arguments for the function in the source program as evaluated under Γ'.

5. The $\uparrow$Inversion rule says that inverting inverse interpretation is to resume computation in the conventional direction
   We can hide the problem of searching for Γ' in the rules for inverse interpretation. In the interest of separating concerns, we have separate rules about searching for context. The form is $\Delta[\![t \downarrow v]\!] \rightsquigarrow \Gamma$ and it reads "*in Δ, the linear term t evaluated to v because of the unique environment Γ*", and the details can be found in Fig. 5.

6. The $\rightarrow$Variable rule says that if x was a linear term, and it evaluated to v, it must have been because of the unique environment, containing a single binding $x \mapsto v$.

7. The $\rightarrow$Constructor rule says that the unique environment under which a constructor evaluated to a value is the composition of the unique (and disjoint by linearity) environments under which its parts evaluated.

8. The $\rightarrow$Cases rule, still requires the bidirectional first match policy ψ. See $\downarrow$Cases (bullet point (2)).

9. The $\rightarrow$Application and $\rightarrow$Inversion rules can be found in Fig. 5.

$$\boxed{\Delta\Sigma \vdash t : \tau}$$

$$\tau\text{Variable} : \dfrac{}{\Delta\{x \mapsto \tau\} \vdash x : \tau}$$

$$\tau\text{Constructor} : \dfrac{\Delta\Sigma_i \vdash p_i : \tau_i}{\Delta[\text{data } \tau = [c\ \tau_i]_j](\circ\Sigma_i) \vdash [c\ p_i] : \tau}$$

$$\tau\text{Cases} : \dfrac{\Delta\Sigma \vdash t : \tau \quad \Delta|p_i : [c\ \tau_i] \Downarrow \Sigma_i \quad \Delta\Sigma_i \circ \Sigma_j \vdash t_i : \tau'}{\Delta[\text{data } \tau = [c\ \tau_i]_j](\Sigma \circ \Sigma_j) \vdash \text{case } t : \tau \text{ of } p_i \to t_i : \tau'}$$

$$\tau\text{Application} : \dfrac{\Delta\Sigma \vdash p' : \tau_p \quad \Delta|p : \tau_p \Downarrow \Sigma_p \quad \Delta\Sigma_p \vdash t : \tau_t}{\Delta[f(p : \tau_p) : \tau_t = t]\Sigma \vdash f\ p' : \tau_t}$$

$$\tau\text{Inversion} : \dfrac{\Delta\Sigma \vDash g\ p : \tau}{\Delta\Sigma \vdash (\text{invert } g)\ p : \tau}$$

Fig. 7. Linear typing.

$$\boxed{\Delta\Sigma \vDash t : \tau}$$

$$\tau\text{InverseApplication} : \dfrac{\Delta\Sigma \vDash p' : \tau_t \quad \Delta|t : \tau_t \Uparrow \Sigma_t \quad \Delta\Sigma_t \vdash p : \tau_p}{\Delta[f\ (p : \tau_p) : \tau_t = t]\Sigma \vDash f\ p' : \tau_p}$$

$$\tau\text{InverseInversion} : \dfrac{\Delta\Sigma \vdash g\ p : \tau}{\Delta\Sigma \vDash (\text{invert } g)\ p : \tau}$$

Fig. 8. Inverse linear typing.

Because the rules for environment inference require linearity, we have given typing rules that are usual for linear typing [13,31]. The main judgement form is $\Delta\Sigma \vdash t : \tau$ and it reads, *"in the program Δ, the term t has type τ under Σ"*, where Σ is a mapping between variable names and type names. Moreover, just like the rules for interpretation, typing has a typing environment inference algorithm with the form $\Delta|t : \tau \Downarrow \Sigma$, which reads *"In the program Δ, we know that the linear term t has type τ because of the unique typing environment Σ"*.

As mentioned in Sect. 2, running a program corresponds to applying its main function to a value provided by the caller in an empty context. As such, a desirable property for programs to have is that this application yields a unique result, and that calling the inverted program on the result will yield said provided input. This property has been summarised in Theorems 1 and 2, and the nifty Corollary 1.

Theorem 1. *If t is a linear term then $\Delta\Gamma \vdash t \downarrow v$ if and only if $\Delta[\![t \downarrow v]\!] \rightsquigarrow \Gamma$.*

Proof. By induction on the syntax of t, we consider the derivations $\mathcal{D}$ of $\Delta\Gamma \vdash t \downarrow v$ and $\mathcal{C}$ of $\Delta[\![t \downarrow v]\!] \rightsquigarrow \Gamma$ respectively.

– Suppose t is a variable x, and $\mathcal{D}$ is a derivation of $\Delta\Gamma \vdash x \downarrow v$ for some v. Then, since t is linear and closed under Γ, we must have $\Gamma = \{x \mapsto v\}$. Hence, $\mathcal{C}$ must be a derivation of $\Delta[\![x \downarrow v]\!] \rightsquigarrow \{x \mapsto v\}$, and the $\to$Variable rule happens to agree with this conclusion.
  Conversely, $\mathcal{C}$ must still use the $\to$Variable rule. Consequently, $\mathcal{D}$ must be a derivation of $\Delta\{x \mapsto v\} \vdash x \downarrow v$ and can only use the $\downarrow$Variable rule, and we are done.

$$\boxed{\Delta|p:\tau \Downarrow \Sigma}$$

$$\Downarrow \text{Variable}: \frac{}{\Delta|x:\tau \Downarrow \{x \mapsto \tau\}}$$

$$\Downarrow \text{Constructor}: \frac{\Delta|p_i:\tau_i \Downarrow \Sigma_i}{\Delta[\text{data } \tau = [c\ \tau_i]]|[c\ p_i]:\tau \Downarrow (\circ\Sigma_i)}$$

Fig. 9. Typing environment inference.

$$\boxed{\Delta|t:\tau \Uparrow \Sigma}$$

$$\Uparrow \text{Variable}: \frac{}{\Delta|x:\tau \Uparrow \{x \mapsto \tau\}}$$

$$\Uparrow \text{Constructor}: \frac{\Delta|t_i:\tau_i \Uparrow \Sigma_i}{\Delta[\text{data } \tau = [c\ \tau_i]]|[c\ t_i]:\tau \Uparrow (\circ\Sigma_i)}$$

$$\Uparrow \text{Cases}: \frac{\Delta|t_i:\tau \Uparrow \Sigma_{t_i} \quad \Delta|p_i:\tau_p \Downarrow \Sigma_{p_i} \quad \Delta|t:\tau_p \Uparrow \Sigma}{\Delta|\text{case } t:\tau_p \text{ of } p_i \to t_i:\tau \Uparrow (\Sigma_{t_i} - \Sigma_{p_i}) \circ \Sigma} \quad (\psi)$$

$$\Uparrow \text{Application}: \frac{\Delta|p:\tau' \Uparrow \Sigma}{\Delta[f(\cdot:\tau):\tau' = \cdot]|fp:\tau \Uparrow \Sigma}$$

$$\Uparrow \text{Inversion}: \frac{\Delta|g\ p:\tau \Downarrow \Sigma}{\Delta|(\text{invert } g)\ p:\tau \Uparrow \Sigma}$$

Fig. 10. Inverse typing environment inference.

- If t is a pattern, then $\mathcal{D}$ is a derivation of $\Delta[\text{data } \tau = [c\tau_i]_j]\Gamma \vdash [c\ p_i] \downarrow [c\ v_i]$ for some constructor c, and (possibly 0) subpatterns p_i. As such, $\mathcal{D}$ can only use the $\downarrow$Pattern rule, in which case we may apply the induction hypothesis to each proof of $\Delta\Gamma \vdash p_i \downarrow v_i$ to get a derivation C_i of $\Delta[\![p_i \downarrow v_i]\!] \rightsquigarrow \Gamma_i$. Moreover, $\mathcal{C}$ can only use the $\rightarrow$Pattern rule with the $\mathcal{C}_i$ as its premises.
  In the converse case, we may use the induction hypothesis with each $\mathcal{C}_i$ to obtain proofs $\mathcal{D}_{0i}$. Now, since t is linear the variables in Γ_i cannot occur free in p_j whenever $i \neq j$. Hence, we may extend each proof $\mathcal{D}_{0i}$ of $\Delta\Gamma_i \vdash p_i \downarrow v_i$ to an equivalent proof including the composition of the environments, obtaining D_i of $\Delta \circ \Gamma_i \vdash p_i \downarrow v_i$. In this case $\mathcal{D}$ must use the $\downarrow$Variable rule and take exactly these $\mathcal{D}_i$ as premises. - We are done.
- Suppose t is a function applied in the conventional direction. Then t looks like $f\ p$, and $\mathcal{D}$ is a derivation of $\Delta\Gamma \vdash f\ p \downarrow v$, and so it must have used the $\downarrow$Application rule. As such, $\mathcal{D}$ must be constructed from a derivation $\mathcal{D}_1$ of $\Delta\Gamma \vdash p \downarrow v'$ and another derivation $\mathcal{D}_2$ of $\Delta(\text{unify}(v',p')) \vdash t' \downarrow v$ where p' and t' are the argument pattern and function body of f as defined in Δ. Furthermore, by the definition of $\text{unify}(v', p')$ and the fact that v' is a value (and thereby variable-free): If p' is a variable, then $\Delta(\text{unify}(v',p')) \vdash p' \downarrow v'$ holds by the $\downarrow$Variable rule, and otherwise, p' is a constructor and we can use the $\downarrow$Constructor rule to obtain the same proof. In either case, we can construct a derivation $\mathcal{D}_3$ of $\Delta(\text{unify}(v',p')) \vdash p' \downarrow v'$.
  Now, by the induction hypothesis on $\mathcal{D}_1$, we get a derivation $\mathcal{C}_1$ of $\Delta[\![p \downarrow v']\!] \rightsquigarrow \Gamma$, and by the induction hypothesis on $\mathcal{D}_2$, we get a derivation $\mathcal{C}_2$ of $\Delta[\![t' \downarrow v]\!] \rightsquigarrow \text{unify}(v',p')$. And finally, we can apply the $\rightarrow$Application rule to $\mathcal{C}_2$, $\mathcal{D}_3$ and $\mathcal{C}_1$ we obtain a derivation $\mathcal{C}$ of $\Delta[\![f\ p \downarrow v]\!] \rightsquigarrow \Gamma$.

Conversely, we can throw away $\mathcal{D}_3$ and use the induction hypothesis on $\mathcal{C}_1$ and $\mathcal{C}_2$ to reconstruct $\mathcal{D}_1$ and $\mathcal{D}_2$, which we may use reconstruct $\mathcal{D}$.

– Finally, t is a case statement. Hence, $\mathcal{D}$ is a derivation of $\Delta\Gamma \vdash$ case t' : τ of $p_i \to t_i \downarrow v_i$ and it must use the $\downarrow$Cases rule. So we get a proof $\mathcal{D}_{t'}$ of $\Delta\Gamma \vdash t' \downarrow v$ for some value v, and another proof $\mathcal{D}_i$ of $\Delta(\Gamma \circ \mathrm{unify}(v, p_i)) \vdash t_i \downarrow v_i$. Now, $\mathcal{C}$ has to be a derivation of $\Delta[\![\text{case } t' : \tau \text{ of } p_i \to t_i \downarrow v_i]\!] \leadsto \Gamma_i \circ \Gamma'$ where $\Gamma = \Gamma_i \circ \Gamma'$. $\mathcal{C}$ must furthermore use the $\to$Cases rule for which we shall provide the premises as follows: Because the derivation satisfies ψ, we can use the induction hypothesis on t_i with $\mathcal{D}_i$ to get corresponding $\mathcal{C}_i$ of $\Delta[\![t_i \downarrow v_i]\!] \leadsto (\Gamma \circ \mathrm{unify}(v, p_i))$ for each of the first premises of $\mathcal{C}$. Then, in each case, $\mathcal{C}_i$ contains the unifier of p_i with v, so of course $\Delta(\Gamma \circ \mathrm{unify}(v, p_i)) \vdash p_i \downarrow v$. The third premise is derived by the induction hypothesis with t' and $\mathcal{D}_{t'}$ and we are done. – The converse case is analogous. $\qquad\square$

Theorem 2. *Let $\Delta[(f(p : \tau_p) : \tau_t) = t.]$ be a program in which a function f has been declared, and consider two values v and w such that $\Delta\emptyset \vdash v : \tau_p$ and $\Delta\emptyset \vdash w : \tau_t$ holds. Then $\Delta\emptyset \vdash f\ v \downarrow w$ if and only if $\Delta\emptyset \vdash f\ w \uparrow v$.*

Proof. Suppose $\Delta\emptyset \vdash f\ v \downarrow w$, then the derivation must have used the $\downarrow$Application rule. Consequently, we get a derivation derivation of $\Delta\mathrm{unify}(v, p) \vdash t \downarrow w$. Now, by Theorem 1, we get another derivation of $\Delta[\![t \downarrow w]\!] \leadsto \mathrm{unify}(v, p)$, and from the definition of the most general unifier, we derive $\Delta\mathrm{unify}(v, p) \vdash p \downarrow v$. Since w is a value, clearly $\Delta\emptyset \vdash w \downarrow w$. So, we can apply the $\uparrow$Application rule to show that $\Delta\emptyset \vdash f\ w \uparrow v$. The converse proof is similar. $\qquad\square$

From this theorem and the $\downarrow$Invert rule follows that inversion is well-behaved:

Corollary 1. *Let Δ be a program, and f an arbitrary function defined in Δ. Then $\Delta\Gamma \vdash f\ v \downarrow w$ if and only if $\Delta\Gamma \vdash (\mathrm{invert}\ f)\ w \downarrow v$.*

4   Designing Invertible Semantics

Programs such as `first-inverse` from the introduction section, do not evaluate under conventional semantics, since its body is not a closed term. In order assign semantics to open terms, one can allow free *existential* variables (unification variables). To remain functional while doing so, requires us to deterministically find unique bindings (e.g. by unification) for such variables before they are used.

That is, functions could behave like Horn clauses which, by a separate program analysis, are known to succeed exactly once, and that all existential variables are bound (i.e., constrained to be equal to a ground term) by the time they are evaluated.

Such existential values allow us to defer a computation into a future that may provide additional information. And a lazily evaluated functional logic language may allow functions to complete the existential parts of such structures by unification at the time they are needed.

As an example, the following predicates (expressed in SWI Prolog) are semantically equivalent to the functions introduced in Sect. 1:

```
first(P, A)   :- P = pair(A, _).
second(P, B) :- P = pair(_, B).
swap(P, Q)    :- Q = pair(B, A), first(P, A), second(P, B).
```

When querying SWI Prolog about swap, it will try to unify the arguments with the rule for swap, and when it matches, infer a (possibly partial) structure. For instance a query might look like:

```
?- swap(pair(1,2), Q).
Q = pair(2, 1).
```

However, the control flow in Prolog is not limited in this direction. We may also ask the related query for the "argument" for swap, that may be swapped in to this particular structure:

```
?- swap(P, pair(2,1)).
P = pair(1, 2).
```

Now, consider the following Haskell program, which may be written in a particular style in the interest of being comparable

```
first  p = a where (a, _) = p
second p = b where (_, b) = p

swap    p = q
  where a = first  p
        b = second p
        q = (b, a)
```

which may naively be inverted as follows

```
first1_inverse  a = (a, _)
second1_inverse b = (_, b)

swap1_inverse q = p
  where  (b, a)  = q
         p       = second1_inverse b
         p       = first1_inverse  a
```

As discussed in Sect. 1 this does not work. However, it is somewhat surprising that it does not, since it worked for the Prolog program: The difference is that Prolog separates the concern of introducing a variable symbol and binding it to a value, and so bindings happen through a unification algorithm which computes a substitution that makes its operands equal. Haskell (and other functional languages) refrain from such symbolic liberation by introducing names and binding simultaneously. So called let-bindings, are immutable and a variable may never change its meaning during execution.

One possible solution to this problem is to allow names to be introduced independently of binding them to a value, using unification for binding exactly as in Prolog. For this purpose, we introduce the syntax ?x to mean the unbound variable x, and the syntax t1 <> t2 to mean the result of applying the most general unifier of t1 and t2 to either.

Equipped with these new operations, we can postpone anything that contains a unification variable until all of the information needed to compute it is available. For instance, we can rewrite the opposite swap program to

```
first2_inverse  a = (a, ?b)
second2_inverse b = (?a, b)

swap2_inverse q = p
  where  (b, a) = q
         ?p1     = second2_inverse b
         ?p2     = first2_inverse  a
         p       = ?p1 <> ?p2
```

It requires little effort to show that <> is both associative and commutative, and that it combines partial data structures (containing *"free"* parts) into equivalent complete (*"closed"*) data structures whenever the structures combined contain all of the information represented by the input structure.

5   Implementing Invertible Semantics

We have seen in Sect. 2.1 that in some cases, it is sufficient to extend the bi-directional first match policy of RFun and CoreFun to include information that is implicitly provided by the caller. To this end, we have developed a program analysis, based on the *available expressions analysis* specified in Nielson, Nielson, and Hankin [24], called *implicitly available arguments analysis* [15]. Based on this analysis, one can extend the judgements for evaluating programs with a statically available environment that contains bindings, available to, but not explicitly provided as arguments by the caller, and the side condition in Figs. 3 and 5 will be an extended notion of orthogonality that is allowed to look at the pattern in each case as well. This leads the way for a number of program transformations that eliminate certain branching constructions in which branching symmetry is not locally decidable (e.g. by syntactic orthogonality). For instance, the static environment of bindings can be utilised for transforming programs into equivalent programs that thread around this information explicitly. As an example, a program like add from Sect. 2, be transformed into one that copies one (or both) of its arguments in order to obtain branching symmetry like so

```
add_and_copy_first (m, n) =
  case m of
  ; [zero ] -> (m, n)
  ; [suc k] ->
    case add_and_copy_first (k, [suc n]) of
    ; (_, k+suc_n) -> (m, k+suc_n).
```

Where the underscore can be inferred in both directions because it is redundant, as m must unify with [suc k], and the underscore must unify with k.

Functions that provide this argument implicitly, like fibber from the same section, can be specialised to use the specialised version in order to become symmetric as well, like so

```
fibber_specialized_for_add_and_copy_first (m, n) =
  case add_and_copy_first (m, n) of
  ; (_, m+n) -> (m+n, m).
```

In general, reversibilisation introduces additional output, sometimes called *garbage*, due to its irrelevance to the user [8]. We call garbage that is specific to the algorithm implemented by a program *intensional garbage*. Similarly, we call garbage that is specific to the function implemented by a program *extensional garbage*. In a certain sense, that above does write a specialised version of add, that produces extensional garbage. However, it does so for intensional reasons: We are pattern matching on m, so its implicit availability is what makes the case statement first-match-symmetric. The transformation can be applied statically, up to bounded recursion and does not introduce a garbage globally [15]. The information it provides can also be used to improve the performance of inverse algorithms, by pruning the search space of algorithms, such as the one found in Fig. 5. In this regard, we conjecture that online partial evaluation can be used to eliminate branches from a case-statement that do not agree with the implicitly provided arguments in the opposite direction of interpretation. An extended type system could also use available expressions to generate a set of constraints in order to conservatively verify that the program complies with this extended notion of term-pattern orthogonality, and that ψ does not need to be checked at runtime in such cases.

In the last example from Sect. 4, the term ?p1 <> ?p2 is immediately closed, so ?p1 and ?p2 are really only *locally* existential variables. In this case, we can generalise the program transformation employed for add above, that turn globally existential variables into locally existential ones, by introducing locally extensional garbage that move the binding time closer to the point where the variable was introduced.

For instance, in the example, implicitly available arguments analysis eliminates the existential variables completely, since the specialisations are all essentially the identity function:

```
first_and_copy_second (a, b) = (b, a)
second_and_copy_first (a, b) = (a, b)

swap_specialised_for_the_copy_versions_of_first_and_Second q =
  let (b, a) = q
      p1      = (invert second_and_copy_first) (a, b)
      p2      = (invert second_and_copy_first) (b, a)
      p       = p1 <> p2 -- no free variables here.
```

The caveat of this kind of analysis is that it is syntax directed, and as seen with the map-f example in Sect. 2.1, this is not always sufficient.

Instead of a syntax directed analysis, we can instead produce a graph structure in the style of [20]. When combined with size-change termination, this could check if a function terminates in a unique case for each possible constructor in the data type definition for its input. However, it will be restricted to programs that we know are terminating in a particular sense.

6 Conclusion

The study of invertible computation has, historically, proven useful in understanding energy and entropy preservation, and in understanding information preserving transformations and transmission. However, there is still something to be learned about program inversion, in particular regarding how to make invertible programming less syntactically restrictive, and how to implement this in a reasonably efficient way.

To this end we presented Jeopardy, with user-definable algebraic data types and inverse function invocation. Here invertibility is a global property, that is ensured by static analysis. Since program invertibility is undecidable in general, all an invertibility analysis can hope to achieve is a reasonable approximation. In other words, any static analysis will split the expressible programs into three groups: those which are found to be invertible, those which are found to *not* be invertible, and those for which the analysis can provide no definite answer.

So far we have provided a reversible semantics for Jeopardy, in and effort to make globally invertible programs a conservative superset of reversible programs. We have presented these semantics and their proof of correctness.

Furthermore, we have investigated several competing ideas for designing and implementing the invertible semantics of Jeopardy. It is left as future work to determine to which extend Jeopardy to express a larger class of statically provable invertible functions.

When comparing to existing designs for reversible functional programming languages, such as RFun [28,32] and CoreFun [13], the introduction of choice by pattern matching in the forward direction introduces search in the form of backtracking under reverse interpretation. However, a set of operations such as ? and <> allows us, when applicable, to introduce pattern matching *without* introducing backtracking in inverted programs.

References

1. Abramov, S., Glück, R.: The universal resolving algorithm and its correctness: inverse computation in a functional language. Sci. Comput. Program. **43**(2–3), 193–229 (2002)
2. Bennett, C.H.: Logical reversibility of computation. IBM J. Res. Dev. **17**(6), 525–532 (1973)
3. Carette, J., Heunen, C., Kaarsgaard, R., Sabry, A.: With a few square roots, quantum computing is as easy as Pi. Proc. ACM Program. Lang. **8**(POPL), 546–574 (2024)
4. Dijkstra, E.W.: Program Inversion, pp. 54–57. Springer, Heidelberg (1979). https://doi.org/10.1007/BFb0014657
5. Futamura, Y.: Partial computation of programs. In: Goto, E., Furukawa, K., Nakajima, R., Nakata, I., Yonezawa, A. (eds.) RIMS Symposia on Software Science and Engineering. LNCS, vol. 147, pp. 1–35. Springer, Heidelberg (1983). https://doi.org/10.1007/3-540-11980-9_13
6. Giachino, E., Lanese, I., Mezzina, C.A.: Causal-consistent reversible debugging. In: Gnesi, S., Rensink, A. (eds.) FASE 2014. LNCS, vol. 8411, pp. 370–384. Springer, Heidelberg (2014). https://doi.org/10.1007/978-3-642-54804-8_26
7. Girard, J.Y.: Linear logic. Theor. Comput. Sci. **50**(1), 1–101 (1987)
8. Glück, R., Yokoyama, T.: Reversible computing from a programming language perspective. Theor. Comput. Sci. **953**, 113429 (2023)
9. Heunen, C., Kaarsgaard, R.: Bennett and Stinespring, together at last. In: Proceedings 18th International Conference on Quantum Physics and Logic (QPL 2021). Electronic Proceedings in Theoretical Computer Science, vol. 343, pp. 102–118. OPA (2021)
10. Heunen, C., Kaarsgaard, R.: Quantum information effects. Proc. ACM Program. Lang. **6**(POPL) (2022)
11. Heunen, C., Kaarsgaard, R., Karvonen, M.: Reversible effects as inverse arrows. In: Mathematical Foundations of Programming Semantics XXXIV, Proceedings. Electronic Notes in Theoretical Computer Science, vol. 341, pp. 179–199. Elsevier (2018)
12. Huffman, D.A.: Canonical forms for information-lossless finite-state logical machines. IRE Trans. Inf. Theory **5**(5), 41–59 (1959)
13. Jacobsen, P.A.H., Kaarsgaard, R., Thomsen, M.K.: CoreFun: a typed functional reversible core language. In: Kari, J., Ulidowski, I. (eds.) RC 2018. LNCS, vol. 11106, pp. 304–321. Springer, Cham (2018). https://doi.org/10.1007/978-3-319-99498-7_21
14. James, R.P., Sabry, A.: Theseus: a high level language for reversible computing (2014). Work in progress paper at RC 2014. www.cs.indiana.edu/~sabry/papers/theseus.pdf
15. Kristensen, J.T., Kaarsgaard, R., Thomsen, M.K.: Branching execution symmetry in jeopardy by available implicit arguments analysis. In: Norwegian Informatics Conference, NIK, vol. 1. 34th Norwegian ICT Conference for Research and Education, NIKT 2022 (2022, to appear)
16. Kristensen, J.T., Kaarsgaard, R., Thomsen, M.K.: Tail recursion transformation for invertible functions. In: Kutrib, M., Meyer, U. (eds.) RC 2023. LNCS, vol. 13960, pp. 73–88. Springer, Cham (2023). https://doi.org/10.1007/978-3-031-38100-3_6
17. Landauer, R.: Irreversibility and heat generation in the computing process. IBM J. Res. Dev. **5**(3), 261–269 (1961)

18. Lanese, I., Nishida, N., Palacios, A., Vidal, G.: CauDEr: a causal-consistent reversible debugger for erlang. In: Gallagher, J.P., Sulzmann, M. (eds.) FLOPS 2018. LNCS, vol. 10818, pp. 247–263. Springer, Cham (2018). https://doi.org/10.1007/978-3-319-90686-7_16

19. Laursen, J.S., Schultz, U.P., Ellekilde, L.P.: Automatic error recovery in robot assembly operations using reverse execution. In: 2015 IEEE/RSJ International Conference on Intelligent Robots and Systems (IROS), pp. 1785–1792. IEEE (2015)

20. Lee, C.S., Jones, N.D., Ben-Amram, A.M.: The size-change principle for program termination. In: Symposium on Principles of Programming Languages, POPL 2001, pp. 81–92. ACM (2001)

21. Lutz, C., Derby, H.: Janus: a time-reversible language. A letter to R. Landauer (1986). http://tetsuo.jp/ref/janus.pdf

22. Matsuda, K., Wang, M.: SPARCL: a language for partially invertible computation. J. Funct. Program. **34**, e2 (2024). https://doi.org/10.1017/S0956796823000126

23. McCarthy, J.: The inversion of functions defined by turing machines. In: Shannon, C.E., McCarthy, J. (eds.) Automata Studies. Princeton University Press (1956)

24. Nielson, F., Nielson, H.R., Hankin, C.: Principles of Program Analysis. Springer, Heidelberg (2015)

25. Schordan, M., Jefferson, D., Barnes, P., Oppelstrup, T., Quinlan, D.: Reverse code generation for parallel discrete event simulation. In: Krivine, J., Stefani, J.-B. (eds.) RC 2015. LNCS, vol. 9138, pp. 95–110. Springer, Cham (2015). https://doi.org/10.1007/978-3-319-20860-2_6

26. Schordan, M., Oppelstrup, T., Thomsen, M.K., Glück, R.: Reversible languages and incremental state saving in optimistic parallel discrete event simulation. In: Ulidowski, I., Lanese, I., Schultz, U.P., Ferreira, C. (eds.) RC 2020. LNCS, vol. 12070, pp. 187–207. Springer, Cham (2020). https://doi.org/10.1007/978-3-030-47361-7_9

27. Schultz, U., Bordignon, M., Stoy, K.: Robust and reversible execution of self-reconfiguration sequences. Robotica **29**(1), 35–57 (2011)

28. Thomsen, M.K., Axelsen, H.B.: Interpretation and programming of the reversible functional language. In: Symposium on the Implementation and Application of Functional Programming Languages, IFL 2015, pp. 8:1–8:13. ACM (2016)

29. Thomsen, M.K., Kaarsgaard, R., Soeken, M.: Ricercar: a language for describing and rewriting reversible circuits with ancillae and its permutation semantics. In: Krivine, J., Stefani, J.-B. (eds.) RC 2015. LNCS, vol. 9138, pp. 200–215. Springer, Cham (2015). https://doi.org/10.1007/978-3-319-20860-2_13

30. Voichick, F., Li, L., Rand, R., Hicks, M.: Qunity: a unified language for quantum and classical computing. Proc. ACM Program. Lang. **7**(POPL), 921–951 (2023)

31. Wadler, P.: Linear types can change the world! In: IFIP TC 2 Working Conference on Programming Concepts and Methods, pp. 347–359. North Holland (1990)

32. Yokoyama, T., Axelsen, H.B., Glück, R.: Towards a reversible functional language. In: De Vos, A., Wille, R. (eds.) RC 2011. LNCS, vol. 7165, pp. 14–29. Springer, Heidelberg (2012). https://doi.org/10.1007/978-3-642-29517-1_2

33. Yokoyama, T., Glück, R.: A reversible programming language and its invertible self-interpreter. In: Partial Evaluation and Program Manipulation, PEPM 2007, pp. 144–153. ACM (2007)

LinguaQuanta: Towards a Quantum Transpiler Between OpenQASM and Quipper

Scott Wesley$^{(\boxtimes)}$

Dalhousie University, Halifax, NS, Canada
scott.wesley@dal.ca

Abstract. As quantum computing evolves, many important questions emerge, such as how best to represent quantum programs, and how to promote interoperability between quantum program analysis tools. These questions arise naturally in the design of quantum transpilers, which translate between quantum programming languages. In this paper, we take a step towards answering these questions by identifying challenges and best practices in quantum transpiler design. We base these recommendations on our experience designing *LinguaQuanta*, a quantum transpiler between Quipper and OpenQASM. First, we provide categorical specifications for quantum transpilers, which aim to encapsulate the core principles of the UNIX philosophy. We then identify quantum circuit decompositions which we expect to be useful in quantum transpilation. With these foundations in place, we then discuss challenges faced during the implementation of LinguaQuanta, such as ancilla management and *stability under round translation*. To show that LinguaQuanta works in practice, a short tutorial is given for the example of quantum phase estimation. We conclude with recommendations for the future of LinguaQuanta, and for quantum software development tools more broadly.

Keywords: Quantum Computing · Source-to-Source Translation · Pipeline Architecture

1 Introduction

In 2018, a perspective article in Quantum Views proclaimed the dawn of quantum computing [29]. At this time IBM had released a small, but universal, quantum computer [25] which reignited interest in quantum programming. Over the five years following this landmark development, researchers have developed considerably faster *superconducting* quantum computers with physical storage exceeding 1000 qubits [6]. In turn, the landscape of quantum programming languages has also exploded, with many new languages emerging (e.g., [5,7,12,16,37]) each with their own compilers and development tools (e.g., [26,30,38]).

© The Author(s), under exclusive license to Springer Nature Switzerland AG 2024
T. Æ. Mogensen and Ł. Mikulski (Eds.): RC 2024, LNCS 14680, pp. 142–160, 2024.
https://doi.org/10.1007/978-3-031-62076-8_10

As we move forward from the dawn of quantum computing, we are now confronted with many important questions, such as how to represent quantum programs, and how best to promote interoperability between quantum program analysis tools. In classical computing, this problem was solved by intermediate representation (IR) languages such as LLVM-IR [22], and by standard logical formulations such as constrained Horn clauses [14]. In this paper, we focus on the first approach, and consider IR languages for quantum computing. One popular contender in this area is the OpenQASM assembly language [11,12].

For OpenQASM to act as an IR language, we must first develop tools to perform source-to-source translation from popular quantum programming languages, to the OpenQASM language. Such source-to-source translators are known as *transpilers*. To date, there has been very little focus on quantum transpilation (outside of circuit optimization), so best practices in this area are poorly defined. However, prior work, such as [23], highlights the need for quantum transpilation in the design and prototyping of new compilation tools. In this paper we set out to identify best practices and challenges for quantum transpilation, through practical experience with a concrete example.

To this end, we propose *LinguaQuanta*, a quantum transpiler between the functional Quipper language [16], and the imperative OpenQASM language. Focus is given to OpenQASM 3 [12], but legacy support is provided for the 2.0 standard [11]. Section 2 reviews quantum computation. Section 3 provides categorical specifications for an abstract quantum transpiler, as informed by best practices in software development. These specifications prioritize small transpilation tools built using compositional design principles. Section 4 identifies standard quantum circuit decomposition techniques which prove useful in LinguaQuanta. Section 5 identifies challenges faced during the design of LinguaQuanta, such as reconciling different measurement abstractions, and circumventing the lack of ancillas in OpenQASM. Section 6 provides an overview of LinguaQuanta, using the quantum phase estimation algorithm as an example. Section 7 discusses lessons learned from the development of LinguaQuanta, and plots a course for future research. Appendices can be found in the extended version of the paper [39].

2   A Brief Introduction to Quantum Computation

This section provides a brief introduction to quantum computation. For a more comprehensive introduction, we refer the reader to [28]. We assume the reader is familiar with linear algebra. If not, we refer the reader to an introductory text such as [2]. A *quantum bit (qubit)* can be in a state of 0 or 1, similar to classical computation. We denote these basis states $|0\rangle$ and $|1\rangle$ respectively, and represent these states by the two-dimensional vectors $|0\rangle = \begin{bmatrix} 1 & 0 \end{bmatrix}^T$ and $|1\rangle = \begin{bmatrix} 0 & 1 \end{bmatrix}^T$. A qubit $|\psi\rangle$ can also exist in a *superposition* of both $|0\rangle$ and $|1\rangle$ [28]. Formally, $|\psi\rangle = \alpha |0\rangle + \beta |0\rangle$ for α and β complex numbers satisfying $|\alpha|^2 + |\beta|^2 = 1$.

An n-qubit quantum system has 2^n possible basis states, corresponding to the 2^n binary strings of length n. As before, the system may also be in a superposition of basis states. The squared norms of these coefficients must still sum to 1. As an example, the basis states for a 2-qubit quantum system are as follows.

$$|00\rangle = \begin{bmatrix} 1 & 0 & 0 & 0 \end{bmatrix}^T \quad |01\rangle = \begin{bmatrix} 0 & 1 & 0 & 0 \end{bmatrix}^T \quad |10\rangle = \begin{bmatrix} 0 & 0 & 1 & 0 \end{bmatrix}^T \quad |11\rangle = \begin{bmatrix} 0 & 0 & 0 & 1 \end{bmatrix}^T$$

An arbitrary 2-qubit state is a linear combination $\alpha|00\rangle + \beta|01\rangle + \gamma|10\rangle + \rho|11\rangle$ satisfying $|\alpha|^2 + |\beta|^2 + |\gamma|^2 + |\rho|^2 = 1$.

In quantum mechanics, the measurement of a qubit $|\psi\rangle$ collapses $|\psi\rangle$ to either state $|0\rangle$ or state $|1\rangle$. This means that if $|\psi\rangle = \alpha|0\rangle + \beta|1\rangle$, it is impossible to determine the values of α and β. However, it is known that the probability $|\psi\rangle$ collapses to $|0\rangle$ is $|\alpha|^2$ and the probability that $|\psi\rangle$ collapses to $|1\rangle$ is $|\beta|^2$, where as before $|\alpha|^2 + |\beta|^2 = 1$ [28]. More generally, if $|\psi\rangle$ can be written as $\alpha|\psi_1\rangle|0\rangle + \beta|\psi_2\rangle|1\rangle$, then the probability of measuring the last qubit in state $|0\rangle$ is $|\alpha|^2$ and the probability of measuring the last qubit in state $|1\rangle$ is $|\beta|^2$.

2.1 Unitary Operations on Quantum Systems

Quantum systems evolve according to unitary dynamics. In quantum computation discrete unitary operations are used to encode computational problems. Before defining unitary operations, some results from linear algebra must be recalled (see, e.g. [2]). The *adjoint* of an $n \times n$ complex matrix M is the conjugate transpose of M, denoted $M^\dagger = \overline{M}^T$. An $n \times n$ matrix M is said to be unitary if $MM^\dagger = M^\dagger M = I$, that is, $M^{-1} = M^\dagger$. For example, both rotations and global phases are examples of unitary operations (see the extended version). The $n \times n$ unitary matrices form a group under multiplication denoted $\mathcal{U}(n)$.

A quantum operation on an n-qubit quantum system is a linear, invertible operator that sends quantum states to quantum states. It turns out that the n-qubit quantum operators are precisely the matrices in $\mathcal{U}(2^n)$ [28]. For example, there exists an operator $X \in \mathcal{U}(2)$ such that $X|0\rangle = |1\rangle$ and $X|1\rangle = |0\rangle$. It is not hard to see that X is the quantum generalization of a classical not-gate. It follows from this analogy that $X^\dagger = X$ since $X^\dagger$ is the inverse to X.

In reversible classical computation, another important gate is the controlled not-gate, denoted $C(X)$ [28]. The $C(X)$ gate belongs to $\mathcal{U}(4)$ and negates the second bit if and only if the first bit is set to 1. That is to say $C(X)|00\rangle = |00\rangle$, $C(X)|01\rangle = |01\rangle$, $C(X)|10\rangle = |11\rangle$, and $C(X)|11\rangle = |10\rangle$. It follows that $C(X)$ is also unitary. The matrix $C(X)$ is the *controlled* version of X. It turns out that every operator $G \in \mathcal{U}(2^n)$ has a controlled version $C(G) \in \mathcal{U}(2^{n+1})$ defined by $C(G) = \begin{bmatrix} I & 0 \\ 0 & G \end{bmatrix}$, where I is the $(2^n) \times (2^n)$ identity matrix.

2.2 Compositionality of Quantum Systems

Quantum operators can be composed in sequence and in parallel, just as gates can be composed in classical computation. The case of sequential composition is the most straightforward. Given operators $M \in \mathcal{U}(2^n)$ and $N \in \mathcal{U}(2^n)$, there exists an operator $N \circ M \in \mathcal{U}(2^n)$ such that applying $N \circ M$ is equivalent to first

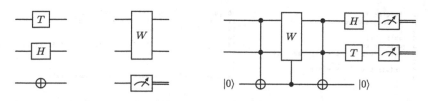

(a) Unitary and measurement gates.   (b) A simple string diagram.

Fig. 1. A collection of quantum gates, and a circuit constructed from those gates.

applying M and then applying N. This sequential composition corresponds to matrix multiplication. It follows almost immediately that $(N \circ M)^\dagger = M^\dagger \circ N^\dagger$.

Parallel composition is more complicated. To understand this challenge, it is sufficient to look at the composition of two quantum systems, each with a single qubit. Before composition, each system has two basis states: $|0\rangle$ and $|1\rangle$. After composition, every combination of the two qubits must be considered. This yields four states: $|00\rangle$, $|01\rangle$, $|10\rangle$, and $|11\rangle$. In general, the composition of an n state system with an m state system yields an $n \cdot m$ state system consisting of all pairwise combinations of states [28]. In the case of qubits, an n qubit system has 2^n states, an m qubit system has 2^m states, and their parallel composition has 2^{n+m} states. This parallel composition, denoted $\otimes$, is known as the Kronecker tensor product and extends to matrix composition in the following way [28].

$$\begin{bmatrix} c_{1,1} & c_{1,2} & \cdots & c_{1,n} \\ c_{2,1} & c_{2,2} & \cdots & c_{2,n} \\ \vdots & \ddots & \vdots & \vdots \\ c_{m,1} & c_{m,2} & \cdots & c_{m,n} \end{bmatrix} \otimes M = \begin{bmatrix} c_{1,1}M & c_{1,2}M & \cdots & c_{1,n}M \\ c_{2,1}M & c_{2,2}M & \cdots & c_{2,n}M \\ \vdots & \ddots & \vdots & \vdots \\ c_{m,1}M & c_{m,2}M & \cdots & c_{m,n}M \end{bmatrix}$$

It follows that $(M \otimes N)(|\psi\rangle \otimes |\varphi\rangle) = (M |\phi\rangle) \otimes (N |\varphi\rangle)$ as desired. By convention $|j\rangle \otimes |k\rangle$ is the concatenation $|jk\rangle$ of j with k. For example, $|0\rangle \otimes |11\rangle = |011\rangle$.

2.3   Circuit Semantics and Compositionality

The formalism discussed so far admits a graphical calculus corresponding to string diagrams in a monoidal category [32]. We use these diagrams freely. However, the resulting diagrams are similar to classical circuits, and it suffices that the reader only knows how to interpret string diagrams as matrices. We do not assume any familiarity with category theory, but we do note that it forms a great basis for compositional reasoning with diagrammatic calculi (e.g., [18,21,32]).

In quantum circuit diagrams, horizontal wires represents program state. A wire consisting of a single horizontal line indicates a single qubit. A wire consisting of two horizontal lines indicates a single classical bit. If $|\varphi\rangle$ is written to the left of a wire, then the wire is initialized in state $|\varphi\rangle$. Likewise, if $|\varphi\rangle$ is written to the right of a wire, then the wire is asserted to be in state $|\varphi\rangle$, before the

```
1  OPENQASM 3;                              10  pow(pow(2,2)) @ ctrl @ t x[0], phi;
2  include "stdgates.inc";                  11  pow(pow(2,1)) @ ctrl @ t x[1], phi;
3                                           12  ctrl @ t x[2], phi;
4  qubit phi;                               13
5  qubit[3] x;                              14  h x[0]; cp(pi / 2) x[1], x[0]; cp(pi / 4) x[2], x[0];
6  reset x[0]; reset x[1]; reset x[2];      15  h x[1]; cp(pi / 2) x[2], x[1];
7                                           16  h x[2];
8  h x[0]; h x[1]; h x[2];                  17
9                                           18  measure x[0]; measure x[1]; measure x[2];
```

Fig. 2. An implementation of QPE in OpenQASM 3 with 3 digits of accuracy.

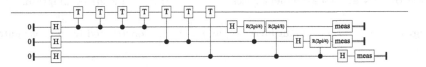

Fig. 3. An implementation of QPE in Quipper with 3 digits of accuracy.

wire is discarded. A wire with a state on both the left and the right represents a temporary variable, and is referred to as an *ancilla* in quantum computation. For example, $|0\rangle === |0\rangle$ depicts a classical ancilla initialized in state $|0\rangle$, and $|1\rangle \text{——} |1\rangle$ depicts a quantum ancilla initialized in state $|1\rangle$.

Quantum operators are depicted as boxes. The qubits acted on by the operator are depicted as wires passing through the box. Since each operator is unitary, the number of wires entering and leaving each box are always equal. Two exceptions to this rule are the not-gate, which is often depicted as an $\oplus$, and the measurement gate, which is often depicted as a gauge. See Fig. 1a for examples of the T and H gates (each acting on one qubit), the W gate (acting on two qubits), the X gate (acting on one qubit), and a single qubit measurement.

Circuits are then constructed from the parallel and sequential composition of these basic building blocks. Sequential composition is depicted by joining wires end-to-end. Parallel composition is depicted by running wires parallel to one-another. Additionally, controls are depicted by running a vertical wire from a dot (on each control qubit) to the controlled gate. See Fig. 1b for a circuit making use of a controlled W gate and two doubly-controlled X gates.

2.4   An Introduction to OpenQASM and Quipper

Two popular languages for quantum algorithm design are OpenQASM 3 [12] and Quipper [16]. Both languages take a circuit-based approach to quantum computation. In this model, a program first declares a finite set of qubits, and optionally, a finite set of classical bits (*cbits*). In OpenQASM, the set of qubits is immutable, whereas in Quipper, the set of qubits can expand or shrink. Using these declarations, a program then specifies a sequence of unitary gates, classical gates, and measurement gates, which are applied to the qubits and cbits in order. In OpenQASM 3, these operations are specified in an imperative style, whereas in Quipper, these operations are declared in a functional style[1]. The functional

---

[1] Quipper also offers an imperative interface to these functional primitives.

programs written in Quipper are categorically equivalent to the circuit diagrams outlined in Sect. 2.3. For ease of presentation, this correspondence is used to depict all Quipper programs as circuit diagrams. In contrast, OpenQASM 3 programs are presented syntactically, as is conventional for imperative languages. Note that this section does not provide a comprehensive introduction to the features of either language. Instead, this section only highlights the language features which are relevant to the design of LinguaQuanta.

For concreteness, we consider the *Quantum Phase Estimation (QPE)* algorithm, which uses quantum computation to approximate the eigenvalues of a predetermined operator U. We take U to be the diagonal gate T, which has entries 1 and $e^{i\pi/4}$ Standard implementations of the QPE algorithm, for both OpenQASM 3 and Quipper, can be found in Fig. 2 and Fig. 3 respectively.

The first major distinction between OpenQASM and Quipper is the way in which qubits are modelled. In OpenQASM, qubits are variables that are referenced by name. For example, the statement `qubit phi;` on line 4 of Fig. 2 declares a new qubit bound to the identifier `phi`. In contrast, Quipper models qubits as wires in circuit diagrams. Each wire in the circuit diagram is assigned a unique index, which is used to reference the corresponding qubit throughout the program. By default, these indices are consecutive starting from zero. For example, the uppermost wire in Fig. 3 has index 0 and corresponds to the variable `phi` in Fig. 2. However, Quipper also supports ancilla initialization, ancilla termination, qubit preparation (casting a cbit to a qubit), and adjoint qubit preparation (casting a qubit in a pure state to a cbit), which can yield non-consecutive indices. In most Quipper programs, only ancilla initialization and ancilla termination are used. These operations are indicated by vertical bars, as illustrated by the bottom three wires in Fig. 3. It should be noted that OpenQASM does not support ancilla management nor qubit preparation, and consequently, the number of qubits in an OpenQASM program is static across program execution.

In terms of unitary operators, OpenQASM and Quipper are quite similar. Both languages allow users to define their own unitary operators, though only OpenQASM allows for the semantics to be declared alongside the syntactic definition. Often, these interfaces are unnecessary, since both OpenQASM and Quipper provide standard libraries for unitary operators (in OpenQASM, these gates are imported explicitly using an include statement, as illustrated on line 2 of Fig. 2). For example, `cx c, t;` is an OpenQASM instruction to apply the standard library controlled not-gate to target qubit t with control qubit c. In Quipper, this same instruction would be represented by an arity-2 gate acting on wires c and t. A full list of standard operators can be found in the extended version. Of note are the rotational gates provided by both languages. A rotational gate $R(\theta)$ is a family of unitary operators defined by a parameter θ. In Quipper, rotational gates are restricted to a single parameter, whereas OpenQASM 3 gates allow for arbitrarily many parameters. For example, OpenQASM 3 provides the $\mathcal{U}(\theta, \rho, \lambda)$ gate which can be used to implement any single-qubit unitary operator up to global phase (i.e., multiplication by a complex scalar of norm 1). In the case of Fig. 8, the rotation operator `cp(pi / 2) x[2], x[1]` on line 15 implements a controlled rotation by a global phase of $\pi/2$.

Both OpenQASM 3 and Quipper allow for unitary operators to be controlled and inverted. Additionally, OpenQASM 3 allows for unitary operators to be exponentiated. In OpenQASM 3, these transformations are indicated using *modifier* annotations. An example of a control modifier appears in the statement `ctrl @ t x[2], phi` on line 12 of Fig. 2, which applies $C(T)$ to `x[2]` $\otimes$ `phi`. Likewise, an example of an *inverse modifier* would be `inv @ t phi`, which applies $T^\dagger$ to qubit `phi`. Finally, an example of a *power modifier* appears in the statement `pow(2) @ ctrl @ t x[1], phi` on line 11 of Fig. 2 which applies $C(U)^2$ to `x[1]` $\otimes$ `phi`. The control modifiers and inverse modifiers in Quipper are depicted graphically as described for circuit diagrams.

Finally, both OpenQASM and Quipper provide primitives for measurement. The semantics of these primitives reflect the fact that OpenQASM is imperative, whereas Quipper is functional. The `bit c = measure q;` statement in OpenQASM can be understood as applying an impure function `measure` to qubit q with output cbit c. In this statement, c is the measurement result, and q collapses according to c as a side-effect of `measure`. This is used on line 18 of Fig. 3, to obtain the first three bits of the eigenvalue approximation. Conversely, the measure gate in Quipper is a pure function, which takes as input a qubit q, and returns as output a cbit c which corresponds to the collapsed state of q. In Fig. 3, this corresponds to the three `meas` boxes which convert wires from qubits to cbits.

3   Pipeline Designs and Categorical Specifications

The *UNIX Philosophy* is a design philosophy which aims to develop software that is simple, general, intelligible, and above all else, effective for programming researchers [27]. In [31], the UNIX Philosophy was summarized as follows: (1) write programs that do one thing and do it well; (2) write programs that work together; (3) write programs to handle text streams. Since transpilation is a classical task, we have followed the UNIX philosophy and designed LinguaQuanta as a collection of simple utilities which compose together to achieve various modes of transpilation. These components are as follows.

1. ELIMCTRLS: A tool to inline control modifiers in an OpenQASM program.
2. ELIMINVS: A tool to inline inversion modifiers in an OpenQASM program.
3. ELIMPOWS: A tool to inline power modifiers in an OpenQASM program.
4. ELIMFUNS: A tool to inline built-in OpenQASM functions.
5. QASMTOQUIP: A tool to transpile from OpenQASM to Quipper.
6. QUIPTOQASM: A tool to transpile from Quipper to OpenQASM.
7. REGMERGE: A tool to combine all registers in an OpenQASM program.
8. TOLSC: A tool to transpile OpenQASM 2.0 to the subset described in [38].
9. TOQASM2: A tool to convert between OpenQASM 2.0 and 3.

Details on how tools compose can be found on the LinguaQuanta GitHub page[2].

The composition of tools in LinguaQuanta can be understood more abstractly as the composition of functions mapping source languages to target languages.

---

[2] https://github.com/onestruggler/qasm-quipper.

Then, it is natural to ask what categorical properties should tool composition satisfy. For concreteness, consider the functions $L_1 \xrightarrow{T_1} L_2 \xrightarrow{T_2} L_1$ where T_1 denotes QASMToQUIP and T_2 denotes QUIPToQASM. Then $T_2 \circ T_1$ is a round translation starting from OpenQASM. It is tempting to require that $T_2 \circ T_1 = 1$, but this is an unreasonable assumption. For example, if T_1 decomposes a gate G, then T_2 must reassemble G exactly. Instead, we require that T_2 is a reflexive inverse to T_1. The reflexive inverse is one of the many generalized inverses in algebra [3], defined by the properties $T_1 \circ T_2 \circ T_1 = T_1$ and $T_2 \circ T_1 \circ T_2 = T_2$. It follows immediately that $(T_2 \circ T_1)^2 = T_2 \circ T_1$ and $(T_1 \circ T_2)^2 = T_1 \circ T_2$. In other words, $T_2 \circ T_1$ and $T_1 \circ T_2$ are idempotent operators [21]. In practice, this means that translating back-and-forth many times between OpenQASM and Quipper is a stable operation, that will not induce arbitrarily large increases in file size.

We can refine these specifications by taking a closer look at each tool in LinguaQuanta. We note that each tool is of the form $L_1 \xrightarrow{R} IR_1 \xrightarrow{T} IR_2 \xrightarrow{W} L_2$ where R is a *reader* that parses the input program, T is a *transformer* that rewrites the parsed input, and W is a *writer* that generates an output program from the result of T. In the case where $(W \circ T \circ R)$ is QASMToQUIP, we have that L_1 is the syntax for the OpenQASM language, IR_1 is an abstract representation of an OpenQASM program, IR_2 is an abstract representation of a Quipper program, and L_2 is the syntax for the Quipper ASCII format.

Returning to our original example, let $L_1 \xrightarrow{R_1} IR_1 \xrightarrow{T_1} IR_2 \xrightarrow{W_2} L_2$ denote QASMToQUIP and $L_2 \xrightarrow{R_2} IR_2 \xrightarrow{T_2} IR_1 \xrightarrow{W_1} L_1$ denote QUIPToQASM. Then consider the equation $(W_1 \circ T_2 \circ R_2) \circ (W_2 \circ T_1 \circ R_1) = (W_1 \circ T_2 \circ T_1 \circ R_1)$. This states that composing QASMToQUIP with QUIPToQASM is equivalent to composing the underlying transformers, as if the composition formed a single executable. This is clearly a desirable property. One way to ensure this property is to require that $R_1 \circ W_1 = 1$ and $R_2 \circ W_2 = 1$. These new properties state that reading back what was previously written constitutes a no-op. Categorically, R_1 is a retract of W_1 and R_2 is a retract of W_2 [21].

Then for any pair of LinguaQuanta tools $L_1 \xrightarrow{R_1} IR_1 \xrightarrow{T_1} IR_2 \xrightarrow{W_2} L_2$ and $L_2 \xrightarrow{R_2} IR_2 \xrightarrow{T_2} IR_1 \xrightarrow{W_1} L_1$, we require that the following rewrite rules hold.

1. **Inversion (i).** $T_i \circ T_j \circ T_i = T_i$ for $i, j \in \{1, 2\}$ with $i \neq j$.
2. **Retraction (i).** $R_i \circ W_i = 1$ for $i \in \{1, 2\}$.

These specifications guide the design of each tool.

Of course, these specifications alone are not sufficient to ensure the correctness of LinguaQuanta. For example, any pair of constant functions C_1 and C_2 satisfy the requirements of **Inversion (1)** and **(2)**. Clearly, these specifications must be extended with a semantic notion of correctness.

For the purposes of a translations pipeline, it suffices to assume that both L_1 and L_2 have the same semantic domain. Then there exists an object SEM with morphisms $L_1 \xrightarrow{[\![-]\!]_1} SEM \xleftarrow{[\![-]\!]_2} L_2$ corresponding to the semantic interpretations of language L_1 and language L_2, respectively. At the very least, each translation should preserve the semantic interpretation of its input. In the case of

QASMTOQUIP, this means that $[\![-]\!]_2 \circ W_2 \circ T_1 \circ R_1 = [\![-]\!]_1$. Note, however, that these specifications do not ensure that reading an input, and then writing it back also preserves semantics. For robust pipelines, this is also a reasonable assumption. In the case of OpenQASM, this would mean that $[\![-]\!]_1 \circ W_1 \circ R_1 = [\![-]\!]_1$. Based on these observations, we require that the following semantic rules hold.

3. **Preservation (i).** $[\![-]\!]_j \circ W_j \circ T_i \circ R_i = [\![-]\!]_i$ for $i, j \in \{1, 2\}$ with $i \neq j$.
4. **Fluency (i).** $[\![-]\!]_i \circ W_i \circ R_i = [\![-]\!]_i$ for $i \in \{1, 2\}$.

We refer to instances of rule 3 as **Preservation** since they specify that each translation should preserve the semantic interpretation of its input text. We refer to instances of rule 4 as **Fluency** since they specify that each pair of readers and writers should maintain the semantic interpretation of their own language. While **Fluency** is not *necessary* for program correctness, it is likely the case that a lack of fluency indicates a yet undiscovered bug in the pipeline.

4   Decompositions for Quantum Transpilation

A large part of transpilation (i.e., defining each T_i) is to decompose gates from a source language into gates of a target language. Naturally, this intersects with prior work on quantum circuit decomposition. For simple gates, the required decompositions exist in the literature [1,10,12,13,28,33,34], as outlined in the extended version. However, the general nature of control and rotation decomposition necessitates more general solutions. In particular, we rely on the following four decomposition techniques to handle multi-controls and arbitrary rotations.

1. Recall $e^{U^\dagger V U} = U^\dagger e^V U$ for any unitary U. Therefore, given any two rotations $R_A(\theta) = e^{iA\theta}$ and $R_B(\theta) = e^{iB\theta}$, if $B = V^\dagger A V$, then the following holds.

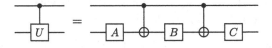

   This provides a change of basis between rotation operators.
2. Assume that $U = CXBXA$ and $CBA = I$. Then the following holds by [4].

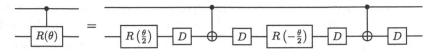

Let $R(\theta)$ be a rotation and D self-inverse. If $V = DXD$, $V \cdot R(\theta) \cdot V = R(-\theta)$, $R(0) = I$, and $R(\theta) \cdot R(\gamma) = R(\theta + \gamma)$, then the following holds by taking $U = R(\theta)$, $C = D$, $B = D \cdot R(-\theta) \cdot D$, and $A = D \cdot R(\theta)$.

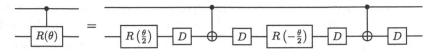

This provides decompositions for many rotations with single controls.

3. A *Toffoli-like gate* is a three-qubit unitary U equipped with two-qubit states $|\varphi_1\rangle$ through to $|\varphi_4\rangle$ such that the following equations hold.

$$U|000\rangle = |\varphi_1\rangle|0\rangle \qquad\qquad U|100\rangle = |\varphi_2\rangle|0\rangle$$
$$U|010\rangle = |\varphi_3\rangle|0\rangle \qquad\qquad U|110\rangle = |\varphi_4\rangle|1\rangle$$

If U is Toffoli-like, then the following holds by [33].

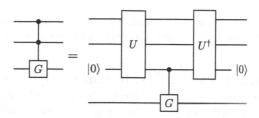

This decomposition can be applied until only a single control remains. Note that the choice of U is not arbitrary, and may impact circuit efficiency.

4. Assume that $U = V^2$. Then the following holds by [4,36].

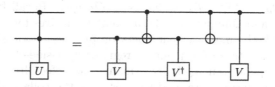

Note that Decomposition 2 also applies to user-defined rotations, provided that the end-user specifies D. In the current version of LinguaQuanta, the list of supported rotations, and their corresponding D operators, is hard-coded.

5   Challenges Faced and Proposed Solutions

Many aspects of LinguaQuanta are routine, such as rewriting gates via known decompositions, or inlining built-in OpenQASM 3 functions. However, certain differences between OpenQASM 3 and Quipper give rise to design problems for which the solutions are far less obvious. In this section, we state these design challenges, and summarize our proposed solutions.

Approximating the Identity on Round Translation. As outlined in Sect. 3, it is unreasonable to require that LinguaQuanta acts as the identity function on round translations. However, it is still desirable to minimize the distance between the round translation function and the identity function. One reason why round translations fail to act as the identity function is that the decomposition of unitary operators is not invertible. For this reason, we attempt to minimize the number of unitary decompositions in LinguaQuanta. In particular, we have implemented every Quipper gate in an OpenQASM library named quipgates. Furthermore, we have backported all OpenQASM 3 gates to OpenQASM 2.0, so that neither Quipper gates nor OpenQASM 3 gates require decompositions

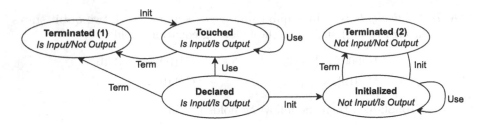

Fig. 4. A DFA to infer the state of a Quipper wire. The alphabet consists of Init, Term, and Use. Missing edges indicate one-way transitions to an error state.

when translated to OpenQASM 2.0. By minimizing the number of decompositions in LinguaQuanta, we also reduce the risk of faults in our implementation (i.e., smaller code surface), while also improving traceability when debugging LinguaQuanta. These techniques should be applicable to any pair of quantum programming languages with distinct gate sets, and support for user-defined unitary operators.

Translating OpenQASM Measurements to Quipper. Recall from Sect. 2.4, that OpenQASM 3 and Quipper provide different primitives for qubit measurement. In OpenQASM, the measurement operator produces a classical bit as output, and collapses the state of a quantum register as a side-effect. In contrast, the measurement operator in Quipper remains side-effect free by first collapsing the state of a quantum wire, and then casting the collapsed quantum wire to a classical wire. It is clear that the semantics of OpenQASM subsumes the semantics of Quipper. To capture the semantics of OpenQASM in Quipper, we introduce the following circuit.

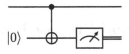

This circuit first prepares an entangled pair of qubits from the wire under measurement, and then measures the second wire in the pair to produce a classical wire as output while collapsing the first wire via entanglement.

Typed Wires and Ancillas in OpenQASM. Recall from Sect. 2.4, that the Quipper circuit model allows for new wires to be allocated (or deallocated) on-the-fly via ancilla management. However, OpenQASM does not support ancilla qubits. Therefore, we have implemented an OpenQASM 3 function with the same semantics as the ancilla allocation and deallocation gates in Quipper. Our goal is to recover all ancilla management data, including the total number of wires in use at the start and end of the circuit. In addition to better approximating a round translation, this also allows us to validate the ancilla management code generated by LinguaQuanta, which facilitates bug detection in LinguaQuanta. To this end, we associate with each register in OpenQASM a deterministic finite-state machine (DFA) of the form shown in Fig. 4. This DFA tracks the allocation state of each conceptual wire, and detects invalid ancilla management (e.g., double initialization, or use before initialization). Essentially, this collection of DFA's form a product DFA indexed by qubits, where the state of each component depends only on the operations that act locally on the associated qubit. In addition to ancilla management, Quipper also supports type-conversion, which is unsupported in OpenQASM. For example, measurement in Quipper casts a quantum wire to a classical wire, whereas measurement in OpenQASM simple produces a new classical register. To overcome this limitation, we make use of shadow memory, as commonly seen in classical program instrumentation [35]. At a high-level, shadow memory allows more than one memory cell to be associated with a single memory address, often to store metadata. In the case of LinguaQuanta, every quantum register can be shadowed by a classical register. Dually, every classical register can be shadowed by a quantum register. These registers are allocated on-the-fly to minimize memory overhead, but are never reclaimed by LinguaQuanta.

Ensuring Controls Remain Inlined. Since OpenQASM 3 and Quipper both support controlled unitary operators, then translating controls between these two languages is straight-forward. However, the OpenQASM 2.0 language does not offer such a feature. This means that when translating from OpenQASM 3 to OpenQASM 2.0, it is necessary to first eliminate all control modifiers. However, the Quipper library already implements most of the control decompositions required for OpenQASM 2.0 legacy support. To avoid rewriting well-tested code, LinguaQuanta performs all control elimination on the level of Quipper programs. This means that control elimination is not possible on the side of OpenQASM. If a new control is introduced during or after the translation from Quipper to OpenQASM, there is no way to eliminate the control. This means that in addition to our categorical requirements, we must also impose the syntactic requirement that pipeline components do not introduce new controls. Here, a control is called *new*, if an uncontrolled gate is translated to one or more controlled gates. Currently, this requirement is enforced manually. In the future, we would like to provide some guarantee for this property, either through formal verification or light-weight formal methods.

6   LinguaQuanta by Example

The design of LinguaQuanta was motivated by real-world examples in quantum program compilation and analysis. In this section, we begin by discussing once such real-world example. Through this example, each tool in the LinguaQuanta pipeline is motivated and described. Following this example, the central tools QASMTOQUIP and QUIPTOQASM are explored in more detail, using the QPE algorithm introduced in Sect. 2.4. Further examples and explanation can be found in the LinguaQuanta documentation.

6.1   An Example Pipeline in LinguaQuanta

In recent work by LeBlonde et. al [23], a prototype of LinguaQuanta was used to compile Quipper programs to fault-tolerant quantum hardware. The goal of this

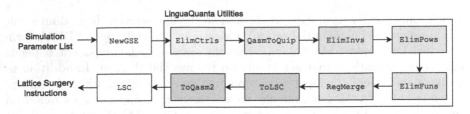

Fig. 5. The translation pipeline implemented in [23]. In this pipeline orange boxes indicate pre-processing, blue boxes indicate post-processing, and green boxes indicate additional steps for legacy support.

paper was to estimate the cost of running certain quantum chemistry simulations on realistic quantum hardware. The simulations were written in Quipper using the NewGSE techniques described in [20]. However, the fault-tolerant hardware targeted by LeBlonde et. al makes use of surface codes, for which operations are performed using lattice surgery instructions rather than high-level quantum gates (see [38], for an introduction to logical lattice instructions). Typically, the Lattice Surgery Compiler (LSC) [38] is used to compile to this lattice surgery instruction set. However, the LSC only supports a subset of OpenQASM 2.0 as its input language. To bridge this gap, LeBlonde et. al made use of LinguaQuanta to translate each simulation to the LSC subset of the OpenQASM 2.0 language.

The pipeline used by LeBlonde et. al can be found in Fig. 5. Recall from Sect. 5 that OpenQASM 2.0 does not support control modifiers. Similarly, Open-QASM 2.0 does not support inverse modifiers, power modifiers, or function calls. As outlined in Sect. 5, control elimination is performed on the level of Quipper programs, since the Quipper library implements many of the control decompositions necessary for OpenQASM 2.0 support. For this reason, the pre-processing stage in the pipeline applies ELIMCTRLS to obtain a Quipper program with only the supported controlled operations. Next, QASMTOQUIP is applied to obtain an OpenQASM 3 program without any controls. The post-processing on this OpenQASM 3 program begins by applying ELIMINVS, ELIMPOWS, and ELIM-FUNS to obtain a valid OpenQASM 2.0 program. Next, REGMERGE is applied to obtain a valid LSC program[3] Following the post-processing stage, TOLSC and TOQASM2 are applied to reformat the output syntax to conform with the LSC subset of the OpenQASM 2.0 language. The full pipeline is expanded in more detail by the `quip_to_lsc.sh` script in LinguaQuanta.

The key step in Fig. 5 is to translate the pre-processed Quipper into a valid OpenQASM 3 program. In this sense, QUIPTOQASM is the most important LinguaQuanta tool featured in Fig. 5. More generally, all LinguaQuanta pipelines will rely on either QUIPTOQASM or QASMTOQUIP to realize a translation between the two languages. For this reason, it is worthwhile exploring QUIP-TOQASM and QASMTOQUIP in more detail. As outlined in Sect. 3, these tools are reflexive inverses which compose to an idempotent operator. To illustrate these tools and their properties, the concrete example of QPE is explored.

---

[3] The LSC requires that all qubits (resp. cbits) appear as a single array.

```
1   OPENQASM 3;
2   include "stdgates.inc";
3   include "quipfuncs.inc";
4
5   qubit[1] input_qwires;
6   qubit qtmp_0; QInit0(qtmp_0);
7   qubit qtmp_1; QInit0(qtmp_1);
8   qubit qtmp_2; QInit0(qtmp_2);
9
10  h qtmp_0; h qtmp_1; h qtmp_2;
11
12  ctrl @ t qtmp_0, input_qwires[0];
13  ctrl @ t qtmp_0, input_qwires[0];
14  ctrl @ t qtmp_0, input_qwires[0];
15  ctrl @ t qtmp_0, input_qwires[0];
16  ctrl @ t qtmp_1, input_qwires[0];
17  ctrl @ t qtmp_1, input_qwires[0];
18  ctrl @ t qtmp_2, input_qwires[0];
19
20  h qtmp_0; cp(π/4.0) qtmp_1, qtmp_0; cp(π/8.0) qtmp_2, qtmp_0;
21  h qtmp_1; cp(π/4.0) qtmp_2, qtmp_1;
22  h qtmp_2;
23
24  bit ctmp_3; ctmp_3 = QMeas(qtmp_0);
25  bit ctmp_4; ctmp_4 = QMeas(qtmp_1);
26  bit ctmp_5; ctmp_5 = QMeas(qtmp_2);
27
28  ctmp_3 = CDiscard(); ctmp_4 = CDiscard(); ctmp_5 = CDiscard();
```

Fig. 6. A translation of Fig. 3 using QuipToQasm. Variables have been renamed.

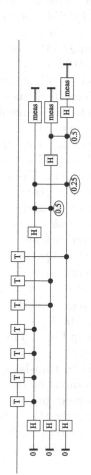

Fig. 7. A round-trip translation of Fig. 3.

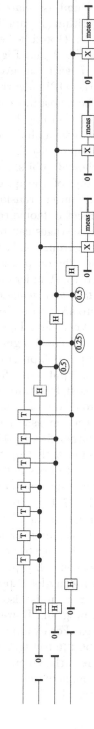

Fig. 8. A translation of Fig. 2 using QasmToQuip. Note that in Quipper X is used rather than $\oplus$.

6.2   Round Translation of the QPE Algorithm

Let U $|\psi\rangle$ and associated eigenvector algorithm. Recall from Sect. 2.4, that the QPE algorithm [19] applies the k-qubit quantum Fourier transform [9] to determine θ from U and $|\psi\rangle$ with an accuracy of k binary digits.

As in Fig. 2 and Fig. 3, we will consider the case where U is the unitary operator T with eigenvector $|1\rangle$ and associated eigenvalue $e^{i\pi/4}$. Then given $k = 3$, the QPE algorithm will produce an estimate of $\pi/4$ up to 3 binary digits. The algorithm can be broken down into three stages. In the first stage (see lines 6–8 in Fig. 2), 3 qubits are prepared in a uniform superposition (i.e., a state from which all 3-qubit sequences can be observed with equal probability). In the second stage (see lines 10–12 in Fig. 2), the T operator is controlled by each of these 3 qubits, and applied to $|\phi\rangle$ exactly 2^{2-j} times, where $j \in \{0, 1, 2\}$ is the index of the qubit. In the third stage (see lines 14–16 in Fig. 2), the quantum Fourier transform is applied to the 3 qubits, to obtain a state whose measurement outcome corresponds to an estimate of $\pi/4$ up to 3 binary digits. These three stages can be clearly visualized in Fig. 3.

Starting from Fig. 3, an OpenQASM 3 program is obtained by running QUIP-TOQASM. The output is illustrated in Fig. 6. Superficially, this output is very similar to the handcrafted OpenQASM program illustrated in Fig. 2. *In particular, the three phases of the QPE algorithm are still distinguishable.* However, there are two major differences. First, note the new function calls QInit0, QMeas, and CDiscard. These functions are defined in LinguaQuanta's quipfuncs.inc library, and allow LinguaQuanta to encode ancilla management metadata within an OpenQASM 3 program. Next, note the input_qwires register. This is used to encode all input wires from the Quipper circuit. Then, for each ancilla, a variable prefixed by qtmp is introduced. These registers stay associated with the wires throughout the entire translation. The first time a type conversion occurs (e.g., at each measurement), a new register is declared, which becomes associated with the wire. In this example, all such registers are prefixed by ctmp. The pair of qtmp and ctmp form the shadow memory outlined in Sect. 5. Note that LinguaQuanta does not depend on variable names to recover ancilla data.

To illustrate a round translation, QASMTOQUIP is then applied to the program in Fig. 7. It is interesting to note that the circuit in Fig. 7 is almost identical to the circuit in Fig. 3. Ancilla recovery in Fig. 7 was facilitated by the ancilla management functions in Fig. 6, together with the ancilla DFA outlined in Fig. 4. The one difference to note is that the $R(2\pi/k)$ gates in Fig. 2 have been replaced by doubly controlled phase gates in Fig. 7. This is because $R(2\pi/k)$ is equivalent to a controlled global phase of $2\pi/k$.

Of course, it is also possible to translate an OpenQASM 3 program to a Quipper program. However, this direction often results in larger changes to the source text. For example, the Quipper program in Fig. 8 is obtained by applying QASMTOQUIP to Fig. 2. Qualitatively, there are two large changes to note. First, each reset in the OpenQASM 3 program has been replaced by qubit termination, followed immediately by qubit initialization. This is equivalent to resetting a qubit. Second, all measurements have been replaced by the measurement circuits presented in Sect. 5. Note that the results are immediately discarded, since the measurement results are never used by the original OpenQASM program.

7 Discussion and Related Work

To the best of our knowledge, we are the first to develop a quantum transpiler with the goal of interoperability, rather than circuit optimization. However, LinguaQuanta is not the first tool to translate between OpenQASM and Quipper. For example, the PyZX circuit optimizer [17] is capable of taking OpenQASM and Quipper programs, both as inputs and as outputs. However, the language support in PyZX is minimal, with many gates unsupported, and no plans for measurement and classical control. Furthermore, tools such as PyZX rely on circuit extraction, and therefore make no guarantee about preserving the structure of the input program. In this respect, LinguaQuanta is the first tool of its kind.

A major challenge faced in the development of LinguaQuanta was support for parameterized unitary gates, otherwise known as *rotation gates* in Quipper. In both Quipper and OpenQASM, users may define their own so-called rotation gates. In OpenQASM, this is achieved through the composition of single-qubit rotations and controlled-not gates. In Quipper, rotations are simply one-parameter opaque gates. It is not hard to see that these rotation gates may not define a rotation about a *fixed axis*. This freedom often contradicts the assumptions a developer might make about rotation gates. For example, one might expect that given a rotation gate $R(\theta)$, the relation $R(\theta) \cdot R(\gamma) = R(\theta + \gamma)$ always holds. However, the R gate in Quipper, as taken from the quantum Fourier transform [15], instead satisfies $R(\theta^{-1}) \cdot R(\gamma^{-1}) = R((\theta + \gamma)^{-1})$. From a compilation and program analysis point-of-view, this lack of standardization is a serious concern.

We note that an important development in classical program design was the introduction of abstract data types (ADTs) [24]. ADTs allow developers to work with common data types, such as lists and arrays, without concern for implementation details. In turn, these ADTs can then be used by compilers and tools to reason compositionally about the program under analysis. For example, consider the gate $C(R(\theta))$ where $R(\theta)$ is an unknown unitary parameterized by an angle $\theta \in [0, 2\pi)$. One might hope that Decomposition 2 in Sect. 4 would yield an implementation for $C(R(\theta))$ using the standard gate set and $R(\theta)$. However, this decomposition requires that $R(0) = I$, $R(\theta) \cdot R(\gamma) = R(\theta + \gamma)$, and $V \cdot R(\theta) \cdot V = R(-\theta)$ for some self-inverse unitary V. Therefore, a compiler would require further specifications about $R(\theta)$ for the decomposition to be possible. Based on such examples, we argue that quantum programming languages are in need of *abstract rotation types*. Abstract rotation types would provide a taxonomy for the parameterized unitary gates used in quantum programming, together with first-order specifications. These types would act as a contract between the developer and the compiler, allowing for better optimizations. Based on our experiments, we start this discussion by proposing a list of abstract specifications.

1. **Zero is Identity:** $R(0) = I$.

2. **Negation is Inversion:** $R(\theta) \cdot R(-\theta) = I$, or $R(\theta)^{-1} = R(-\theta)$.
3. **Negation by G-Conjugation:** $G^{-1} \cdot R(\theta) \cdot G = R(-\theta)$ for some gate G.
4. **Commutativity:** $R(\theta) \cdot R(\gamma) = R(\gamma) \cdot R(\theta)$.
5. **Additivity:** $R(\theta) \cdot R(\gamma) = R(\theta + \gamma)$.
6. **Inverse Addivity:** $R(\theta^{-1}) \cdot R(\gamma^{-1}) = R((\theta + \gamma)^{-1})$.
7. **p-Periodicity:** $R(\theta) = R(\theta + kp)$ for all $k \in \mathbb{N}$.

Dependencies between these properties suggest a hierarchy of abstract rotations. This hierarchy differs from equation theories of quantum circuits (e.g., [8]), since abstract rotations may abstract away details such as the axes of rotation.

Whereas the lack of abstract rotation types is a limitation of all languages, several other limitations we encountered were entirely language-specific. For example, the Quipper framework can generate self-inverse gates with inverse modifiers, but will eliminate those same modifiers when reading back the circuit. This means that the reader is not a retraction of the writer in Quipper. From a semantic perspective, this is inconsequential, but may lead to unexpected behaviour when fit into a program analysis pipeline. Furthermore, whereas Quipper-related tools support angles of arbitrary precision [30], the internal representation used by Quipper is double-precision. For many applications, double-precision is insufficient, though an end-user be unaware of this discrepancy. Finally, we note the lack of ancillas in OpenQASM. The reason stated for this design choice is that qubit allocation is too expensive at runtime. However, OpenQASM is intended as a language for all stages of quantum compilation, including algorithm specification. Thus, OpenQASM couples ancilla management with algorithm specification, and fails to separate concerns. As shown in this paper, recursion-free ancilla allocation can be resolved at compile-time. An interesting direction for future work is to reason about ancillas in the presence of recursion at compile-time.

The current version of LinguaQuanta is limited to the features required to compile Quipper programs to surface code instructions via the OpenQASM tool in [38]. In future work, we plan to extend and improve the design and implementation of LinguaQuanta as follows:

1. Support for hierarchically-defined and opaque unitary gates;
2. Improved power modifier support;
3. Constant value propagation and bounded iteration;
4. White-box pipeline fuzzing and empirical evaluations;
5. Refined categorical foundations.

See the extended version for further details.

Acknowledgements. We would like to thank Xiaoning Bian for his help during the early development stages of LinguaQuanta, and Peter Selinger for his perspectives on the categorical specification of LinguaQuanta. This research was sponsored in part by the United States Defense Advanced Research Projects Agency (DARPA) under the Quantum Benchmarking program, contract # HR001122C0066.

References

1. Amy, M., Maslov, D., Mosca, M., Roetteler, M.: A meet-in-the-middle algorithm for fast synthesis of depth-optimal quantum circuits. Trans. Comput.-Aided Des. Integr. Circuits Syst. **32**(6), 818–830 (2013)
2. Axler, S.: Linear Algebra Done Right, 3rd edn. Springer, Cham (2014). https://doi.org/10.1007/978-3-319-11080-6
3. Baksalary, O.M., Trenkler, G.: The Moore-Penrose inverse: a hundred years on a frontline of physics research. Eur. Phys. J. H **46**, 2102–6467 (2021)
4. Barenco, A., et al.: Elementary gates for quantum computation. Phys. Rev. A **52**, 3457–3467 (1995)
5. Bichsel, B., Baader, M., Gehr, T., Vechev, M.: Silq: a high-level quantum language with safe uncomputation and intuitive semantics. In: PLDI, pp. 286–300. ACM (2020)
6. Choi, C.Q.: An IBM quantum computer will soon pass the 1,000-qubit mark. IEEE Spectrum (2022). Accessed 12 June 2022
7. Circ (2023). https://quantumai.google/cirq. Accessed 13 June 2022
8. Clement, A., Heurtel, N., Mansfield, S., Perdrix, S., Valiron, B.: A complete equational theory for quantum circuits. In: LICS, pp. 1–13 (2023)
9. Coppersmith, D.: An approximate Fourier transform useful in quantum factoring. Technical report RC19642, IBM, 1994
10. Crooks, G.E.: Gates, states, and circuits. Technical report 014, Berkeley Institute for the Theoretical Sciences, 2022
11. Cross, A.W., Bishop, L.S., Smolin, J.A., Gambetta, J.M.: Open quantum assembly language, 2017
12. Cross, A., et al.: OpenQASM 3: a broader and deeper quantum assembly language. ACM Trans. Quantum Comput. **3**(3) (2022)
13. Giles, B., Selinger, P.: Exact synthesis of multiqubit Clifford+T circuits. Phys. Rev. A **87**, 032332 (2013)
14. Grebenshchikov, S., Lopes, N.P., Popeea, C., Rybalchenko, A.: Synthesizing software verifiers from proof rules. In: PLDI, pp. 405–416. ACM (2012)
15. Green, A.S., Lumsdaine, P.L.F., Ross, N.J., Selinger, P., Valiron, B.: An introduction to quantum programming in Quipper. In: Dueck, G.W., Miller, D.M. (eds.) RC 2013. LNCS, vol. 7948, pp. 110–124. Springer, Heidelberg (2013). https://doi.org/10.1007/978-3-642-38986-3_10
16. Green, A.S., Lumsdaine, P.L., Ross, N.J., Selinger, P., Valiron, B.: Quipper: a scalable quantum programming language. SIGPLAN Not. **48**(6), 333–342 (2013)
17. Kissinger, A., van der Wetering, J.: PyZX: large scale automated diagrammatic reasoning. EPTCS **318**, 230–242 (2020)
18. Kissinger, A., Zamdzhiev, V.: Quantomatic: a proof assistant for diagrammatic reasoning. In: Felty, A.P., Middeldorp, A. (eds.) CADE 2015. LNCS (LNAI), vol. 9195, pp. 326–336. Springer, Cham (2015). https://doi.org/10.1007/978-3-319-21401-6_22
19. Kitaev, A.: Quantum measurements and the abelian stabilizer problem, 1995
20. Kornell, A., Selinger, P.: Some improvements to product formula circuits for Hamiltonian simulation, 2023
21. Mac Lane, S.: Categories for the Working Mathematician. Springer, New York (2010). https://doi.org/10.1007/978-1-4757-4721-8
22. Lattner, C., Adve, V.: LLVM: a compilation framework for lifelong program analysis & transformation. In: CGO, pp. 75–88. IEEE (2004)

23. LeBlond, T., Dean, C., Watkins, G., Bennink, R.S.: Realistic cost to execute practical quantum circuits using direct Clifford+T lattice surgery compilation, 2023
24. Liskov, B., Zilles, S.: Programming with abstract data types. SIGPLAN Not. **9**(4), 50–59 (1974)
25. Mandelbaum, R.: Five years ago today, we put the first quantum computer on the cloud. Here's how we did it. IBM Blog (2021). Accessed 12 June 2022
26. McClean, J.R., et al.: OpenFermion: the electronic structure package for quantum computers. Quantum Sci. Technol. **5**(3), 034014 (2020)
27. McIlroy, M.D., Pinson, E.N., Tague, B.A.: UNIX time-sharing system: foreword. Bell Syst. Tech. J. **57**(6), 1899–1904 (1978)
28. Nielsen, M.A., Chuang, I.L.: Quantum Computation and Quantum Information. Cambridge University Press, Cambridge (2011)
29. Ross, N.J.: The dawn of quantum programming. Quantum Views **2**, 4 (2018)
30. Ross, N.J., Selinger, P.: Optimal ancilla-free Clifford+T approximation of z-rotations. Quantum Inf. Comput. **16**(11–12), 901–953 (2016)
31. Salus, P.: A Quarter Century of UNIX. Addison-Wesley Professional, Boston (1994)
32. Selinger, P.: A survey of graphical languages for monoidal categories. In: Coecke, B. (eds.) New Structures for Physics. Lecture Notes in Physics, LNCS, vol. 813, pp. 289–355. Springer, Berlin, Heidelberg (2010). https://doi.org/10.1007/978-3-642-12821-9_4
33. Selinger, P.: Quantum circuits of T-depth one. Phys. Rev. A **87**, 042302 (2013)
34. Selinger, P.: The Quipper System (2014). https://www.mathstat.dal.ca/~selinger/quipper/doc/. Accessed 06 June 2023
35. Seward, J., Nethercote, N.: Using Valgrind to detect undefined value errors with bit-precision. In: USENIX ATC, pp. 17–30. USENIX Assoc. (2005)
36. Sleator, T., Weinfurter, H.: Realizable universal quantum logic gates. Phys. Rev. Let. **74**(20), 4087–4090 (1995)
37. Microsoft Azure Quantum Team. Announcing the Microsoft quantum development kit (2017). https://cloudblogs.microsoft.com/. Accessed 01 July 2023
38. Watkins, G., et al.: A high performance compiler for very large scale surface code computations, 2023
39. Wesley, S.: LinguaQuanta: towards a quantum transpiler between OpenQASM and Quipper (extended), 2024

Connecting Reversible and Classical Computing Through Hybrid SSA

Lukas Gail[(✉)] and Uwe Meyer

Technische Hochschule Mittelhessen, Wiesenstr. 14, 35390 Giessen, Germany
{lukas.gail,uwe.meyer}@mni.thm.de

Abstract. Despite the numerous benefits of reversible computing, non-reversible systems remain relevant in the real world. There are cases where reversibility is even detrimental, for example when performing lossy data compressions, where the removal of information is inherently required. For reversible systems to be more broadly adopted, they need to be able to interact with non-reversible systems in one way or another.

To allow for seamless co-operation between both paradigms, we propose the integration of optional non-reversibility as a first-class citizen into reversible programming languages to create what we call hybrid programming languages. A hybrid programming language can express both reversible and non-reversible computations in a single host language.

This paper describes the hybrid static single assignment form HSSA. Based on the principles of RSSA, HSSA puts reversibility and determinism first, while providing facilities to allow for explicit nondeterminism in either direction.

This also includes forward-nondeterminism while maintaining the useful properties of symmetry and invertibility.

Keywords: reversible computing · reversible programming languages · partial reversibility · intermediate languages · static single assignment

1 Introduction

Reversible computing is an alternative computing approach in which programs can be executed both forwards and backwards. Reversible algorithms can be inverted to produce an algorithm that computes the inverse function. This means that reversible programs compute bijective functions.[1]

Reversible computing promises substantial benefits over traditional computing, including the ability to save energy by avoiding the Landauer effect [9] and the fact that development of an algorithm automatically also provides a reverse algorithm. Many use cases such as reverse debugging [6] or high-performance computing [4] show the potential of reversible computing.

---

[1] Still, as shown by Glück and Yokoyama even non-bijective functions can be computed by reversible machines since any function can be made into a bijection by adding enough additional output data [8].

T. Æ. Mogensen and Ł. Mikulski (Eds.): RC 2024, LNCS 14680, pp. 161–178, 2024.
https://doi.org/10.1007/978-3-031-62076-8_11

Rooted in ambitions to reduce energy consumption of processors due to Landauer's principle [5], research on reversible computing concerns all layers of computing ranging from hardware to programming languages, as well as information and computability theory.

Fundamentally, reversible computing is about determinism. A common notion about the defining difference between reversible and classical computing is that the former is deterministic in both execution directions while the latter is only deterministic in one direction.

In [7] Glück and Yokoyama classify computing approaches based on their (non-)determinism in forwards and backwards direction into the four categories (D, D), (D, N), (N, D), and (N, N).

1. (D, N) contains classical programming languages that are only deterministic in forwards direction, but nondeterministic backwards.
2. (D, D) contains computations that are deterministic in both execution directions and therefore contains reversible programming languages.
3. (N, N) programs are not deterministic in either execution direction. Logic programming languages can be considered to fall into this category.
4. (N, D) is a peculiar class of programs that are only deterministic in backwards direction, but non-deterministic when executed forwards.

As can be seen in this brief description, programming languages can be placed into exactly one of these categories. The reversible programming language Janus [15] for example falls into (D, D), while classical programming languages such as C are categorized as (D, N).

One kind of programming language that is rarely considered are programming languages able to express more than one category of computations. For example, such a programming language could be able to express both reversible (D, D) bijections and non-reversible (D, N) functions in the same program and have them interact. We categorize such a language as (D, *). What distinguishes a (D, *) language from (D, N) is the fact that in (D, *), individual procedures can be proven to be either (D, D) or (D, N), while such a classification is not possible for procedures in a (D, N) language. We call a programming language that can express more than one category 'hybrid'. The partially reversible language Sparcl can be considered a hybrid (D, *) programming language [10].

The aim of hybrid approaches is to create a unified framework for expressing classical and reversible computations, allowing to express program transformations such as reversibilization as a transformation of a program in a hybrid language into a program of the same hybrid language.

Based on insights gained from the reversible static single assignment form RSSA [11], we propose the hybrid intermediate language HSSA. With the inclusion of explicit information loss, i.e., backwards-nondeterminism, we create a hybrid intermediate language that can express (D, D) as well as (D, N) computations. Moreover, with also including forwards-nondeterminism we restore symmetry by also enabling the representation of (N, N) and (N, D) computations, making HSSA a (*, *) language.

The remainder of this paper is organized as follows: In Sect. 2 we define the principles guiding the design of a hybrid intermediate language. In Sect. 3 we define the hybrid (*, *) intermediate language HSSA. In Sect. 4 we show how invalid HSSA programs with implicit nondeterminism can automatically be transformed into valid HSSA using only explicit nondeterminism. We conclude by outlining future work in Sect. 5.

2   Principles of a Hybrid Intermediate Language

Intermediate languages serve an important purpose in compiler construction to simplify code generation and optimization. To achieve this, intermediate languages usually are kept small and only have few and simple language constructs. Complicated user-facing features are compiled down to the simplified intermediate language and can then be analyzed and transformed, before finally being translated to the actual target architecture. Code analysis and transformation is made simple by only having to handle the core of the computational model.

For similar reasons, intermediate languages are also useful for research. They are able to capture the core of a computing approach, allowing us to focus on the essentials. This is why we want to advance hybrid computing models by introducing an appropriate intermediate language.

Since programming languages are usually deterministic, we believe that a hybrid intermediate language should also be primarily deterministic. Nondeterminism (and therefore non-reversibility and information loss) should only exist when used explicitly rather than the other way around. This makes hybrid programs easy to analyze regarding their reversibility for both automated tools as well as users. This leads us to the first principle guiding the design of a hybrid intermediate language:

Principle 1: Programs in a hybrid programming language should be reversible unless nondeterministic constructs are used explicitly.

Consequently, hybrid programming languages should use the general established techniques of reversible programming languages. One such technique is the finalization of variables to consume and transform information. Finalization is the inverse of initialization and undefines a variable during execution. While initializations compute values and assign them to a variable, finalizations uncompute values and mark the end of the variable's lifetime. On program inversion, finalizations and initializations switch roles. For languages that allow updating variables, there also is the concept of reversible updates [15]. A applies state changes to a variable using an injective operator.

A common abstraction of intermediate languages is static single assignment (SSA) code [13]. Static single assignment as a language concept dictates that every variable has exactly one associated assignment. Note that this only affects the static semantics of a SSA language, and not the dynamic semantics. Specifically, an assignment to a variable can be executed more than once through the usage of loops. This property is useful because it simplifies connecting variable usages to their unique defining statement, aiding optimizations such as constant propagation. It also causes the language to be functional in nature since any variables are inherently immutable [1].

For reversible computing, there is the reversible static single assignment form RSSA [11]. In the past, RSSA has proven to be a very suitable intermediate representation for optimizations and program analysis [3]. This is in line with the use of SSA forms for optimization of non-reversible languages [12].

RSSA takes SSA a step further and supports reversibility by extending the concept of static single assignment to also apply to finalization, making RSSA a static single finalization form. Variables are finalized by information preserving statements, which can be reversed. On inversion or reverse execution, finalizations take on the role of assignments and vice versa, so that the inverse of a RSSA program still follows the rules of static single assignment. Given the emphasis on reversibility, hybrid SSA should also employ static single finalization. To intentionally let information leave the system, an explicit instruction that does not preserve information should be used to finalize variables.

For backwards deterministic flowchart languages, it is important to preserve branching information at join points in the control flow graph. Specifically, this means that the information about which branch lead to any given join point must be preserved. RSSA achieves this with a combination of two restrictions: Firstly, it restricts labels to be used as a jump target exactly once, essentially causing the language to be a "static single jump" form. Secondly, at join points of two branches in the control flow graph a condition is used to uncompute the bit of information indicating which edge the control flow came from. On reverse execution, this condition determines which branch to take. Figure 1 depicts the RSSA instructions used to declare jumps and jump targets.

	Unconditional	Conditional
Jump/Exit	$\rightarrow L_1(a)$	$a > 0 \rightarrow L_1(a)L_2$
Jump Target/Entry	$L_1(a) \leftarrow$	$L_1(a)L_2 \leftarrow a > 0$

Fig. 1. Entries and Exits in RSSA

Unconditional jumps behave as expected from jumps in classical languages and pass control flow to the label L_1. Unconditional entries on the other hand can be compared to label definitions. Conditional jumps are also fairly straightforward. The condition on the left $(a > 0)$ decides whether control flow is passed to L_1 when the condition is true or to L_2 otherwise. Conditional entries on the other hand are less intuitive: They correspond to two simultaneous label definitions with an added assertion. The assertion must evaluate to true when a jump to L_1 was used to arrive at that entry point and to false if L_2 was used.

As part of RSSA's control flow the flow of information through the program is also handled in a reversible manner. Rather than variables implicitly existing in multiple basic blocks, information is passed between them through parameterized labels, as can also be seen in Fig. 1. Jump targets declare how many parameters they expect, and the respective jumps must supply that exact number of arguments. Entry instructions initialize the parameters defined in them to the value that was passed to the label, while passing a variable in a jump consequently finalizes that variable. At the end of every basic block, all initialized variables must have been finalized to ensure the information contained within is preserved when moving execution to the next block. This implementation of information flow fits well with the reversibility-first principle, which is why we also use it for HSSA.

The use of entry conditions is not entirely suited for a hybrid variant of RSSA. RSSA enforces that control flow must always be backwards deterministic, while a hybrid program can allow for nondeterministic control flow. Thus, a hybrid SSA variant needs to be more flexible in how the branching information is handled.

In our past work on analyzing and optimizing RSSA code, the property of invertibility proved to be very useful. Invertibility can be leveraged by implementing optimization techniques for just one execution direction and reuse them by inverting the program instead of implementing them twice. This property should be preserved for hybrid computing, leading us to the second principle:

Principle 2: A well-formed hybrid program can be inverted into a well-formed hybrid program of the same language. Inverting an inverted program should produce the original program.

This means that even non-reversible (D, N) programs need to be expressible in our hybrid SSA form. Inverting a (D, N) program produces a (N, D) program, which is nondeterministic going forwards, but deterministic in reverse. If a language can express both forwards and backwards nondeterminism, it can also combine both and express (N, N) programs. Consequently, while (D, *) languages are also considered 'hybrid' by the explanation in the introduction, a proper hybrid programming language should be (*, *).

With the inclusion of forwards nondeterminism, there is the looming question about how programs that are forwards nondeterministic are even executed. As touched on in the introduction, there are execution models for nondeterministic languages, for example in the logic paradigm. Does this mean that any hybrid language with forwards nondeterminism should also employ backtracking or similar to execute nondeterministic programs? For classical (D, N) programs, no backwards semantics are defined, neither would we expect them to be. Executing them in reverse would require an oracle to guess the correct values wherever information is lost during forwards execution. For (D, N) programs in a hybrid programming language, this does not change, and execution would also require an oracle. While hybrid programming languages should be able to statically express nondeterminism in any direction in accordance with principle

2, we do not expect hybrid programming languages to define executable runtime semantics for nondeterminism. This leads us to the final principle:

Principle 3: Hybrid programs do not necessarily need to be executable in a nondeterministic direction.

Although this principle is inherently met by any language, we consider it important to state explicitly that our understanding of hybrid programming languages does not necessitate runtime semantics for nondeterminism.

3   Hybrid Single Static Assignment (HSSA)

With these design principles in place, we now introduce the hybrid static single assignment form HSSA. As a notational convention, an overline like in $\overline{S}$ is used to denote repetition in the abstract syntax, including the empty sequence. The value domain HSSA operates on is the set $\mathbb{V}$, which is constructed by the abstract syntax in Fig. 2.

$$
\begin{array}{lll}
\mathbf{V} ::= & & \textbf{Values } \mathbb{V} \\
& \textbf{Int } c & \textit{Integer} \\
& \textbf{Pair } (V, V) & \textit{Pair} \\
& \textbf{Unit} & \textit{Unit}
\end{array}
$$

Fig. 2. Values in HSSA

As you can see, in addition to integers, the value domain also contains pairs of values as well as the value **Unit**. Operators with multiple operands operate on pairs and parameterless operators are expressed with **Unit**.

The full abstract syntax of HSSA is given in Fig. 3. An HSSA program is a sequence of user-defined procedures, which compute relations. A procedure in turn consists of a sequence of statements, which make use of expressions as well as parameterized relations. Statements are generally assignments, as can be seen by the abundant use of the assignment operator := in the abstract syntax.

Regarding its overall structure, HSSA is a flowchart language like RSSA. The statements forming a procedure can be organized into basic blocks that are the nodes of a control flow graph. Basic blocks start with an entry statement and end with an exit statement. To form a valid control flow graph, the first and last statement must be the unique usages of **begin** and **end** respectively within that procedure. Any other contained exit must be immediately followed by an entry. Procedures that do not adhere to this structure are ill-formed.

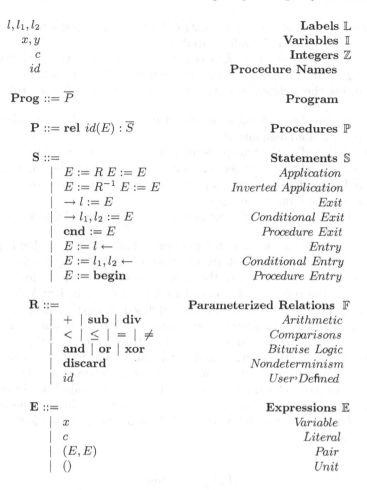

$$l, l_1, l_2 \qquad\qquad \textbf{Labels } \mathbb{L}$$
$$x, y \qquad\qquad \textbf{Variables } \mathbb{I}$$
$$c \qquad\qquad \textbf{Integers } \mathbb{Z}$$
$$id \qquad\qquad \textbf{Procedure Names}$$

$$\textbf{Prog} ::= \overline{P} \qquad\qquad \textit{Program}$$

$$\textbf{P} ::= \textbf{rel } id(E) : \overline{S} \qquad\qquad \textbf{Procedures } \mathbb{P}$$

$$\textbf{S} ::= \qquad\qquad \textbf{Statements } \mathbb{S}$$
$$\mid\ E := R\ E := E \qquad\qquad \textit{Application}$$
$$\mid\ E := R^{-1}\ E := E \qquad\qquad \textit{Inverted Application}$$
$$\mid\ \rightarrow l := E \qquad\qquad \textit{Exit}$$
$$\mid\ \rightarrow l_1, l_2 := E \qquad\qquad \textit{Conditional Exit}$$
$$\mid\ \textbf{end} := E \qquad\qquad \textit{Procedure Exit}$$
$$\mid\ E := l \leftarrow \qquad\qquad \textit{Entry}$$
$$\mid\ E := l_1, l_2 \leftarrow \qquad\qquad \textit{Conditional Entry}$$
$$\mid\ E := \textbf{begin} \qquad\qquad \textit{Procedure Entry}$$

$$\textbf{R} ::= \qquad\qquad \textbf{Parameterized Relations } \mathbb{F}$$
$$\mid\ + \mid \textbf{sub} \mid \textbf{div} \qquad\qquad \textit{Arithmetic}$$
$$\mid\ < \mid \leq \mid = \mid \neq \qquad\qquad \textit{Comparisons}$$
$$\mid\ \textbf{and} \mid \textbf{or} \mid \textbf{xor} \qquad\qquad \textit{Bitwise Logic}$$
$$\mid\ \textbf{discard} \qquad\qquad \textit{Nondeterminism}$$
$$\mid\ id \qquad\qquad \textit{User-Defined}$$

$$\textbf{E} ::= \qquad\qquad \textbf{Expressions } \mathbb{E}$$
$$\mid\ x \qquad\qquad \textit{Variable}$$
$$\mid\ c \qquad\qquad \textit{Literal}$$
$$\mid\ (E, E) \qquad\qquad \textit{Pair}$$
$$\mid\ () \qquad\qquad \textit{Unit}$$

Fig. 3. Abstract Syntax of HSSA

3.1   Initialization and Finalization Using Parameterized Relations

Besides entries and exits for control flow, the only other statements in HSSA are assignments. They form the body of every basic block and are used to finalize variables as well as initialize new ones. They transform information given by the expression on the right-hand side by applying a parameterized relation to it. Let us ignore the fact that relations are parameterized for a moment and focus on the transformation of information instead.

For every assignment, the expression on the right-hand side is first evaluated to construct a value out of constants and variables. Any variable used in this expression is finalized. Finalization is the counterpart of initialization, and undefines the variable, so that it can not be used anymore after finalization. To be valid HSSA code, every variable initialized inside of a basic block must be finalized by the end of the block. Control flow instructions discussed in the next section also initialize and finalize variables.

The constructed value is then transformed by applying a relation, before being assigned to the expression on the left-hand side which takes on the role of a pattern. For the assignment of values to patterns, the following rules apply:

1. Values assigned to a variable associate the value with that variable identifier, as expected of an assignment.
2. Values assigned to the unit-pattern () are required to be a **Unit** value.
3. Values assigned to an integer constant c are required to be **Int** c.
4. A pair **Pair**(a, b) assigned to a pair-pattern (x, y) assigns a to x and b to y, recursively applying these rules.
5. Any other combination of value and pattern is a reversibility violation error.

These rules ensure that any information contained in the value is preserved on execution, by either being stored in a variable or by being invariant and their value available as a constant in the program's source code. Rules 2 and 3 are equivalent to the behavior of assignments to constants in RSSA. The runtime behavior of reversibility violations is not defined. As explored in [2], assuming reversibility violations to never happen creates additional optimization potential, which is why there are no runtime semantics attached to reversibility violations.

To be reversible, the relation used to transform information is required to be injective and univalent. Assuming neither it nor its inverse are ever applied to a value they are not defined on, it can also be seen as a bijection. In accordance with the reversibility-first principle, most primitive built-in relations are in fact bijective. Of course, with HSSA being a hybrid language, non-bijective relations are also available.

(D, D)	one-to-one
(D, N)	many-to-one
(N, D)	one-to-many
(N, N)	many-to-many

Fig. 4. Correspondence between language classification and relation classes

In fact, relations can be categorized using the same classification as for programming languages into (D, D), (D, N), (N, D), and (N, N). The correspondence between classes of relations and the computation category is listed in Fig. 4. The intuition behind this correspondence is that forwards/nondeterministic computations have multiple possible outcomes for the same input, hence they map one value to many values. Conversely, deterministic programs map values to a unique result.

Relations that are functions (one-to-one and many-to-one) are applied like expected of functions. The application of forwards-nondeterministic relations will be discussed in detail in Sect. 3.5 where the primitive relation **discard** and its inverse are introduced.

As indicated above, the relations used in assignments are instantiated parameterized relations. To understand why this is useful, we consider some examples, starting with a relation defining the addition of integers. Addition viewed as a relation from pairs of integers to integers is a non-injective function. To be backwards-deterministic, an injective alternative must be used. Non-injective relations can be turned into injective relations by a process known as injectivization. Every non-injective computable function can be injectivized into an equivalent computable injective function [16]. A specific and straightforward way to do injectivization is the preservation of (parts of) the input in the output of the relation. In the extreme case, where a relation is not injective in any subset of its input, we can simply return the complete input in addition to the actual output to preserve it. Applied to integer addition, one viable result of this process is a relation between pairs formally defined as $\{((a,b),(a,a+b)) \mid a,b \in \mathbb{Z}\}$. As we can see, the value of the first operand is always preserved as part of the output pair. We only need to preserve one of the operands, because addition is injective in the other one.

One example of operators falling into the extreme case mentioned before are comparisons such as $<$, which are not injective in any of their operands. To remain in the domain of integers, we define $a < b$ as 1 if a is less than b, and as 0 otherwise. Formally expressed, such a relation is defined as the relation mapping pairs of integers to the set $\{0,1\}$. To injectivize this relation by means of input-preservation, we need to preserve the entire input pair:

$$\{((a,b),((a,b),(\begin{cases} 1 & \text{if } a < b \\ 0 & \text{else} \end{cases}))) \mid a,b \in \mathbb{Z}\}$$

For analysis and optimization techniques such as constant propagation it is vital for the analysis to be able to trace constants. If the application of a relation obscures the preservation of input in its output, tracing constants becomes a hard (and potentially undecidable) problem. To allow analysis tools to know about such preservation in both user-defined and built-in relations by means of constructions, we use parameterized relations instead of raw relations.

Definition 1. *A (partial) function $P : \mathbb{V} \to \wp(\mathbb{V} \times \mathbb{V})$ is called a parameterized relation on $\mathbb{V}$. For any $v \in dom(P)$, $P(v)$ is called an instantiation of P.*

Parameterized relations factor out the parts of the input that are exactly preserved as part of the output. Values that are used to instantiate a relation for use in HSSA are consequently not finalized.

Definition 2. *$R_P = \{((a,b),(a,c)) \mid a \in dom(P), b,c \in \mathbb{V} : (b,c) \in P(a)\}$ is called the expanded relation for the parameterized relation P.*

Instantiating a parameterized relation with an operand outside of its domain is considered undefined behavior. The same applies for the application of the instantiated relation. The set of variables used to instantiate a parameterized relation must be disjoint from the set of variables used on either the left or right-hand side of the assignment. The rationale behind this is simple; if a value used to instantiate the relation is consumed by the very same relation, it is not available to instantiate the same relation during reverse execution. Using a variable that is finalized in the same statement can be interpreted as a duplication followed by discarding the duplicate afterwards. This is implicit backwards-nondeterminism and therefore disallowed.

Parameterized relations are inverted using the R^{-1} syntax. This swaps the domain and codomain of the instantiated relations and therefore inverts it.

Definition 3. P^{-1} *defined by* $P^{-1}(v) = \{(b,a) \mid (a,b) \in P(v)\}$ *is called the inverted parameterized relation of* P.

Basic built-in relations available in HSSA cover arithmetic, comparisons and bitwise operations and are constructed using the techniques outlined above. In accordance with the reversibility-first principle, they all produce bijective relations and are listed in Fig. 5. Additionally, we define the synonyms − for $+^{-1}$ and **mul** for $\mathbf{div}^{-1}$. For brevity, the definitions of the bitwise **or**, which is defined the same way as **and**, as well as for the comparison operators $\leq$, $=$ and $\neq$, which follow the scheme of $<$, have been omitted.

$$+(\mathbf{Int}\ a) = \{(\mathbf{Int}\ b, \mathbf{Int}\ b + a) \mid b \in \mathbb{Z}\}$$
$$\mathbf{sub}(\mathbf{Int}\ a) = \{(\mathbf{Int}\ b, \mathbf{Int}\ a - b) \mid b \in \mathbb{Z}\}$$
$$\mathbf{div}(\mathbf{Int}\ a) = \{(\mathbf{Int}\ b, \mathbf{Pair}\ (\mathbf{Int}\ \lfloor \tfrac{b}{a} \rfloor \mid \mathbf{Int}\ b - \lfloor \tfrac{b}{a} \rfloor)) \mid a, b \in \mathbb{Z}, b \neq 0\}$$
$$< (\mathbf{Pair}\ (\mathbf{Int}\ a, \mathbf{Int}\ b)) = \{(\mathbf{Unit}, \mathbf{Int}\ \begin{cases} 1 & \text{if } a < b \\ 0 & \text{else} \end{cases})\}$$
$$\mathbf{and}(\mathbf{Pair}\ (\mathbf{Int}\ a, \mathbf{Int}\ b)) = \{(\mathbf{Unit}, \mathbf{Int}\ a\ \text{AND}\ b)\}$$
$$\mathbf{xor}(\mathbf{Int}\ a) = \{(\mathbf{Int}\ b, \mathbf{Int}\ a\ \text{XOR}\ b \mid b \in \mathbb{Z})\}$$

Fig. 5. built-in parameterized relations. Logical operators are bitwise.

3.2   Control Flow Using Entries and Exits

As mentioned, HSSA is primarily a flowchart language. Control flow is implemented by using entry and exit instructions to pass control as well as information between basic blocks. This concept was established by RSSA and is mostly kept in HSSA as well with some minor changes.

As indicated by the use of the := operator in the abstract syntax, control flow statements can be viewed in the context of initialization and finalization. In general, exit statements (jumps) finalize the variables on the right-hand side of the assignment operator. The value constructed by that expression (and thus the information contained within) is passed to the target block named by the label, where it is used to initialize the pattern used in the respective entry statement following the previously mentioned rules of assignment.

Conditional exits require an additional bit of information to decide which of the two labels the control flow is passed to. To do so, the conditional exit actually requires a pair of values. Only the first element of that pair is passed to the next block. The other element is used as the condition to decide which label to follow. If the condition is 1, the first label is used; if it is 0 the other label is used. Values other than 1 and 0 used as a condition are a reversibility violation.

Conversely, conditional entry instructions produce a pair of values to initialize the pattern on the left-hand side. The first element of the pair is the value passed to the jump that leads to this entry, while the second element is either 1 or 0, depending on which of the two labels was used to jump to this block. This is slightly different from the handling of conditional entries and exits in RSSA, where a condition is directly part of the respective instruction. This means that the bit of information on join points in the control flow graph must be uncomputed immediately, whereas in HSSA the handling of branching information is slightly more flexible. The user can decide whether to store it, uncompute it, or discard it to introduce backwards-nondeterminism.

$$
\begin{aligned}
&\textbf{rel } \mathrm{count}\,(max) : \\
&\quad () := \quad\;\; \textbf{begin} \\
&\quad\;\; a := \qquad +0 \qquad := 0 \\
&\qquad\qquad\quad \to l_1 \qquad := a \\[4pt]
&\;(a_1, c_1) := \quad l_1, l_2 \leftarrow \\
&\qquad () := \;=^{-1} (a_1, 0) := c_1 \\
&\qquad a_2 := \qquad +1 \qquad := a_1 \\
&\qquad c_2 := \; < (a_2, max) := () \\
&\qquad\qquad\quad \to l_2, l_3 \;\; := (a_2, c_2) \\[6pt]
&\quad\;\; a := \qquad l_3 \leftarrow \\
&\qquad\qquad\;\; \textbf{end} \qquad := a \\[8pt]
&\textbf{rel } \mathrm{main}\,(()) : \\
&\quad () := \quad\;\; \textbf{begin} \\
&\quad\;\; a := \quad \mathrm{count}\; 10 \;\; := () \\
&\quad\;\; b := \quad \mathrm{count}^{-1}\, a \;\; := 10 \\
&\qquad\qquad\;\; \textbf{end} \qquad := (a, b)
\end{aligned}
$$

Fig. 6. Exemplary procedures making use of all types of statements.

In addition to (un-)conditional entries and exits, there are also the special cases **begin** and **end**. They mark the entry and exit of the user-defined relation and must be the first, respectively last statement of the definition. The begin statement initializes a pattern to the value passed in the application of the relation, while the end statement returns the value constructed by the expression on the right.

Figure 6 depicts two user-defined parameterized relations that use all variants of entries and exits. The *count* relation is parameterized on the variable *max*, which is expected to be an integer. Variables defined in the pattern in the relation's signature are in scope for the entire procedure and can never be finalized. This way, user-defined relations can make use of being parameterized the same way as built-in relations do.

The instantiated relation maps the **Unit** value to *max*, and is therefore essentially a constant function in either direction. The instance *count* 10 has this value set to 10, so the relation is the set $\{(\mathbf{Unit}, \mathbf{Int}\ 10)\}$. The implementation of count uses a looping basic block to increment a variable until it reaches the value *max*. It is then returned in the final basic block.

In *main*, *count* is instantiated and applied twice. First, it is used to initialize the variable *a* to 10. Next, its inverse is instantaited with the value of *a* which is now 10, and then applied to the value 10, the result of which is used to initialize *b*. *b* now has the value **Unit**. Consequently, the result of the entire program defined by the end statement in *main* is **Pair** (**Int** 10, **Unit**)

3.3   Inverting HSSA

With the established understanding of assignments and control flow, we can now define inversion rules to comply with the invertibility-principle. Given the symmetry of control flow statements and the availability of two assignment variants, the rules for statements are simple as seen in Fig. 7.

$$
\begin{array}{ccc}
e := l_1 \leftarrow & \leftrightarrow & \rightarrow l_1 := e \\
e := l_1, l_2 \leftarrow & \leftrightarrow & \rightarrow l_1, l_2 := e \\
e := \mathbf{begin} & \leftrightarrow & \mathbf{end} := e \\
e_1 := f\ e_2 := e_3 & \leftrightarrow & e_3 := f^{-1}\ e_2 := e_1
\end{array}
$$

Fig. 7. Symmetric inversion rules for HSSA statements

To invert a user-defined relation, its contained statements need to be inverted and their order reversed. This is a context-sensitive operation, since any reference to an inverted relation must also be inverted to restore its original meaning, including recursive usages within the inverted procedure. To adjust for the inversion of a user-defined relation f, any usage $e_1 := f\ e_2 := e_3$ must be converted to $e_1 := f^{-1}\ e_2 := e_3$ and vice versa. Note that the roles of the expressions on the left and right of the respective assignments are not switched back.

3.4   Correct Initialization and Finalization

As briefly mentioned before, every variable defined in a basic block must also be finalized in it. This is part of the implementation of the reversibility-first principle. The dual counterpart of this requirement is that any finalized variable in a basic block must also be initialized in it. While this seems obvious for any programming language, it is worth mentioning that for reversible languages, not finalizing variables is the same class of programming error as using variables that are not defined. The algorithm given in Fig. 8 checks a basic block for consistency regarding initialization, use, and finalization of variables. In it, $init(s)$ determines the set of variables initialized by the statement s, i.e., variables used in the pattern on the left of the assignment. $final(s)$ does the same for finalized variables, and $use(s)$ names the set of variables used to instantiate a parameterized relation.

procedure $consistent(block = S_1...S_n)$
> $L \leftarrow \emptyset$
> **foreach** $s \in block$ **do**
>> **if** $use(s) \cap init(s) \neq \emptyset \vee use(s) \cap final(s) \neq \emptyset$ **then return** *false*
>> **if** $final(s) \nsubseteq L \vee (init(s) \cap L) \neq \emptyset$ **then return** *false*
>> $L \leftarrow (L \setminus final(s)) \cup init(s)$
>
> **return** $L \neq \emptyset$

Fig. 8. Checking the consistency of variable use

3.5 Nondeterminism

What we have discussed so far makes HSSA a reversible programming language. Every step of evaluation is information preserving and there are clearly defined semantics for reverse execution. The instances of every built-in parameterized relation we have introduced so far are bijective relations. Programs that make use of only these relations are reversible (D, D) programs by construction. This is a consequence of the determinism-first principle but restricts HSSA to reversible programs instead of being able to express all four categories of programs.

To introduce the ability to express (D, N) programs too, we need a built-in relation that is not bijective. Specifically, to express backwards-nondeterminism, we need a many-to-one relation. Many-to-one, non-injective relations map at least two elements of the domain to the same element of the co-domain. Applying such a function during execution while discarding the input (through finalization) allows information to leave the system[2], which is the definition of backwards-nondeterminism. Inverting such a relation produces a non-univalent

---

[2] Actually, information only leaves the system if the function's value has two or more domain counterparts. Relations that are injective on a subset of their domain are partially reversible. This is an interesting topic, but not investigated further in this paper.

relation (i.e., not a function), which when applied to a value produces an ambiguous result.

The simplest possible many-to-one relation on the set of values $\mathbb{V}$ is the constant function mapping every input value to the same output value. A suitable candidate for this is the **Unit** value, but any other constant would serve the same purpose. Since such a function effectively discards the entire information contained in the value that it is applied to, we appropriately name it **discard**. To fit within the framework of HSSA using parameterized relations, discard is also a parameterized relation. But since it does not need any additional constant information, the value it is instantiated with is required to be the **Unit**-value. Keeping that in mind, **discard** is defined as follows:

$$\mathbf{discard}(\mathbf{Unit}) = \{(v, \mathbf{Unit}) \mid v \in \mathbb{V}\}$$

The **discard** relation enables us to use backwards-nondeterminism by explicitly removing information. This is in line with the idea of forcing nondeterminism to be explicitly present in the source code, compared to information implicitly vanishing for example by not preserving a variable. Since **discard** is the only possible source of information loss in HSSA, it also makes it easy to identify where information is lost. Reversibilization techniques for programs written in HSSA can then be concerned with the elimination of **discard** usages.

The introduction of **discard** as a parameterized relation also allows us to use its inverse by writing $x := \mathbf{discard}^{-1}$ () := (). The inversion of the **discard** relation produces a one-to-many relation that maps the **Unit** value to any other value of the (infinite) set of values $\mathbb{V}$. Such a relation would create information out of thin air. Since it is not a function, it can not be evaluated to a single value when applied. To actually execute it, the application would need to guess a correct value out of all the possibilities, which would make it an **oracle**. Appropriately we can write **oracle** as a synonym for **discard**$^{-1}$. The application of **oracle** has no runtime semantics associated with it. While there are execution models for nondeterministic programs in general for example using backtracking, HSSA does not define such a model for nondeterminism in accordance with principle 3 defined earlier. Still, the ability to express forwards-nondeterminism in HSSA ensures that all HSSA programs are invertible, which is a useful property to have for optimizations and analysis techniques [3].

With the many-to-one relation **discard** and the one-to-many **oracle**, user-defined relations that are also many-to-one (D, N), one-to-many (N, D) or even many-to-many (N, N) can be constructed. User-defined relations can be classified into the four categories using a straightforward process to find a fix-point:

1. Assume all user-defined relations are (D, D).
2. Any relation that uses a (D, N) or (N, N) relation has its kind set to (_, N).
3. Any relation that uses a (N, D) or (N, N) relation has its kind set to (N, _).
4. Repeat from 2 until nothing changes anymore.

$$
\begin{aligned}
&\textbf{rel } \text{manytomany}\,(max): \\
&in := \quad \textbf{begin} \\
&\quad () := \textbf{discard } () := in \\
&out := \quad \textbf{oracle } () := () \\
&\qquad\qquad \textbf{end} \quad := out
\end{aligned}
$$

Fig. 9. The simplest possible (N, N) relation.

4   Repairing Invalid HSSA Programs

HSSA places two major restrictions similar to those of RSSA on programs to follow the reversibility-first principle, namely the finalization of variables and the requirement for labels to be used exactly once as a jump target. For the implementation of code generation in a compiler for a higher-level programming language, it might be convenient to forgo these restrictions when translating non-reversible code and produce invalid HSSA code instead. Not finalizing a variable can be interpreted as the intention of discarding the information contained in the variable. Using a label as a jump target more than once on the other hand may express the intention of discarding the branching information. Both can also be explicitly expressed using **discard**. We propose two techniques to automatically repair such implicit intentions and make them explicit.

4.1   Non-finalized Variables

Automatically discarding unfinalized variables is a straightforward process. In every basic block, find variables that are initialized but never finalized. An adaption of the algorithm in Fig. 8 can easily achieve this. For every such variable a, a discard statement $() := \textbf{discard } () := a$ is added to the end of the block.

The reverse of that logic is adding **oracle** statements for variables that are finalized, but never initialized. Instead of implementing the reverse logic, a code transformer can also invert the program, run the original technique, and then invert the program again to get to the same result.

4.2   Labels Used More Than once

Explicitly discarding branching information for labels used more than once is slightly more complicated. Figure 10 depicts an example of the process.

For every two usages of the same label, a new block with a conditional entry with two new unique labels is generated. Here, the branching information is explicitly discarded, and the value passed in the jump is passed on to the original label with an unconditional exit. This process is repeated until there is only one usage left. Every added block reduces the number of usages by one, so for n usages of the same label, a total of $n - 1$ blocks following this scheme must be added.

As with discarding unfinalized variables, this process can also be applied in the inverse direction. For labels that are used in multiple entries, blocks with

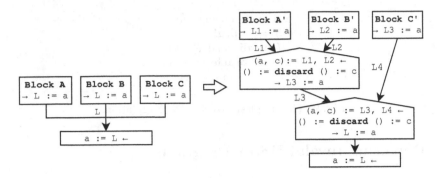

Fig. 10. Automatic repair of duplicate labels.

conditional exits are generated that create the branching bit using **oracle**. This captures the intuition of nondeterministic control flow, where there are multiple possible jump targets.

5   Future Work and Conclusion

We have proposed a hybrid intermediate language, HSSA, that allows the representation of classical computing (D, N) and reversible computing (D, D), as well as the two non-deterministic cases (N, D) and (N, N). HSSA uses relations instead of functions to allow for the expression of nondeterminism. As opposed to RSSA, HSSA unifies the various assignments within only one syntactic construct. Non-determinism in backwards-direction is achieved by means of adding a 'discard' relation to explicitly erase information; its inverse, called 'oracle', is used to allow for nondeterminism in forwards direction. HSSA offers a controlled way to express nondeterminism/loss of information and may be used in cases where full reversibility is not required. For example, it can be used as an intermediate representation for analysis and optimization in the translation of higher level partially reversible languages such as Sparcle [10].

Regarding future work, an implementation of a HSSA toolkit is currently underway based on a new implementation of the RC3 compiler [14]. A full formalization of HSSA's semantics is also underway. One idea for future research is a more fine-grained view of partially deterministic relations by employing a potent type-system. Instead of classifying procedures as either reversible or non-reversible, a dependent type system could be used to express dependent reversibility for procedures that are injective in a subset of their domain. Applying reversibility techniques in the context of hybrid programs by implementing them in terms of removing usages of **discard** or statistically analyzing the amount of lost information can also be interesting.

A limitation of the current definition of **discard** is that it does not consider the possible set of values to be discarded. For example, discarding the branching information produced by a conditional entry only ever discards the values 0 or

1. On inversion, the corresponding **oracle** should only be able to produce the same set of values. In other words, the actual domain of a specific instance of **discard** is not the same as its formal domain (i.e., the entire set of values).

Acknowledgements. We would like to thank the reviewers for their valuable and insightful feedback.

References

1. Appel, A.W.: SSA is functional programming. ACM SIGPLAN Notices **33**(4), 17–20 (1998). http://dblp.uni-trier.de/db/journals/sigplan/sigplan33.html#Appel88
2. Deworetzki, N., Gail, L.: Optimization of reversible control flow graphs. In: Kutrib, M., Meyer, U. (eds.) Reversible Computation. RC 2023. LNCS, vol. 13960, pp. 57–72. Springer, Cham (2023). https://doi.org/10.1007/978-3-031-38100-3_5
3. Deworetzki, N., Meyer, U.: Program analysis for reversible languages. In: Proceedings of the 10th ACM SIGPLAN International Workshop on the State Of the Art in Program Analysis, pp. 13–18 (2021)
4. Frank, M.P.: Introduction to reversible computing: motivation, progress, and challenges. In: Proceedings of the 2nd Conference on Computing Frontiers. p. 385-390. CF '05, Association for Computing Machinery, New York, NY, USA (2005). https://doi.org/10.1145/1062261.1062324
5. Frank, M.P.: The future of computing depends on making it reversible. IEEE Spectr. **25**(08), 2017 (2017)
6. Giachino, E., Lanese, I., Mezzina, C.A.: Causal-consistent reversible debugging. In: Gnesi, S., Rensink, A. (eds.) Fundamental Approaches to Software Engineering. FASE 2014. LNCS, vol. 8411, pp. 370–384. Springer, Berlin, Heidelberg (2014). https://doi.org/10.1007/978-3-642-54804-8_26
7. Glück, R., Yokoyama, T.: Reversible computing from a programming language perspective. Theor. Comput. Sci. **953**, 113429 (2023). https://doi.org/10.1016/J.TCS.2022.06.010
8. Glück, R., Yokoyama, T.: Making programs reversible with minimal extra data. N. Gener. Comput. (2022). https://doi.org/10.1007/s00354-022-00169-z
9. Landauer, R.: Irreversibility and heat generation in the computing process. IBM J. Res. Dev. **5**(3), 183–191 (1961). https://doi.org/10.1147/rd.53.0183
10. Matsuda, K., Wang, M.: Sparcl: a language for partially-invertible computation. Proc. ACM Program. Lang. **4**(ICFP), 118:1–118:31 (2020). http://dblp.uni-trier.de/db/journals/pacmpl/pacmpl4.html#MatsudaW20
11. Mogensen, T.Æ.: RSSA: a reversible SSA form. In: Mazzara, M., Voronkov, A. (eds.) PSI 2015. LNCS, vol. 9609, pp. 203–217. Springer, Cham (2016). https://doi.org/10.1007/978-3-319-41579-6_16
12. Muchnick, S., et al.: Advanced Compiler Design Implementation. Morgan Kaufmann, Burlington (1997)
13. Rosen, B.K., Wegman, M.N., Zadeck, F.K.: Global value numbers and redundant computations. In: Proceedings of the 15th ACM SIGPLAN-SIGACT Symposium on Principles of Programming Languages, pp. 12–27 (1988)
14. Technische Hochschule Mittelhessen: Reversible computing compiler collection (rc3). https://git.thm.de/thm-rc3/release

15. Yokoyama, T., Axelsen, H.B., Glück, R.: Principles of a reversible programming language. In: Proceedings of the 5th Conference on Computing Frontiers, pp. 43–54. CF '08, Association for Computing Machinery, New York, NY, USA (2008). https://doi.org/10.1145/1366230.1366239
16. Yokoyama, T., Axelsen, H.B., Glück, R.: Reversible flowchart languages and the structured reversible program theorem. In: Aceto, L., Damgård, I., Goldberg, L.A., Halldórsson, M.M., Ingólfsdóttir, A., Walukiewicz, I. (eds.) ICALP 2008. LNCS, vol. 5126, pp. 258–270. Springer, Heidelberg (2008). https://doi.org/10.1007/978-3-540-70583-3_22

Synthesis, Verification, and Analysis
of Reversible and Quantum Systems

Concurrent RSSA for CRIL: Flow Analysis for a Concurrent Reversible Programming Language

Shunya Oguchi and Shoji Yuen$^{(\boxtimes)}$ (iD)

Graduate School of Informatics, Nagoya University, Nagoya, Japan
{oguchi321,yuen}@sqlab.jp

Abstract. We present the CRSSA (Concurrent Reversible Static Single Assignment) form for a concurrent reversible intermediate language called CRIL, which the authors proposed. A CRIL program is a collection of basic blocks where each basic block consists of a single 3-address code with labels for forward and backward control flow. CRIL extends RIL by Mogensen, allowing the multiple calls of basic blocks to execute concurrently in forward and backward directions. The operational semantics of CRIL enjoy causal safety and causal liveness as the fundamental correctness for reversibility. RSSA proposed by Mogensen assigns a value to a pair of unique variables for both directions. In addition to ϕ functions to present bidirectional splits and joins of sequential flow, we incorporate π functions for possible joins of concurrent flow via shared variables, where the π functions are proposed by Lee et al. to present the joins of the concurrent flow of parallel programs. We extend π functions for the backward execution to present bidirectional splits and joins of CRIL behavior. We give a translation from a CRIL program into a CRSSA form given a bidirectional data flow analysis. We apply the optimization technique using the CRSSA form, such as conditional constant propagation, dead code elimination, and copy propagation to CRIL programs. A CRSSA form is translated back to a CRIL program.

1 Introduction

Reversible programming languages have been proposed to describe reversible computation where the control flows both forward and backward [7,8,19,20]. They not only directly specify reversible computation but also develop new aspects of software because reversibility holds all information at any point of execution. Since this is an advantage for behavioral analysis such as optimization and debugging, reversible debugging tools have been investigated as well as compiler optimization [1,9].

In the forward-only computation, intermediate results unnecessary for the further computation can be lost since they do not affect the result of the computation. However, to enable backward computation, history information has to be preserved to track the backward control and data flow. Therefore, the flow analysis of reversible programming languages describes the flow in both directions.

T. Æ. Mogensen and L. Mikulski (Eds.): RC 2024, LNCS 14680, pp. 181–200, 2024.
https://doi.org/10.1007/978-3-031-62076-8_12

The SSA form is an intermediate language where each variable is defined at exactly one assignment used in compilers. In the SSA form, a variable is renamed by indices and the value with the same index for the variable is the same. This syntactic property is very useful for program analyses such as optimization. Mogensen extends SSA (static single assignment) with reversibility and proposes the RSSA (reversible SSA) form [14] where each basic block is attributed by splits and joins of data flow as reversible ϕ functions and the optimization techniques for Janus language using RSSA developed by Deworetzki et al. [5,6]. The RSSA form is used as the intermediate representation of Janus language for flow analysis and optimization. For concurrent programs, CSSA (concurrent SSA) [13] is proposed where updates of shared variables in interleaving concurrent blocks are considered as joins of flow in the form of π functions.

The authors proposed a concurrent reversible intermediate language, called CRIL [16]. CRIL is an extension of RIL [15] by calling multiple blocks as concurrent processes with the PV operation commonly used in the process synchronization in operating systems. The controlled semantics of CRIL combined with "Annotation DAGs" enjoy causal safety and causal liveness [11,12] as the fundamental reversibility. A CRIL program consists of 3-address level codes suitable for machine-independent flow analysis. A control flow graph is straightforwardly constructed from a CRIL program to apply the existing flow analysis to the control flow graph in both directions according to the syntactic structure of programs. A static flow analysis is sound if it approximates all possible data flows of the executions. The authors proposed the bidirectional flow analysis for CRIL as the relation between basic blocks [17] according to the CRIL's call structure and the process synchronization by the PV operation.

Given a sound bidirectional flow analysis, this paper proposes the CRSSA (concurrent RSSA) form by incorporating the π functions of CSSA [13] into RSSA. Adding reversible ϕ functions as well as reversible π functions, we present the CRSSA form as a collection of the basic blocks with extra information at entry and exit. A π function has the form: $\pi(x_1, \cdots, x_n)$ and π represents the value of shared x between the concurrently running processes. The CRSSA form explicitly represents possible data flow equivalent to the given CRIL program in both directions. It preserves the local reversibility of the CRIL program. Combining with an Annotation DAG preserves the reversibility as a whole.

In the CRSSA form, a basic block may have the assignments of ϕ functions and π functions at the entry and exit parts. A ϕ function at the entry point receives the forward flow of unshared variables. Symmetrically, the ϕ function at the exit point receives the flow in the backward execution. The ϕ function assignment mechanism follows the conventional technique like in [3]. Similarly, a π function receives the flow of shared variables from the other processes that are running concurrently.

We apply the optimization techniques [2,3] such as conditional constant propagation, dead-code elimination, and common subexpression elimination extending with π functions. After applying these optimizations, the CRSSA form is translated back to the corresponding CRIL program removing ϕ and π functions. The optimized CRIL program provides the equivalent behavior to that of the original CRIL program so that its controlled operational semantics enjoy the reversibility.

This paper is organized as follows. Section 2 presents CRIL and Sect. 3 explains the flow analysis of CRIL. Section 4 shows the conversion from CRIL to CRSSA based on a sound flow analysis, and we apply the optimization techniques to CRIL programs using the CRSSA form in Sect. 5. In Sect. 6, we provide the concluding remark.

2 CRIL: Concurrent Reversible Intermediate Language

This section provides a brief review of CRIL [16] proposed by the authors. CRIL is a reversible language with concurrency intended to be an "intermediate language" between a high-level abstract language and a low-level machine-oriented language. All variables and one heap are referred by the global scope.

Figure 1 gives the syntax of CRIL. A CRIL program is a collection of basic blocks, each of which consists of an entry part, an atomic single 3-address level instruction, and an exit part. Given a basic block b, the entry part $\mathsf{entry}(b)$ is one of $\mathsf{begin}\ \ell$, $\ell\ \texttt{<-}$, and $\ell_1; \ell_2\ \texttt{<-}e$, $\mathsf{inst}(b)$ is the instruction in b, and the exit part $\mathsf{exit}(b)$ is one of $\mathsf{end}\ \ell$, $\texttt{->}\ \ell$, and $e\texttt{->}\ell_1; \ell_2$. $\mathsf{in}(b)$ is the set of labels appearing in the form of $\ell\ \texttt{<-}$ or $\ell_1; \ell_2\texttt{<-}e$, and $\mathsf{out}(b)$ is those appearing in the form of $\texttt{->}\ell$ or $e\texttt{->}\ell_1; \ell_2$. b and b' are *immediately connected* each other when $\mathsf{out}(b) \cap \mathsf{in}(b') \neq \varnothing$ or $\mathsf{out}(b') \cap \mathsf{in}(b) \neq \varnothing$, written as $b \bowtie b'$. b and b' are *connected* when $b \bowtie^* b'$.

$$
\begin{aligned}
Pg &::= b^* \\
b &::= instb \mid callb \\
instb &::= entry\ inst\ exit \\
entry &::= \ell\ \texttt{<-}\ \mid\ \ell; \ell\ \texttt{<-}\ e\ \mid\ \mathsf{begin}\ \ell \\
exit &::= \texttt{->}\ \ell\ \mid\ e\ \texttt{->}\ \ell; \ell\ \mid\ \mathsf{end}\ \ell \\
inst &::= left\ \oplus\texttt{=}\ e\ \mid\ left\ \texttt{<=>}\ left \\
 &\ \mid\ \mathsf{V}\ x\ \mid\ \mathsf{P}\ x\ \mid\ \mathsf{assert}\ e\ \mid\ \mathsf{skip} \\
callb &::= \ell\ \texttt{<-}\ \mathsf{call}\ \ell(,\ \ell)^*\ \texttt{->}\ \ell \\
e &::= right \odot right\ \mid\ !\,right \\
left &::= x\ \mid\ \mathsf{M}[x] \\
right &::= k\ \mid\ left \\
\oplus &::= +\ \mid\ -\ \mid\ \char`\^ \\
\odot &::= \oplus\ \mid\ \texttt{==}\ \mid\ \texttt{!=}\ \mid\ \texttt{<}\ \mid\ \texttt{<=}\ \mid\ \texttt{>} \\
 &\ \mid\ \texttt{>=}\ \mid\ \texttt{\&\&}\ \mid\ \texttt{||}
\end{aligned}
$$

Fig. 1. Syntax of CRIL

For a basic block b whose instruction is $left\oplus\texttt{=}\ e$, we write $\mathsf{write}(b) = \{x\}$ when $left = x$, or $\mathsf{write}(b) = \{\mathsf{M}\}$ when $left = \mathsf{M}[x]$. $\mathsf{read}(b)$ is a set of variables and M appearing in b.

The fundamental bidirectional behavior of a basic block is as follows: A basic block (1) receives a control flow from the connected block, (2) executes the instruction in either direction and (3) passes the flow to the connected block. A conditional exit of $e\ \texttt{->}\ \ell; \ell'$ passes the control to ℓ when e evaluates to true, and passes to ℓ' otherwise. A conditional entry of $\ell; \ell'\ \texttt{<-}\ e$ receives the control from ℓ when e evaluates to true, and receives from ℓ' otherwise.

For consistent behavior, a CRIL program needs to be *well-formed* [16]. For each label ℓ, there must be a unique pair of immediately connected basic blocks by ℓ. This ensures that b with the exit of $\texttt{->}\ell$ deterministically passes the control flow to b' with the entry of $\ell\texttt{<-}$ in the forward execution, and vice versa in the backward execution. A *process block* is a set of connected basic blocks. To be well-formed, a process block has a pair of basic blocks with $\mathsf{begin}\ \ell$ and $\mathsf{end}\ \ell$, where **begin** ℓ is the unique source and **end** ℓ is the unique sink with respect to the connections by labels[1].

CRIL extends **call** of RIL [15] to multiple labels, passing control flows to multiple process blocks simultaneously. In the forward execution, **call** $\ell_1, \cdots, \ell_n$ creates processes of process blocks labelled by $\ell_1, \ldots, \ell_n$ and simultaneously passes the forward control flows to those processes to wait until those controls reach to the basic blocks with **end** $\ell_1, \cdots,$ **end** ℓ_n. In the backward execution, the call instruction passes the backward control flows to the newly created processes whose exit labels **end** $\ell_1, \cdots$ **end** ℓ_n to wait until those controls reach backward to the basic blocks with **begin** $\ell_1, \cdots,$ **begin** ℓ_n. To control the synchronization among multiple control flows, CRIL has the instruction of **P** x and **V** x where x is a special variable called a *synchronization variable* that ranges over $\{0, 1\}$. **P** x waits until x is set to 1 and set x to 0 after the instruction is executed. **V** x works symmetrically. **V** x waits until x is set to 0 and set x to 1 after the execution.

A process block with **begin** ℓ and **end** ℓ is denoted by $\mathsf{PB}(\ell)$. The variables appearing in a process block B and the heap M are denoted by $\mathsf{Res}(B)$. For process blocks B and $\mathsf{PB}(\ell)$, $B \Rightarrow_{call} \mathsf{PB}(\ell)$ if for some $b \in B$ whose instruction is **call** $\ell_1, \cdots, \ell_n$ with $\ell \in \{\ell_1, \cdots, \ell_n\}$. Process blocks B_1 and B_2 are *concurrent* unless $B_1 \Rightarrow^*_{call} B_2$ or $B_2 \Rightarrow^*_{call} B_1$. A variable x is shared if there are some concurrent process blocks B_1 and B_2 and $x \in \mathsf{Res}(B_1) \cap \mathsf{Res}(B_2)$ with $B_1 \neq B_2$. The set of shared variables in Pg and the heap is written as $\mathsf{ShR}(Pg)$ and the set of non-shared variables in Pg is $\mathsf{NShR}(Pg)$.

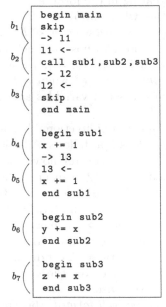

In the appendix, we show the operational semantics of CRIL. A configuration of CRIL program is (Pg, ρ, σ, Pr) where Pg is a CRIL program, ρ is a value assignment to variables and σ is a value assignment of the heap M. Pr is the mapping from process ids to basic blocks, where a process id is a sequence of natural numbers. The i-th subprocess of process p is identified by $p \cdot i$. We write PID for the set of process ids. The root process is identified by ε. $Pr(p)$ gives the basic block with the control flow in the process whose id is p. The basic reversible semantics is $(Pg, \rho, \sigma, Pr) \underset{prog}{\overset{p, Rd, Wt}{\rightleftharpoons}} (Pg, \rho', \sigma', Pr')$ meaning that the state (ρ, σ, Pr) in Pg evolves to (ρ', σ', Pr') in forward by process p, referring to variables of Rd, and updating variables of Wt and (ρ', σ', Pr') evolves back to (ρ, σ, Pr) in backward by undoing the updates of variables of Wt by referring to variables of Rd.

Fig. 2. Example of CRIL

---

[1] Note that the connection relation of basic blocks is defined by labels of **in** and **out** not by those of **call**.

Figure 2 shows a small example of CRIL. The program is well-formed and consists of 7 basic blocks, which are partitioned into four process blocks: $\{b_1, b_2, b_3\}, \{b_4, b_5\}, \{b_6\}, \{b_7\}$. In b_2, call passes the controls to processes of process blocks labelled by sub1, sub2, and sub3. Depending on the timing to execute b_6 and b_7, the values of y and z vary at the end because x is shared. For example, $b_1 b_2 b_4 b_6 b_7 b_5 b_3$ results in x=2, y=1, and z=1 assuming x,y, and z are initially 0. By $\xrightleftharpoons[\text{prog}]{p, Rd, Wt}$, the whole behavior of the program is not reversible since the backward execution of b_2 does not ensure order in the forward execution. If $b_3 b_2 b_7 b_5 b_4 b_6 b_1$, then the result is x=0, y=1 and z=-1 back at begin main. Since this is not the initial state of all 0, the program is not reversible according to this semantics. Here, besides reversing the forward order exactly, $b_3 b_2 b_5 b_6 b_7 b_4 b_1$ also reaches back to the initial state since there is no causality between y and z. This order should be allowed as the backward execution.

Reversibility by Annotation DAG. To gain reversibility, we incorporate a data structure called "Annotation DAG" to record the causality of variable updates.

An *annotation DAG* is a DAG (V, E_R, E_W) satisfying the following conditions:

1. $V \subseteq (\text{PID} \times \mathbb{N}) \cup \{\bot\}$ where $\mathbb{N}$ is the set of natural numbers;
2. $\bot \in V$, and if $(p, n) \in V$ then for all $n' \leq n$, $(p, n') \in V$;
3. $E_R, E_W \subseteq V \times \mathcal{R} \times V$ where $(v', r, v), (v'', r, v) \in E_R \cup E_W$ implies $v' = v''$;
4. $E_R \cap E_W = \varnothing$ and $(V, E_R \uplus E_W)$ is a DAG with the finite set of nodes V;
5. $(v', r, v) \in E_W$ and $v' \neq \bot$ imply $(v'', r, v') \in E_W$; and
6. $(v, r, v'), (v, r, v'') \in E_W$ implies $v' = v''$

$\mathcal{A}$ is the set of all annotation DAGs, and A_{init} is $(\{\bot\}, \varnothing, \varnothing)$.

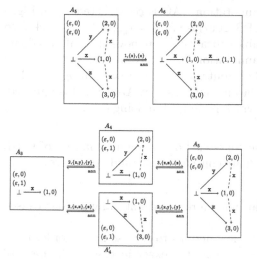

An annotation DAG starts with A_{init} synchronizes with the control flow of a CRIL program by $A_1 \xrightleftharpoons[\text{ann}]{p, Rd, Wt} A_2$. $(p, n) \in V$ represents the state of the n-th basic block in the process p. $(v', r, v) \in E_W$ means the variable (or the heap element) of r is updated by the forward transition from v' to v. $(u, r, u') \in E_R$ means the variable (or the heap element) of r is referred by the forward transition from u to u'. When $A_1 \xrightleftharpoons[\text{ann}]{p, Rd, Wt} A_2$, a fresh node (p, n') is appended where n' is the next basic block of p, and add the edges for updating

Fig. 3. Annotation DAG

Wt and referring to Rd for the forward transition of the CRIL program. For the backward transition, (p, n') and the edges with Rd and Wt are removed from A_2 to obtain A_1.

Given an annotation DAG (V, E_R, E_W), we write $\max_p(V)$ for $max_{(p,n) \in V}\, n$ for some $(p, n) \in V$. $\max_p(V) = -1$ when $(p, n) \notin V$ for all n. For $r \in \mathcal{R}$, there is a unique sequence of E_W with the label of r from $\bot$ to v: $(\bot, r, v_1), (v_1, r, v_2), \cdots, (v_n, r, v)$ such that $\forall v'.(v, v') \notin E_W$. $\mathsf{last}(r, E_W)$ denotes the last node v of such sequence.

Definition 1 *For* $A_1, A_2 \in \mathcal{A}$, $A_1 = (V_1, E_{R1}, E_{W1}) \underset{\text{ann}}{\overset{p, Rd, Wt}{\rightleftharpoons}} A_2 = (V_2, E_{R2}, E_{W2})$

1. $V_2 = V_1 \cup \{v\}$;
2. $E_{R2} = E_{R1} \cup \{\mathsf{newedge}(r, E_{W1}, v) \mid r \in Rd - Wt\}$; and
3. $E_{W2} = E_{W1} \cup \{\mathsf{newedge}(r, E_{W1}, v) \mid r \in Wt\}$

where $v = (p, \max_p(V_1) + 1)$ *and* $\mathsf{newedge}(r, E_W, v) = (\mathsf{last}(r, E_W), r, v)$.

The *operational semantics controlled by annotation DAG* over program configurations $(C, A) \overset{p, Rd, Wt}{\rightleftharpoons} (C', A')$ is defined by:

$$\frac{C \underset{\text{prog}}{\overset{p, Rd, Wt}{\rightleftharpoons}} C' \qquad A \underset{\text{ann}}{\overset{p, Rd, Wt}{\rightleftharpoons}} A'}{(C, A) \overset{p, Rd, Wt}{\rightleftharpoons} (C', A')} \textbf{ProgAnn}$$

A computation is a sequence of $(C_i, A_i) \overset{p_i, Rd_i, Wt_i}{\rightleftharpoons} (C_{i+1}, A_{i+1})$ $(i \geq 0)$ beginning with $(C_0, A_0) = (C_{init}, A_{init})$.

For the example in Fig. 2, by the forward computation of $b_1 b_2 b_4 b_6 b_7 b_5 b_3$ with $\rho_4 = [\mathtt{x} \mapsto 2, \mathtt{y} \mapsto 1, \mathtt{z} \mapsto 2]$. The annotation DAG is constructed A_6 in Fig. 3 where pid of $\mathsf{PB}(\mathtt{main})$ is ε and pid of $\mathsf{PB}(\mathtt{sub}i)$ is i for $i = 1, 2, 3$. In the backward execution starting with b_3, the resolvable causality is to remove $(1, 1)$ after redoing b_3 as in Fig. 3. After this undo, the annotation DAG becomes A_5 and $(2, 0)$ and $(3, 0)$ can be removed. In the forward computation, z is increased by b_5, but $(2, 0)$ can be removed to be A_4' without violating any causality. After $(2, 0)$ is removed, $(3, 0)$ can be removed to become A_3 which is same of undoing $b_3 b_5$.

Properties for Reversibility. The controlled operational semantics of CRIL enjoy causal safety and liveness, which are considered the fundamental reversibility for concurrent behavior [11, 12].

Causal Safety (CS): An action can not be reversed until any actions caused by it have been reversed.

Causal Liveness (CL): We should allow actions to reverse in any order compatible with Causal Safety not necessarily the exact inverse of the forward order.

Theorem 1 ([16]). $\xrightarrow{p,Rd,Wt}$ *satisfies the causal safety and the causal liveness.*

For CRIL, causal safety ensures that the same value is used for a variable in both directions. Causal liveness ensures that a program does not deadlock without returning to its initial state in the backward direction. To implement the proper reversibility, combining with an annotation DAG is essential. Otherwise, in the backward execution, a CRIL program may reach a state that is not reachable in the forward execution.

3   Bidirectional Data Flow of CRIL

For a CRIL program, we analyze the data flow through variables. In particular, data flow via shared variables among parallel blocks depends on the synchronization constraints. This section presents a static analysis to approximate data flow obtained from the syntactic information and the synchronization by P-V operations [17].

For $C_1 = (Pg, \rho, \sigma, Pr)$ and $C_2 = (Pg, \rho', \sigma', Pr')$, $C_1 \xrightleftharpoons[prog]{p,Rd,Wt} C_2$, we write $C_1 \xrightleftharpoons[prog]{p,b} C_2$ if the transition is by the basic block of $Pr(p)$ is executed, where $Pr(p) = (l, \mathsf{run})$ or $Pr(p) = (l, \mathsf{begin})$ with entry(b) whose label is l and $Pr'(p) = (l', \mathsf{run})$ or $Pr(p) = (l', \mathsf{end})$ with exit(b) whose label is l'. Or, $b = l\texttt{<-call } l_1, \cdots, l_n \texttt{->} l'$ at forking subprocesses where $Pr(p) = (l, \mathsf{run})$, $Pr'(p) = (l', \mathsf{run})$, and $Pr'(p \cdot i) = (l_i, \mathsf{begin})$ for $(1 \leq i \leq n)$ and at merging subprocesses where $Pr(p) = (l, \mathsf{run})$, $Pr(p \cdot i) = (l_i, \mathsf{end})$, and $Pr'(p) = (l', \mathsf{run})$ for $1 \leq i \leq n$.

An execution of Pg is a sequence: $C_0 \xrightleftharpoons[prog]{p_1,b_1} C_1 \xrightleftharpoons[prog]{p_2,b_2} \cdots \xrightleftharpoons[prog]{p_n,b_n} C_n$ where $C_0 = (Pg, \rho_0, \sigma_0, [\varepsilon \mapsto (\mathsf{begin}, \mathsf{main})])$ and $C_n = (Pg, \rho_n, \sigma_n, [\varepsilon \mapsto (\mathsf{end}, \mathsf{main})])$

A forward data flow via a variable r exists from b_i to b_j (b_i, r, b_j) if:

- $C_0 \xrightleftharpoons[prog]{\gamma} C_{i-1} \xrightleftharpoons[prog]{(p_i,b_i)} \cdots \xrightleftharpoons[prog]{(p_j,b_j)} C_j \xrightleftharpoons[prog]{\gamma'} C_n$
- $r \in (\mathsf{write}(b_i) \cap (\mathsf{read}(b_j)) \backslash (\cup_{k=i}^{j} \mathsf{write}(b_k))$

Symmetrically, there exists a backward data flow from b_j to b_i $\langle b_j, r, b_i \rangle$ if:

- $r \in (\mathsf{write}(b_j) \cap \mathsf{read}(b_i)) \backslash (\cup_{k=i}^{j} \mathsf{write}(b_k))$

fwddflow$(Pg) = \{(b, r, b') \mid b, b' \in Pg, r \in \mathsf{Res}(Pg)\}$, and bkwdflow$(Pg) = \{\langle b', r, b \rangle \mid b, b' \in Pg, r \in \mathsf{Res}(Pg)\}$

fwddflow(Pg) and bkwdflow(Pg) are defined by all executions of Pg. In general, given Pg, b, b' and r, checking whether $(b, r, b') \in$ fwddflow(Pg) and checking whether $(b, r, b') \in$ bkwdflow(Pg) are both undecidable since CRIL can implement the while loop structure and has the integers as the data domain. Thus, a data flow analysis is to approximate data flows according to the syntactical structure of Pg. A data flow analysis is *sound* if the forward data flow analysis includes fwddflow(Pg) and the backward data flow analysis includes bkwdflow(Pg).

An obvious data flow analysis in both directions is $F = \{(b, r, b'), \langle b', r, b \rangle \mid r \in$ read(b) $\cap$ write(b')$\}$ ignoring the execution order of basic blocks. If it is shown that b cannot be executed before b' in any forward execution or b cannot be executed after b' in any backward execution, no such data flow exists. Or, r is overwritten by some execution in either a forward execution or a backward execution.

To obtain a more precise data flow analysis, we construct a control flow graph to remove the impossible data flows from F. In this paper, we give an overview of getting a more precise bidirectional data flow analysis using the following syntactical information.

1. **UD and DU chain relationship:** Among process blocks in $\Rightarrow^*_{call}$, by applying the conventional data flow analysis, it is possible to remove (b, r, b') and $\langle b', r, b \rangle$ if r is defined in the execution path from b to b';
2. **Synchronization:** Two processes are executed concurrently where one process has $P\ x$ and the other has $V\ x$. Since a block b after $P\ x$ has no flow to a block b' after $V\ x$ since the blocks after $P\ x$ wait until $V\ x$ is executed, (b, r, b') and $\langle b', r, b \rangle$ are removed.
3. **Critical region:** If a set of connected basic blocks whose source of control is $V\ y$ and whose sink of control is $P\ y$ and there exist the blocks $B_1, \cdots, B_n$, y works as the semaphore and B_i's are mutually excluded and B_i's are critical regions. The flows between basic blocks in those critical regions do not exist. When $b \in B_i$ and $b' \in B_j$ (b, r, b') and $\langle b', r, b \rangle$ are removed.

By applying the above, a sound forward data flow analysis of FAE(Pg) and a sound backward data flow analysis of BAE(Pg) are derived [17]. FAE and BAE give reasonably precise data flow analysis.

In this paper, we only consider shared variables assuming the heap is a store for irreversible data. Although it is possible to use the heap M in the analysis, the heap is identified if all the values in the heap are identical since it is treated as a single memory. Since this does not contribute to a data flow analysis, we exclude M from ShR(Pg) at the moment.

An Example of Bidirectional Data Flow Analysis

For a program shown in Fig. 4, there are three process blocks $\{b_0, \cdots, b_9\}$, $\{b_{10}, \cdots, b_{15}\}$, and $\{b_{16}, \cdots, b_{24}\}$, where we abbreviate the matching labels between basic blocks. Two processes labelled sub1 and sub2 run concurrently.

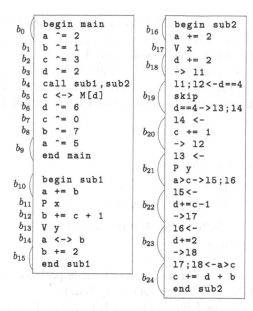

Fig. 4. Example for data flow

Table 1. write and read

x	$\{b \mid x \in \text{write}(b)\}$
a	$\{b_0, b_9, b_{10}, b_{14}, b_{16}\}$
b	$\{b_1, b_8, b_{10}, b_{12}, b_{14}, b_{15}\}$
c	$\{b_2, b_5, b_7, b_{20}, b_{24}\}$
d	$\{b_3, b_6, b_{18}, b_{22}, b_{23}\}$
x	$\{b \mid x \in \text{read}(b)\}$
a	$\{b_0, b_9, b_{10}, b_{14}, b_{16}, b_{21}, b_{24}\}$
b	$\{b_1, b_8, b_{10}, b_{12}, b_{14}, b_{15}, b_{24}\}$
c	$\{b_2, b_5, b_7, b_{12}, b_{20}, b_{22}, b_{24}\}$
d	$\{b_3, b_5, b_6, b_{18}, b_{19}, b_{22}, b_{23}, b_{24}\}$

Table 1 shows the blocks with write and read for each shared variable. For a pair of basic blocks (b, b') such that $\text{write}(b) \cap \text{read}(b') \neq \varnothing$, there exists a potential data flow (b, r, b') in forward and $\langle b', r, b \rangle$ in backward via variables or the heap $r \in \text{write}(b) \cap \text{read}(b')$.

In the following, we apply the data flow analysis FAE and BAE in [17] to the example as a more precise data flow analysis.

We define $F(r)$ as the forward flows to the basic block whose instruction is $r \oplus = e$ or $r \text{<->} r'$, where r is defined immediately after it is used. A flow of $F(r)$ terminates at the basic block of the destination.

$$F(\text{a}) = \{(b_0, \text{a}, b_{10}), (b_0, \text{a}, b_{16}), (b_{10}, \text{a}, b_{16}), (b_{16}, \text{a}, b_{10}), (b_{10}, \text{a}, b_{14}), (b_{16}, \text{a}, b_{14}),$$
$$(b_{14}, \text{a}, b_9)\}$$
$$F(\text{b}) = \{(b_1, \text{b}, b_{12}), (b_{12}, \text{b}, b_{14}), (b_{14}, \text{b}, b_{15}), (b_{15}, \text{b}, b_8)\}$$
$$F(\text{c}) = \{(b_2, \text{c}, b_{20}), (b_2, \text{c}, b_{24}), (b_{20}, \text{c}, b_{20}), (b_{20}, \text{c}, b_{24}), (b_{24}, \text{c}, b_5), (b_5, \text{c}, b_7)\}$$
$$F(\text{d}) = \{(b_3, \text{d}, b_{18}), (b_{18}, \text{d}, b_{22}), (b_{18}, \text{d}, b_{23}), (b_{22}, \text{d}, b_6), (b_{23}, \text{d}, b_6)\}$$

The following $F'(r)$ is the forward flow to the right values in the basic blocks, where the values may be used by the other basic blocks.

$$F'(\text{a}) = \{(b_{10}, \text{a}, b_{21}), (b_{14}, \text{a}, b_{21}), (b_{16}, \text{a}, b_{21}), (b_{10}, \text{a}, b_{24}), (b_{14}, \text{a}, b_{24}), (b_{16}, \text{a}, b_{23})\}$$
$$F'(\text{b}) = \{(b_1, \text{b}, b_{10}), (b_{12}, \text{b}, b_{24}), (b_{14}, \text{b}, b_{24}), (b_{15}, \text{b}, b_{24})\}$$
$$F'(\text{c}) = \{(b_2, \text{c}, b_{12}), (b_2, \text{c}, b_{21}), (b_2, \text{c}, b_{22}), (b_{20}, \text{c}, b_{12}), (b_{20}, \text{c}, b_{21}), (b_{20}, \text{c}, b_{22})\}$$
$$F'(\text{d}) = \{(b_3, \text{d}, b_{16}), (b_{18}, \text{d}, b_{19}), (b_{22}, \text{d}, b_5), (b_{22}, \text{d}, b_{24}), (b_{23}, \text{d}, b_5), (b_{23}, \text{d}, b_{24})\}$$

A forward flow analysis FAE is a collection of F and F' for all variables and the heap. (In this case, no heap memory is used.) $\mathsf{FAE}(Pg) = \cup_{r \in \{a,b,c,d\}} F(r) \cup F'(r)$

For backward flows, the reversed flows in $F(r)$ become the backward data flows since a backward flow of r starts with a basic block in the form of $r \oplus = e$. Meanwhile, the flows in $F'(r)$ cannot be immediately reversed for backward data flows. A backward flow of r starts with the last referred basic block in the forward executions.

$$G(\mathsf{a}) = \{\langle b_{14}, \mathsf{a}, b_{21}\rangle, \langle b_{14}, \mathsf{a}, b_{24}\rangle, \langle b_9, \mathsf{a}, b_{21}\rangle, \langle b_9, \mathsf{a}, b_{24}\rangle\}$$
$$G(\mathsf{b}) = \{\langle b_8, \mathsf{b}, b_{24}\rangle, \langle b_{14}, \mathsf{b}, b_{24}\rangle, \langle b_{15}, \mathsf{b}, b_{24}\rangle, \langle b_{12}, \mathsf{b}, b_{10}\rangle\}$$
$$G(\mathsf{c}) = \{\langle b_{24}, \mathsf{c}, b_{22}\rangle, \langle b_{24}, \mathsf{c}, b_{21}\rangle, \langle b_{24}, \mathsf{c}, b_{12}\rangle, \langle b_{20}, \mathsf{c}, b_{12}\rangle\},$$
$$G(\mathsf{d}) = \{\langle b_6, \mathsf{d}, b_5\rangle, \langle b_6, \mathsf{d}, b_{24}\rangle, \langle b_{22}, \mathsf{d}, b_{19}\rangle, \langle b_{23}, \mathsf{d}, b_{19}\rangle, \langle b_{18}, \mathsf{d}, b_{16}\rangle\}$$
$$\mathsf{BAE}(Pg) = \cup_{r \in \{a,b,c,d\}} F^{-1}(r) \cup G(r)$$

Both of $\mathsf{FAE}(Pg)$ and $\mathsf{BAE}(Pg)$ are sound. In this example, it is possible to derive the exact data flows $\mathsf{fwddflow}(Pg)$ and $\mathsf{bkwdflow}(Pg)$ by hand.

$\mathsf{fwddflow}(Pg)$ is obtained by removing the following flows: $\{(b_2, \mathsf{c}, b_{20}), (b_{20}, \mathsf{c}, b_{20}), (b_{20}, \mathsf{c}, b_{24}), (b_{20}, \mathsf{c}, b_{12}), (b_{20}, \mathsf{c}, b_{21}), (b_{20}, \mathsf{c}, b_{22}), (b_{18}, \mathsf{d}, b_{23}), (b_{23}, \mathsf{d}, b_6), (b_{23}, \mathsf{d}, b_5), (b_{23}, \mathsf{d}, b_{24})\}$

$\mathsf{bkwdflow}(Pg)$ is obtained by removing the following flows: $\{\langle b_{24}, \mathsf{c}, b_{20}\rangle, \langle b_{20}, \mathsf{c}, b_{20}\rangle, \langle b_{20}, \mathsf{c}, b_2\rangle, \langle b_{20}, \mathsf{c}, b_{12}\rangle, \langle b_{23}, \mathsf{d}, b_{18}\rangle, \langle b_6, \mathsf{d}, b_{23}\rangle, \langle b_{23}, \mathsf{d}, b_{19}\rangle\}$

These flows are related to b_{20} and b_{23}. b_{19} and b_{20} form a loop structure whose entry is by l1 and whose exit is by l3.

4   CRSSA: Concurrent Reversible SSA Form

In the SSA form, some built-in functions are defined to represent possible data flow. Those functions are not compiled to compute values but are just used to show one of their arguments is assigned to the lefthand side variable in the execution. By the built-in functions, possible data flow is represented in the form of assignments. In addition to the ϕ function used for non-shared variables, we introduce the π function for shared variables as follows.

π **function** A π-function term $\pi(x_{i_1}, \cdots, x_{i_n})$ means that one of x_{i_j} is chosen from the shared variables of the concurrently running processes.

For $x \in \mathsf{ShR}(Pg)$, $x_{i_0} := \pi(x_{i_1}, \cdots, x_{i_n})$ at the entry of a basic block indicates that a fresh variable x_{k_0} is from one of $x_{i_1}, \cdots, x_{i_n}$ when the basic block is executed in the forward direction, and $\pi(x_{j_1}, \cdots, x_{j_m}) := x_{j_0}$ at the exit indicates that x_{j_0} is recovered from one of $x_{j_1}, \cdots, x_{j_m}$ in the backward execution.

ϕ **function** At a ϕ assignment $x_{i_0} := \phi(x_{i_1}, \cdots, x_{i_n})$, the possible flow of $x \in \mathsf{NShR}(Pg)$ joins and the value of x used afterward is stored in x_{i_0} in forward direction. Symmetrically, at an inverted ϕ assignment $\phi(x_{i_1}, \cdots, x_{i_n}) := x_{i_0}$, the possible flow of x joins and the used value is stored in x_{i_0} in backward direction.

4.1 Basic Blocks of CRSSA

A block in CRIL contains an instruction. Data flow among variables exists if there is an execution path to produce update causality. Depending on the order of parallel blocks, the sound analysis of data flow covers all possible data flow. A π function presents flow candidates by synchronization, while a ϕ function presents flow candidates by conditionals.

Variable Updates. Let $\text{invop}(+) = -$, $\text{invop}(-) = +$, and $\text{invop}(\hat{}) = \hat{}$. To convert instructions which define variables into assignment form, we introduce the instruction forms: $x_i := \hat{e}$, $\hat{e} := x_i$, $x_j := x_i \oplus \hat{e}$, $x_j, y_{j'} := y_{i'}, x_i$, $x_j := M[z_h] := x_i$.

- $x_i := \hat{e}$ assigns the value of $\hat{e}$ to x_i in forward direction.
- $\hat{e} := x_i$ assigns the value of $\hat{e}$ to x_i in backward direction.
- $x_j := x_i \oplus \hat{e}$ assigns the value of $x_i \oplus e$ to x_j and assigns the value of $x_j \ominus e$ to x_i in backward direction, where $\ominus = \text{invop}(\oplus)$.
- $x_j, y_{j'} := y_{i'}, x_i$ assigns the value of x_i to x_j and the value of $y_{i'}$ to $y_{j'}$ in forward direction and from x_j to x_i and $y_{j'}$ to $y_{i'}$ in backward direction.
- $x_j := M[z_h] := x_i$ assigns the value of $M[z_h]$ to x_j and the value of x_i to $M[z_h]$ in forward direction. It assigns the value of $M[z_h]$ to x_i and the value of x_j to $M[z_h]$ in backward direction.

We write the defining variables in block b $\text{Def}(b)$: $\text{Def}(b) = \text{write}(b) - \{M\}$. $\text{Ref}(b)$ is the set of other variables appearing in b. $\text{Ref}(b)$ appears on the right side of the update or in the conditional part at the entry and exit.

Variables at Entry and Exit. The variables appearing in conditional entry and exit parts of basic blocks are indexed as $\ell_1; \ell_2$ <- $\hat{c}$ and $\hat{e}$ -> $\ell_1; \ell_2$.

Non-translated Instructions. For other types of instructions, we put the instructions of CRIL without translation.

V x, P x, assert e, and skip, or call $\ell_1, \cdots, \ell_n$.

A synchronization variable appearing in a PV operation is not indexed since PV operations essentially differ from updates and exchanges in that they synchronize processes where no data flow occurs. Here, we do not track the data flow between heap elements. We do not translate the following types of instructions: $M[x_i] \oplus= \hat{e}$, and $M[x_i]$ <-> $M[x_j]$.

4.2 Translation from CRIL to CRSSA

We add the π-function assignments of the variables appearing in the basic block. An update instruction of $r \oplus = e$ is replaced by assignment $x_{i_0} := x_{j_0} \oplus \hat{e}$ in the SSA form, where $\hat{e}$ is the expression whose variables are replaced by the indexed variables and x_i is unique in the program. If x is a shared variable, a π-assignment of $x_{i_0} := \pi(x_{i_1}, \cdots, x_{i_n})$ is placed at the entry and $\pi(x_{j_1}, \cdots, x_{j_m}) := x_{j_0}$ at the exit, where $x_{i_1}, \cdots, x_{i_n}$ and $x_{j_1}, \cdots, x_{j_m}$ are the lists of indexed variables according to the flows. For a shared variable y_k in $\hat{e}$, $y_{k_0} := \pi(y_{k_1}, \cdots, y_{k_n})$ at the entry and $\pi(y_{k_1}, \cdots, y_{k_m}) := y_{k_0}$ at the exit. Note that the index is the same for y both at the entry and exit since y is read-only and creates no fresh definition in that basic block.

Let a sound forward and backward flow be *Fflow* and *Bflow*. For simplicity, assume that $\text{inst}(b) = x\char`\^=e$ if for all $b'.(b', b) \notin$ *Fflow* at the initialization of $x$, and $\text{inst}(b) = x\char`\^=e$ if for all $b'.(b', b) \in$ *Bflow* at a finalization of x.

The translation is done in the following 7 steps:

Step 1: **(Translation to assignment forms)** For each $b \in Pg$, we convert $\text{inst}(b)$ into an assignment form $\text{af}(b)$, which is defined as follows:

- If $\text{inst}(b) = x \oplus= e$, then $\text{af}(b) = \begin{cases} x := e & \text{if } \forall b'.(b', x, b) \notin \textit{Fflow} \\ e := x & \text{if } \forall b'.\langle b', x, b\rangle \notin \textit{Bflow} \\ x := x \oplus e & \text{otherwise.} \end{cases}$

- If $\text{inst}(b) = x\texttt{<->}y$, then $\text{af}(b) = x, y := y, x$.
- If $\text{inst}(b) = x\texttt{<->M}[z]$, then $\text{af}(b) = x := \texttt{M}[z] := x$.
- Otherwise, $\text{af}(b) = \text{inst}(b)$.

Let $\hat{Pg} = \{\hat{b} \mid \text{inst}(\hat{b}) = \text{af}(b) \in Pg\}$. $\hat{Pg}$ is the set of basic blocks of CRSSA where the instructions are replaced by af. $\hat{b}$ has the one-to-one correspondence between the basic blocks of Pg and its CRSSA form.

Step 2: **(Construct the RSSA form of $\hat{Pg}$ for $\text{NShR}(Pg)$)** Following the procedure of [14], construct $(\hat{Pg}, \phi entry, \phi exit)$ where $\phi entry$ is the set of ϕ assignments to $\text{NShR}(Pg)$ placed at the entry of $\hat{b}$,and $\phi exit$ is the set of inverted ϕ assignments to $\text{NShR}(Pg)$ placed at the exit of ϕb.

Step 3: **(Assign indices to defining variables)** For each $x \in \text{ShR}(Pg)$ appearing in b, assign unique indices to $x \in \text{Def}(b)$ as $\text{DefLIdx}(b, x)$ and $\text{DefRIdx}(b, x)$, and assign indices to $z \in \text{Ref}(b)$ as $\text{UseIdx}(b, z)$. DefLIdx, DefRIdx and UseIdx are disjoint from each other and all unique in the program for each variable.

Step 4: **(Add indices to variables)** Add the index $j = \text{DefLIdx}(b, x)$ and $j' = \text{DefLIdx}(b, y)$ to x and y appearing on the left side of instructions in the forms: $x_j := e$, $x_j := x \oplus e$, $x_j, y_{j'} := y, x$, and $x_j := \texttt{M}[z] := x$. Then add the index $k = \text{DefRIdx}(b, x)$ and $k' = \text{DefRIdx}(b, y)$ to x and y appearing on the right side of the instruction in the forms: $e := x_k$, $x := x_k \oplus e$, $x, y := y_k, x_{k'}$ and $x := \texttt{M}[z] := x_k$. Assign $z \in \text{Ref}(b)$ to $\text{UseIdx}(b, z)$.

Step 5: **(Place π assignments)** The π assignments for $\text{Var}(b)$ are placed at the entry of $\hat{b}$. The variables appearing in b

$$\pi entry(\hat{b}) = \bigcup_{x \in \text{Def}(b)} \{x_{i_0} := \pi(x_{i_1}, \cdots, x_{i_n}) \mid i_0 = \text{DefRIdx}(b, x),$$
$$\{i_1, \cdots, i_n\} = \cup_{(b', x, b) \in Fflow} \text{DefLIdx}(b', x)\}$$
$$\cup \bigcup_{z \in \text{Ref}(b)} \{z_{k_0} := \pi(z_{k_1}, \cdots, z_{k_n}) \mid k_0 = \text{UseIdx}(b, z),$$
$$\{k_1, \cdots, k_n\} = \cup_{(b', z, b, \in,)Fflow} \text{UseIdx}(b', z)\}$$

$$\pi exit(\hat{b}) = \bigcup_{x \in \text{Def}(b)} \{\pi(x_{j_1}, \cdots, x_{j_m}) := x_{j_0} \mid j_0 = \text{DefLIdx}(b, x),$$
$$\{j_1, \cdots, j_m\} = \cup_{\langle b, x, b'\rangle \in Bflow} \text{DefRIdx}(b', x)\}$$
$$\cup \bigcup_{z \in \text{Ref}(b)} \{z_{k_0} := \pi(z_{k_1}, \cdots, z_{k_m}) \mid k_0 = \text{UseIdx}(b, z),$$
$$\{k_1, \cdots, k_m\} = \cup_{\langle b, z, b'\rangle \in Bflow} \text{UseIdx}(b', z)\}$$

Step 6: (**Add indices to other uses of variables**) For each use of unindexed x except for PV operations, by following all paths backward from the use until we reach a definition of x_i on the dominator tree, we can find the unique definition of x_i.

Step 7: (**Remove redundant assignments**) Remove a pair of $x_i := \pi(x_j)$ and $\pi(x_i) := x_j$ and replace all the occurrences of x_i with x_j. Remove a pair of $x_i := \pi(x_j)$ and $\pi(x_j) := x_i$ and replace all the occurrences of x_i with x_j. Similar to π, remove redundant ϕ assignments.

By translation above, we obtain the CRSSA form of Pg as a control flow graph: $G = (\hat{P}g, \phi entry, \phi exit, \pi entry, \pi exit)$.

4.3   Examples for Translation from CRIL into CRSSA

The example in Fig. 4 is converted into the CRSSA shown in Fig. 5 using FAE(Pg) and BAE(Pg) in [17]. The data flow of a, b, and c which are operated in main, sub1, and sub2 is syntactically represented by indices and π assignments. For example, a1 := π(a0, a6) in $\hat{b}_{10}$ indicates that the data of a flow from $\hat{b}_0$ where a0 is defined or $\hat{b}_{16}$ where a6 is defined into $\hat{b}_{10}$ in forward direction. π(a3, a5) := a2 indicates that the data of a flow from $\hat{b}_{14}$ or $\hat{b}_{16}$ into $\hat{b}_{10}$ in backward direction. Note that a4, b2 := b1, a3 defines a3 (and b1) and a6:=a5+d0 defines a5 in backward direction. The data flow of d which is sequentially operated in main and sub2 is represented by indices and ϕ assignments like RSSA.

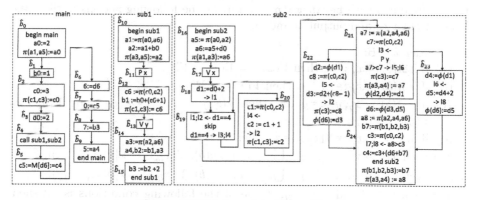

Fig. 5. CRSSA translated from Fig. 4

5   Application of Optimization

We apply the existing optimization techniques. In the following, we show conditional constant propagation, dead code elimination, and copy propagation. After optimization is applied, we eliminate π and ϕ functions. Finally, we illustrate our optimization by showing examples.

5.1 Conditional Constant Propagation

The "simple" constant propagation tracks the assignments whose righthand side expressions are constants in forward and whose lefthand side expressions are constants in backward [17]. The conditional constant propagation checks if a block is possible to be executed. Here, we present the bidirectional version of the conditional constant propagation shown in [3, (Section 19.3)].

We determine all the variables in CRSSA to be constant integers, $\bot$ (never assigned), or $\top$ (assigned with different values). We define $* : (\mathbb{Z} \cup \{\bot, \top\})^2 \to \mathbb{Z} \cup \{\bot, \top\}$ as in Table 2, where $\mathsf{eq}(m, m') = m$ if $m = m'$, $\mathsf{eq}(m, m') = \top$ otherwise. Let $\widehat{Vars}$ be the set of indexed variables. For $\mathcal{V} : \widehat{Vars} \to \mathbb{Z} \cup \{\bot, \top\}$, we defines $\mathcal{V}[t]$ as follows:

Table 2. Definition of $*$

$$\mathcal{V}[t] = \begin{cases} \mathcal{V}(x_i) & \text{if } t = x_i \\ \top & \text{if } t = \mathbb{M}[x_i] \\ \mathcal{V}[t'] \odot \mathcal{V}[t''] & \text{if } t = t \odot t' \text{ and } \mathcal{V}[t'], \mathcal{V}[t''] \in \mathbb{Z} \\ \top & \text{if } t = t \odot t' \text{ and } \top \in \{\mathcal{V}[t'], \mathcal{V}[t'']\} \\ \bot & \text{otherwise} \end{cases}$$

$*$	$\bot$	$\top$	m
$\bot$	$\bot$	$\top$	m
$\top$	$\top$	$\top$	$\top$
m'	m'	$\top$	$\mathsf{eq}(m, m')$

In addition, let $\mathcal{V}[\pi(x_{i_1, \cdots, i_n})] = \mathcal{V}[\phi(x_{i_1, \cdots, i_n})] = \mathcal{V}(x_{i_1}) * \cdots * \mathcal{V}(x_{i_n})$. We define $\mathcal{V}_\bot : \widehat{Vars} \to \mathbb{Z} \cup \{\bot, \top\}$ by $\mathcal{V}_\bot(x_i) = \bot$ for all $x_i \in \widehat{Vars}$.

Forward Conditional Constant Propagation. First, $\mathcal{V} := \mathcal{V}_\bot$ and $\mathcal{B} := \{\hat{b}\}$ for the unique $\hat{b}$ with **begin main**. We repeat the following actions until $\mathcal{B}$ and $\mathcal{V}$ never changes and output $\mathcal{V}$ and $\mathcal{B}$.

1. For each $\hat{b} \in \mathcal{B}$:
   (a) if $\mathsf{inst}(\hat{b}) = x_j := \hat{e}$, then $\mathcal{V}(x_j) := \mathcal{V}(x_j) * \mathcal{V}[\hat{e}]$;
   (b) if $\mathsf{inst}(\hat{b}) = x_j := x_i \oplus \hat{e}$, then $\mathcal{V}(x_j) := \mathcal{V}(x_j) * \mathcal{V}[x_i \oplus \hat{e}]$;
   (c) if $\mathsf{inst}(\hat{b}) = x_j, y_{j'} := y_{i'}, x_i$, then $\mathcal{V}(x_j) := \mathcal{V}(x_j) * \mathcal{V}(y_{i'})$; and $\mathcal{V}(y_{j'}) := \mathcal{V}(y_{j'}) * \mathcal{V}(x_i)$; and
   (d) if $\mathsf{inst}(\hat{b}) = x_j := \mathbb{M}[z_h] := x_i$, then $\mathcal{V}(x_j) := \top$.
2. For each $x_{i_0} := \pi(x_{i_1, \cdots, i_n}) \in \bigcup_{\hat{b} \in \mathcal{B}} \pi entry(\hat{b})$, $\mathcal{V}(x_{i_0}) := \mathcal{V}[\pi(x_{i_1, \cdots, i_n})]$.
3. For each $x_{i_0} := \phi(x_{i_1, \cdots, i_n}) \in \bigcup_{\hat{b} \in \mathcal{B}} \phi entry(\hat{b})$, $\mathcal{V}(x_{i_0}) := \mathcal{V}[\phi(x_{i_1, \cdots, i_n})]$.
4. For each $\hat{b} \in \mathcal{B}$ and $\hat{b}' \in \hat{P}g$, if one of the following conditions is satisfied, then $\mathcal{B} := \mathcal{B} \cup \{\hat{b}'\}$:
   (a) $\mathsf{exit}(\hat{b}) = \text{->}\ell$ and $\ell \in \mathsf{in}(\hat{b}')$;
   (b) $\mathsf{exit}(\hat{b}) = \hat{e}\text{->}\ell; \ell'$, $\mathcal{V}[\hat{e}]$ is $\top$ or not 0, and $\ell \in \mathsf{in}(\hat{b}')$;
   (c) $\mathsf{exit}(\hat{b}) = \hat{e}\text{->}\ell'; \ell$, $\mathcal{V}[\hat{e}]$ is $\top$ or 0, and $\ell \in \mathsf{in}(\hat{b}')$;
   (d) $\mathsf{inst}(\hat{b}) = \text{call } \ell_1, \cdots, \ell_n$ and $\exists i.\mathsf{entry}(\hat{b}') = \text{begin } \ell_i$

Backward Conditional Constant Propagation. First, $\mathcal{V} := \mathcal{V}_\perp$ and $\mathcal{B} := \{\hat{b}\}$ for the unique $\hat{b}$ with end main. We repeat the following actions until $\mathcal{V}$ and $\mathcal{B}$ never changes and output $\mathcal{V}$ and $\mathcal{B}$.

1. For each $\hat{b} \in \mathcal{B}$:
   (a) if $\mathsf{inst}(\hat{b}) = \hat{e} := x_i$, then $\mathcal{V}(x_i) := \mathcal{V}(x_i) * \mathcal{V}[\hat{e}]$;
   (b) if $\mathsf{inst}(\hat{b}) = x_j := x_i \oplus \hat{e}$, then $\mathcal{V}(x_i) := \mathcal{V}(x_i) * \mathcal{V}[x_j \ominus \hat{e}]$, where $\ominus = \mathsf{invop}(\oplus)$;
   (c) if $\mathsf{inst}(\hat{b}) = x_j, y_{j'} := y_{i'}, x_i$, then $\mathcal{V}(x_i) := \mathcal{V}(x_i) * \mathcal{V}(y_{j'})$; and $\mathcal{V}(y_{i'}) := \mathcal{V}(y_{i'}) * \mathcal{V}(x_j)$; and
   (d) if $\mathsf{inst}(\hat{b}) = x_j := \mathsf{M}[z_h] := x_i$, then $\mathcal{V}(x_i) := \top$.
2. For each $\pi(x_{i_1}, \cdots, x_{i_n}) := x_{i_0} \in \bigcup_{\hat{b} \in \mathcal{B}} \pi exit(\hat{b})$, $\mathcal{V}(x_{i_0}) := \mathcal{V}[\pi(x_{i_1, \cdots, i_n})]$.
3. For each $\phi(x_{i_1}, \cdots, x_{i_n}) := x_{i_0} \in \bigcup_{\hat{b} \in \mathcal{B}} \phi exit(\hat{b})$, $\mathcal{V}(x_{i_0}) := \mathcal{V}[\phi(x_{i_1, \cdots, i_n})]$.
4. For each $\hat{b} \in \mathcal{B}$ and $\hat{b}' \in \hat{P}g$, if one of the following conditions is satisfied, then $\mathcal{B} := \mathcal{B} \cup \{\hat{b}'\}$:
   (a) $\mathsf{entry}(\hat{b}) = \ell\mathtt{<-}$ and $\ell \in \mathsf{out}(\hat{b}')$;
   (b) $\mathsf{entry}(\hat{b}) = \ell; \ell'\mathtt{<-}\hat{e}$, $\mathcal{V}[\hat{e}]$ is $\top$ or not 0, and $\ell \in \mathsf{out}(\hat{b}')$;
   (c) $\mathsf{entry}(\hat{b}) = \ell'; \ell\mathtt{<-}\hat{e}$, $\mathcal{V}[\hat{e}]$ is $\top$ or 0, and $\ell \in \mathsf{out}(\hat{b}')$;
   (d) $\mathsf{inst}(\hat{b}) = \mathtt{call}\ \ell_1, \cdots, \ell_n$ and $\exists i.\mathsf{exit}(\hat{b}') = \mathtt{end}\ \ell_i$

Constant Folding. By using the result of $\mathcal{V}$ of forward or backward conditional constant propagation, we replace some variable uses with constants and some instructions with skip.

Replacement of variable use: If $\mathcal{V}(x_i)$ is a constant k, then replace all the x_i in expressions with k. After the replacement, remove $x_i := \pi(\cdots)$ and $\pi(\cdots) := x_i$ if x_i does not appear elsewhere.

Forward folding: If $x_i := \hat{e}$ and $x_j := x_i \oplus \hat{e}'$ exist, x_i does not appear elsewhere, and there is $\hat{e}''$ equivalent to $\hat{e}' \oplus \hat{e}$ (for example, $x + 6$ is equivalent to $(x + 3) + (1 + 2)$), then replace $x_i := \hat{e}'$ with skip and $x_j := x_i \oplus \hat{e}$ with $x := \hat{e}''$.

Backward folding: If $\hat{e} := x_j$ and $x_j := x_i \oplus \hat{e}'$ exist, x_j does not appear elsewhere, and there is $\hat{e}''$ equivalent to $\hat{e} \ominus \hat{e}'$, then replace $\hat{e} := x_j$ with skip and $x_j := x_i \oplus \hat{e}'$ with $\hat{e}'' := x_i$, where $\ominus = \mathsf{invop}(\oplus)$.

Replacement of unused definitions: If $x_i := \hat{e}$ and $\hat{e}' := x_i$ exist and x_i does not appear elsewhere, then replace $x_i := \hat{e}$ and $\hat{e}' := x_i$ with skip.

Elimination of skip: If $\mathsf{inst}(\hat{b}) = \mathtt{skip}$, $\mathsf{exit}(\hat{b}') = \mathtt{->}\ell$, and $\mathsf{entry}(\hat{b}) = \ell\mathtt{<-}$, then $\mathsf{exit}(\hat{b}') := \mathsf{exit}(\hat{b})$ and remove $\hat{b}$. If $\mathsf{inst}(\hat{b}) = \mathtt{skip}$, $\mathsf{exit}(\hat{b}) = \mathtt{->}\ell$ and $\mathsf{entry}(\hat{b}') = \ell\mathtt{<-}$, then $\mathsf{entry}(\hat{b}') := \mathsf{entry}(\hat{b})$ and remove $\hat{b}$.

5.2   Dead Code Elimination

Following [3, (Section 19.3)] and [2, (Section 9.1.6)], we consider the bidirectional dead code elimination. By using the result $\mathcal{B}$ of forward or backward conditional constant propagation, we remove unreachable $\hat{b} \in \hat{P}g - \mathcal{B}$ from G. For each $\hat{b} \in \hat{P}g - \mathcal{B}$:

1. Remove x_i from the parameters of all the π and ϕ functions if $\hat{b}$ is assigned with $x_i := \pi(\cdots)$, $x_i := \phi(\cdots)$, $\pi(\cdots) := x_i$, or $\phi(\cdots) := x_i$.
2. If there are $\hat{b}', \hat{b}'' \in \mathcal{B}$ such that $\mathsf{out}(\hat{b}') \cap \mathsf{in}(\hat{b}) = \{\ell_1\}$ and $\mathsf{out}(\hat{b}') \cap \mathsf{in}(\hat{b}'') = \{\ell_2\}$, then $\mathsf{exit}(\hat{b}') := \texttt{->}\ell_1$ and $\mathsf{entry}(\hat{b}'') := \ell_1 \texttt{<-}$.
3. If there are $\hat{b}', \hat{b}'' \in \mathcal{B}$ such that $\mathsf{out}(\hat{b}) \cap \mathsf{in}(\hat{b}') = \{\ell_1\}$ and $\mathsf{out}(\hat{b}'') \cap \mathsf{in}(\hat{b}') = \{\ell_2\}$, then $\mathsf{exit}(\hat{b}'') := \texttt{->}\ell_1$ and $\mathsf{entry}(\hat{b}') := \ell_1 \texttt{<-}$.
4. Remove $\hat{b}$ from G.

5.3 Copy Propagation

The copy propagation [2, (Section 9.1.5)] is extended bidirectionally by checking the lefthand sides of assignments in the backward execution. If $x_i := y_j \texttt{ ^ } 0$ or $y_j \texttt{ ^ } 0 := x_i$ exists, then we replace the use of x_i which is not a parameter of π or ϕ with y_j.

5.4 Conversion from CRSSA into CRIL

Remove indices from all the variables and replace $x := e, e := x$ with $x\texttt{^=}e$, $x := x \oplus e$ with $x \oplus= e$, and $x := \mathtt{M}[z] := x$ with $x \texttt{<->} \mathtt{M}[z]$. By removing all the π and ϕ assignments, the conversion from CRSSA to CRIL is completed.

5.5 An Example

We use the CRSSA in Fig. 5 as an example for optimization. By forward conditional constant propagation, we find $\mathtt{a0} = 2, \mathtt{b0} = 1, \mathtt{b1}, \mathtt{b2} = 5, \mathtt{b3} = 7, \mathtt{c0}, \mathtt{c3}, \mathtt{c6}, \mathtt{c7}, \mathtt{c8} = 3, \mathtt{d0} = 2, \mathtt{d1}, \mathtt{d2}, \mathtt{d4} = 4, \mathtt{d3}, \mathtt{d5}, \mathtt{d6} = 6$, and $\hat{b}_{20}$ is unreachable. By backward conditional constant propagation, we find $\mathtt{a3}, \mathtt{a4}, \mathtt{a7}, \mathtt{a8} = 5, \mathtt{b0} = 1, \mathtt{b1}, \mathtt{b2} = 5, \mathtt{b3} = 7, \mathtt{c5} = 0, \mathtt{d4} = 4, \mathtt{d3}, \mathtt{d5}, \mathtt{d6} = 6$. Since $\hat{b}_{20}$ is unreachable, remove $\hat{b}_{20}$, $\mathtt{c1}$, and $\mathtt{c2}$ from the CRSSA. $\hat{b}_{19}$ is also removed since its instruction is $\mathtt{skip}$. Since $\pi(\mathtt{c3}) := \mathtt{c0}$ in $\hat{b}_2$ and $\mathtt{c3} := \pi(\mathtt{c0})$ in $\hat{b}_{24}$ are redundant after removing $\mathtt{c1}$ and $\mathtt{c2}$, they are removed and $\mathtt{c3}$ is replaced with $\mathtt{c0}$. Since $\mathtt{c0} = 3$ and $\mathtt{d6} = 6$, $\hat{b}_2$ is removed and the instruction of $\hat{b}_{24}$ is replaced with $\mathtt{c4:=(9+b7)}$. By replacing $\mathtt{a7}$, $\mathtt{a8}$, $\mathtt{c6,c7}$, and $\mathtt{c8}$ in expressions with the constants, π assignments of $\mathtt{a}$ and $\mathtt{c}$ in $\hat{b}_{12}$, $\hat{b}_{21}$, $\hat{b}_{22}$, and $\hat{b}_{24}$ can be removed. Since the conditional expressions in $\hat{b}_{21}$ and $\hat{b}_{24}$ are replaced with $\mathtt{5>3}$, $\hat{b}_{23}$ is found to be unreachable by doing constant propagation again. By removing redundant ϕ assignments and doing constant folding, basic blocks where $\mathtt{d}$ is updated can be removed. We obtain the optimized CRSSA shown in Fig. 6, which is reverted to the optimized CRIL program shown in Fig. 7.

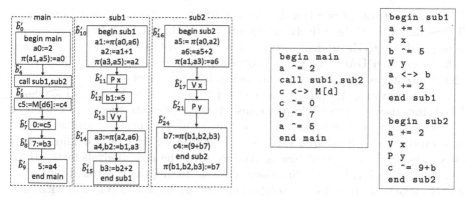

Fig. 6. CRSSA optimized from Fig. 5   **Fig. 7.** CRIL optimized from Fig. 4

6 Conclusion

We presented the CRSSA (concurrent reversible SSA) form for the reversible intermediate language CRIL based on the bidirectional data flow analysis. Given a sound data flow analysis, we add ϕ functions and π functions at the entry and exit points of basic blocks, showing the data flow to convert to the CRSSA form. A ϕ function represents the data for a non-shared variable that may flow from one of its arguments in the same process. A π function represents the data for a shared variable that may flow from other processes. Due to concurrency, the data flows vary for each execution. Like SSA and RSSA formats, a CRSSA format reflects the possible data flow as syntax, ensuring that an indexed variable holds a single value in the program execution. We have presented the application of some optimization techniques in compilers such as conditional constant propagation, dead-code elimination, and copy propagation. The backward flow analysis is useful even when a forward analysis is terminated. More identification of flows is possible if we track the flow at the end of programs.

The CRSSA form is derived from a static data flow analysis of a CRIL program to be used for program analysis such as optimization. For any sound data flow analysis, the CRSSA form is derived, but the more precise analysis is given, the better optimization is possible. Besides optimization, π functions denote the possible data flow in both directions. Detecting unexpected data flow would help to find the insufficient synchronization control. Concrete application to reversible debugging needs further research.

The correctness of our translation to CRSSA can be explained in terms of FR-bisimilarity [18]. Intuitively, an update in a CRIL program has a one-to-one correspondence to the update in the CRSSA form in both directions. Combined with Annotation DAG, the whole program preserves the reversible properties. Giving formal proof to show the correctness is future work.

As related work, [10] presents a compiler from Janus to RSSA and [5] shows the optimization of reversible programs. And [4] presents the optimization of reversible control flow graphs. [4] does not deal with concurrency, and we mainly focus on data flow via shared variables. We obtain CRSSA by providing a flow analysis between concurrent blocks. And we used the flow analysis for CRIL in [17]. And we deal with the bidirectional flows assuming the controlled semantics of CRIL where no reversibility violation occurs, while [4] and [14] deal with such property using the assertion mechanism. Such an argument is one direction of our future work.

As the perspective of optimization, the effect of speeding up executions is limited due to the nature of reversible concurrency since it provides very fine-grained operational semantics. We expect that CRSSA formats and the optimization help to find a cause of *concurrency bugs*. A π function explicitly denotes the possible source of data flow. Deriving the π function with fewer arguments simplifies the synchronization structure of the concurrent programs.

For future work, we may apply the technique to the reversible debugging of concurrent programs. For reversible debugging, controlling concurrently running processes in both directions is complex. The CRSSA information simplifies the consistent controls to deal with the asynchronous behavior in concurrency.

A   Appendix

A.1   Semantics of CRIL

The following SOS rules are the basic operational semantics of CRIL. $(Pg, \rho, \sigma, Pr) \xrightleftharpoons[\text{prog}]{p, Rd, Wt} (Pg, \rho', \sigma', Pr')$ is defined as the relation applying the rules.

Expressions:

$$\frac{k \text{ is a constant}}{(\rho,\sigma) \rhd k \rightsquigarrow k} \text{ Con} \qquad \frac{}{(\rho[x \mapsto m],\sigma) \rhd x \rightsquigarrow m} \text{ Var} \qquad \frac{}{(\rho[x \mapsto m_1],\sigma[m_1 \mapsto m_2]) \rhd \texttt{M}[x] \rightsquigarrow m_2} \text{ Mem}$$

$$\frac{(\rho,\sigma) \rhd right_1 \rightsquigarrow m_1 \qquad (\rho,\sigma) \rhd right_2 \rightsquigarrow m_2 \qquad m_3 = m_1 \odot m_2}{(\rho,\sigma) \rhd right_1 \odot right_2 \rightsquigarrow m_3} \text{ Exp1}$$

$$\frac{(\rho,\sigma) \rhd right \rightsquigarrow 0}{(\rho,\sigma) \rhd \,!right \rightsquigarrow 1} \text{ Exp2} \qquad \frac{(\rho,\sigma) \rhd right \rightsquigarrow m \qquad m \neq 0}{(\rho,\sigma) \rhd \,!right \rightsquigarrow 0} \text{ Exp3}$$

Instructions:

$$\frac{(\rho,\sigma) \rhd e \rightsquigarrow m_3 \qquad m_2 = m_1 \oplus m_3}{x \oplus\!= e \rhd (\rho[x \mapsto m_1],\sigma) \rightarrowtail (\rho[x \mapsto m_2],\sigma)} \text{ AssVar}$$

$$\frac{(\rho,\sigma) \rhd e \rightsquigarrow m_3 \qquad m_2 = m_1 \oplus m_3}{\texttt{M}[x] \oplus\!= e \rhd (\rho[x \mapsto m_4],\sigma[m_4 \mapsto m_1]) \rightarrowtail (\rho[x \mapsto m_4],\sigma[m_4 \mapsto m_2])} \text{ AssArr}$$

$$\frac{}{x \texttt{ <-> } y \rhd (\rho[x,y \mapsto m_1,m_2],\sigma) \rightarrowtail (\rho[x,y \mapsto m_2,m_1],\sigma)} \text{ SwapVarVar}$$

$$\frac{}{x \texttt{ <-> } \texttt{M}[y] \rhd (\rho[x,y \mapsto m_1,m_3],\sigma[m_3 \mapsto m_2]) \rightarrowtail (\rho[x,y \mapsto m_2,m_3],\sigma[m_3 \mapsto m_1])} \text{ SwapVarArr}$$

$$\frac{}{\texttt{M}[y] \texttt{ <-> } x \rhd (\rho[x,y \mapsto m_1,m_3],\sigma[m_3 \mapsto m_2]) \rightarrowtail (\rho[x,y \mapsto m_2,m_3],\sigma[m_3 \mapsto m_1])} \text{ SwapArrVar}$$

$$\frac{}{\texttt{M}[x] \texttt{ <-> } \texttt{M}[y] \rhd (\rho[x,y \mapsto m_3,m_4],\sigma[m_3,m_4 \mapsto m_1,m_2]) \rightarrowtail (\rho[x,y \mapsto m_3,m_4],\sigma[m_3,m_4 \mapsto m_2,m_1])} \text{ SwapArrArr}$$

$$\frac{}{\texttt{V } x \rhd (\rho[x \mapsto 0],\sigma) \rightarrowtail (\rho[x \mapsto 1],\sigma)} \text{ V-op} \qquad \frac{}{\texttt{P } x \rhd (\rho[x \mapsto 1],\sigma) \rightarrowtail (\rho[x \mapsto 0],\sigma)} \text{ P-op}$$

$$\frac{}{\texttt{skip} \rhd (\rho,\sigma) \rightarrowtail (\rho,\sigma)} \text{ Skip} \qquad \frac{(\rho,\sigma) \rhd e \rightsquigarrow m \qquad m \neq 0}{\texttt{assert } e \rhd (\rho,\sigma) \rightarrowtail (\rho,\sigma)} \text{ Assert}$$

Entry and exit points:

$$\frac{}{\texttt{begin } \ell \vdash (\rho,\sigma,\ell,\texttt{begin})} \qquad \frac{}{\ell \texttt{ <-} \vdash (\rho,\sigma,\ell,\texttt{run})} \qquad \frac{(\rho,\sigma) \rhd e \rightsquigarrow 0}{\ell_1 ; \ell_2 \texttt{ <- } e \vdash (\rho,\sigma,\ell_2,\texttt{run})} \qquad \frac{(\rho,\sigma) \rhd e \rightsquigarrow m \qquad m \neq 0}{\ell_1 ; \ell_2 \texttt{ <- } e \vdash (\rho,\sigma,\ell_1,\texttt{run})}$$

$$\frac{}{\texttt{end } \ell \dashv (\rho,\sigma,\ell,\texttt{end})} \qquad \frac{}{\texttt{-> } \ell \dashv (\rho,\sigma,\ell,\texttt{run})} \qquad \frac{(\rho,\sigma) \rhd e \rightsquigarrow 0}{e \texttt{ -> } \ell_1 ; \ell_2 \dashv (\rho,\sigma,\ell_2,\texttt{run})} \qquad \frac{(\rho,\sigma) \rhd e \rightsquigarrow m \qquad m \neq 0}{e \texttt{ -> } \ell_1 ; \ell_2 \dashv (\rho,\sigma,\ell_1,\texttt{run})}$$

Basic Blocks:

$$\frac{\text{isleaf}(Pr_{act},p) \quad b \in Pg \quad entry(b) \vdash (\rho,\sigma,\ell,stage) \quad inst(b) \rhd (\rho,\sigma) \rightarrowtail (\rho',\sigma') \quad exit(b) \dashv (\rho',\sigma',\ell',stage')}{(Pg,\rho,\sigma,Pr[p \mapsto (\ell,stage)]) \xrightleftharpoons[\text{prog}]{p,read(b),write(b)} (Pg,\rho',\sigma',Pr[p \mapsto (\ell',stage')])} \text{ Inst}$$

$$\frac{\text{isleaf}(Pr_{act},p) \qquad (\ell' \texttt{ <-,call } \ell_1,\cdots,\ell_n,\texttt{-> } \ell'') \in Pg}{(Pg,\rho,\sigma,Pr[p \mapsto (\ell',\texttt{run})]) \xrightleftharpoons[\text{prog}]{p,\varnothing,\varnothing} (Pg,\rho,\sigma,Pr[p \mapsto (\ell'',\texttt{run}),p \cdot 1 \mapsto (\ell_1,\texttt{begin}),\cdots,p \cdot n \mapsto (\ell_n,\texttt{begin})])} \text{ CallFork}$$

$$\frac{\text{isleaf}(Pr_{act},p) \qquad (\ell' \texttt{ <-,call } \ell_1,\cdots,\ell_n,\texttt{-> } \ell'') \in Pg}{(Pg,\rho,\sigma,Pr[p \mapsto (\ell'',\texttt{run}),p \cdot 1 \mapsto (\ell_1,\texttt{end}),\cdots,p \cdot n \mapsto (\ell_n,\texttt{end})]) \xrightleftharpoons[\text{prog}]{p,\varnothing,\varnothing} (Pg,\rho,\sigma,Pr[p \mapsto (\ell'',\texttt{run})])} \text{ CallMerge}$$

References

1. GDB: The GNU project debugger. https://www.sourceware.org/gdb/
2. Aho, A.V., Sethi, R., Ullman, J.D.: Compilers: Principles, Techniques, and Tools. Addison-Wesley series in computer science / World student series edition. Addison-Wesley, Boston (1986)
3. Appel, A.W., Palsberg, J.: Modern Compiler Implementation in Java, 2nd edn. Cambridge University Press, Cambridge (2002)
4. Deworetzki, N., Gail, L.: Optimization of reversible control flow graphs. In: Kutrib, M., Meyer, U. (eds.) Reversible Computation. Lecture Notes in Computer Science, vol. 13960, pp. 57–72. Springer, Cham (2023). https://doi.org/10.1007/978-3-031-38100-3_5

5. Deworetzki, N., Kutrib, M., Meyer, U., Ritzke, P.: Optimizing reversible programs. In: Mezzina, C.A., Podlaski, K. (eds.) Reversible Computation. Lecture Notes in Computer Science, vol. 13354, pp. 224–238. Springer, Cham (2022). https://doi.org/10.1007/978-3-031-09005-9_16
6. Deworetzki, N., Meyer, U.: Program analysis for reversible languages. In: SOAP@PLDI 2021, pp. 13–18. ACM (2021)
7. Hay-Schmidt, L., Glück, R., Cservenka, M.H., Haulund, T.: Towards a unified language architecture for reversible object-oriented programming. In: Yamashita, S., Yokoyama, T. (eds.) Reversible Computation. Lecture Notes in Computer Science(), vol. 12805, pp. 96–106. Springer, Cham (2021). https://doi.org/10.1007/978-3-030-79837-6_6
8. Hoey, J., Ulidowski, I.: Reversing an imperative concurrent programming language. Sci. Comput. Program. **223**, 102873 (2022)
9. Ikeda, T., Yuen, S.: A reversible debugger for imperative parallel programs with contracts. In: Mezzina, C.A., Podlaski, K. (eds.) Reversible Computation. Lecture Notes in Computer Science, vol. 13354, pp. 204–212. Springer, Cham (2022). https://doi.org/10.1007/978-3-031-09005-9_14
10. Kutrib, M., Meyer, U., Deworetzki, N., Schuster, M.: Compiling Janus to RSSA. In: Yamashita, S., Yokoyama, T. (eds.) Reversible Computation. Lecture Notes in Computer Science(), vol. 12805, pp. 64–78. Springer, Cham (2021). https://doi.org/10.1007/978-3-030-79837-6_4
11. Lanese, I., Phillips, I., Ulidowski, I.: An axiomatic theory for reversible computation. ACM Trans. Comput. Logic (2024). https://doi.org/10.1145/3648474
12. Lanese, I., Phillips, I.C.C., Ulidowski, I.: An axiomatic approach to reversible computation. In: Goubault-Larrecq, J., Konig, B. (eds.) Foundations of Software Science and Computation Structures. Lecture Notes in Computer Science(), vol. 12077, pp. 442–461. Springer, Cham (2020). https://doi.org/10.1007/978-3-030-45231-5_23
13. Lee, J., Midkiff, S.P., Padua, D.A.: Concurrent static single assignment form and constant propagation for explicitly parallel programs. In: Li, Z., Yew, P.C., Chatterjee, S., Huang, C.H., Sadayappan, P., Sehr, D. (eds.) Languages and Compilers for Parallel Computing. Lecture Notes in Computer Science, vol. 1366, pp. 114–130. Springer, Berlin (1997). https://doi.org/10.1007/bfb0032687
14. Mogensen, T.Æ.: RSSA: a reversible SSA form. In: Mazzara, M., Voronkov, A. (eds.) Perspectives of System Informatics. Lecture Notes in Computer Science(), vol. 9609, pp. 203–217. Springer, Cham (2015). https://doi.org/10.1007/978-3-319-41579-6_16
15. Mogensen, T.Æ.: Reversible garbage collection for reversible functional languages. New Gener. Comput. **36**(3), 203–232 (2018)
16. Oguchi, S., Yuen, S.: CRIL: a concurrent reversible intermediate language. In: EXPRESS/SOS 2023, vol. 387, pp. 149–167 (2023)
17. Oguchi, S., Yuen, S.: Constant propagation in CRIL by bidirectional data flow analysis. J. Inf. Process., 1–12 (2024). (to appear)
18. Phillips, I.C.C., Ulidowski, I.: Reversing algebraic process calculi. J. Log. Algebraic Methods Program. **73**(1–2), 70–96 (2007)
19. Yokoyama, T.: Reversible computation and reversible programming languages. Electron. Notes Theor. Comput. Sci. **253**(6), 71–81 (2010)
20. Yokoyama, T., Axelsen, H.B., Glück, R.: Towards a reversible functional language. In: De Vos, A., Wille, R. (eds.) Reversible Computation. Lecture Notes in Computer Science, vol. 7165, pp. 14–29. Springer, Berlin (2011). https://doi.org/10.1007/978-3-642-29517-1_2

Is Simulation the only Alternative for Effective Verification of Dynamic Quantum Circuits?

Liam Hurwitz[1], Kamalika Datta[1,2(✉)], Abhoy Kole[2], and Rolf Drechsler[1,2]

[1] Institute of Computer Science, University of Bremen, Bremen, Germany
{kdatta,hurwitz,drechsler}@uni-bremen.de
[2] Cyber-Physical Systems, DFKI GmbH, Bremen, Germany
abhoy.kole@dfki.de

Abstract. This paper investigates the verification gap of *Dynamic Quantum Circuits (DQC)* by analyzing state-of-the-art equivalence checking approaches. Today's *Noisy Intermediate-Scale Quantum (NISQ)* devices are limited in the number of qubits. DQCs drastically reduce the number of qubits required by guiding the outcome based on the intermediate results of the computations. Investigation of feasibility of existing verification tools with respect to DQC verification is needed. In order to verify the equivalence of DQCs, verification tools often transform dynamic primitives in order to reveal the underlying functionality of the circuits. This leads to restoration of their unitary functionality and allows existing equivalence checkers to reason about DQCs. Our objective is to provide empirical data that can be used to improve these tools by examining their capabilities and effectiveness. Equivalence checking methods that use ZX-Calculus, *Quantum Multi Valued Decision Diagrams (QMDD)* and simulators are considered in this regard. In order to gauge the effectiveness of the present tools, we use the Bernstein-Vazirani, Deutsch-Jozsa and Quantum Phase Estimation algorithms and their dynamic variants. Experiments reveal that the existing equivalence checking tools are limited in their effectiveness, while simulation based approaches provide correct verifications at the expense of high runtime overhead. Our results show that the different verification methods never achieves accuracy of more than 50%.

Keywords: Dynamic Quantum Circuit · Equivalence Checking · Verification · QMDD · ZX-Calculus · Quantum Simulation

1 Introduction

Quantum computing is a rapidly advancing field with the potential to revolutionize how we solve complex problems. Quantum computers take advantage of quantum mechanical principles, such as *superposition* and *entanglement* to solve certain problems. Currently, we are in the *Noisy Intermediate Scale Quantum (NISQ)* era, where the fabricated quantum computing devices are noisy and have

T. Æ. Mogensen and L. Mikulski (Eds.): RC 2024, LNCS 14680, pp. 201–217, 2024.
https://doi.org/10.1007/978-3-031-62076-8_13

limited number of qubits. While current quantum computers, such as the IBM Condor, can scale up to 1211 qubits, they are not advanced enough for fault-tolerant computing. The long-term goal in quantum computation is to achieve *Fault-Tolerant Quantum Computing*, thus providing robustness and opening the door to more applications. Recently with the introduction of non-unitary operations such as mid-circuit measurement, active resets and classically controlled quantum operations, a new class of circuits known as *Dynamic Quantum Circuits (DQC)* have emerged [7]. The mid-circuit measurements in a computation enable the measurement of an outcome during the execution of an intermediate stage, where subsequent gate operations depend on this measurement. This allows non-unitary operations to be combined with unitary operations. One fundamental difference between *Static Quantum Circuits (SQC)* and DQC is that, future states of DQC depend on the outcome of measurements that occur in the circuit. Also, the measurement always occurs at the end of the circuit for SQC i.e. states of a SQC, have no dependencies [7]. This brings us one step closer to overcoming the limitations of NISQ era by reducing the number of qubits required for executing any algorithm.

DQCs allow the realization of any quantum algorithm with fewer qubits. Recent works have targeted the design of dynamic versions of Toffoli gate [14] thereby paving the way for dynamic realization of *Deutsch-Jozsa (DJ)* algorithm [8]. Another work [13] targets the dynamic realization of *Multiple Control Toffoli (MCT)* gate that further allows for dynamic realization of many more quantum algorithms. Now the task is to verify whether the functionality of the dynamically realized algorithm is correct, as compared to its static counterpart.

Existing verification tools have their merits and demerits with respect to dynamic circuit verification [4,10]. To verify the equivalence of DQCs, the verification tools transform the dynamic primitives to represent the underlying functionality of the circuits. This leads to restoration of their unitary functionality and permits existing equivalence checkers to reason about DQCs. Even when we transform a DQC to a SQC, there still exist some issues because of which available tools for SQC verification fail. The challenge is that the qubit order is lost during the unitary reconstruction of the DQC to the SQC, and hence exiting methods cannot be directly applied. In this paper we primarily focus on analyzing existing equivalence checking methods based on ZX-Calculus, and *Quantum Multi-Valued Decision Diagrams (QMDD)*. We also use the Qiskit Aer simulator [16] for verifying our results. We use the *Bernstein-Vazirani (BV)*, *Deutsch-Jozsa (DJ)* and *Quantum Phase Estimation (QPE)* algorithms and their dynamic variants [7,14] for the experiments. The goal of this work is to provide empirical data for evaluating the effectiveness of equivalence checkers for DQCs, as well as finding the best candidate from a set of DQCs for a quantum algorithm. Experimental results show that existing verification tools have certain limitations while verifying DQCs. In contrast, simulation based approaches provide accurate results; however, they are not scalable and become very expensive in terms of memory and run-time when the circuit size increases. Our experiments reveal that the accuracy level of the considered verification methods does not exceed 50% and depends on their implementation.

2   Background

2.1   Quantum Gates and Quantum Circuits

The state of a quantum system is manipulated by *quantum operations*, known as *quantum gates*. Every such operation on a quantum system is reversible and must yield a valid quantum state; thus, the operation is represented by a $2^n \times 2^n$ unitary matrix U, where n is the number of qubits on which the gate operates. The only constraint for a quantum operation is that the matrix U needs to be unitary.

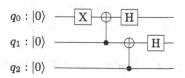

Fig. 1. A Quantum Circuit

Figure 1 shows a 3-qubit quantum circuit consisting of NOT (X), CNOT (CX) and *Hadamard (H)* gates. Generally, circuits are evaluated on physical quantum computers. This mode of computation is considered static, as the result of the outcome is available only after the execution of all the gates, and it does not have the capability to perform computations based on intermediate outcomes.

2.2   Dynamic Quantum Circuit

The traditional quantum circuit model forms the basis for implementing quantum circuits on physical quantum devices. Recently, IBM has introduced the capability to manipulate quantum circuits in real-time and perform mid-circuit measurements [7]. These advancements have laid the groundwork for the realization of DQCs. DQCs have the potential to realize any n qubit quantum circuit using minimum 2 qubits only, as opposed to traditional or static circuits requiring at least n-qubits.

Many recent works have shown the advantage of using DQCs for realizing various algorithms like QPE, BV and DJ. In [14] two methods were introduced for converting a Toffoli gate into its dynamic analogue. This work in particular shows the dynamic implementations of 3-qubit DJ circuits using two different dynamic Toffoli designs, namely *dynamic 1* and *dynamic 2*.

Figure 2(a) shows the BV algorithm to determine a 3-qubit hidden string 111 from a given black-box function that implements the function $\mathcal{F}(x) = xyz$. This uses three data qubits (q_0, q_1 and q_2) that are initialized to $|0\rangle$ state, and an answer qubit (q_3) initialized to $|-\rangle$ ($= \frac{1}{\sqrt{2}}(|0\rangle - |1\rangle)$) state. The main idea of dynamic transformation is to transform the static circuit consisting of various data and answer qubits into a single data qubit and equal number of answer

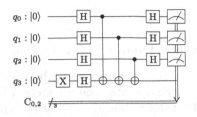

(a) BV Algorithm

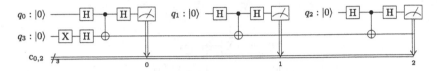

(b) Dynamic Realization of BV Algorithm

Fig. 2. Static and Dynamic Representation of BV Algorithm

qubits. In the case of the BV algorithm, we use one data qubit and one answer qubit. It may be noted that while performing the transformation, we need to consider independent and dependent 1- and 2-qubit operations. This information allows us to determine how the dynamic transformation will follow.

Figure 2(b) shows the dynamic realization of BV algorithm. It can be observed that we require three iterations, involving one data qubit and one answer qubit. All the operations present between a reset and a measurement on the data qubit are performed within an iteration. The three iterations entail evaluation of all the gate operations between qubits (q_0, q_3), (q_1, q_3) and (q_2, q_3) respectively, along with a reset operation on the data qubit after the first and second iteration.

2.3 Verification of Quantum Circuits

Design and verification of quantum circuits is a challenging task due to the inherent complexity of quantum systems. Simulation can be an effective tool for small quantum circuits and their verification. It allows for the comparison of the measurement outcomes of circuits. However, quantum simulators are not effective for complex or large-scale quantum systems. Current scalable approaches to address this challenge use *Quantum Multiple-Valued Decision Diagrams (QMDDs)*, *Tensor Decision Diagrams (TDDs)* and ZX-Calculus. All of these approaches have been shown to be effective in verifying the equivalence of static quantum circuits, yet have different strengths and weaknesses.

Tensor Decision Diagrams *(TDD)* [10] offer a compact representation of Boolean functions and are inspired by tensor networks. They are used widely for formal verification, artificial intelligence and cryptography. In recent years,

TDDs have attracted attention in the field of quantum computing, due to their ability to efficiently represent and manipulate quantum circuits. In [10] Hong et al. have provided efficient methods for verifying the equivalence of static and dynamic quantum circuits. They formally define DQCs and have characterized their functionality in terms of ensembles of linear operators. Equivalence is checked by verifying that the two DQCs have the same functionality. Here, the authors present a unified representation for each component of the DQC as a tensor. This allows DQCs to be interpreted as a tensor decision network and represented as a TDD. The equivalence checking operation then checks if the two DQCs share the same TDD representation.

Quantum Multivalued Decision Diagrams (QMDD) are a type of decision diagrams capable of representing multiple values simultaneously, making them well-suited for depicting quantum states. The fundamental concept behind QMDDs involves portraying a quantum state as a tree structure, where each node signifies a superposition of quantum states, and the edges denote transitions between different superpositions. Leveraging QMDDs allows for the efficient representation and manipulation of quantum states, a crucial aspect in verifying the equivalence of quantum circuits.

Several studies use QMDDs for verifying the equivalence of quantum circuits. For instance, in [20], the authors proposed a method for verifying the equivalence of two quantum circuits by constructing their corresponding QMDDs and comparing them. The authors demonstrated that their approach is efficient and scalable [21]. It is shown that decision diagrams can efficiently represent large quantum states by leveraging the principles of quantum mechanics [3].

ZX-Calculus has drawn the attention of researchers from different fields such as quantum circuit optimization, error correcting codes, circuit simulation, extraction and equivalence checking, as well as measurement based computing, tensor networks, variational circuits and quantum natural language processing [18]. A literature survey [6] was published by Bob Coecke. It has several advantages over traditional methods for equivalence checking. First, it provides a graphical representation of quantum circuits that is easy to understand and analyze [6]. Second, algorithms for equivalence checking exist [9,12]. The disadvantage of ZX-Calculus is that it is not efficient for quantum circuits containing Toffoli gates, as the rewrite rules take longer to terminate due to gate decomposition. The ZH-Calculus is a promising alternative for quantum circuits with multiple controlled Toffoli gates [1]. Equivalence checking using the ZX-Calculus has not yet been proven to be complete for quantum circuits. If the rewrite rules cannot prove equivalence, no conclusion can be drawn. In an earlier work Seiter et al. [17] have exploited the QMDD data structure for property checking in quantum circuits. As a future work we can also extend the concept for dynamic quantum circuit.

3 Verification of Dynamic Quantum Circuits (DQC)

Checking the equivalence of two quantum circuits relies on the reversibility of quantum operations [15]. Every quantum operation is unitary and hence reversible. The product of any quantum operation and its inverse (adjoint) will always yield identity. G is an abstract representation of a quantum circuit such as QMDD or ZX-Calculus, while U represents the matrix operator of the circuit. If U is equivalent to U', this implies G is equivalent to G' and vice versa. Given two quantum circuits G and G', where g and g' are the individual gates of each circuit, their equivalence is defined as:

Definition 1. *Given two quantum circuits*

$$G = g_o \ldots g_{m-1} \text{ and } G' = g'_0 \ldots g'_{n-1}$$

and the respective system matrices for the two circuits

$$U = U_{m-1} \ldots U_0 \text{ and } U' = U'_{n-1} \ldots U'_0,$$

the problem of equivalence checking *is to verify, whether*

$$U = e^{i\sigma} U' \text{ or } UU'^{\dagger} = e^{i\sigma}\mathbb{I},$$

given $\sigma \in (-\pi, \pi]$ *denotes a physically unobservable global phase.*

In general, checking the equivalence of quantum circuits becomes increasingly difficult because the size of the matrices grows exponentially with the number of qubits. Equivalence checking is *Quantum Merlin Arthur (QMA)-Complete*. Problems that are QMA-Complete can be solved efficiently using quantum computing algorithms.

Definition 1 is not complete as it does not always consider circuits equivalent when the number of qubits differ, or the circuit has non-unitary operations or even when the system matrices differ. The cause for the non-equivalence between the system matrices could be numerical inaccuracies or permutations in the input or outputs of the circuits [4]. In order to ensure that compiled or optimized quantum circuits do not alter the functionality or the intended behavior, equivalence checking needs to be able to deal with the variations that exist in the system matrices [3]. Current equivalence checking tools [11,20] try to avoid using the matrix based operator representation (system matrix), since the representation of an n qubit quantum circuit requires a matrix of the size $M^{2^n \times 2^n}$.

3.1 QMDD Based Verification

The QMDD equivalence checking algorithm verifies the equality of two quantum circuits G and G' according to Definition 1. It first constructs a decision diagram representation of each circuit's functionality: first by applying each gate

g from the circuit G onto the initial identity, and next by applying the inverse functionality of G'^{-1} as individual gates g'^{-1}.

$$G'^{-1} \cdot G = (g_{m'-1}'^{-1} \cdots g_0'^{-1}) \cdot (g_0 \cdots g_{m-1}) = G' \rightarrow \mathbb{I} \leftarrow G \qquad (1)$$

If the resulting diagram is the identity decision diagram, the circuits are equivalent; otherwise, they are not [20]. Figure 3 exemplifies the process of verifying the equality of two quantum circuits, G and G' with QMDD. Figure 3(a), labeled 'Initial Identity $\mathbb{I}$', shows the QMDD representing the initial identity operator. Next, Fig. 3(b) displays the QMDD of the given circuit G, In Fig. 3(c), referred to as 'Intermediate', we observe an intermediate state during the construction of the QMDD for the inverted circuit G'. Specifically, all the gates of the first qubit have already been applied to the previous diagram. Figure 3(d) exhibits the resulting QMDD when applying $G' \rightarrow \mathbb{I} \leftarrow G$, proving they yield the identity. MQT DDVis [19] is a tool for visualizing simulation and verification for QMDD.

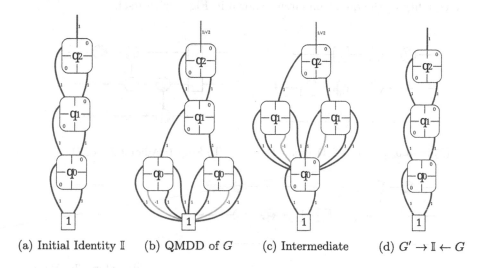

(a) Initial Identity $\mathbb{I}$ (b) QMDD of G (c) Intermediate   (d) $G' \rightarrow \mathbb{I} \leftarrow G$

Fig. 3. Example of QMDD verification using MQT DDVis for Fig. 1.

While QMDDs typically enable compact representation of quantum systems, their size can still grow exponentially with the number of qubits in the worst-case scenario, where no redundancy in the state description can be exploited, resulting in minimal node sharing and exponential node growth [3]. They should be used for computing the full state vector, since the QMDD remains compact [2]. In conclusion, QMDDs have emerged as a powerful tool for verifying the equivalence of quantum circuits. Numerous studies have explored their application for this purpose, proposing innovative techniques for constructing, manipulating and visualizing QMDDs [20].

3.2   ZX-Calculus Based Verification

ZX-Calculus is a rigorous graphical language for reasoning about quantum circuits and algorithms. It extends the categorical quantum mechanics school of reasoning [5], using the paradigms of *monoidal category theory*. ZX-Calculus provides a solution to the problem of equivalence checking. By representing quantum circuits as diagrams referred to as ZX-Diagrams, it is possible to manipulate these diagrams using a set of graphical rewrite rules [18]. These rules allow us to verify, if two quantum circuits, which were transformed into ZX-Diagrams, are equivalent [20].

The transformations utilized by the ZX-Calculus equivalence miter [11], proves that $G' \cdot G^\dagger = I$, where G and G' are quantum circuits and $G^\dagger$ is the adjoint (transposed complex conjugated) of G. The equivalence checking miter leverages Definition 1, which states that if two quantum circuits are equivalent, the adjoint of one circuit applied to the second circuit can be rewritten as the identity. If the reduced ZX-Diagram consists only of bare wires, both circuits are equivalent [18]. Figure 4 shows how the equivalence checking miter proves the equality of the quantum circuit shown in Fig. 1 with itself.

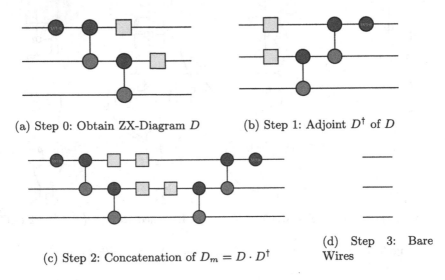

(a) Step 0: Obtain ZX-Diagram D (b) Step 1: Adjoint $D^\dagger$ of D

(c) Step 2: Concatenation of $D_m = D \cdot D^\dagger$

(d) Step 3: Bare Wires

Fig. 4. Equivalence Check using ZX-Calculus [4,11] of Fig. 1

The equivalence miter checking method involves several steps, that are depicted in Fig. 4(b), 4(c), and 4(d). A key benefit of utilizing ZX-Calculus rewrite rules lies in their non-deterministic nature, which enables the application of each rule until exhaustive application of the rule, followed by a subsequent rewrite rule without requiring a reapplication of the prior rewrite rule [12]. This non-deterministic rewrite rule application in ZX-Calculus allows for a flexible and efficient approach for reducing ZX-Diagrams. First, the adjoint

ZX-Diagram $D^\dagger$ of Fig. 1 is obtained, as shown in Fig. 4(b). The adjoint operation switches the inputs with the outputs and vice versa, implicitly reversing the order of the operations for each wire. Additionally, every phase is negated; for instance, the X gate has a phase of π, which becomes $-\pi$ after negation. Because phases have the range $0 \le \varphi < 2\pi$ and are periodic, the phase remains π. It can be observed that $-\pi = \pi \mod 2\pi$, since it represents the same angle in the periodic domain. The concatenation $D_m = D \cdot D^\dagger$ is formed by connecting the output of the first diagram with the inputs of the second diagram, as displayed in Fig. 4(c). The resulting diagram D_m is reduced as much as possible using ZX-Graph rules, resulting in the simplified diagram shown in Fig. 4(d). Finally, it is checked whether the reduced diagram consists of only bare wires. This can be done efficiently by verifying whether every input directly connects to an output. If so, the two original circuits are equivalent up to global phases, as demonstrated in [4,11].

The advantage of the ZX-Calculus for equivalence checking is that computing the equivalence becomes computationally cheap, after the $D \cdot D'^\dagger = D_m$ has been reduced, since checking if a ZX-Diagram contains only 'bare' wires requires checking if every input node is directly connected to output node. If two circuits are not equal, Definition 1 will yield the difference between both circuits instead of the identity. The difference can be quantified with various methods, such as the trace-distance, fidelity or the Hilbert-Schmidt inner product. This provides a measure of how well the first circuit matches the behavior of the second circuit. Quantifying this difference in a memory efficient way is an active research topic.

3.3 Simulation

Our informal definition for equivalence of quantum circuits states that two quantum circuits are equal, if they have the same measurement distribution. To simulate a quantum circuit, the quantum registers should be initialized to the $|0\rangle$ state. After each operation is applied, measurements are conducted. This process is then repeated multiple times. The simulator returns the number of occurrences of a specific measurement result. The following points are considered for simulation based method:

1. Two circuits are equal if their measurement distributions are identical.
2. Two circuits can be considered similar if the difference in their measurement distributions falls within a certain percentage, attributable to their probabilistic nature.
3. If there is a significant discrepancy between the measurement distributions, we conclude that the circuits are unequal.

We utilized the Qiskit Aer simulator [16] to acquire the measurements for each quantum circuit. This requires transpiling the quantum circuits for the Aer simulator (a successor to the previously deprecated Qasm simulator). If a SQC and a DQC produce identical measurements, they are regarded as equivalent. However, when they differ, the degree of similarity is determined using Eq. 2, where s represents the number of shots, n denotes the measurement distribution of the desired outcome for the SQC, and m signifies the corresponding measurement count for the DQC.

$$\text{Similarity} = \left(1 - \frac{|n-m|}{s}\right) \times 100 \tag{2}$$

3.4 Unitary Reconstruction for DQCs

Another approach to verify DQCs is known as unitary reconstruction that was proposed in [4]. This method involves transforming the dynamic primitives to reveal their underlying unitary functionality by overcoming mid-circuit resets, and applying the deferred measurement principle to delay all measurements to the end of the circuit.

The first step transforms a n-qubit circuit containing r active reset operations into a $(n + r)$-qubit quantum circuit and eliminates qubit reuse. In the second step, all phase rotations controlled by measurement outcomes are replaced by phase gates controlled directly by the respective qubit, that was measured previously. Next all measurements are moved to the end of the circuit, thus removing any mid-circuit measurements [4], applying the principle of deferred measurement [15]. The verification of the original and reconstructed SQCs is not straight forward, as their qubit order differs. Figure 5 shows the unitary reconstruction of the dynamic BV-111 from Fig. 2(b).

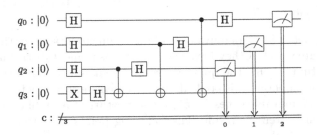

Fig. 5. Unitary Reconstruction of Fig. 2(b)

Unitary reconstruction enables existing equivalence checking tools to verify the equivalence of DQCs, as only unitary quantum operations are present.

4 Experimental Evaluation

To evaluate the effectiveness of existing equivalence checkers for verifying DQC, we perform the following series of experiments:

1. Compare the similarity between static and DQCs using Qiskit Aer quantum simulator.

2. Performance evaluation of existing verification tools for DQCs.

For performing the experiments, following algorithms are used as benchmarks:

- *Deutsch-Josza (DJ)* algorithm: A quantum algorithm designed to determining whether a boolean function is constant or balanced with just one query when given access to a quantum oracle. This circuit also consists of Hadamard, CNOT, and measurement gates.
- *Bernstein-Vazirani (BV)* algorithm: An extension of the DJ algorithm capable of finding the hidden string within a black box function using exponentially fewer queries compared to classical methods. The circuit involves Hadamard gates, controlled-NOT gates, and measurement operations.
- *Quantum Phase Estimation (QPE)*: A fundamental subroutine in many quantum algorithms, including Shor's factoring algorithm. It estimates the eigenvalues of a unitary operator with high precision.

One goal of this experiment is to publish a reproducible benchmark for increasing the accessibility and effectiveness of quantum circuit equivalence checkers. The benchmarking tool requires that all .qasm files follow the naming convention of MQT Bench. Each equivalence checker verifies the equivalence between variations of a quantum circuit and their hardware-independent versions, and exports the results in a CSV or XLS format. The source code for this Benchmark and Unitary Reconstruction can be found at https://codeberg.org/QuantumHB/equivalence. The benchmark folder contains a README file with a step-by-step guide to reproduce the results of this experiment, as well as further benchmarks that can be used to assess the efficiency and effectiveness of SQCs and DQCs.

4.1 Similarity Comparison

In this experiment, we simulate a set of SQC benchmarks, namely the *Bernstein-Vazirani (BV)* algorithm, *Deutsch-Josza (DJ)* algorithm, and *Quantum Phase Estimation (QPE)* algorithms along with their dynamic counterparts from [14]. Simulation is performed to verify the equality of DQCs. The simulation results and details are presented in Table 1. We use Qiskit's Aer simulator for this purpose. But it may not always be efficient or practical due to the resource requirements in simulating large quantum systems.

Table 1 shows the simulation results for SQC and DQC. The first column represent the name of the quantum circuit, the second column specifies which type of the quantum circuit was instantiated. Third to sixth column provide details about number of inputs N, depth D, number of single-qubit gates G_1, and number of two-qubit gates G_2 required for the static quantum circuit. The seventh till eleventh column show the version Ver, i.e. which dynamic variant from [14] was evaluated, number of inputs N, depth D, number of single-qubit gates G_1, and number of two-qubit gates G_2 required for the DQC. The last column contains the similarity between the SQCs and DQCs, which is calculated

Table 1. Similarity Comparison of Execution Outcome of SQC and DQC

Circuit	Type	SQC				DQC					Similarity
		N	D	G_1	G_2	Ver	N	D	G_1	G_2	
BV	001	4	5	8	1	–	2	13	8	1	100
	010	4	5	8	1	–	2	13	8	1	100
	011	4	6	8	2	–	2	14	8	2	100
	100	4	5	8	1	–	2	13	8	1	100
	101	4	6	8	2	–	2	14	8	2	100
	110	4	6	8	2	–	2	14	8	2	100
	111	4	7	8	3	–	2	15	8	3	100
DJ	And	3	15	12	6	1	2	23	17	6	75
						2	2	26	21	6	99
	Carry	4	35	26	18	1	2	60	41	18	100
						2	2	68	49	18	100
	Const 0	3	3	6	1	–	2	7	6	2	100
	Const 1	3	3	7	0	–	2	7	7	1	100
	Imply 1	3	17	13	7	1	2	26	18	7	74
						2	2	29	22	7	97
	Imply 2	3	17	13	7	1	2	25	18	7	74
						2	2	28	22	7	97
	Inhib 1	3	16	12	7	1	2	24	17	7	76
						2	2	27	21	7	99
	Inhib 1	3	16	12	7	1	2	25	17	7	73
						2	2	28	21	7	99
	Invert 1	3	6	7	1	–	2	10	7	2	100
	Invert 2	3	6	7	1	–	2	8	7	2	100
	Nand	3	16	13	6	1	2	24	18	6	72
						2	2	27	22	6	97
	Nor	3	18	13	8	1	2	27	18	8	74
						2	2	30	22	8	97
	Or	3	17	12	8	1	2	26	17	8	75
						2	2	29	21	8	99
	Pass 1	3	5	6	1	–	2	9	6	2	100
	Pass 2	3	5	6	1	–	2	8	6	2	100
	Xnor	3	7	7	2	–	2	11	7	2	100
	Xor	3	6	6	2	–	2	10	6	2	100
QPE	00	3	8	5	0	–	2	11	6	0	100
	01	3	8	5	0	–	2	11	6	0	100
	10	3	8	5	0	–	2	11	6	0	100
	11	3	8	5	0	–	2	11	6	0	100

by running the Qiskit Aer simulator 1024 times. If both circuits both generate the same measurements distributions, they have a similarity of 100% and are considered equivalent and are marked green. Otherwise, their similarity is calculated with Eq. 2. Yellow indicates that they behave similarly, and red signifies greater variance between the measurements counts.

4.2 Evaluation of Equivalence Checkers

In this evaluation, we have considered MQT and PyZX equivalence checkers. These tools are publicly available. Several TDD based checkers are available as well; however, all the TDD implementations are plagued by runtime errors, making it impossible to include them in the evaluation study. In order to compare the accuracy of the PyZX and MQT ZX-Calculus implementations for DQCs, a preprocessor was added to PyZX benchmark, which applies the unitary reconstruction if necessary.

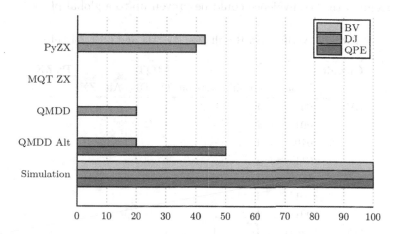

Fig. 6. Accuracy of PyZX, MQT QCEC and the Qiskit Aer Simulator

In Fig. 6, we present the result of various equivalence checkers after evaluating on our considered benchmarks. Only benchmarks, that were 100% equivalent using simulation are included in this part of the experiment. The Y-axis represents different methods for equivalence checking, and the X-axis represents the accuracy in percent. *PyZX* (version 0.8.0) coupled with the unitary reconstruction preprocessor achieved an accuracy of 42% for BV instances, 40% for DJ instances, and failed for all QPE instances, because the custom unitary reconstruction algorithm, which was added for this experiment, does not support all gates that are necessary for QPE.

Next, we evaluated different equivalence checking methods supported by version 2.4.3 of the *Quantum Circuit Equivalence Checker (QCEC)*, that is part of the *Munich Quantum Toolkit (MQT)* [3]. MQT ZX, the ZX-Calculus method,

did not perform any correct evaluations, indicated by zero percent across all
benchmark BV, DJ, and QPE instances.

The *Construction Equivalence Checker (QMDD)* [3] did not perform correct
verifications for BV and QPE instances but managed to achieve an accuracy
of 20% for the DJ instances (Invert2 and XNOR). It reported equivalence up
to a global phase. The *Alternate Equivalence Checker Method (QMDD Alt)* [3],
correctly classified 2 out of 4 QPE circuits and managed to correctly verify the
equality of the Const-1 and Const-2 version of the DJ algorithm achieving an
accuracy of 50% and 20%. Both QMDD methods combined achieved an accuracy
of 30% for all circuits.

Table 2 provides a more in depth comparison of various state-of-the-art equivalence checkers. The table offers analysis consisting of individual equivalence
check for each type of equivalence checker and for individual circuit version,
that are 100% similar using simulation. An X indicates a false negative when
the checker returned not equivalent, timeout or undecidable for an equivalent
circuit. The ✓ denotes a correct verification and ⋆ represents a software crash.
The p signifies that equivalence could be proven up to a global phase.

Table 2. Verification Results for BV, DJ and QPE Circuits

Circuit				MQT			PyZX
	Type	Qubits	Version	QMDD	Alt	ZX	
BV	001	4	–	X	X	X	X
	001	4	–	X	X	X	✓
	010	4	–	X	X	X	X
	011	4	–	X	X	X	X
	100	4	–	X	X	X	✓
	101	4	–	X	X	X	X
	001	4	–	X	X	X	✓
DJ	Carry	4	1	X	X	X	X
			2	X	X	X	X
	Const 0	3	1	X	✓	X	✓
	Const 1	3	1	X	✓	X	✓
	Invert 1	3	1	X	X	X	X
	Invert 2	3	1	p	X	X	X
	Pass 1	3	1	X	X	X	X
	Pass 2	3	1	X	X	X	X
	Xnor	3	1	p	X	X	✓
	Xor	3	1	X	X	X	✓
QPE	00	3	–	X	✓	X	⋆
	01	3	–	X	X	X	⋆
	01	3	–	X	✓	X	⋆
	01	3	–	X	X	X	⋆

4.3   Critical Analysis

We can safely say that no tool achieved an accuracy higher than 50% for any of the three quantum algorithms. This emphasizes the imperative for further development and improvement of equivalence checking methodologies tailored for DQCs. There is a need for refining tools for verifying equivalence of DQCs. Additionally, there is a call for defining missing functionality in current equivalence checkers, such as a similarity metric. Overall, the study provides valuable data for critical evaluation of existing equivalence checkers and motivation for proposing new approaches for checking the equivalence of DQCs. Furthermore, it is assumed that the accuracy of MQT-QCEC is low for DQCs because MQT-QCEC does not correctly handle the qubit permutations that occur during the unitary reconstruction of DQCs. The experiment has revealed that no equivalence checking method except simulation is effective for dynamic quantum circuits, as their accuracy reaches, at best, a limited level. Figure 7 is a depiction of the verification gap for DQCs. It shows that the current state-of-the-art equivalence checkers are not effective and efficient for verifying the equivalence of DQCs. State-of-the-art equivalence checkers need to enhance their accuracy to be effective for DQCs.

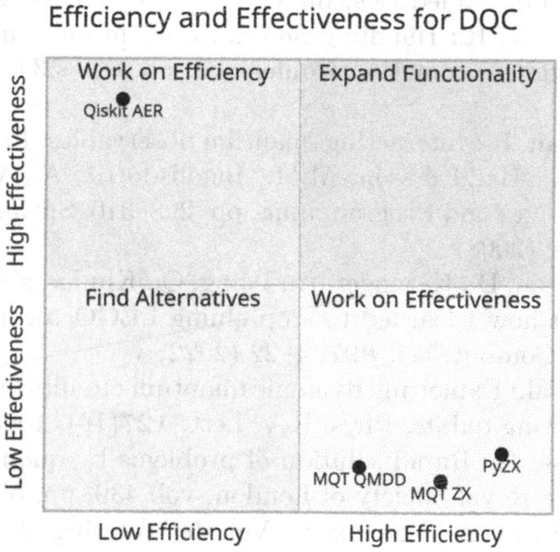

Fig. 7. Efficiency and Effectiveness for Dynamic Quantum Circuits

5   Conclusion

In this paper we investigate and analyze the verification gap of the existing state-of-the-art equivalence checking approaches for DQCs. In the current NISQ era, DQCs are considered a viable alternative because it reduces the number of qubits required to realize any algorithm. We particularly study and analyze the existing tools to verify the DQCs. We can safely say that none of the existing tools can fully verify the DQCs. The highest accuracy achieved by these tools for various benchmarks is 50%. This clearly demonstrates the need for designing improved verification tool for DQCs. Only simulation based method using Qiskit Aer provide 100% accuracy for a set of benchmarks. This answers the question that we raise in the title of the paper. As a future work we can also exploit various decision diagrams for property checking in quantum circuits.

Acknowledgment. We are grateful to Lennart Weingarten for his support in designing the quantum circuits and helpful guidance.

References

1. Backens, M., Kissinger, A.: ZH: a complete graphical calculus for quantum computations involving classical non-linearity. Electron. Proc. Theor. Comput. Sci. **287**, 23–42 (2019)
2. Burgholzer, L., Ploier, A., Wille, R.: Tensor networks or decision diagrams? guidelines for classical quantum circuit simulation. arXiv preprint: arXiv:2302.06616 (2023)
3. Burgholzer, L., Wille, R.: Advanced equivalence checking for quantum circuits. IEEE Trans. Comput. Aided Des. Integr. Circuits Syst. **40**(9), 1810–1824 (2020)
4. Burgholzer, L., Wille, R.: Handling non-unitaries in quantum circuit equivalence checking. In: Design Automation Conference, pp. 529–534. ACM, San Francisco California (2022)
5. Coecke, B., Duncan, R.: Interacting quantum observables. In: Aceto, L., Damgård, I., Goldberg, L.A., Halld órsson, M.M., Ingólfsdóttir, A., Walukiewicz, I. (eds.) Automata, Languages and Programming, pp. 298–310. Springer Berlin Heidelberg, Berlin, Heidelberg (2008)
6. Coecke, B., Horsman, D., Kissinger, A., Wang, Q.: Kindergarden quantum mechanics graduates ...or how I learned to stop gluing LEGO together and love the ZX-Calculus. Theor. Comput. Sci. **897**, 1–22 (2022)
7. Córcoles, A.D., et al.: Exploiting dynamic quantum circuits in a quantum algorithm with superconducting qubits. Phys. Rev. Lett. **127**(10), 100501 (2021)
8. Deutsch, D., Jozsa, R.: Rapid solution of problems by quantum computation. In: Proceedings of the Royal Society of London, vol. 439, pp. 553–558 (1992)
9. Duncan, R., Kissinger, A., Perdrix, S., Van de Wetering, J.: Graph-theoretic simplification of quantum circuits with the ZX-Calculus. Quantum **4**, 279 (2020)
10. Hong, X., Feng, Y., Li, S., Ying, M.: Equivalence checking of dynamic quantum circuits. In: International Conference on Computer-Aided Design (ICCAD), pp. 1–8 (2022)
11. Kissinger, A., Van de Wetering, J.: PyZX: large scale automated diagrammatic reasoning. Electron. Proc. Theor. Comput. Sci. **318**, 229–241 (2020)
12. Kissinger, A., Van de Wetering, J.: Reducing the number of non-Clifford gates in quantum circuits. Phys. Rev. A **102**(2), 022406 (2020)
13. Kole, A., Deb, A., Datta, K., Drechsler, R.: Dynamic realization of multiple control Toffoli gate. In: Design, Automation & Test in Europe Conference & Exhibition, DATE 2024, pp. 1–6 (2024)

14. Kole, A., Deb, A., Datta, K., Drechsler, R.: Extending the design space of dynamic quantum circuits for Toffoli based network. In: Design, Automation & Test in Europe Conference & Exhibition, DATE 2023, pp. 1–6. IEEE (2023)
15. Nielsen, M.A., Chuang, I.L.: Quantum Computation and Quantum Information. Cambridge University Press, Cambridge (2010)
16. Qiskit contributors: Qiskit: An open-source framework for quantum computing (2023). https://doi.org/10.5281/zenodo.2573505
17. Seiter, J., Soeken, M., Wille, R., Drechsler, R.: Property checking of quantum circuits using quantum multiple-valued decision diagrams. In: Gluck, R., Yokoyama, T. (eds.) Reversible Computation. Lecture Notes in Computer Science, vol. 7581, pp. 183–196. Springer, Berlin (2013). https://doi.org/10.1007/978-3-642-36315-3_15
18. Van de Wetering, J.: ZX-Calculus for the working quantum computer scientist, arXiv preprint: arXiv:2012.13966 (2020)
19. Wille, R., Burgholzer, L., Artner, M.: Visualizing decision diagrams for quantum computing. In: Design, Automation and Test in Europe, pp. 768–773 (2021)
20. Wille, R., Burgholzer, L., Hillmich, S., Grurl, T., Ploier, A., Peham, T.: The basis of design tools for quantum computing. In: Design Automation Conference, pp. 1367–1370. ACM (2022)
21. Zulehner, A., Hillmich, S., Wille, R.: How to efficiently handle complex values? Implementing decision diagrams for quantum computing. In: International Conference on Computer-Aided Design (ICCAD), pp. 1–7 (2019)

Model Checking Reversible Systems: Forwardly

Federico Dal Pio Luogo[1], Claudio Antares Mezzina[2]([✉])(iD),
and G. Michele Pinna[1]([✉])(iD)

[1] Dipartimento di Matematica e Informatica, Università di Cagliari, Cagliari, Italy
[2] Dipartimento di Scienze Pure e Applicate, Università di Urbino, Urbino, Italy
claudio.mezzina@uniurb.it

Abstract. Reversibility is nowadays playing a major role when dealing with systems, allowing to revert to safe states of systems evolutions. For instance reversibility can be applied to causal-consistent debugging. On the other hand, Linear Temporal Logic (LTL) has been used to formalize properties that a system may fulfil, and it may be equipped with past operators. This makes this logic appealing to express and prove properties of a reversible system. In this paper we investigate this feature, and we use the classical approaches to model check LTL formulas on unfoldings, in order to deal with reversible systems.

1 Introduction

Reversibility has attracted interests since the 70's for its promise of reaching low-energy computations. Recently, reversibility has found applications in modelling biochemical reactions [26,28], enhancing parallel discrete event simulators [29], formalising fault-tolerant systems [3,13,22,31], and improving reversible debuggers [10,16]. Due to this versatility, several classical formalisms have been adapted to model reversible systems: reversible process calculi [2,14,27], reversible Petri nets [20,21,23] and reversible event structures [19,30], just to name a few. Although many formalisms have emerged for modelling reversible computations, especially in concurrency, the verification of such systems has received little attention mainly focusing on equivalence theory [15,24,25].

Model checking is a well-know verification technique. It involves building a finite state model of the system to be verified, and then proving that desired

This work was supported by the Project PRIN 2022 DeLiCE (F53D23009130001) funded under the MUR National Recovery and Resilience Plan funded by the European Union - NextGenerationEU, by the Italian MUR PRIN 2020 project NiRvAna, by the Italian Ministry of Education, University and Research through the PRIN 2022 project "Developing Kleene Logics and their Applications" (DeKLA), project code: 2022SM4XC8, and the European Union - NextGenerationEU SEcurity and RIghts in the CyberSpace (SERICS) Research and Innovation Program PE00000014, projects STRIDE and SWOP.

T. Æ. Mogensen and L. Mikulski (Eds.): RC 2024, LNCS 14680, pp. 218–237, 2024.
https://doi.org/10.1007/978-3-031-62076-8_14

Main	Thread A	Thread B
...	...	
$x = 1;$	$a = x;$	$b = x;$
...	...	...

Fig. 1. A shared memory scenario involving two threads

properties, expressed as logic formulae, hold on the model. Usually properties are expressed using a temporal logic, for instance *linear temporal logic* (LTL). Such a logic has modal operators to deal with the future of events, and its applications to forward-only systems have been studied thoroughly (e.g. [1,5] and quotation herein).

In a reversible system we can observe two directions of computation: the classical forward one, and a backward one aiming at undoing the effects of the forward computation. Hence, a natural question arises: how can we model check a reversible system? One option is to equip LTL with modal operators dealing with the past. In fact LTL can be endowed with past modal operators and the interesting result is that this extension does not add expressivity to LTL [17]. Therefore a logic with past operators seems promising in the capability of describing the two computational directions of a reversible systems.

However the act of *undoing* the effect of a forward computational step can be seen itself as a forward action. This observation suggests that one can use just a *future* temporal logic only. Since LTL with past (PLTL) and LTL without past have the same expressive power, and there are various ways to encode PLTL into LTL (see for example [8]), we can just focus on LTL. The choice of considering LTL instead of other logics is also motivated by the fact that in the reversible system we are not interested in branching time, but rather on the linear line on which we can go also backward.

Consider the following shared memory scenario, depicted in Fig. 1, in which two threads read the value of a variable shared with the main method: the threads can read the initial value of the variable, which is 0, or 1 depending on whether they have read the value of x before or after the main method has modified it.

Assuming sequential consistency, if we were to reverse debug such a program we would like to check the following property: if thread A reads the value 1 this means that it has never read 0 before, or it has read in the past 0 but then it has undone this action. This is a kind of property that can be expressed in a temporal logic with past operators. However, if we think in terms of future we could rephrase the above property as follows. If the thread A reads 1 then two situations are possible: either it will never read 0 or it can read 0 and then it will have undone this read. The above scenario can be described using *future* operators only.

We now turn our attention on how to describe the forward and backward computations of a reversible systems. A concurrent system can be seen as a product of several components that run in parallel and synchronise on some actions.

Such components run sequentially without internal concurrency, but they exhibit internal nondeterminism due to some choices. This model of concurrency is not different from the real world ones. Take for example the actor-model (made popular by Erlang) where actors are sequential computational units and they can synchronise with each other by message exchange. Hence, we consider our system as a *multi-clock net* (*mcn*-net), introduced in [6], which precisely captures the idea of single-threaded components running in parallel.

The choice of modelling a system with *mcn*-nets allows us to describe their behaviours with unfoldings that in this particular case turn out to be *mcn*-nets as well. Also, the unfolding produces an occurrence net, and we can reason about reversibility as it is done in [21], by simply adding for every transition we want to reverse an exact opposite one (e.g., consuming tokens in the postset and producing tokens in the preset). Despite these transitions, the unfolding remains a product of state machines without concurrency, or transition systems. Therefore, the final result is still a transition system, and we can use standard techniques to verify LTL formulae, as in [5].

We sum up our approach to model check forwardly properties regarding reversible computations of a reversible system:

1. we describe a concurrent system as a parallel composition of sequential processes,
2. we unfold the system to obtain a representation of all its possible behaviours,
3. we add reversible transitions to the unfolded system following [21], which can be *unfolded* again to obtain a *forward* representation of all the possible behaviours of a reversible system, and
4. we use standard LTL model checking to model check the obtained system.

Structure of the Paper: We start, in the next section, by revising nets, multi-clock nets and unfoldings, and in Sect. 3 we describe the temporal logic we will use. In Sect. 4 we show how to add reversibility to the transition systems and in Sect. 5 we describe how properties of our reversible systems can be verified. Finally we draw some conclusions.

2   Petri Nets, Multi-clock Nets and Unfoldings

A concurrent system can be modelled by a suitable class of Petri nets, and its computations can be still expressed as a Petri net. Hence in this section, we will first introduce the class of Petri nets we will be using to model a concurrent system and then show how it is possible to express its behavious.

With $\mathbb{N}$ we denote the set of natural numbers. Let X be a set, with $|X|$ we denote the cardinality of the set.

We start reviewing the notions of (safe) labeled Petri nets and of token game. We fix a set Σ of transition names.

Definition 1. *A labeled* Petri net *over Σ is a 5-tuple $N = \langle S, T, F, m, \ell \rangle$, where S is a set of places and T is a set of* transitions *(with $S \cap T = \emptyset$), $F \subseteq (S \times T) \cup$*

$(T \times S)$ *is the* flow *relation,* $m \colon S \to \mathbb{N}$ *is the* initial marking, *and* $\ell \colon T \to \Sigma$ *is a labeling mapping.*

Ordinary Petri nets are those where the labeling is the identity. Subscripts or superscript on the net name carry over the names of the net components. Given $x \in T \cup S$, ${}^\bullet x = \{y \mid (y, x) \in F\}$ and $x^\bullet = \{y \mid (x, y) \in F\}$. ${}^\bullet x$ and $x^\bullet$ are called the *preset* and *postset* respectively of x. A net $\langle S, T, F, m, \ell \rangle$ is as usual graphically represented as a bipartite directed graph where the nodes are the places and the transitions, and where an arc connects a place s to a transition t iff $(s, t) \in F$ and an arc connects a transition t to a place s iff $F(t, s) \in F$. We assume that all nets we consider are such that $\forall t \in T$ ${}^\bullet t$ and $t^\bullet$ are not empty.

A transition t is enabled at a marking m, if m *contains* the pre-set of t, where contain here means that $m(s) \geq 1$ for all $s \in {}^\bullet t$. If a transition t is enabled at a marking m it may *fire*, yielding to a new marking m' defined as $m'(s) = m(s) - |{}^\bullet t \cap \{s\}| + |t^\bullet \cap \{s\}|$. The firing of t at m giving m' is denoted as $m [t\rangle m'$ and with $m [t\rangle$ we say that t is enabled at m. A marking $m' \colon S \to \mathbb{N}$ is *reachable* whenever there exists a sequence of transitions $t_0, \ldots, t_n$ and markings $m_0, \ldots, m_{n+1}$ such that $m_i [t_i\rangle m_{i+1}$ for all $i \leq n$, m_0 is the initial marking and m_{n+1} is m'. The set of reachable markings of a net N is denoted with $\mathcal{M}_N$. A net N is said to be *safe* whenever its places hold at most one token in all possible evolutions, namely $\forall m \in \mathcal{M}_N$ it holds that m can be seen as a set (the only possible values are 0 and 1). We will consider safe nets only, and we will identify markings with the subsets of places carrying a token.

We recall some notions that will come in handy in the following.

State Machines: A state machine net is a safe net where only choices are allowed, and at each reachable marking if two or more transitions are enabled, then only one can fire. Formally:

Definition 2. *Let* $N = \langle S, T, F, m, \ell \rangle$ *be a safe net.* N *is said to be a* state machine net *whenever* $\forall t \in T$ *it holds that* $|{}^\bullet t| = 1 = |t^\bullet|$, *and* $\forall m' \in \mathcal{M}_N$ *it holds that for all* $t, t' \in T$ *if* $m' [t\rangle$ *and* $m' [t'\rangle$ *then* ${}^\bullet t \cap {}^\bullet t' \neq \emptyset$.

Net Morphisms: The notion of morphism between safe nets [32] formalizes how labeled safe nets are related.

Definition 3. *Let* $N = \langle S, T, F, m, \ell, \Sigma \rangle$ *and* $N' = \langle S', T', F', m', \ell', \Sigma' \rangle$ *be safe nets over* Σ *and* Σ' *respectively. A morphism* $\phi \colon N \to N'$ *is a pair* $\langle \phi_T, \phi_S \rangle$, *where* $\phi_T \colon T \to T'$ *is a partial function and* $\phi_S \subseteq S \times S'$ *is a relation such that*

- *for each* $s' \in m'$ *there exists a unique* $s \in m$ *and* $s \, \phi_S \, s'$,
- *if* $s \, \phi_S \, s'$ *then the restriction* $\phi_T \colon {}^\bullet s \to {}^\bullet s'$ *and* $\phi_T \colon s^\bullet \to s'^\bullet$ *are total functions,*
- *if* $t' = \phi_T(t)$ *then* $\phi_S^{op} \colon {}^\bullet t' \to {}^\bullet t$ *and* $\phi_S^{op} \colon t'^\bullet \to t^\bullet$ *are total functions, where* ϕ_S^{op} *is the opposite relation to* ϕ_S,
- ϕ_T *preserves labels, i.e.* $\ell'(\phi_T(t)) = \ell(t)$.

Morphisms among safe nets preserve reachable markings. Consider $\phi \colon N \to N'$, then for each $m, m' \in \mathcal{M}_N$ and transition t, if $m [t\rangle m'$ then $\phi_S(m) [\phi_T(t)\rangle \phi_S(m')$ where $\phi_S(m) = \{s' \in S' \mid \exists p \in m \text{ and } p \, \phi_S \, s'\}$.

Restriction of a Net: A subnet is obtained by restricting places and transitions, and accordingly the flow relation and the initial marking.

Definition 4. *Let $N = \langle S, T, F, m, \ell \rangle$ be a labeled Petri net and let $S' \subseteq S$ be a subset of places and $T' = {}^\bullet S' \cup S'^\bullet$. The subnet generated by S', denoted with $N|_{S'}$ is the net $\langle S', T', F', m', \ell' \rangle$, where F' is the restriction of F to S' and T', m' is the multiset on S' obtained by m restricting to the places in S' and ℓ' is the restriction of ℓ to the transitions in T'.*

Product of Safe Nets: We define how to combine components represented as safe nets. The idea is that the components may *share* transitions with the same labels, synchronising on them. We assume w.l.o.g. that nets have disjoint places and transitions.

Definition 5. *Given two safe nets $N = \langle S, T, F, m, \ell \rangle$ and $N' = \langle S', T', F', m', \ell' \rangle$ on Σ and Σ' respectively, such that $S \cap S' = \emptyset$ and $T \cap T' = \emptyset$, their product is defined as the safe net $N \times N' = \langle S \cup S', \hat{T}, \hat{F}, m + m', \hat{\ell} \rangle$ on $\Sigma \cup \Sigma'$ where*

- $\hat{T} = T \setminus \{t \in T \mid \ell(t) \in \ell'(T')\} \cup T' \setminus \{t' \in T' \mid \ell'(t') \in \ell(T)\} \cup \{\{t\} \cup \{t'\} \mid t \in T, t' \in T' \wedge \ell(t) = \ell'(t')\}$,
- $(s, \{x, y\}) \in \hat{F}$ *iff* $(s, x) \in F$ *or* $(s, y) \in F'$, $(\{x, y\}, s) \in \hat{F}$ *iff* $(x, s) \in F$ *or* $(y, s) \in F'$, *and*
- $\hat{\ell}(t) = \ell(t)$ *if* $t \in T \setminus \{t \in T \mid \ell(t) \in \ell'(T')\}$, $\hat{\ell}(t) = \ell'(t)$ *if* $t \in T' \setminus \{t' \in T' \mid \ell'(t') \in \ell(T)\}$ *and* $\hat{\ell}(\{t, t'\}) = \ell(t) = \ell'(t')$.

The projections from $N \times N'$ to N and N' are defined in the obvious way: the places of each component are related with the same places in the product and the mapping on transitions is undefined for the transitions of the other component, and it is the identity on the ones of the component.

We observe that the product on safe nets is commutative and associative.

Proposition 1. *The product of safe nets is associative and commutative, i.e. $N \times N' = N' \times N$ and $N \times (N' \times N'') = (N \times N') \times N''$.*

2.1   Multi-clock Nets

Safe nets can be seen as formed by various *sequential* components (automata) synchronizing on common transitions. This intuition is formalized in the notion of *multi-clock* nets, introduced by Fabre in [6].

Definition 6. *A multi-clock net (mcn-net) N is the pair (N, ν) where $N = \langle S, T, F, m, \ell \rangle$ is a safe net and $\nu : S \to m$ is a mapping such that*

- *for all $s, s' \in m$, it holds that $s \neq s'$ implies $\nu^{-1}(s) \cap \nu^{-1}(s') = \emptyset$,*
- $\bigcup_{s \in m} \nu^{-1}(s) = S$,
- *ν is the identity when restricted to m, and*
- *for all $t \in T$. ν is injective on ${}^\bullet t$ and on $t^\bullet$, and $\nu({}^\bullet t) = \nu(t^\bullet)$.*

The cardinality *of a mcn-net* N, *denoted with* $\upsilon(N)$, *is the cardinality of* m.

Given $s \in S$, with $\bar{s}$ we denote the subset of places defined by $\nu^{-1}(\nu(s))$. The consequence of the last two requirements, namely (i) $\nu(m) = m$, (ii) ν is injective on the preset (postset) of each transition and that $\nu(^\bullet t) = \nu(t^\bullet)$, is that, for each $s \in m$, the net $\langle \bar{s}, T_{\bar{s}}, F_{\bar{s}}, \{s\}, \ell_{\bar{s}} \rangle$ is a net automaton, *i.e.* the preset and the postset of each transition has exactly one element, where $T_{\bar{s}}$ are the transitions of N such that $\forall t \in T_{\bar{s}}$ $^\bullet t \cap \bar{s} \neq \emptyset$ and $t^\bullet \cap \bar{s} \neq \emptyset$, and $F_{\bar{s}}$ is the restriction of F to $\bar{s}$ and $T_{\bar{s}}$. Each place s in the initial marking can be identified with an index in $\{1, \ldots, \upsilon(N)\}$, hence we denote N_i as the net $\langle \bar{s}, T_{\bar{s}}, F_{\bar{s}}, \{s\}, \ell_{\bar{s}} \rangle$ where i is the *index* of s.

Proposition 2. *Let* (N, ν) *be a mcn-net, with* $N = \langle S, T, F, m, \ell \rangle$. *Then* $N|_{\bar{s}}$ *is a state machine net.*

State-machine nets can be considered as finite state automata, and the consequence of what stated above is that $N = \langle S, T, F, m \rangle$ can be seen as *formed* by the various components. More precisely N is the product of the nets N_s where $s \in m$ and each N_s is $\langle \bar{s}, T_{\bar{s}}, F_{\bar{s}}, m_{\bar{s}} \rangle$.

Proposition 3. *Let* (N, ν) *be a mcn-net, with* $N = \langle S, T, F, m, \ell \rangle$. *Then* $N = \times_{s \in m} N|_{\bar{s}}$.

Sometimes multi-clock nets will be identified with the underlying safe net $N = \langle S, T, F, m \rangle$ and the partition mapping will be denoted with $\nu(N)$. It should be stressed out that the partition is not unique.

We have now enough material to re-elaborate the shared memory example given in the Introduction, casting it as a multi clock net.

Example 1. Let us consider the following shared memory scenario:

Main	Thread A	Thread B	Possible Values
...	...	...	$x = 1; a = 0; b = 0;$
$x = 1;$	$a = x;$	$b = x;$	$x = 1; a = 1; b = 0;$
...	...	...	$x = 1; a = 0; b = 1;$
			$x = 1; a = 1; b = 1;$

where a global variable x is shared among two threads and the main program. We assume that x is initialized to 0. The two threads read the value of x and copy it to their local variables (respectively a and b), while the main program modifies the value of the variable x by assigning 1 to it. Under sequential consistency, we can have four possible combinations of values, depending on the scheduling: either the two threads read x before the main method changes its value or one of the threads reads 0 and the other reads 1, or they both perform the reads after that the value of x has been changed. The above scenario can be modelled by the mcm-net in the top part of Fig. 2. We can see that as long as the main program does not overwrite the value of x the two threads can only read 0 independently. This is modelled by the pink and light green transitions, which are independent (occur in different components). The act of assigning 1 to x,

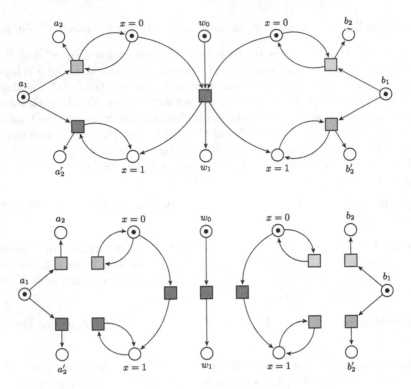

Fig. 2. An *mcn*-net and its components (Color figure online)

by the main program, is rendered by the w transition which consumes the old value of the variable and produces the new value of the variable. Hence if the transition w takes place, the pink and light green transition cannot fire, while the red and green transition are enabled. These last transitions mimic the fact that the threads can potentially read 1, and they are modelled so that their execution is independent of the other. The bottom part of Fig. 2 shows the state machine nets whose product is the mcm-net (according to Proposition 3).

When we turn our attention to *mcn*-nets, we consider morphisms that preserve the partitions.

Definition 7. *Let* $N = (\langle S, T, F, m, \ell \rangle, \nu)$ *and* $N' = (\langle S', T', F', m', \ell' \rangle, \nu')$ *be two multi-clock nets. A morphism* $\phi : N \to N'$ *is a mcn-morphism iff* $\forall s \in S$, $\forall s' \in S'$, $s \; \phi_S \; s'$ *implies that* $\nu(s) \; \phi_S \; \nu'(s')$.

2.2   Occurrence Nets

Once we have modelled a system using (multi-clock) nets, we turn our attention on how to describe the behaviours of the system. And on such behaviours we will prove properties of the original system. The behaviour of a Petri net can be described using a suitable net ([4,11,32] among others). The idea is that a net can be *unrolled*, yielding to an acyclic net called *occurrence net*, which describes all the possible executions of a net.

Let $N = \langle S, T, F, m, \ell \rangle$ be a labeled safe Petri net, the *causality relation* $<$ is the transitive closure of F and $\leq$ is its reflexive transitive closure. The set of causes of a node x is defined as $\lfloor x \rfloor = \{y \in T \cup S \mid y \leq x\}$. Two different nodes x and y are in *conflict*, written $x \# y$ if there are transitions t_1 and t_2 such that $^\bullet t_1 \cap {}^\bullet t_2 \neq \emptyset$ and $t_1 \leq x$ and $t_2 \leq y$. Execution paths of the Petri net branch at the conditions where the conflict originates. Finally, the concurrency relation **co** holds between nodes $x, y \in S \cup T$ that are neither ordered nor in conflict, i.e. $x \textbf{ co } y \Leftrightarrow \neg(x \leq y) \wedge \neg(y \leq x) \wedge \neg(x \# y)$.

Definition 8. *A Petri net $N = \langle S, T, F, m, \ell \rangle$ is an* occurrence net *whenever*

- $\leq$ *is a partial order;*
- *for all $s \in S$, $|^\bullet s| \leq 1$;*
- *for all $x \in S \cup T$, the set $\lfloor x \rfloor$ is finite;*
- *no node is in self-conflict, i.e. there is no $x \in B \cup E$ such that $x \# x$; and*
- *for all $s \in m$. $^\bullet s = \emptyset$.*

In literature, places and transitions of occurrence nets are called respectively *conditions* and *events* and denoted with B and E respectively. Therefore an occurrence net will be denoted with $C = \langle B, E, F, c \rangle$ with $c \subseteq B$ being the initial marking. The initial marking is such that the conditions $b \in B$ have the property that $^\bullet b = \emptyset$. The occurrence net associated to a safe net N, together with a way relating places and transitions of this occurrence net to those of the net N, is called *unfolding* of the net. The unfolding holds useful properties that can be exploited to make the semantic of a net a reversible one.

Definition 9. *Let $N = \langle S, T, F, m, \ell \rangle$ be a safe net on Σ, $C = \langle B, E, F, c, \ell_C \rangle$ be an occurrence net on Σ and let $\phi = (\phi_S, \phi_T) : C \to N$ be a net-morphism such that*

- $\forall e \in E$, $\ell_C(e) = \ell(\phi_T(e))$,
- ϕ_S^{-1} *and $\phi_S|_m$ are total functions; and*
- $\phi_S|_m$ *is injective.*

Then (C, ϕ) is an unfolding *of N. The morphism ϕ is the* folding morphism.

The construction of the unfolding, i.e. of the occurrence net and of the folding morphism, is standard and it is omitted here. When considering nets with cycles, as the unfolding represents all the computations, the resulting occurrence net may be infinite. However it is enough to consider, of the unfolding, only a finite part, provided that it is *complete*, namely all the possible computations are somehow represented (see [12,18] among others). Here we consider unfoldings that are complete prefixes of an unfolding.

We now characterize better the unfolding obtained from a *mcn*-net.

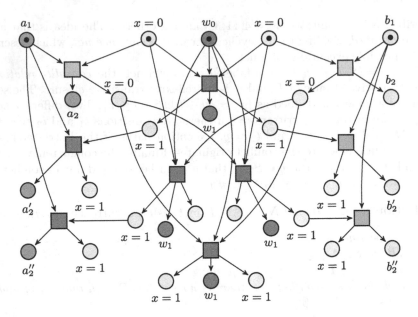

Fig. 3. The unfolding of the *mcn*-net in Fig. 2. The conditions arising from the places of each state machine are coloured in the same way.

Proposition 4. *Let* (N, ν) *be an mcn-net on* Σ, *C* $= \langle B, E, F, c, \ell_C \rangle$ *be an occurrence net on* Σ *and* $\phi : C \to N$ *be a net-morphism such that* (C, ϕ) *is an unfolding of* N. *Define* $\nu_C : B \to c$ *as follows:* $\nu_C(b) = b'$ *when* $\forall s, s' \in \phi_S^{-1}(b)$. $\nu(s) = \nu(s')$ *and* $\nu(s)\phi_S b'$. *Then* (C, ν_C) *is an mcn-net.*

The relevant result is that the unfolding of an *mcn*-net, which is the product of some components, is an occurrence net which is still the product of some components.

Proposition 5. *Let* (N, ν) *be an mcn-net on* Σ *and* (C, ϕ) *be an unfolding of* N, *with* $N = \langle S, T, F, m, \ell \rangle$ *and* $C = \langle B, E, F, c, \ell_C \rangle$. *Then* $C = \times_{b \in c} C|_{\overline{b}}$.

Example 2. Figure 3 depicts the complete unfolding of the *mcn*-net in the Example 1. Observe that there are four writes (depending on whether or not $x = 0$ has been read by one of the readers) and each reader can read $x = 1$ in two different ways. When restricting the net to various components we have the various unfoldings that keep memory of the previous interactions.

3   Past Linear Temporal Logic

Past Linear Temporal Logic (PLTL) is a *modal temporal logic* that extends propositional logic with time operators (formally, modalities) to reason on (the future or the past of) paths of events. In the context of system verification, the atomic propositions of the formulae are state labels, or basic assertions about the states of the system under consideration.

Syntax: We fix a set AP of atomic propositions. A PLTL formula, ranged over by Greeks letters, obeys to the grammar

$$\psi ::= \text{true} \mid a \mid \psi_1 \wedge \psi_2 \mid \neg\psi \mid \bigcirc \psi \mid \odot \psi \mid \psi_1 \mathsf{U} \psi_2 \mid \psi_1 \mathsf{S} \psi_2$$

where $a \in AP$. The temporal modalities are $\bigcirc$ (pronounced *next*), $\odot$ (pronounced *previous*), U (pronounced *until*) and S (pronounced *since*). We indicate with $PLTL$ the set of all the possible formulae generated by the above grammar. The until operator allows to derive the future temporal modalities $\Diamond$ (*eventually*, sometime in the future) and $\square$ (*always* in the future, from now on forever) as follows $\Diamond\psi \overset{\text{def}}{=} \text{true}\,\mathsf{U}\,\psi$ and $\square\psi \overset{\text{def}}{=} \neg\Diamond\neg\psi$, whereas the since operator allows to derive the temporal modalities $\Diamond$ (*once*, sometime in the past) and $\boxdot$ (*always* in the past), hence $\Diamond\psi \overset{\text{def}}{=} \text{true}\,\mathsf{S}\,\psi$ and $\boxdot\psi \overset{\text{def}}{=} \neg\Diamond\neg\psi$.

Semantics: PLTL views time as a discrete domain, whose *ticks* (advances of a single time unit) correspond to transitions of the system under observation. The present refers to the current state (e.g., state i) and the next moment corresponds to the immediate successor state (e.g., $i+1$). The system behavior is assumed to be observable at the time points $0, 1, 2, \dots$.

The semantics of PLTL is defined over infinite sequences of sets of atomic propositions. Intuitively, these sets correspond to the conditions that the system satisfies in a given time frame. The occurrence of a transition triggers a change in the state of the system and consequently in the basic assertions (i.e. atomic propositions) that hold in the next frame. The i-th letter $A_i \subseteq AP$ of a word $\sigma = A_0 A_1 A_2 \dots$ corresponds to the assertions that hold at the i-th time frame, where $i \geq 0$. With (σ, j) we denote the suffix of σ starting at index $j \geq 0$.

Definition 10 (Semantics of PLTL). *The relation* $\models \,\subseteq (2^{AP})^\omega \times \mathbb{N} \times PLTL$ *is defined inductively as follows:*

$(\sigma, i) \models \text{true}$ always

$(\sigma, i) \models a$ iff $a \in A_i$

$(\sigma, i) \models \psi_1 \wedge \psi_2$ iff $(\sigma, i) \models \psi_1$ and $(\sigma, i) \models \psi_2$

$(\sigma, i) \models \neg\psi$ iff $(\sigma, i) \not\models \psi$

$(\sigma, i) \models \bigcirc\psi$ iff $(\sigma, i+1) \models \psi$

$(\sigma, i) \models \odot\psi$ iff $i > 0$ and $(\sigma, i-1) \models \psi$

$(\sigma, i) \models \psi_1 \mathsf{U} \psi_2$ iff $\exists j \geq i \, (\sigma, j) \models \psi_2$ and $\forall k. \, i \leq k < j \, (\sigma, k) \models \psi_1$

$(\sigma, i) \models \psi_1 \mathsf{S} \psi_2$ iff $\exists j. \, 0 \leq j \leq i. \, (\sigma, j) \models \psi_2$ and $\forall k. \, j < k \leq i \, (\sigma, k) \models \psi_1$

The PLTL *property* induced by the formula ψ (or equivalently the *model of* ψ), denoted by $Words(\psi)$, is the language comprising the infinite words that satisfy the property: $Words(\psi) = \left\{ \sigma \in (2^{AP})^\omega \mid (\sigma, 0) \models \psi \right\}$

Example 3. Consider the propositional letters $AP = \{a, b\}$ and the PLTL formula $\psi = \Diamond (\Diamond \, a \wedge \bigcirc b)$ which says simply that there will be a point where b holds and before that in a point a held. The word $\sigma = \emptyset^n \{a\} \emptyset^m \{b\} \ldots$ is such that $(\sigma, 0) \models \psi$. Observe the ψ can be written using forward modalities only as $\phi = \Diamond (a \wedge \Diamond \bigcirc b)$, as it is easy to observe that $\forall \sigma \in (2^{AP})^\omega$ it holds that $(\sigma, 0) \models \psi$ iff $(\sigma, 0) \models \phi$, hence $Words(\psi) = Words(\phi)$.

3.1   Modeling a (P)LTL Formula and Model Checking It

According to [17] past modalities do not add expressive power to LTL, but are useful to express formulae more succinctly. Hence, any formula with past modalities can be rewritten into one using just forward modalities as done for example in [7,8]. Therefore, we will be considering just forward LTL formulae.

We recall that the model of any LTL formula ψ can be represented as the language accepted by a nondeterministic Büchi automaton (NBA), which is a nondeterministic finite state automaton where accepting states have to be visited infinitely often. Given an NBA $\mathcal{A} = (Q, 2^{AP}, \delta, Q_0, F)$ the language recognized by it is denoted as $\mathcal{L}^\omega(\mathcal{A})$ and it is the set of infinite words $A_0 A_1 A_2 \ldots$ such that there exists an infinite sequence of states $q_0 q_1 q_2 \ldots$ such that $\forall i \in \mathbb{N}$. $q_{i+1} \in \delta(g_i, A_i)$ with $q_0 \in Q_0$ and there exists infinite indexes j such that $q_j \in F$.

Proposition 6. *Given an LTL formula ψ, there exists an NBA automaton $\mathcal{A}_\psi$ such that $\mathcal{L}^\omega(\mathcal{A}_\psi) = Words(\psi)$.*

Example 4. The following NBA accepts the words $\sigma \in (2^{\{a,b\}})^\omega$ modeling the formulae in Example 3:

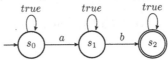

Once that the automaton is built, it is sufficient to build a *product* of the automaton with the representation of the behaviours of the system (on which we want to verify a formula) and then check whether there exists a way to fulfil the accepting conditions of $\mathcal{A}$. If this is the case, then the formula is satisfied by the system.

The unfolding of a multi-clock net can be seen as the product of components, hence given a multi-clock net, we can compute its unfolding, and then construct the product of the unfolding with the automaton $\mathcal{A}$. This is possible since the unfolding of a *mcn*-net can be seen as the product of several state machines (see Property 5), and the automaton itself is a state machine.

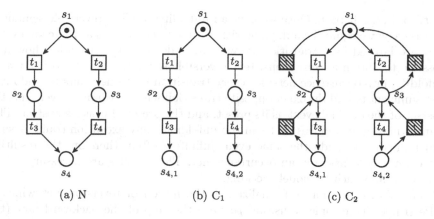

(a) N   (b) C_1 (c) C_2

Fig. 4. A net with backward conflict (left), its unfolding (center) and its reversible version (right).

4   How to Model Reversibility

A reversible computational model is a model which is able of describing not only the forward direction of the computation but also the backward one. Starting from a system modeled as mcn-net we are able to represent its forward behaviour as an unfolding. It is worth recalling that unfolding a mcn-net produces an occurrence net which is still a mcn-net. For example, if we take the unfolding of our running example, which is depicted in Fig. 3 it is easy to check that the net is an occurrence one, where the initial markings is represented by all the places (conditions) with no incoming arc. One important property of the unfolding is the absence of *backward conflicts* (e.g., a token in a place can be produced by two or more transitions). Backward conflicts are not desirable in reversibility because they do not allow to distinguish between transitions putting a token in the same place. Graphically, a backward conflict is represented by a place with two or more input edges. The unfolding removes backward conflicts by creating a copy of this state for each of its input transitions, explicitly rendering the different execution paths that lead to it. Hence, for each place it is always possible to know which transition generated a token in it.

Since all the places (or conditions) have a unique path, adding reversibility is quite straightforward: to undo any transition, we simply add its *inverse*, where the postset of the original transition becomes the preset of the undoing transition, and vice versa. For example, let us consider the net N on the left of Fig. 4. If we have a token in the place s_4, we really cannot tell whether the token has been produced by transition t_3 (e.g., left branch) or by transition t_4 (e.g., right branch). By unfolding the net on the left of Fig. 4, we obtain the net C_1 on the center, where now the place s_4 has been duplicated into two places: each one having a unique history. Now, the resulting net can be easily *reversed*, by just adding for each transition we want to reverse a transition which is the exact inverse. For example, the inverse of transition t_1, consumes the token produced by t_1 and puts it back. Once we have an unfolding, adding reversible semantics to it is easy: we equip the unfolding with as many *undo* events as there are events that are labeled by a transition we wish to undo. In [21] it is shown how it is possible to obtain a causal-consistent reversible semantics of a Petri net via its unfolding into occurrence nets: for every transition that one wants to undo it is just sufficient to add the exact opposite transition where each undo event has the postset of the original event as its preset, and the preset of it as its postset. This transformation introduces cycles in the unfolding - any execution could execute and immediately undo the same event infinitely often, therefore the resulting net cannot be considered an occurrence net. These cycles are necessary in the automata approach to model checking.

The above intuition is formalized in the notion of reversible net which is a Petri net where some transition *perform* the step of the backward flow (the reversing transitions) and removing these ones we have an occurrence net, which is related to the original system under consideration via a folding morphism.

Definition 11. *Let $N = \langle S, T, F, m \rangle$ be a net and let $\underline{T} \subseteq T$ be a subset of transitions such that*

- *$\forall \underline{t} \in \underline{T}$ there exists a unique $t \in T \backslash \underline{T}$ with $\bullet t = \underline{t}^\bullet$ and $t^\bullet = \bullet \underline{t}$;*
- *$\forall t, t', t'' \in T$, it $\bullet t = t'^\bullet = t''^\bullet$ and $t^\bullet = \bullet t' = \bullet t''$ then $t' = t''$; and*
- *$\langle S, \overline{T}, \overline{F}, m \rangle$ is an occurrence net, where $\overline{T} = T \backslash \underline{T}$ and $\overline{F} = F \cap ((S \times \overline{T}) \cup (\overline{T} \times S))$.*

Then $(N, \underline{T})$ is a reversing *net with $\underline{T}$ as reversing transitions.*

The first condition stipulates that for each reversing transition there is just one forward one, and the second says that the set of forwards transitions having a reverse is bijectively related with the set of reversing transitions.

Operatively, given an occurrence net C, we can add reversing transition as follows.

Definition 12. *Let $C = \langle B, E, F, c \rangle$ be an occurrence net and let $E' \subseteq E$ be a subset of transitions to be reversed. Let $\overleftarrow{C} = \langle B, E \cup \overleftarrow{E'}, \overleftarrow{F}, c \rangle$ where $\overleftarrow{E'} = \{(e, \mathtt{r}) \mid e \in E'\}$ and $\overleftarrow{F} = F \cup \{(b, (e, \mathtt{r})) \mid (e, b) \in F\} \cup \{((e, \mathtt{r}), b) \mid (b, e) \in F\}$. Then $(\overleftarrow{C}, \overleftarrow{E'})$ is a reversing net with $\overleftarrow{E'}$ as reversing transitions.*

We simply add the reversing transitions that have the effect of undoing the forward one.

Example 5. Given the net N in Fig. 4, the net C_1 is the unfolding of N into an occurrence net. The net C_2 is the reversing net of C_1, that is $C_2 = (\overleftarrow{C_1}, \{(t_1, \mathtt{r}), (t_2, \mathtt{r}), (t_3, \mathtt{r}), (t_4, \mathtt{r})\})$.

With this approach we add reversibility to our model.

Example 6. Figure 5 reports the reversible variant of Fig. 3. For the sake of clarity, we have just added one backward transition (the one labelled with $\uparrow$), which corresponds to the undoing of the read of the thread A when it reads 0. In the model we have considered (and model checked) all the transitions have been reversed.

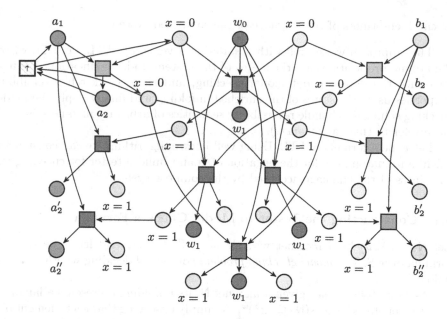

Fig. 5. Adding reversible transitions

Let us note that by adding reversing transitions to the unfold of a mcn-net, we still obtain an mcn-net, which is still a product of sequential components.

Proposition 7. *Let $((C, \nu_C), \phi)$ be an unfolding of an mcn-net (N, ν) and let $E' \subseteq E$ be a set of reversing transitions, then $\overleftarrow{C}$ is a reversing net and $(\overleftarrow{C}, \nu_C)$ is a mcn-net.*

We do not care too much about the morphism from the enriched unfolding to the original net as it is not important for our purposes. We just notice that the extension of the mapping on transitions which is undefined on the reversing transition would work perfectly.

By adding reversible transitions we obtain a net which is not any longer an occurrence net, it is however the model of the behaviour we are interested in, and on these we can reason about the properties we want to check.

5   Model Checking a Formula

To prove that the behaviours of a system or program satisfies some property, a standard method is to use model checking. The method we use to perform model checking is very classical and it is known as the *automata-theoretic approach*. It can be summed up in three steps:

1. translate the negation of the formula to be checked into a Büchi automaton,
2. synchronize the system and the Büchi automaton in an adequate way to yield a composed system, and

3. check emptiness of the language of the composed system.

This approach works well with a *state-based* version of LTL, i.e. LTL where the atomic propositions are the states of the system under verification. We first introduce the details about model checking, and then we sketch reversibility properties using the states of the enriched unfolding and finally apply the model checking solution to handle reversibility semantics of arbitrary *mcn*-nets (we will often refer to these as *products*).

Let ψ be a formula of LTL. Using well known algorithms we can construct a Büchi automaton $\mathcal{A}_{\neg\psi}$ for the negation of ψ and build a tester for checking the emptiness of the language accepted by the compose system.

5.1   Constructing the Tester to Model Check a Formula

Let $\mathsf{N} = (N, \nu)$ be a *mcn*-net with $N = \langle S, T, F, m, \ell \rangle$ and let ψ be an LTL formula over S. The *model checking problem* consists of deciding whether $\mathsf{N} \models \psi$ holds.

We first observe that, given a *mcn*-net N, its unfolding represents a language that we denote as $Traces(\mathsf{N}) \subseteq (2^S)^\omega$, by simply observing that each element of a trace is indeed a reachable marking of the unfolding. Now, being N a multi-clock net, also its unfolding is a multi-clock net, which implies that in the reachable marking just one place of each component is marked. A Büchi automaton $\mathcal{A}_{\neg\psi}$ for the negation of the formula recognizes the language $Words(\neg\psi)$ containing all the infinite words that satisfy $\neg\psi$, i.e. $\forall \sigma \in Words(\neg\psi). (\sigma, 0) \models \neg\psi$. The classic construction of the automaton for the LTL formula (e.g. see [1]) yields an NBA that is exponential in the size of the formula.

Therefore checking whether ψ holds for N reduces to verifying whether the language $Traces(\mathsf{N}) \cap Words(\neg\psi)$ is empty. Formally we have:

$$
\begin{aligned}
\mathsf{N} \models \psi \quad &\text{iff} \quad Traces(\mathsf{N}) \subseteq Words(\psi) \\
&\text{iff} \quad Traces(\mathsf{N}) \cap ((2^S)^\omega \backslash Words(\psi)) = \emptyset \\
&\text{iff} \quad Traces(\mathsf{N}) \cap (Words(\neg\psi)) = \emptyset \\
&\text{iff} \quad Traces(\mathsf{N}) \cap (\mathcal{L}_\omega(\mathcal{A}_{\neg\psi})) = \emptyset
\end{aligned}
$$

In order to provide an answer to the emptiness problem of $Traces(\mathsf{N}) \cap (\mathcal{L}_\omega(\mathcal{A}_{\neg\psi}))$, we need to construct a new device recognizing the intersection of the two languages. Such a device can be obtained by the synchronous product of N and $\mathcal{A}_{\neg\psi}$. Observe that any automaton can be seen as a state machine, hence the product we are going to use is well defined.

Definition 13. *Let* $\mathsf{N} = (N, \nu)$ *be a mcn-net with* $N = \langle S, T, F, m, \ell \rangle$ *and let* $\mathcal{A}_{\neg\psi} = \langle S', T', F', m', \ell' \rangle$ *be a state machine net encoding the Büchi automaton recognizing* $\neg\psi$ *labelled over* $\Sigma = T$. *The full synchronization of* N *and* $\mathcal{A}_{\neg\psi}$ *is the product* $\mathsf{N} \times \mathcal{A}_{\neg\psi} = \langle S \cup S', \hat{T}, \hat{F}, m + m', \hat{\ell} \rangle$ *given by Definition 5.*

In the full synchronization the Büchi tester participates pervasively in every transition of the product.

Therefore to check whether ψ holds for N one first constructs the NBA for the negation of the input formula ψ, representing in this way the infinite histories that violate the property, and then one constructs the product $N \times \mathcal{A}_{\neg\psi}$ whose language is the language we are interested in, namely $Traces(N) \cap (\mathcal{L}_\omega(\mathcal{A}_{\neg\psi}))$. Loosely speaking, the emptiness check on $\mathcal{L}_\omega(N \times \mathcal{A}_{\neg\psi})$ reduces nicely to checking whether a final state of lies on a cycle in $N \times \mathcal{A}_{\neg\psi}$. This translates to model checking the fixed LTL persistence property *"eventually forever $\neg F$"* where F is the disjunction of all final states of $\mathcal{A}_{\neg\psi}$. This property formalizes the requirement that no accepting state of $\mathcal{A}_{\neg\psi}$ will be visited infinitely often in a run, or, equivalently, that from a certain point on the state sequences induced by the histories of N never visit accepting states. Therefore:

$$N \models \psi \quad \text{iff} \quad \mathcal{L}_\omega(N \times \mathcal{A}_{\neg\psi}) = \emptyset$$

$$\text{iff} \quad N \times \mathcal{A}_{\neg\psi} \models \Diamond \Box \neg F$$

Checking the formula $\Diamond \Box \neg F$ amounts to checking whether no global transition leading to a marking containing a final state of the tester can be executed infinitely often. This is a *persistence checking problem*, and can be solved by means of algorithms that perform cycle detection, such as Nested DFS illustrated in [1].

Theorem 1. *Let* $N = (N, \nu)$ *be a mcn-net with* $N = \langle S, T, F, m, \ell \rangle$ *and let* ψ *be an LTL formula over* $AP = S$. *Let* $\mathcal{A}_{\neg\psi} = \langle S', T', F', m', \ell' \rangle$ *be the state machine net encoding the Büchi automaton for* $\neg\psi$ *labelled over* $\Sigma = T$. *Then* $N \models \psi$ *iff the product* $N \times \mathcal{A}_{\neg\psi}$ *does not contain a reachable final state of* $\mathcal{A}_{\neg\psi}$ *that lies on a cycle.*

Notes About Performance: The automata-based model checking approach we work with is PSPACE-hard, but there is room for optimizations in each step. In step (1), an LTL to Büchi automata naive translation produces very large automata which states can be reduced by using on-the-fly techniques as in [9], increasing performance of subsequent steps; in step (2) a more compact synchronization of the system and the automaton can be obtained by coupling only those transitions that trigger a change in the truth value of the states observed by the Büchi automaton and idling the others; this is the *stuttering synchronization* illustrated in [5] (it is however worth to note that this theory works nicely only on the fragment of LTL without the next operator - and consequently on the fragment of PLTL also without the previous modality). Many algorithms have been studied to solve the persistence check of step (3), [5] again studies a method that employs the unfolding procedure equipped with search strategies that intelligently exploits the concurrency of the stuttering synchronization.

5.2   Model Checking Reversible Systems

We combine all the results seen so far to handle reversibility semantics in testing LTL formulae against arbitrary mcn-nets. Let $N = (N, \nu)$ be an mcn-net and let $C = ((C, \nu_C), \phi)$ be its unfolding, where $C = \langle B, E, F, c \rangle$ is an occurrence net, let $E' \subseteq E$ be a set of reversing transitions and let ψ be an LTL formula over $AP = B$:

1. Let $\overleftarrow{C} = (\overleftarrow{C}, \nu_C)$ be the reversing net of N over E' as defined in Sect. 4,
2. Construct the Büchi automaton $\mathcal{A}_{\neg\psi}$ for the negation of ψ labeled by the events of $(\overleftarrow{C}, \nu_C)$ as hinted at Sect. 5.1,
3. Construct the product $\Sigma = \overleftarrow{C} \times \mathcal{A}_{\neg\psi}$ as shown previously;
4. Test for illegal ω-traces in Σ, which is an infinite sequence violating the property (operatively a trace where accepting states of the NBA are visited infinitely often). If the test is positive, then there exists an infinite run of $\overleftarrow{C}$ that violates ψ, and the model checker returns FALSE together with a sample run; otherwise it returns TRUE.

Example 7. Consider the Example 1, the unfolding is shown in Fig. 3, and its enriching is partially depicted in Fig. 5. We may try to prove that the thread A reads 1 then either she/he has never read 0 or if this is the case then the action of reading 0 has been undone. This property can be formalized in either PLTL (formula 1) or LTL (formula 2) as follows:

$$\Diamond (L1 \Rightarrow \boxdot \neg L0 \vee \Diamond(L0 \wedge \bigcirc \overline{L0})) \tag{1}$$

$$\Diamond L1 \Rightarrow (\Box \neg L0 \vee \Diamond (L0 \wedge \Diamond \overline{L0})) \tag{2}$$

where variables $L1$, $L0$ and $\overline{L0}$ represent the actions "*read 1*", "*read 0*" "*undo read 0*" respectively. The formula (1) reads as follows: "if the thread A has read 1 this implies that back in the past either he/she has never read 0 or he/she has read 0 and then afterwards that operation has been reversed". This formula can be re-written by just using forward modalities as (2). We instantiate these variables using the states of the unfolding of Fig. 5, choosing $L1 = a_2'$, $L0 = a_2$ and $\overline{L0} = a_1$. These atomic propositions only concern thread A, its copy of the global variable x and the writing agent. We are able to verify the property which can be written using only *forward* operators.

6   Conclusions

In this paper, we have proposed a strategy to verify properties of reversible systems using model checking. This is, to the best of our knowledge, the first work to address this problem.

We model the system under verification as a product of sequential automata without internal concurrency. The unfolding of such a model captures all its possible behaviours. We then introduce reversibility at this level, following the approach of [21]. Once we have enriched the unfolding with reversible transitions, we can apply again the unfolding, obtaining a *forward* only model which has the same behaviour (in terms of visited states) of the enriched one.

In model checking, properties are usually written in some logic. Linear temporal logic (LTL) is one of the most common logics, which enables writing formulae with future modalities. Past linear temporal logic (PLTL) extends LTL with past modalities, enabling reasoning about past. A well-known result [17] shows that PLTL and LTL have the same expressive power, so every PLTL formula can be rewritten as an equivalent LTL formula. Hence, classic LTL can be used to prove properties on reversible systems.

After reducing the model and the logic to only forward transitions, we have applied classical automata-based model checking consisting of constructing a Büchi automaton for the formula, and then building the product of the automaton with the system. We then have shown how this approach can be used to reason about reversibility with a shared memory example.

To the best of our knowledge, our approach is a first attempt to tackle the problem of model checking reversible systems. The closest work to ours is [33], where linear-time model checking techniques are applied to the verification of (closed) quantum systems. The idea is that a closed quantum system is inherently reversible, hence it is modelled by a class of reversible automaton called quantum automaton. We leave as future work a deeper comparison with [33].

Our work can be improved in several ways, for instance by implementing several optimisation algorithms to minimise the formula and the complexity of Büchi automaton. To reduce the complexity we could also resort to bounded model checking algorithms. Finally, we plan to build a fully-fledged tool with an usable interface wherein a user can model a reversible system and verify an arbitrary formula against the model.

Acknowledgments. The authors thank the anonymous reviewers for their helpful comments that improved the quality of the paper.

References

1. Baier, C., Katoen, J.: Principles of Model Checking. MIT Press, Cambridge (2008)
2. Danos, V., Krivine, J.: Reversible communicating systems. In: Gardner, P., Yoshida, N. (eds.) CONCUR 2004. LNCS, vol. 3170, pp. 292–307. Springer, Heidelberg (2004). https://doi.org/10.1007/978-3-540-28644-8_19
3. Danos, V., Krivine, J.: Transactions in RCCS. In: Abadi, M., de Alfaro, L. (eds.) CONCUR 2005. LNCS, vol. 3653, pp. 398–412. Springer, Heidelberg (2005). https://doi.org/10.1007/11539452_31
4. Engelfriet, J.: Branching processes of Petri nets. Acta Informatica **28**(6), 575–591 (1991)
5. Esparza, J., Heljanko, K.: Unfoldings - A Partial-Order Approach to Model Checking. Monographs in Theoretical Computer Science. An EATCS Series, Springer, Heidelberg (2008). https://doi.org/10.1007/978-3-540-77426-6

6. Fabre, E.: Trellis processes: a compact representation for runs of concurrent systems. Discrete Event Dyn. Syst. **17**(3), 267–306 (2007)
7. Gabbay, D.M.: The declarative past and imperative future: executable temporal logic for interactive systems. In: Banieqbal, B., Barringer, H., Pnueli, A. (eds.) Temporal Logic in Specification. LNCS, vol. 398, pp. 409–448. Springer, Heidelberg (1989). https://doi.org/10.1007/3-540-51803-7_36
8. Geatti, L., Gigante, N., Montanari, A., Venturato, G.: Past matters: supporting LTL+past in the BLACK satisfiability checker. In: TIME 2021. LIPIcs, vol. 206. Schloss Dagstuhl - Leibniz-Zentrum für Informatik (2021)
9. Gerth, R., Peled, D.A., Vardi, M.Y., Wolper, P.: Simple on-the-fly automatic verification of linear temporal logic. In: Protocol Specification, Testing and Verification XV. IFIP Conference Proceedings, vol. 38. Chapman & Hall (1995)
10. Giachino, E., Lanese, I., Mezzina, C.A.: Causal-consistent reversible debugging. In: Gnesi, S., Rensink, A. (eds.) FASE 2014. LNCS, vol. 8411, pp. 370–384. Springer, Heidelberg (2014). https://doi.org/10.1007/978-3-642-54804-8_26
11. Goltz, U., Reisig, W.: The non-sequential behavior of Petri nets. Inf. Control **57**(2/3), 125–147 (1983)
12. Khomenko, V., Koutny, M., Vogler, W.: Canonical prefixes of Petri net unfoldings. Acta Informatica **40**(2), 95–118 (2003)
13. Lanese, I., Lienhardt, M., Mezzina, C.A., Schmitt, A., Stefani, J.-B.: Concurrent flexible reversibility. In: Felleisen, M., Gardner, P. (eds.) ESOP 2013. LNCS, vol. 7792, pp. 370–390. Springer, Heidelberg (2013). https://doi.org/10.1007/978-3-642-37036-6_21
14. Lanese, I., Mezzina, C.A., Stefani, J.-B.: Reversibility in the higher-order π-calculus. Theor. Comput. Sci. **625**, 25–84 (2016)
15. Lanese, I., Phillips, I.: Forward-reverse observational equivalences in CCSK. In: Yamashita, S., Yokoyama, T. (eds.) RC 2021. LNCS, vol. 12805, pp. 126–143. Springer, Cham (2021). https://doi.org/10.1007/978-3-030-79837-6_8
16. Lanese, I., Schultz, U.P., Ulidowski, I.: Reversible computing in debugging of Erlang programs. IT Prof. **24**(1), 74–80 (2022)
17. Lichtenstein, O., Pnueli, A., Zuck, L.D.: The glory of the past. In: Parikh, R. (ed.) Logics of Programs. LNCS, vol. 193, pp. 196–218. Springer, Heidelberg (1985). https://doi.org/10.1007/3-540-15648-8_16
18. McMillan, K.L.: Using unfoldings to avoid the state explosion problem in the verification of asynchronous circuits. In: von Bochmann, G., Probst, D.K. (eds.) CAV 1992. LNCS, vol. 663, pp. 164–177. Springer, Heidelberg (1993). https://doi.org/10.1007/3-540-56496-9_14
19. Melgratti, H.C., Mezzina, C.A., Pinna, G.M.: A distributed operational view of reversible prime event structures. In: LICS 2021. IEEE (2021)
20. Melgratti, H.C., Mezzina, C.A., Pinna, G.M.: Relating reversible petri nets and reversible event structures, categorically. In: Huisman, M., Ravara, A. (eds.) FORTE 2023. LNCS, vol. 13910, pp. 206–223. Springer, Cham (2023). https://doi.org/10.1007/978-3-031-35355-0_13
21. Melgratti, H.C., Mezzina, C.A., Ulidowski, I.: Reversing place transition nets. Log. Methods Comput. Sci. **16**(4), 5:1–5:28 (2020)
22. Mezzina, C.A., Tiezzi, F., Yoshida, N.: Rollback recovery in session-based programming. In: Jongmans, S.S., Lopes, A. (eds.) COORDINATION 2023. LNCS, vol. 13908, pp. 195–213. Springer, Cham (2023). https://doi.org/10.1007/978-3-031-35361-1_11
23. Philippou, A., Psara, K.: Reversible computation in nets with bonds. J. Log. Algebraic Methods Program. **124**, 100718 (2022)

24. Phillips, I., Ulidowski, I.: A hierarchy of reverse bisimulations on stable configuration structures. Math. Struct. Comput. Sci. **22**(2), 333–372 (2012)
25. Phillips, I., Ulidowski, I.: Event identifier logic. Math. Struct. Comput. Sci. **24**(2), e240204 (2014)
26. Phillips, I., Ulidowski, I., Yuen, S.: A reversible process calculus and the modelling of the ERK signalling pathway. In: Glück, R., Yokoyama, T. (eds.) RC 2012. LNCS, vol. 7581, pp. 218–232. Springer, Heidelberg (2012). https://doi.org/10.1007/978-3-642-36315-3_18
27. Phillips, I.C.C., Ulidowski, I.: Reversing algebraic process calculi. J. Log. Algebraic Methods Program. **73**(1–2), 70–96 (2007)
28. Pinna, G.M.: Reversing steps in membrane systems computations. In: Gheorghe, M., Rozenberg, G., Salomaa, A., Zandron, C. (eds.) CMC 2017. LNCS, vol. 10725, pp. 245–261. Springer, Cham (2017). https://doi.org/10.1007/978-3-319-73359-3_16
29. Schordan, M., Oppelstrup, T., Jefferson, D.R., Barnes Jr., P.D.: Generation of reversible C++ code for optimistic parallel discrete event simulation. New Gener. Comput. **36**(3), 257–280 (2018)
30. Ulidowski, I., Phillips, I., Yuen, S.: Reversing event structures. New Gener. Comput. **36**(3), 281–306 (2018)
31. Vassor, M., Stefani, J.-B.: Checkpoint/rollback vs causally-consistent reversibility. In: Kari, J., Ulidowski, I. (eds.) RC 2018. LNCS, vol. 11106, pp. 286–303. Springer, Cham (2018). https://doi.org/10.1007/978-3-319-99498-7_20
32. Winskel, G.: Event structures. In: Brauer, W., Reisig, W., Rozenberg, G. (eds.) ACPN 1986. LNCS, vol. 255, pp. 325–392. Springer, Heidelberg (1986). https://doi.org/10.1007/3-540-17906-2_31
33. Ying, M., Li, Y., Yu, N., Feng, Y.: Model-checking linear-time properties of quantum systems. ACM Trans. Comput. Log. **15**(3), 1–31 (2014)

Exact Synthesis of Multiqubit Clifford-Cyclotomic Circuits

Matthew Amy[1]👤, Andrew N. Glaudell[2]👤, Shaun Kelso[3]👤,
William Maxwell[3,4]👤, Samuel S. Mendelson[3]👤, and Neil J. Ross[5(✉)]👤

[1] Simon Fraser University, Burnaby, BC, Canada
matt_amy@sfu.ca
[2] Photonic Inc., Vancouver, BC, Canada
[3] NSWC Dahlgren Division, Dahlgren, VA, USA
shaun.f.kelso.civ@us.navy.mil
[4] Sandia National Laboratories, Albuquerque, NM, USA
wjmaxwell@sandia.gov
[5] Dalhousie University, Halifax, NS, Canada
neil.jr.ross@dal.ca

Abstract. Let $n \geq 8$ be divisible by 4. The Clifford-cyclotomic gate set $\mathcal{G}_n$ is the universal gate set obtained by extending the Clifford gates with the z-rotation $T_n = \mathrm{diag}(1, \zeta_n)$, where ζ_n is a primitive n-th root of unity. In this note, we show that, when n is a power of 2, a multiqubit unitary matrix U can be exactly represented by a circuit over $\mathcal{G}_n$ if and only if the entries of U belong to the ring $\mathbb{Z}[1/2, \zeta_n]$. We moreover show that $\log(n) - 2$ ancillas are always sufficient to construct a circuit for U. Our results generalize prior work to an infinite family of gate sets and show that the limitations that apply to single-qubit unitaries, for which the correspondence between Clifford-cyclotomic operators and matrices over $\mathbb{Z}[1/2, \zeta_n]$ fails for all but finitely many values of n, can be overcome through the use of ancillas.

Keywords: Quantum circuits · Exact synthesis · Clifford-cyclotomic

1 Introduction

1.1 Background

Let $n \geq 8$ be an integer divisible by 4. The **single-qubit Clifford-cyclotomic gate set of degree** n was introduced in [7] and consists of the gates

$$H' = \frac{1}{2} \begin{bmatrix} 1+i & 1+i \\ 1+i & -1-i \end{bmatrix} \quad \text{and} \quad T_n = \begin{bmatrix} 1 & \cdot \\ \cdot & \zeta_n \end{bmatrix},$$

where $\zeta_n = e^{2\pi i/n}$ is a primitive n-th root of unity, $H' = \zeta_8 H$ is equal to the usual **Hadamard gate** H up to a global phase of ζ_8, and T_n is a z-rotation gate of order n. The gate $S = T_n^{n/4}$ is the usual **phase gate** and the gate T_8 is simply known as the T **gate**. The single-qubit Clifford-cyclotomic gate set is a universal extension of the **single-qubit Clifford gate set** $\{H', S\}$; it coincides with the well-studied **single-qubit Clifford+T gate set** when $n = 8$.

The entries of H' and T_n lie in $\mathbb{Z}[1/2, \zeta_n]$, the smallest subring of $\mathbb{C}$ containing $1/2$ and ζ_n. As a consequence, if a 2-dimensional unitary matrix U can be exactly represented by a single-qubit Clifford-cyclotomic circuit of degree n, then the entries of U belong to $\mathbb{Z}[1/2, \zeta_n]$. In their seminal 2012 paper [14], Kliuchnikov, Maslov, and Mosca proved that the converse implication holds when $n = 8$: every 2-dimensional unitary matrix with entries in $\mathbb{Z}[1/2, \zeta_8]$ can be exactly represented by a Clifford+T circuit. Thus, single-qubit Clifford+T operators correspond precisely to elements of $\mathrm{U}_2(\mathbb{Z}[1/2, \zeta_8])$, the group of 2×2 unitary matrices over $\mathbb{Z}[1/2, \zeta_8]$. Forest et al. later showed in [7] that such a correspondence holds when n is one of 8, 12, 16, or 24, but, disappointingly, that it fails for almost all other values of n. Ingalls et al. put the nail in this coffin in 2019 by proving that 8, 12, 16, and 24 are in fact the only values of n for which such a correspondence holds [10], as had been previously conjectured by Sarnak [18].

The **multiqubit Clifford-cyclotomic gate set of degree** n, which we denote $\mathcal{G}_n$, is obtained by adding the **controlled-NOT gate**

$$CX = I_2 \oplus \begin{bmatrix} \cdot & 1 \\ 1 & \cdot \end{bmatrix}$$

to the single-qubit Clifford-cyclotomic gate set of degree n. In other words, $\mathcal{G}_n$ is the extension of the **multiqubit Clifford gate set** $\{H', S, CX\}$ by the z-rotation T_n. For convenience, we set $\mathcal{G}_2 = \{X, CX, CCX, H \otimes H\}$ and $\mathcal{G}_4 = \{X, CX, CCX, S, H'\}$, where

$$X = \begin{bmatrix} \cdot & 1 \\ 1 & \cdot \end{bmatrix}, \qquad CCX = I_6 \oplus X, \qquad \text{and} \qquad H \otimes H = \frac{1}{2} \begin{bmatrix} 1 & 1 & 1 & 1 \\ 1 & -1 & 1 & -1 \\ 1 & 1 & -1 & -1 \\ 1 & -1 & -1 & 1 \end{bmatrix}.$$

The gates X and CCX are the usual **NOT gate** and **doubly-controlled-NOT gate** (or **Toffoli gate**), respectively.

In [8], Giles and Selinger extended Kliuchnikov, Maslov, and Mosca's 2012 result to the multiqubit setting by proving that a unitary matrix U of dimension 2^m can be represented by an m-qubit circuit over $\mathcal{G}_8$ if and only if the entries of U lie in the ring $\mathbb{Z}[1/2, \zeta_8]$. In [4], some of the present authors showed how to adapt the methods of Giles and Selinger to a handful of other gate sets, including $\mathcal{G}_2$ and $\mathcal{G}_4$. In the multiqubit context, circuits can use ancillary qubits, provided that they are initialized and terminated in the computational basis state $|0\rangle$. It was shown in [4] and [8] that a single ancilla is always sufficient to construct the desired circuits.

Clifford-cyclotomic circuits, and in particular those of degree 2^k for some positive integer k, are ubiquitous in quantum computation; they appear in Shor's factoring algorithm [19], the study of the Clifford hierarchy [9], and protocols for state distillation [6].

1.2 Contributions

Let k and m be positive integers. In the present note, we show that a 2^m-dimensional unitary matrix U can be exactly represented by an m-qubit Clifford-cyclotomic circuit of degree 2^k if and only if the entries of U lie in the ring $\mathbb{Z}[1/2, \zeta_{2^k}]$. To construct a circuit for U, a single ancilla suffices, when $k \leq 2$, and $k - 2$ ancillas suffice, when $k > 2$.

Our results extend those of [4] and [8] to an infinite family of multiqubit gate sets, but our proof is surprisingly simple. It relies on the fact that the root of unity ζ_{2^k} can be represented by a 2-dimensional unitary matrix over $\mathbb{Z}[1/2, \zeta_{2^{k-1}}]$, and that this representation can be used to define a well-behaved function $\phi_k : U(\mathbb{Z}[1/2, \zeta_{2^k}]) \to U(\mathbb{Z}[1/2, \zeta_{2^{k-1}}])$ mapping unitary matrices over $\mathbb{Z}[1/2, \zeta_{2^k}]$ to unitary matrices over $\mathbb{Z}[1/2, \zeta_{2^{k-1}}]$. The function ϕ_k generalizes the standard real representation of complex numbers which was used by Aharonov in [1] to prove the universality of the Toffoli-Hadamard gate set and is an example of a **catalytic embedding** [2]. One can think of our results as circumventing the no-go theorems of [7] and [10] through the use of ancillas: there are elements of $U_2(\mathbb{Z}[1/2, \zeta_{2^k}])$ that cannot be represented by an ancilla-free single-qubit circuit over $\mathcal{G}_{2^k}$, but every such element becomes representable if sufficiently many additional qubits are available.

1.3 Contents

The note is organized as follows. In Sect. 2, we briefly review some important properties of the ring $\mathbb{Z}[1/2, \zeta_{2^k}]$. We introduce catalytic embeddings in Sect. 3 and define the catalytic embedding ϕ_k. Section 4 contains the proof of our main result. We discuss future work in Sect. 5.

2 Cyclotomic Integers

We start by briefly discussing the rings of **cyclotomic integers** that will be of interest in the rest of the note. For further details, the reader is encouraged to consult [20].

Let k be a positive integer. The ring $\mathbb{Z}[\zeta_{2^k}]$ is the smallest subring of $\mathbb{C}$ containing ζ_{2^k}. Hence, $\mathbb{Z}[\zeta_{2^1}] = \mathbb{Z}$. Moreover, when $k > 1$, we have $\zeta_{2^k}^2 = \zeta_{2^{k-1}}$ and therefore $\mathbb{Z}[\zeta_{2^{k-1}}] \subseteq \mathbb{Z}[\zeta_{2^k}]$. It will be useful for our purposes to further note that, for $k > 1$,

$$\mathbb{Z}[\zeta_{2^k}] = \{a + b\zeta_{2^k} \mid a, b \in \mathbb{Z}[\zeta_{2^{k-1}}]\}. \tag{1}$$

The linear combinations in Eq. (1) are unique. That is, every element of $\mathbb{Z}[\zeta_{2^k}]$ can be uniquely written as $a + b\zeta_{2^k}$, for some $a, b \in \mathbb{Z}[\zeta_{2^{k-1}}]$.

We will be interested in an extension of $\mathbb{Z}[\zeta_{2^k}]$ obtained by localizing $\mathbb{Z}[\zeta_{2^k}]$ at 2, i.e., by adding denominators that are powers of 2. The resulting ring is

$$\mathbb{Z}[1/2, \zeta_{2^k}] = \{a/2^\ell \mid a \in \mathbb{Z}[\zeta_{2^k}], \ell \in \mathbb{Z}\}. \tag{2}$$

For brevity, and in keeping with prior work (see, e.g., [4,8]), we denote $\mathbb{Z}[1/2, \zeta_{2^k}]$ by $\mathbb{D}[\zeta_{2^k}]$ in what follows. This notation emphasizes the fact that $\mathbb{Z}[1/2, \zeta_{2^k}]$ can be seen as the extension by ζ_{2^k} of the ring $\mathbb{D} = \{a/2^\ell \mid a \in \mathbb{Z}, \ell \in \mathbb{Z}\}$ of **dyadic rationals**.

Lemma 1. *Let $k \geq 2$. Every element of $\mathbb{D}[\zeta_{2^k}]$ can be uniquely written as $a + b\zeta_{2^k}$ for some $a, b \in \mathbb{D}[\zeta_{2^{k-1}}]$.*

Proof. Equations (1) and (2) jointly imply that every element of $\mathbb{D}[\zeta_{2^k}]$ can be written as $a + b\zeta_{2^k}$ for some $a, b \in \mathbb{D}[\zeta_{2^{k-1}}]$. To see that this expression is unique, let $a, b, a', b' \in \mathbb{D}[\zeta_{2^{k-1}}]$ and suppose that $a + b\zeta_{2^k} = a' + b'\zeta_{2^k}$. By choosing ℓ large enough, $2^\ell(a + b\zeta_{2^k}) = 2^\ell(a' + b'\zeta_{2^k})$ becomes an equation over $\mathbb{Z}[\zeta_{2^k}]$, from which we get $a = a'$ and $b = b'$.

3 Catalytic Embeddings

We now define **catalytic embeddings**. The definition introduced below is a special case of the more general notion of catalytic embedding used in [2], but it suffices for our purposes.

Let $\mathcal{U}$ and $\mathcal{V}$ be collections of unitaries. An **ℓ-dimensional catalytic embedding** of $\mathcal{U}$ into $\mathcal{V}$ is a pair $(\phi, |\lambda\rangle)$ consisting of a function $\phi : \mathcal{U} \to \mathcal{V}$ and a quantum state $|\lambda\rangle \in \mathbb{C}^\ell$ such that if $U \in \mathcal{U}$ has dimension d then $\phi(U) \in \mathcal{V}$ has dimension $d\ell$, and

$$\phi(U)(|u\rangle \otimes |\lambda\rangle) = (U|u\rangle) \otimes |\lambda\rangle \tag{3}$$

for every $|u\rangle \in \mathbb{C}^d$. We refer to the state $|\lambda\rangle$ as the **catalyst** and to Eq. (3) as the **catalytic condition**. We sometimes write $(\phi, |\lambda\rangle) : \mathcal{U} \to \mathcal{V}$ to indicate that $(\phi, |\lambda\rangle)$ is a catalytic embedding of $\mathcal{U}$ into $\mathcal{V}$. If $(\phi, |\lambda\rangle) : \mathcal{U} \to \mathcal{V}$ and $(\psi, |\omega\rangle) : \mathcal{V} \to \mathcal{W}$ are catalytic embeddings, then $(\psi \circ \phi, |\lambda\rangle \otimes |\omega\rangle)$ is a catalytic embedding of $\mathcal{U}$ into $\mathcal{W}$, since

$$\psi(\phi(U))(|u\rangle \otimes |\lambda\rangle \otimes |\omega\rangle) = (\phi(U)(|u\rangle \otimes |\lambda\rangle)) \otimes |\omega\rangle = (U|u\rangle) \otimes |\lambda\rangle \otimes |\omega\rangle.$$

We refer to this catalytic embedding as the **concatenation** of $(\phi, |\lambda\rangle)$ and $(\psi, |\omega\rangle)$. The concatenation of catalytic embeddings is associative and $(I_{\mathcal{U}}, [1]) : \mathcal{U} \to \mathcal{U}$ acts as the identity for concatenation.

Now let $U(\mathbb{D}[\zeta_{2^k}])$ denote the collection of all unitary matrices over $\mathbb{D}[\zeta_{2^k}]$. The rest of this section is dedicated to constructing, for every $k \geq 2$, a 2-dimensional catalytic embedding $U(\mathbb{D}[\zeta_{2^k}]) \to U(\mathbb{D}[\zeta_{2^{k-1}}])$. To this end, we define the state $|\lambda_k\rangle$ and the matrix Λ_k as

$$|\lambda_k\rangle = \frac{1}{\sqrt{2}} \begin{bmatrix} 1 \\ \zeta_{2^k} \end{bmatrix} \quad \text{and} \quad \Lambda_k = \begin{bmatrix} 0 & 1 \\ \zeta_{2^{k-1}} & 0 \end{bmatrix},$$

respectively. Note that Λ_k is a unitary matrix and $|\lambda_k\rangle$ is an eigenvector of Λ_k for eigenvalue ζ_{2^k}. To verify the latter claim, we compute:

$$\Lambda_k |\lambda_k\rangle = \begin{bmatrix} 0 & 1 \\ \zeta_{2^{k-1}} & 0 \end{bmatrix} \frac{1}{\sqrt{2}} \begin{bmatrix} 1 \\ \zeta_{2^k} \end{bmatrix} = \frac{1}{\sqrt{2}} \begin{bmatrix} \zeta_{2^k} \\ \zeta_{2^{k-1}} \end{bmatrix} = \frac{1}{\sqrt{2}} \begin{bmatrix} \zeta_{2^k} \\ \zeta_{2^k}^2 \end{bmatrix} = \zeta_{2^k} |\lambda_k\rangle. \tag{4}$$

Note further that $\zeta_{2^k}^\dagger = \zeta_{2^{k-1}}^\dagger \zeta_{2^k}$ and that $\Lambda_k^\dagger = \zeta_{2^{k-1}}^\dagger \Lambda_k$. In order to define the desired catalytic embedding, we start by showing that the matrix Λ_k can be used to define a function $U(\mathbb{D}[\zeta_{2^k}]) \to U(\mathbb{D}[\zeta_{2^{k-1}}])$.

Lemma 2. *Let $k \geq 2$, let A and B be matrices over $\mathbb{D}[\zeta_{2^{k-1}}]$, and assume that $A + B\zeta_{2^k} \in U(\mathbb{D}[\zeta_{2^k}])$. Then $A \otimes I + B \otimes \Lambda_k \in U(\mathbb{D}[\zeta_{2^{k-1}}])$.*

Proof. Let k, A, and B be as stated. Since $A + B\zeta_{2^k}$ is unitary and $\zeta_{2^k}^\dagger = \zeta_{2^{k-1}}^\dagger \zeta_{2^k}$, we have

$$I = (A + B\zeta_{2^k})^\dagger (A + B\zeta_{2^k}) = (A^\dagger A + B^\dagger B) + (A^\dagger B + B^\dagger A \zeta_{2^{k-1}}^\dagger)\zeta_{2^k}.$$

Hence, $A^\dagger A + B^\dagger B = I$ and $A^\dagger B + B^\dagger A \zeta_{2^{k-1}}^\dagger = 0$. Now, since $\Lambda_k^\dagger = \zeta_{2^{k-1}}^\dagger \Lambda_k$ and Λ_k is unitary, we have

$$(A \otimes I + B \otimes \Lambda_k)^\dagger (A \otimes I + B \otimes \Lambda_k) = (A^\dagger A + B^\dagger B) \otimes I + (A^\dagger B + B^\dagger A \zeta_{2^{k-1}}^\dagger) \otimes \Lambda_k = I.$$

Reasoning analogously, one can also show that $(A \otimes I + B \otimes \Lambda_k)(A \otimes I + B \otimes \Lambda_k)^\dagger = I$. This proves that $A \otimes I + B \otimes \Lambda_k$ is indeed unitary.

Proposition 1. *Let $k \geq 2$ and let $\phi_k : U(\mathbb{D}[\zeta_{2^k}]) \to U(\mathbb{D}[\zeta_{2^{k-1}}])$ be the function defined by*

$$\phi_k : A + B\zeta_{2^k} \mapsto A \otimes I + B \otimes \Lambda_k.$$

Then the pair $(\phi_k, |\lambda_k\rangle)$ is a 2-dimensional catalytic embedding of $U(\mathbb{D}[\zeta_{2^k}])$ into $U(\mathbb{D}[\zeta_{2^{k-1}}])$.

Proof. Every element U of $U(\mathbb{D}[\zeta_{2^k}])$ can be uniquely written as $U = A + B\zeta_{2^k}$, where A and B are matrices over $\mathbb{D}[\zeta_{2^{k-1}}]$. Hence, Lemma 2 implies that $\phi_k : U(\mathbb{D}[\zeta_{2^k}]) \to U(\mathbb{D}[\zeta_{2^{k-1}}])$ is indeed a function. Moreover, by construction, $\phi_k(U) \in U(\mathbb{D}[\zeta_{2^{k-1}}])$ has dimension $2d$, if $U \in U(\mathbb{D}[\zeta_{2^k}])$ has dimension d. Now let $|u\rangle \in \mathbb{C}^n$. Then

$$
\begin{aligned}
\phi_k(U)(|u\rangle \otimes |\lambda_k\rangle) &= (A \otimes I + B \otimes \Lambda_k)(|u\rangle \otimes |\lambda_k\rangle) \\
&= A|u\rangle \otimes I|\lambda_k\rangle + B|u\rangle \otimes \Lambda_k|\lambda_k\rangle \\
&= A|u\rangle \otimes |\lambda_k\rangle + B|u\rangle \otimes \zeta_{2^k}|\lambda_k\rangle \\
&= A|u\rangle \otimes |\lambda_k\rangle + B\zeta_{2^k}|u\rangle \otimes |\lambda_k\rangle \\
&= (A|u\rangle + B\zeta_{2^k}|u\rangle) \otimes |\lambda_k\rangle \\
&= (U|u\rangle) \otimes |\lambda_k\rangle.
\end{aligned}
$$

Thus, $(\phi_k, |\lambda_k\rangle)$ is a 2-dimensional catalytic embedding $U(\mathbb{D}[\zeta_{2^k}]) \to U(\mathbb{D}[\zeta_{2^{k-1}}])$.

Remark 1. The catalytic embedding of Proposition 1 is an example of what is called a **standard catalytic embedding** in [2]. At the heart of this construction lies the fact that ζ_{2^k} can be represented by the matrix Λ_k, whose characteristic polynomial is also the minimal polynomial of ζ_k over $\mathbb{Q}[\zeta_{2^{k-1}}]$. A more general description of this construction can be found in [2].

4   Exact Synthesis

We now prove our main result. While it is clear that if a unitary U can be represented by a circuit over $\mathcal{G}_{2^k}$ then it is an element of $U(\mathbb{D}[\zeta_{2^k}])$, the challenge is to show that the converse implication is also true. The main idea behind the proof is to use Proposition 1 to inductively reduce the problem for $U(\mathbb{D}[\zeta_{2^k}])$ to the problem for $U(\mathbb{D}[\zeta_{2^{k-1}}])$, and so on until one reaches a case for which the result is known, such as $U(\mathbb{D}[\zeta_{2^3}])$, $U(\mathbb{D}[\zeta_{2^2}])$, or $U(\mathbb{D}[\zeta_{2^1}])$. We formalize this intuition in the proposition below.

Theorem 1. *Let k and m be positive integers. A $2^m \times 2^m$ unitary matrix U can be exactly represented by an m-qubit circuit over $\mathcal{G}_{2^k}$ if and only if $U \in U_{2^m}(\mathbb{D}[\zeta_{2^k}])$. Moreover, to construct a circuit for U, a single ancilla suffices, when $k \leq 2$, and $k - 2$ ancillas suffice, when $k > 2$.*

Proof. The left-to-right direction is an immediate consequence of the fact that the elements of $\mathcal{G}_{2^k}$ have entries in $\mathbb{D}[\zeta_{2^k}]$. For the right-to-left direction, we proceed by induction on k. The cases of $k = 1, 2, 3$ follow from [4, Corollary 5.6], [4, Corollary 5.27], and [8, Theorem 1], respectively. Now suppose that $k > 3$, let $U \in U_{2^m}(\mathbb{D}[\zeta_{2^k}])$, and let $(\phi_k, |\lambda_k\rangle) : U(\mathbb{D}[\zeta_{2^k}]) \rightarrow U(\mathbb{D}[\zeta_{2^{k-1}}])$ be the catalytic embedding of Proposition 1. Then $\phi_k(U) \in U_{2^{m+1}}(\mathbb{D}[\zeta_{2^{k-1}}])$. Thus, by the induction hypothesis, there exists an $(m+1)$-qubit circuit C for $\phi_k(U)$ over $\mathcal{G}_{2^{k-1}}$ that uses no more than $k - 3$ ancillas. For every state $|u\rangle$, we then have

$$C(|u\rangle \otimes |\lambda_k\rangle) = \phi_k(U)(|u\rangle \otimes |\lambda_k\rangle) = (U|u\rangle) \otimes |\lambda_k\rangle. \tag{5}$$

Now let D be the circuit defined by $D = (I \otimes (T_{2^k} H))^\dagger \circ C \circ (I \otimes (T_{2^k} H))$. This is a circuit over $\mathcal{G}_{2^k}$, since $X = H'S^2 H'^\dagger$ implies that H can be expressed as

$$H = \zeta_8^\dagger H' = X(T_{2^k}^\dagger)^{2^{k-3}} X(T_{2^k}^\dagger)^{2^{k-3}} H'$$

when $k \geq 3$. By Eq. (5), and since $|\lambda_k\rangle = T_{2^k} H|0\rangle$, we then have

$$
\begin{aligned}
D(|u\rangle \otimes |0\rangle) &= (I \otimes (T_{2^k} H))^\dagger \circ C \circ (I \otimes (T_{2^k} H))(|u\rangle \otimes |0\rangle) \\
&= (I \otimes (T_{2^k} H))^\dagger \circ C(|u\rangle \otimes |\lambda_k\rangle) \\
&= (I \otimes (T_{2^k} H))^\dagger ((U|u\rangle) \otimes |\lambda_k\rangle) \\
&= (U|u\rangle) \otimes |0\rangle.
\end{aligned}
$$

That is, D represents U exactly and uses no more than $k - 2$ ancillas, which completes the proof.

The circuit constructed in the inductive step of Theorem 1 is depicted in Fig. 1. The ancillary qubits used by C are not represented in Fig. 1 (just as they are kept implicit in the proof of the theorem).

The construction of Theorem 1 can be used to give an alternative proof of [4, Corollary 5.27] and [8, Theorem 1], albeit one that uses more ancillas than is necessary. In the proof of Theorem 1, the cases of $k = 1$, $k = 2$, and $k = 3$ are

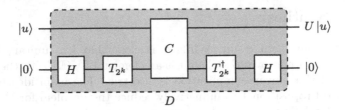

Fig. 1. The circuit constructed in the proof of Theorem 1.

all treated as base cases. Instead, one could use only the case of $k = 1$ as the base case and establish the cases of $k = 2$ and $k = 3$ inductively. The resulting circuit would then use k ancillas to represent an element of $U(\mathbb{D}[\zeta_{2^k}])$ for all k, rather than $k - 2$ ancillas when $k > 2$, as in the current proof.

5   Conclusion

Several questions arise from this work. Firstly, can the proof Theorem 1 be modified so as to produce smaller circuits? The size of the circuits produced by the theorem depends on the exact synthesis algorithm applied in the base case, but the produced circuits are likely to remain large, even if improved synthesis methods such as [3, 12, 15, 17] are used. Lowering this cost is an important avenue for future work. Secondly, can Theorem 1 be generalized to Clifford-cyclotomic gate sets of degree $n \neq 2^k$ or can such an extension be shown to be impossible? Preliminary research indicates that arbitrary roots of unity can be represented using circuits over $\{X, CX, CCX, H \otimes H\}$ in the presence of appropriate catalysts, but the construction is more intricate than the one presented here. Finally, and further afield, can Theorem 1 be used to develop algorithms for the approximation of unitaries using Clifford-cyclotomic circuits, following prior work such as [5, Appendix A], [13], or [16]?

Acknowledgements. The authors would like to thank Sarah Meng Li, Vadym Kliuchnikov, Kira Scheibelhut, and Peter Selinger for insightful comments on an earlier version of this note. The circuit diagram in this note was typeset using Quantikz [11].

Disclosure of Interests. MA was supported by the Canada Research Chairs program. MA and NJR were supported by the Natural Sciences and Engineering Research Council of Canada (NSERC). SK was supported by ONR, whose sponsorship and continuing guidance of the ILIR program has made this research possible. These efforts were funded under ONR award N0001423WX00070. SK, SSM, and WM were supported by Naval Innovative Science and Engineering funding. WM was supported by the U.S. Department of Energy, Office of Science, National Quantum Information Science Research Centers, Quantum Systems Accelerator.

References

1. Aharonov, D.: A simple proof that Toffoli and Hadamard are quantum universal (2003). arXiv preprint quant-ph/0301040
2. Amy, M., Crawford, M., Glaudell, A.N., Macasieb, M.L., Mendelson, S.S., Ross, N.J.: Catalytic embeddings of quantum circuits (2023). arXiv preprint 2305.07720
3. Amy, M., Glaudell, A.N., Li, S.M., Ross, N.J.: Improved synthesis of Toffoli-Hadamard circuits. In: Reversible Computation: 15th International Conference, RC 2023, Proceedings, pp. 169–209 (2023)
4. Amy, M., Glaudell, A.N., Ross, N.J.: Number-theoretic characterizations of some restricted Clifford+T circuits. Quantum **4**, 252 (2020)
5. Beverland, M., Campbell, E.T., Howard, M., Kliuchnikov, V.: Lower bounds on the non-Clifford resources for quantum computations. Quantum Sci. Technol. **5** (2019)
6. Duclos-Cianci, G., Poulin, D.: Reducing the quantum-computing overhead with complex gate distillation. Phys. Rev. A **91**(4), 042315 (2015)
7. Forest, S., Gosset, D., Kliuchnikov, V., McKinnon, D.: Exact synthesis of single-qubit unitaries over Clifford-cyclotomic gate sets. J. Math. Phys. **56**(8), 082201 (2015)
8. Giles, B., Selinger, P.: Exact synthesis of multiqubit Clifford+T circuits. Phys. Rev. A **87**(3), 032332 (2013)
9. Gottesman, D., Chuang, I.L.: Demonstrating the viability of universal quantum computation using teleportation and single-qubit operations. Nature **402**(6760), 390–393 (1999)
10. Ingalls, C., Jordan, B.W., Keeton, A., Logan, A., Zaytman, Y.: The Clifford-cyclotomic group and Euler-Poincaré characteristics. Can. Math. Bull. **64**(3), 651–666 (2021)
11. Kay, A.: Tutorial on the Quantikz package (2018). arXiv preprint 1809.03842
12. Kliuchnikov, V.: Synthesis of unitaries with Clifford+T circuits (2013). arXiv preprint 1306.3200
13. Kliuchnikov, V., Lauter, K., Minko, R., Paetznick, A., Petit, C.: Shorter quantum circuits (2022). arXiv preprint 2203.10064
14. Kliuchnikov, V., Maslov, D., Mosca, M.: Fast and efficient exact synthesis of single-qubit unitaries generated by Clifford and T gates. Quantum Inf. Comput. **13**(7–8), 607–630 (2013)
15. Niemann, P., Wille, R., Drechsler, R.: Improved synthesis of Clifford+T quantum functionality. In: 2018 Design, Automation & Test in Europe Conference & Exhibition, DATE 2018, Proceedings, pp. 597–600 (2018)
16. Ross, N.J., Selinger, P.: Optimal ancilla-free Clifford+T approximation of z-rotations. Quantum Inf. Comput. **16**(11–12), 901–953 (2016)
17. Russell, T.: The exact synthesis of 1- and 2-qubit Clifford+T circuits (2014). arXiv preprint 14086202
18. Sarnak, P.: Letter to Scott Aaronson and Andy Pollington on the Solavay-Kitaev theorem (2015). https://publications.ias.edu/sarnak/paper/2637
19. Shor, P.W.: Polynomial-time algorithms for prime factorization and discrete logarithms on a quantum computer. SIAM J. Comput. **26**(5), 1484–1509 (1997)
20. Washington, L.C.: Introduction to Cyclotomic Fields. Springer, New York, NY (1982). https://doi.org/10.1007/978-1-4612-1934-7

Author Index

T. Æ. Mogensen and Ł. Mikulski (Eds.): RC 2024, LNCS 14680, p. 247, 2024.
https://doi.org/10.1007/978-3-031-62076-8

Printed in the United States
by Baker & Taylor Publisher Services

Printed in the United States
by Baker & Taylor Publisher Services